Armed Conflict and Displacement

With 'displacement' as the guiding threa
twofold. First, it derives from the relevant provisions of international humanitarian law a legal framework for the protection of displaced persons in armed conflict, both from and during displacement. It contains a case study of Israeli settlements in the Occupied Palestinian Territory and the recent Advisory Opinion on the Separation Wall, and addresses such issues as humanitarian assistance for displaced persons, the treatment of refugees in the hands of a party to a conflict and the militarization of refugee camps.

Second, it examines the issue of displacement within the broader context of civilian war victims and identifies and addresses the normative gaps of international humanitarian law, including the inadequacy of concepts such as 'protected persons' and the persistence of the dichotomy between international and non-international armed conflicts, which is at odds with the realities of contemporary armed conflicts.

MÉLANIE JACQUES is a visiting research fellow and teaching associate at Queen Mary, University of London, where her interests lie in the fields of public international law and international humanitarian law, with a particular emphasis on issues of forced migration.

CAMBRIDGE STUDIES IN INTERNATIONAL AND COMPARATIVE LAW

Established in 1946, this series produces high quality scholarship in the fields of public and private international law and comparative law. Although these are distinct legal sub-disciplines, developments since 1946 confirm their interrelations.

Comparative law is increasingly used as a tool in the making of law at national, regional and international levels. Private international law is now often affected by international conventions, and the issues faced by classical conflicts rules are frequently dealt with by substantive harmonization of law under international auspices. Mixed international arbitrations, especially those involving state economic activity, raise mixed questions of public and private international law, while in many fields (such as the protection of human rights and democratic standards, investment guarantees and international criminal law) international and national systems interact. National constitutional arrangements relating to 'foreign affairs', and to the implementation of international norms, are a focus of attention.

The series welcomes works of a theoretical or interdisciplinary character, and those focusing on the new approaches to international or comparative law or conflicts of law. Studies of particular institutions or problems are equally welcome, as are translations of the best work published in other languages.

A list of books in the series can be found at the end of this volume.

Armed Conflict and Displacement

The Protection of Refugees and Displaced Persons under International Humanitarian Law

Mélanie Jacques

CAMBRIDGE
UNIVERSITY PRESS

CAMBRIDGE
UNIVERSITY PRESS

University Printing House, Cambridge CB2 8BS, United Kingdom

Cambridge University Press is part of the University of Cambridge.

It furthers the University's mission by disseminating knowledge in the pursuit of education, learning and research at the highest international levels of excellence.

www.cambridge.org
Information on this title: www.cambridge.org/9781107538399

First published 2012
First paperback edition 2015

A catalogue record for this publication is available from the British Library

Library of Congress Cataloguing in Publication data

Jacques, Mélanie.
Armed conflict and displacement : the protection of refugees and displaced persons under international humanitarian law / By Mélanie Jacques.
p. cm. – (Cambridge studies in international and comparative law)
Includes bibliographical references and index.
ISBN 978-1-107-00597-6 (hardback : alk. paper)
1. Refugees – Legal status, laws, etc. 2. Internally displaced persons – Legal status, laws, etc. 3. Humanitarian law. I. Title.
KZ6530.J33 2012
341.4′86 – dc23 2012024121

ISBN 978-1-107-00597-6 Hardback
ISBN 978-1-107-53839-9 Paperback

To Alec, Nina and Joe

Contents

Table of treaties and statutes

Hague Convention IV Respecting the Laws and Customs of War on Land and Annexed Regulations, 18 October 1907 (1908) 2 AJIL Supplement, 90–117

Agreement for the establishment of an International Military Tribunal for the prosecution and punishment of the major war criminals of the European Axis, London, 8 August, 1945, 82 UNTS 279

Geneva Convention I for the Amelioration of the Condition of the Wounded and Sick in Armed Forces in the Field of 12 August 1949, 75 UNTS 31

Geneva Convention II for the Amelioration of the Condition of Wounded, Sick and Shipwrecked Members of the Armed Forces at Sea of August 12, 1949, 75 UNTS 85

Geneva Convention III relative to the Treatment of Prisoners of War of 12 August 1949, 75 UNTS 135

Geneva Convention IV relative to the Protection of Civilian Persons in Time of War of 12 August 1949, 75 UNTS 287

European Convention for the Protection of Rights and Fundamental Freedoms, Rome, 4 November 1950, 213 UNTS 222

Convention Relating to the Status of Refugees, Geneva, 28 July 1951, 189 UNTS 137

International Covenant on Civil and Political Rights, New York, 16 December 1966, 999 UNTS 171

International Covenant on Economic, Social and Cultural Rights (ICESCR), New York, 16 December 1966, 993 UNTS 3

Protocol relating to the Status of Refugees, New York, 4 October 1967, 606 UNTS 267

Convention Governing Specific Aspects of the Refugee Problems in Africa, Addis Ababa, 10 September 1969, 1001 UNTS 45

American Convention on Human Rights 'Pact of San José, Costa Rica', San José, 22 November 1969, 1144 UNTS 123

Protocol Additional to the Geneva Conventions of 12 August 1949, and relating to the Protection of Victims of International Armed Conflicts, Geneva, 8 June 1977, 1125 UNTS 3

Protocol Additional to the Geneva Conventions of 12 August 1949, and relating to the Protection of Victims of Non-International Armed Conflicts, Geneva, 8 June 1977, 1125 UNTS 60

African Charter on Human and Peoples' Rights, Nairobi, 27 June 1981, 1520 UNTS 217

Convention Against Torture or Other Cruel, Inhuman or Degrading Treatment or Punishment, New York, 10 December 1984, 1465 UNTS 85

Cartagena Declaration on Refugees, 22 November 1984, Annual Report of the Inter-American Commission on Human Rights, OAS Doc. OEA/Serv.L/V/II.66/doc.10, rev.1

Convention on the Rights of the Child, New York, 20 November 1989, 1577 UNTS 3

Turku Declaration of Minimum Humanitarian Standards, 2 December 1990, UN Doc. E/CN.4/1995/116

Statute of the International Criminal Tribunal for the Former Yugoslavia (ICTY), UN Doc. S/25704, adopted by Security Council on 25 May 1993, UN Doc. S/RES/827 (1993)

Statute of the International Criminal Tribunal for Rwanda (ICTR), adopted by Security Council on 8 November 1995, UN Doc. S/RES/955 (1994)

Guiding Principles on Internal Displacement, 1998, E/CN.4/1998/53/Add.2

Rome Statute of the International Criminal Court, Rome, 17 July 1998, UN Doc. A/CONF.183/9

UN Transitional Administration in East Timor (UNTAET), Regulation 2000/15, On the Establishment of Panels with Exclusive Jurisdiction over Serious Criminal Offences, 6 June 2000, UNTAET/REG/2000/15

Statute of Special Court for Sierra Leone, 16 January 2002, appended to a letter dated 6 March 2002 from the Secretary-General addressed to the President of the Security Council, UN Doc. S/2002/246

Selected abbreviations

ACHR	American Convention on Human Rights
AD	*Annual Digest*
AI	Amnesty International
AJIL	*American Journal of International Law*
Am. U. J. Int'l. L. & Pol'y	*American University Journal of International Law and Policy*
Am. U. L. Rev.	*American University Law Review*
ASIL	American Society of International Law
Case W. Res. J. Int. L.	*Case Western Reserve Journal of International Law*
CJIL	*Chicago Journal of International Law*
CESCR	Committee on Economic, Social and Cultural Rights
Dick. J. Int'l L.	*Dickinson Journal of International Law*
ECHR	European Convention on Human Rights
EJIL	*European Journal of International Law*
FMR	*Forced Migration Review*
Fordham Int'l L. J.	*Fordham International Law Journal*
Ga. J. Intl & Comp. L.	*Georgia Journal of International and Comparative Law*
Harv. Int'l L.J.	*Harvard International Law Journal*
HRC	Human Rights Committee
HRW	Human Rights Watch
ICC	International Criminal Court
ICCPR	International Covenant on Civil and Political Rights
ICESCR	International Covenant on Economic, Social and Cultural Rights
ICG	International Crisis Group

ICJ	International Court of Justice
ICLQ	*International and Comparative Law Quarterly*
ICRC	International Committee of the Red Cross
ICTR	International Criminal Tribunal for Rwanda
ICTY	International Criminal Tribunal for the Former Yugoslavia
IDMC	Internal Displacement Monitoring Centre
IDP	internally displaced person
IHL	international humanitarian law
IHRL	international human rights law
IJRL	*International Journal of Refugee Law*
ILR	International Law Reports
IMT	International Military Tribunal
IRRC	*International Review of the Red Cross*
IRL	international refugee law
Isr. Y. B. Hum. Rts.	*Israel Yearbook on Human Rights*
Israel L. Rev.	*Israel Law Review*
JCSL	*Journal of Conflict and Security Law*
JICJ	*Journal of International Criminal Justice*
JRS	*Journal of Refugee Studies*
LJIL	*Leiden Journal of International Law*
MLR	*Modern Law Review*
NGO	non-governmental organization
NILR	*Netherlands International Law Review*
NLJ	*New Law Journal*
Nord. J. Int'l L.	*Nordic Journal of International Law*
NYU L Rev.	*New York University Law Review*
OCHA	UN Office for the Coordination of Humanitarian Affairs
OPT	Occupied Palestinian Territory
ORC	open relief centre
Stan. J. Int'l L.	*Stanford Journal of International Law*
UCLA Pac. Basin L. J.	*UCLA Pacific Basin Law Journal*
UDHR	Universal Declaration on Human Rights
UN	United Nations
UNCHR	United Nations Commission on Human Rights
UNGA	United Nations General Assembly
UNHCR	United Nations High Commissioner for Refugees

UNHRC	United Nations Human Rights Council
UNSC	United Nations Security Council
UNTS	United Nations Treaty Series
UNYB	*Yearbook of the United Nations*
USCRI	US Committee for Refugees and Immigrants
Vanderbilt J. Transnatl. L.	*Vanderbilt Journal of Transnational Law*
Virginia J. Intl. L.	*Virginia Journal of International Law*
YIHL	*Yearbook of International Humanitarian Law*

Introduction

Armed conflict and displacement: the issue

There is an indisputable correlation between armed conflict and displacement. Armed conflict and internal strife are widely considered to be major causes of population movement, within and outside borders.[1] As observed in the 2005 Human Security Report:

> For four decades the number of refugees around the world has tracked the number of armed conflicts – growing inexorably, though unevenly, from the 1960s to the early 1990s, then falling commensurably as the numbers of wars declined in the 1990s.[2]

At the end of 2010, the United Nations High Commissioner for Refugees (UNHCR) recorded some 43.7 million people displaced worldwide, as a result of armed conflict or persecution, the highest in more than fifteen years.[3] According to the Internal Displacement Monitoring Centre (IDMC), displacement in 2010 was mostly caused by conflict between governments and armed groups, or by generalized violence.[4]

The tragedy is that the majority of those displaced never really escape conflict. Indeed, people fleeing situations of danger increasingly choose or are forced to remain within their own country and to become internally displaced persons (IDPs). As of December 2010, the total number of

[1] In a 1992 report, the Secretary-General on Internally Displaced Persons identified 'armed conflict and internal strife' as a major cause of displacement. UNCHR, 'Analytical report by the Secretary-General on internally displaced persons' (14 February 1992) E/CN/4/1992/23, para. 18. Similarly, a group of governmental experts observed, in 1986, that 'wars and armed conflicts have been and continue to be a major cause of massive flows of refugees' (UNGA, 'Report of the Group of Governmental Experts on international cooperation to avert new flows of refugees' (13 May 1986) A/41/324, para. 31)).

[2] Human Security Centre, *Human Security Report 2005*, 2005, p. 103.

[3] UNHCR, *Global Trends 2010*, 2011, p. 5. [4] IDMC, *Global Overview*, 2010, p. 14.

internally displaced persons worldwide was estimated at 27.5 million,[5] nearly twice the number of refugees.[6] The reasons for internal, rather than external, displacement are numerous. People generally prefer to stay within or close to, their own community and their homes, hoping for a speedy return, as soon as the hostilities end.[7] In certain situations, geographical and topographical considerations may stand in the way of external flight.[8] Military operations on the border may also constitute an obstacle. Recently, the obstacles have tended to be political, with governments growing progressively more reluctant to accept large numbers of refugees within their frontiers. Persons displaced by armed conflicts have thus faced closed borders, stringent travel restrictions and check points, forcing them to remain in camps at the frontier.[9] Consequently, while they may be able to escape the fighting, internally displaced persons never escape the conflict, which eventually catches up with them, particularly during civil wars.

Alternatively, people may flee across international borders and seek refuge in neighbouring or third countries. However, as observed by Lischer, 'often the resulting refugee crisis leads to an expansion of violence rather than an escape'.[10] Many analyses have demonstrated that there is a link between large-scale population movements and the spread of conflict.[11] A 2006 study suggested that countries that experienced an influx of refugees from neighbouring states were significantly more likely to experience civil wars themselves.[12] The presence of refugees may indeed threaten ethnic or inter-communal balance or endanger social and economic stability in the host country, thus sparking insurrection.[13] Additionally, mass influxes of refugees bring with them 'arms, combatants and ideologies that are conducive to violence'.[14] Militarized refugee camps may cause frictions between the host state and the state of origin,

[5] *Ibid.*, p. 8.

[6] At the end of 2010, the UNHCR recorded 15.4 million refugees worldwide, including 10.55 million under UNHCR mandate and 4.82 million Palestinian refugees under mandate of the UN Relief and Works Agency for Palestinian Refugees in the Near East (UNRWA) (UNHCR, *Global Trends 2010*, 2011, p. 5).

[7] Phuong, *International Protection of Internally Displaced Persons*, 2004, p. 3.

[8] UNHCR, *State of the World's Refugees*, 1997, ch. 3.

[9] *Ibid.* [10] Lischer, *Dangerous Sanctuaries*, 2005, p. 2.

[11] *Ibid.*; Salehyan and Gleditsch, 'Refugees and the spread of civil war', 2006, 335; Weiner, 'Bad neighbors, bad neighborhoods', 1996, 5.

[12] Salehyan and Gleditsch, 'Refugees and the spread of civil war', 338.

[13] Dowty and Loescher, 'Refugee flows', 1996, 48; Lischer, *Dangerous Sanctuaries*, pp. 13–14; Salehyan and Gleditsch, 'Refugees and the spread of civil war', 342–3.

[14] Salehyan and Gleditsch, 'Refugees and the spread of civil war', 338.

for which refugees constitute a potential military threat.[15] Accordingly, 'those uprooted by armed conflict in one country are increasingly likely to include people who are already refugees from another'.[16] As conflict spreads across borders, it becomes more difficult for civilians to escape violence. Many refugees caught up in armed conflict find themselves once again on the road. Some become internally displaced within their state of asylum, while others elect to return to their country of origin and face the violence all over again.[17]

Objective and structure of the study

As conflict creates displacement and displacement in turn spreads conflict, it is clear that the two issues are intrinsically related. In this context, it is apposite to examine how the law applicable in situations of armed conflict, namely international humanitarian law (IHL), deals with the issue of displacement. International humanitarian law protects civilians from becoming internally displaced persons or refugees by expressly prohibiting forced displacement. The question remains whether international humanitarian law sufficiently protects civilians from *all* instances of forced displacement in armed conflict. Failing that, how does international humanitarian law protect displaced persons caught up in armed conflict? The Geneva Conventions and Protocol I specifically refer to refugees in a few provisions, but no mention is made of internally displaced persons. Is the protection afforded to civilian victims of war sufficient to tackle displacement-related issues?

Several of these issues have been addressed by other authors.[18] However, the protection of both refugees and internally displaced persons in time of war has never been dealt with in a comprehensive fashion. In addition, consideration of the issue of displacement in armed conflict from the perspective of refugee law has received extensive coverage

[15] Lischer, *Dangerous Sanctuaries*, p. 2. [16] UNHCR, *State of the World's Refugees*, 1993.

[17] E.g. when conflict erupted in Côte d'Ivoire in 2002, thousands of Liberian refugees fled back to Liberia, itself engulfed in civil war.

[18] Bugnion, 'Réfugiés, personnes déplacées et droit international humanitaire', 2001, 277–88; Partsch, 'Refugees in armed conflict and internal disturbances', 1983, 419–28; Patrnogic, 'Protection of refugees in armed conflict', 1981, 1–11; Dinstein, 'Refugees and the law of armed conflict', 1982, 94–109; Jacquemet, 'Cross-fertilization', 2001, 651–74; Obradovic, 'La protection des réfugiés dans les conflits armés internationaux', 1987, pp. 147–61; Krill, 'ICRC action in aid of refugees', 1988, 328–50; Lavoyer, 'Refugees and internally displaced persons', 1995, 162–80; Kälin, 'Flight in times of war', 2001, 628–48; Hulme, 'Armed conflict and the displaced', 2005, 91–116.

in the literature.[19] Similarly, the protection of internally displaced persons under international law has been widely covered.[20] While this study inevitably builds on those earlier developments, it takes a different perspective by looking at the global issue of displacement mainly from the viewpoint of humanitarian law. This book thus intends to produce a holistic study of the protection of 'war migrants' under international humanitarian law. With 'displacement' as the guiding thread, the purpose of this study is twofold. First, it seeks to derive from the relevant provisions of international humanitarian law a comprehensive legal framework for the protection of displaced persons in armed conflict. It will indeed be demonstrated that the regime forms a continuum of protection, both from and during displacement. Second, it aims to apply the issue of displacement within the broader context of civilian war victims generally and to identify and address the shortcomings of international humanitarian law in this respect.

The structure of this book is as follows. Chapters 1 and 2 focus on the protection against forced displacement in international and non-international armed conflicts. It is argued that, while international humanitarian law expressly and adequately prohibits the displacement in certain situations of armed conflict, it does not deal with all cases of forced displacement, and that the traditional state-centric concept of nationality and the dichotomy on which IHL is based no longer reflect the reality of contemporary armed conflicts. Chapter 3 focuses on the practice of population transfers in occupied territory, commonly used by occupying powers as a way to create *faits établis* in occupied territory. This chapter explores the legal issues arising from such practices through a study of Israel's settlement policy and the recent International Court of Justice Advisory Opinion on the legality of the construction of a Separation Wall in Occupied Palestinian Territory. Chapter 5 examines the concept of forced displacement as an international crime. Chapter 6 analyses the specific, if limited, protection of refugees under international humanitarian law, while Chapter 7 concentrates on internally displaced persons as civilians in time of war. Finally, it is asserted, in Chapter 8, that the rules of international humanitarian law regulating the conduct of hostilities reinforce the prohibition of armed attacks on refugee and

19 I. C. Jackson, *The Refugee Concept in Group Situations* (The Hague: Martinus Nijhoff, 1999); P. Kourula, *Broadening the Edges: Refugee Definition and International Protection Revisited* (The Hague: Martinus Nijhoff, 1997).

20 Phuong, *International Protection of Internally Displaced Persons.*

IDP camps, particularly through the creation of protected zones immune from attacks.

Legal framework

International humanitarian law

In time of armed conflict, the legal regime applicable is international humanitarian law, also known as the international law of armed conflicts. The International Committee of the Red Cross (ICRC) defines 'international humanitarian law applicable in armed conflict' as:

> international rules, established by treaties or custom, which are specifically intended to solve humanitarian problems directly arising from international or non-international armed conflicts and which, for humanitarian reasons, limit the right of Parties to a conflict to use the methods or means of warfare of their choice or protect persons and property that are, or may be, affected by conflict.[21]

The principal sources of conventional international humanitarian law are the 1907 Hague Conventions, in particular Convention IV respecting the Laws and Customs of War on Land and the Regulations annexed to it,[22] the four Geneva Conventions of 1949[23] and their two Additional Protocols of 1977.[24] In addition, an authoritative study published in 2005 under the auspices of the ICRC identified over 160 customary rules of international humanitarian law applicable in international and non-international armed conflicts.[25]

IHL is based on a strong dichotomy between international and non-international armed conflicts and the extent of the protection afforded

21 Sandoz *et al.*, *Commentary on the Protocols*, 1987, p. xxvii.

22 Hague Convention IV Respecting the Laws and Customs of War on Land and Annexed Regulations, 18 October 1907, AJIL Supplement, 2 (1908), 90–117.

23 Geneva Convention I for the Amelioration of the Condition of the Wounded and Sick in Armed Forces in the Field, 12 August 1949, 75 UNTS 31; Geneva Convention II for the Amelioration of the Condition of Wounded, Sick and Shipwrecked Members of the Armed Forces at Sea, 12 August 1949, 75 UNTS 85; Geneva Convention III relative to the Treatment of Prisoners of War, 12 August 1949, 75 UNTS 135; Geneva Convention IV relative to the Protection of Civilian Persons in Time of War, 12 August 1949, 75 UNTS 287.

24 Protocol Additional to the Geneva Conventions, 12 August 1949, and relating to the Protection of Victims of International Armed Conflicts, 8 June 1977, 1125 UNTS 3; Protocol Additional to the Geneva Conventions, 12 August 1949, and relating to the Protection of Victims of Non-International Armed Conflicts, 8 June 1977, 1125 UNTS 609.

25 Henckaerts and Doswald-Beck (eds.), *Customary International Humanitarian Law*, 2 vols., 2005.

to the victims of war will depend on the qualification of the situation. Humanitarian law applicable to international armed conflicts is much more developed and detailed than that of internal armed conflicts. International armed conflicts, namely conflicts opposing two or more states,[26] are governed by the four Geneva Conventions, as well as the First Protocol and an extended body of customary law, which regulates the conduct of hostilities. In addition, the law of belligerent occupation, which regulates the relationship between the occupying power and the occupied population, is governed by the Hague Regulations,[27] the 1949 Civilians Convention[28] and Protocol I. Non-international armed conflicts, on the other hand, enjoy a much more restricted legal framework. Common Article 3 to the four Geneva Conventions applies to 'armed conflict not of an international character' and lays down minimum humanitarian principles for the protection of persons not or no longer taking part in hostilities. Protocol II is the first instrument entirely dedicated to non-international armed conflicts. However, its high threshold of applicability and a lack of ratification have meant that the Protocol has rarely been applied in practice. In addition, internal disturbances and tensions fall below the threshold of armed conflict and, as a result, are excluded from the scope of application of international humanitarian law.[29]

The 1949 Geneva Conventions are mainly concerned with the treatment of enemy nationals in the hands of a party to an armed conflict. Entitlement to full protection under international humanitarian is clearly linked to a traditional concept of nationality, and vast categories of civilians and other war victims are consequently excluded from its scope of application.[30] Nevertheless, all civilians, irrespective of their nationality, are protected against the effects of hostilities. The ICRC commentary on the First Protocol clearly states that: '[i]n protecting civilians against the dangers of war, the important aspect is not so much their nationality as the inoffensive character of the persons to be spared and the situation in which they find themselves'.[31]

Refugees and internally displaced persons caught in the middle of an armed conflict are entitled, as civilians, to the protection of international humanitarian law. The extent of this protection will depend on various factors, including the characterization of the conflict and the nature of

26 Geneva Conventions, Common Article 2(1).
27 Section III, 'Military Hostility over Hostile Territory'.
28 Arts. 27 to 34 and Section III 'Occupied Territories'.
29 Protocol II, Art. 1(2). 30 See below Chapter 1.
31 Sandoz *et al.*, *Commentary on the Protocols*, p. 610.

their relationship with the power whose hands they are in. The various issues pertaining to the protection of displaced persons in armed conflict will be addressed in this book. However, no international legal framework should be seen as an isolated system. It is therefore necessary, as a preliminary matter, to place this issue within the wider context of international law, as a unified system of correlated and interdependent branches, and to examine the interaction between international humanitarian law and other branches of international law.

Interplay between international humanitarian law and other 'human' branches of international law

Similarities and differences

The three humanitarian branches of international law, i.e. international human rights law (IHRL), international humanitarian law and international refugee law (IRL), share a common interest in the protection of humanity. This ideological common ground was recognized by the International Tribunal for the Former Yugoslavia (ICTY) in the 1998 *Furundžija* decision:

> The general principle of respect for human dignity is the basic underpinning and indeed the very *raison d'être* of international humanitarian law and human rights law; indeed in modern times it has become of such paramount importance as to permeate the whole body of international law.[32]

However, the scope and conditions of application of each legal regime differ on a several important points. First, while international humanitarian law only applies in situations of armed conflict, human rights law and refugee law apply in principle at all time. However, most human rights instruments contain a derogation clause, which enables a state party to derogate from certain rights 'in time of public emergency threatening the life of the nation' and other exceptional circumstances.[33] Human rights may be derogated only 'to the extent strictly required by the exigencies of the situation' and the validity of these derogations will depend on the fulfilment of a number of strict requirements laid down in each

[32] *Prosecutor* v. *Furundžija*, Trial Judgment, IT-95-17/1, 10 December 1998, para. 183.

[33] [European] Convention for the Protection of Rights and Fundamental Freedoms (ECHR), Rome, 4 November 1950, 213 UNTS 222, Art. 15(1); International Covenant on Civil and Political Rights (ICCPR), New York, 16 December 1966, 999 UNTS 171, Art. 4(1); American Convention on Human Rights 'Pact of San José, Costa Rica' (ACHR), San José, 22 November 1969, 1144 UNTS 123, Art. 27(1).

instrument's derogation clause.[34] This clearly indicates that, unless an affirmative step is taken to derogate and all the conditions are met, states involved in an armed conflict will continue to be bound by their obligations under international human rights law.[35]

Not all human rights may be derogated from. Certain rights, including the right to life, the prohibition of torture or cruel or degrading treatment, prohibition of slavery and the prohibition of retroactive criminal laws, are so-called 'non-derogable rights' and must be applied in all circumstances.[36] In addition, certain human rights instruments, including the International Covenant on Economic, Social and Cultural Rights (ICESCR)[37] and the African Charter on Human and Peoples' Rights[38] do not contain a derogation clause. They do, however, allow for restrictions or limitations to most human rights under certain circumstances.[39] As for refugee law, unlike most human rights law instruments, the 1951 Refugee Convention[40] does not contain a clause which would allow states to suspend or derogate from Convention rights in time of emergency.[41]

[34] ICCPR, Art. 4(2); ECHR, Art. 15(2) and ACHR, Art. 27(2) require, as conditions of validity of the derogations: (a) the existence of a public emergency threatening the life of the nation; (b) proportionality to the exigencies of the situation; (c) consistency with other international obligations; and (d) notification of the state of emergency to other state parties and the relevant supervisory bodies. In addition, Art. 4(2) of ICCPR requires an official proclamation of a state of emergency. Finally, ICCPR, Art. 4(2) and ACHR, Art. 27(2) both require that the derogation does not involve 'discrimination on the ground of race, colour, sex, language, religion, or social origin'.

[35] Olson, 'Practical challenges of implementing complementarity', 2009, 444.

[36] ECHR, Art. 15(2); ICCPR, Art. 4(2); ACHR, Art. 27(2).

[37] International Covenant on Economic, Social and Cultural Rights (ICESCR), New York, 16 December 1966, 993 UNTS 3.

[38] African [Banjul] Charter on Human and Peoples' Rights, Nairobi, 27 June 1981, 1520 UNTS 217.

[39] The ICESCR contains a general limitation clause. Article 4 provides that: 'The States Parties to the present Covenant recognise that, in the enjoyment of those rights provided by the State in conformity with the present Covenant, the State may subject such rights only to such limitations as are determined by law only in so far as this may be compatible with the nature of these rights and solely for the purpose of promoting the general welfare in a democratic society.'

In addition, most human rights instruments allow for restrictions of or limitations on the enjoyment of specific human rights, for reasons of national security, public order, public health or morals, or the rights and freedoms of others. See, for instance, ICCR, Art. 12 (freedom of movement), ICESCR, Art. 8 (right of trade unions), African Charter, Art. 8 (freedom of conscience).

[40] Convention relating to the Status of Refugees (Refugee Convention), Geneva, 28 July 1951, 189 UNTS 137, modified by the Protocol relating to the Status of Refugees, 4 October 1967, 606 UNTS 267.

[41] Hathaway, *The Rights of Refugees under International Law*, 2005, p. 261.

It does, however, provide for certain provisional measures to be taken against specific individuals 'in time of war or other grave exceptional circumstances'.[42] An antithetic interpretation of Article 9 leads to the conclusion that 'the Convention is to be applied not only in normal peace time, but also in time of war or national emergency'.[43] In contrast, as a body of law specifically designed to apply in situations of emergency, no derogation to the rules of international humanitarian law is ever allowed.[44]

The three branches of international law also differ in terms of their passive scope of application. International humanitarian law is designed primarily to protect victims of war, i.e. persons who do not or are no longer taking part in hostilities and who find themselves in the hands of the enemy. International human rights law, on the other hand, governs the relationship between a state and its own nationals or individuals who are under its territorial jurisdiction.[45] International refugee law seeks to provide protection and assistance to persons who, owing to well-founded fear of persecution, have fled across international borders and do not enjoy the protection of their country of origin.[46] It therefore regulates the relationship between the asylum state and the refugee.

[42] Article 9 states that 'in time of war or other grave exceptional circumstances', a contracting state may take 'provisionally measures which it considers to be essential to the national security in the case of a particular person, pending a determination by the Contracting State that that person is in fact a refugee and that the continuance of such measures is necessary in his case in the interest of national security.'

[43] Grahl-Madsen, *Commentary on the Refugee Convention*, 1997, p. 42.

[44] With the exception of Article 5 of the Fourth Geneva Convention, which provides that a person in the territory of a party to an armed conflict 'definitely suspected of or engaged in activities hostile to the security of the State' may see their rights and privileges under the Fourth Convention withdrawn by the party concerned. Similarly, spies, saboteurs or any person detained as 'a person under definite suspicion of active hostilities to the security of the occupying power' may, where absolute military security so requires, be regarded as having forfeited rights of communication under the Fourth Convention.

[45] Vinuesa, 'Interface, correspondence and convergence', 1998, 71.

[46] Article 1A(2) of the Refugee Convention. Regional refugee instruments have elected a broader definition of the term 'refugee', which also includes armed conflict and internal disturbances as a ground for refugee protection. The 1969 OAU Convention thus states that 'The term "refugee" shall also apply to every person who, owing to external aggression, occupation, foreign domination or events seriously disturbing public order in either part or whole of his country of origin or nationality, is compelled to leave his place of habitual residence in order to seek refuge in another place outside his country of origin or nationality' (OAU Convention Governing Specific Aspects of the Refugee Problems in Africa, Addis Ababa, 10 September 1969, 1001 UNTS 45). Similarly, the Cartagena Declaration on Refugees cites 'generalized violence, foreign aggression, internal conflicts, massive violation of human rights or other circumstances which have seriously disturbed public order' as grounds for refugee protection (Cartagena

With regard to the active personal scope of application, it is widely accepted that international humanitarian law is binding on all parties to an armed conflict, states and non-state actors alike.[47] Thus, as soon as a situation of internal violence reaches a certain threshold, it qualifies as a non-international armed conflict and all actors involved, including rebels and other armed groups, become consequently bound by the rules of international humanitarian law, at least those obligations contained in Common Article 3 of the Geneva Conventions. In *Nicaragua*, the International Court of Justice (ICJ) indeed expressly recognized that the acts of the *contras* towards the Nicaraguan government were governed by the law applicable to conflicts 'not of an international character'.[48] The provisions of Protocol II have similarly been recognized as applicable to all parties to an internal armed conflict.[49]

In contrast, international human rights law – and, by analogy, refugee law – has traditionally been regarded as imposing obligations on governments only.[50] However, there is a growing body of opinion which considers that armed opposition groups have human rights obligations; particularly if they exercise governmental functions.[51] The issue remains nonetheless widely controversial. Whatever the outcome of this debate, it should be borne in mind that the statutes of the international tribunals for the former Yugoslavia[52] and Rwanda,[53] as well as that of the International Criminal Court (ICC),[54] provide for the individual criminal responsibility

Declaration on Refugees, 22 November 1984, Annual Report of the Inter-American Commission on Human Rights, OAS Doc. OEA/Serv.L/V/II.66/doc.10, rev. 1, 190–3).

[47] For a detailed discussion on the binding force of Common Article 3 and Protocol II for non-state actors, see Zegveld, *Accountability of Armed Opposition Groups in International Law*, 2002, p. 9; Moir, *The Law of Internal Armed Conflict*, 2002, pp. 52, 96; Cassese, 'The status of rebels', 1981, 416.

[48] *Military and paramilitary activities in and against Nicaragua (Nicaragua* v. *United States of America)*, Merits, Judgment, ICJ Reports 1986, p. 14, para. 219.

[49] Zegveld, *Accountability of Armed Opposition Groups in International Law*, p. 11.

[50] Cohen and Deng, *Masses in Flight*, 1998, pp. 74–5. See also Lindsay Moir, who considers that: 'Human rights obligations are binding on governments only, and the law has not yet reached the stage whereby, during internal armed conflict, insurgents are bound to observe the human rights of government forces, let alone of opposing insurgents' (*Law of Internal Armed Conflict*, p. 194).

[51] For a detailed discussion on human rights obligations of non-state actors, see Clapham, 'Human rights obligations of non-state actors in conflict situations', 2006, 491.

[52] Statute of the International Criminal Tribunal for the former Yugoslavia (ICTY), UN Doc. S/25704, adopted by Security Council on 25 May 1993, UN Doc. S/RES/827 (1993).

[53] Statute of the International Criminal Tribunal for Rwanda (ICTR), adopted by Security Council on 8 November 1995, UN Doc. S/RES/955 (1994).

[54] Rome Statute of the International Criminal Court (ICC), Rome, 17 July 1998, 2187 UNTS 3.

of perpetrators of crimes against humanity, which are largely derived from international human rights law,[55] and which may be committed in peacetime as in time of war.

Continued applicability of international human rights law and refugee law in armed conflict

The continued applicability of international human rights law in armed conflict, although subject to debate until the 1970s,[56] is now widely accepted within the international community.[57] Ever since the 1968 International Conference on Human Rights in Tehran, which recognized for the first time the applicability of human rights in armed conflict,[58] the UN General Assembly has consistently made reference to human rights in resolutions dealing with conflict situations.[59] Similarly, the Security Council has repeatedly condemned violations of both international humanitarian law and human rights in specific situations of armed conflicts,[60] while generally reaffirming the continuing relevance of human rights law and refugee law in situations of armed conflict. In its Resolution 1894 (2009) on the protection of civilians in armed conflicts, the Security Council demanded 'that parties to armed conflict comply strictly with the obligations applicable to them under international humanitarian, human

55 Hadden and Harvey, 'The law of internal crisis and conflict', 1999, 129.

56 In 1973, Pictet indeed observed that 'the two legal systems are fundamentally different, because whilst humanitarian law is valid only in the case of armed conflicts, human rights are essentially applicable in peacetime' (*Le droit humanitaire et la protection des victimes de la guerre*, 1973, p. 13).

57 Provost, *International Human Rights and Humanitarian Law*, 2002; Meron, *The Humanization of International Law*, 2006; Greenwood, 'Rights at the frontier', 1999, 277; Doswald-Beck and Vité, 'International humanitarian law and human rights law', 1993, 94; Droege, 'Elective affinities?', 2008, 501; Sassòli and Olson, 'The relationship between international humanitarian law and human rights law where it matters', 2008, 599; Heintze, 'On the relationship between human rights law and international humanitarian law', 2004, 789; Krieger, 'A conflict of norms', 2006, 265; Watkin, 'Controlling the use of force', 2004, 1; Vinuesa, 'Interface, correspondence and convergence', 1998, 69.

58 Final Act of the International Conference on Human Rights, Tehran, 22 April–13 May 1968, UN Doc. A/Conf.32/41.

59 UN Commission on Human Rights (CHR) (Sub-Commission), 'Working paper on the relationship between human rights law and international humanitarian law by Françoise Sampson and Ibrahim Salama', 21 June 2005, UN Doc. E./CN.4/Sub.2/2005/14, p. 14.

60 E.g. UNSC Res. 1592 (2005) of 30 March 2005, UN Doc. S/RES/1592 (2005), on the situation concerning the Democratic Republic of the Congo; UNSC Res. 1833 (2008) of 22 September 2008, UN Doc. S/RES/1833 (2008) on the situation in Afghanistan.

rights and refugee law' and called on states to ratify and implement the relevant international treaties.[61]

The ICJ has addressed the issue of the applicability of international human rights law in armed conflict on three separate occasions.[62] In its 1996 Advisory Opinion on *The Legality of Threat or Use of Nuclear Weapons*, the ICJ stated that:

> the protection of the International Covenant on Civil and Political Rights does not cease in times of war, except by operation of Article 4 of the Covenant whereby certain provisions may be derogated from in time of national emergency.[63]

In 2004, the Court confirmed that, more generally, 'the protection offered by human rights conventions does not cease in case of armed conflict, save through the effect of provisions for derogations of the kind to be found in Article 4 [ICCPR]'.[64] Furthermore, the Court also found that the ICCPR, ICESCR and the Convention on the Rights of the Child[65] were applicable 'in respect of acts done by the State in the exercise of its jurisdiction outside its own territory', including in occupied territories.[66] This ruling was upheld in the legally binding decision of the ICJ in *Armed Activities on the Territory of the Congo* (*DRC* v. *Uganda*).[67] The European Court on Human Rights (ECtHR) has also recognized the extraterritorial applicability of the European Convention on Human Rights (ECHR) to situations of armed conflict, most notably to the Turkish occupation of Northern Cyprus, and has held that states' human rights obligations under the ECHR also extended outside their territory, to areas under their 'effective control'.[68] There is also a considerable body of domestic judicial decisions in this regard. UK courts, for instance, have applied human rights law

[61] UNSC Res. 1894 (2009) of 11 November 2009, S/RES/1894 (2009).

[62] *Legality of the Threat or Use of Nuclear Weapons*, Advisory Opinion, ICJ Reports 1996, 226, para. 25; *Legal Consequences of the Construction of a Wall in the Occupied Palestinian Territory*, Advisory Opinion, ICJ Reports 2004, 136, para. 106; *Armed Activities on the Territory of the Congo* (*Democratic Republic of the Congo* v. *Uganda*), Judgment, ICJ Reports 2005, 168, para. 216.

[63] *Legality of the Threat or Use of Nuclear Weapons*, para. 25.

[64] *Legal Consequences of the Construction of a Wall in the Occupied Palestinian Territory*, Advisory Opinion, para. 106.

[65] Convention on the Rights of the Child, New York, 20 November 1989, 1577 UNTS 3.

[66] *Legal Consequences of the Construction of a Wall in the Occupied Palestinian Territory*, Advisory Opinion, paras. 107–13.

[67] *Armed Activities on the Territory of the Congo* (*Democratic Republic of the Congo* v. *Uganda*), para. 216.

[68] ECtHR, *Loizidou* v. *Turkey* (Preliminary Objections), Judgment of 23 March 1995, Series A No. 310, para. 62.

extraterritorially when assessing the conduct of British troops in Iraq and the UK's obligations in this regard.[69]

Interrelationship between IHL, IHRL and IRL

As a consequence of the simultaneous application of international humanitarian law, human rights law and international refugee law in situations of armed conflict, there will inevitably be circumstances where all three legal regimes overlap. The question of the interplay between the three branches of international law is therefore of considerable importance, particularly when substantive rules come into conflict with one another.

Two theories are often advanced to explain the nature of the relationship between international humanitarian law and human rights law. The first theory adopts the *lex specialis* principle[70] as a method of interpretation of a belligerent's duties in armed conflict.[71] The second theory, often called the 'complementarity' or 'convergence' theory, posits the simultaneous application of both bodies of international law, for an optimal protection of individuals in armed conflicts.[72] Professor Schabas talks of a 'belt and suspenders' approach: 'The norm that better protects the individual, whether it is drawn from international human rights or international humanitarian law, is to be applied.'[73] Although at first glance fundamentally opposed, these two approaches may lead to similar results; particularly in situations where the two legal rules in question are similar

69 *Al Skeini and others* v. *Secretary of State for Defence*, 13 June 2007, [2007] UKHL 26; *R. (on application of Al-Jedda)* v. *Secretary of State for Defence*, 12 December 2007 [2007] UKHL 58; *Secretary of State for Defence* v. *R. (on the application of Smith)*, 18 May 2009 [2009] EWCA Civ 441.

70 *Lex specialis derogat lex generalis*: the special law derogates from the general law.

71 In its *Nuclear Weapons*, Advisory Opinion, the ICJ held that although the applicability of the ICCPR did 'not cease in times of war', the law of armed conflict was nevertheless *lex specialis*. Consequently, in case of conflict between the two bodies, relevant provisions of human rights law had to be interpreted in light of the law applicable in armed conflict (at para. 25).

72 Heintze, 'On the relationship between human rights law and international humanitarian law', 794; Krieger, 'A conflict of norms', 271; this approach was adopted by the Human Rights Committee (HRC), which stated, in its General Comment No. 31, that: 'the Covenant applies also in situations of armed conflict to which the rules of international humanitarian law are applicable. While, in respect of certain Covenant rights, more specific rules of international humanitarian law may be especially relevant for the interpretation of Covenant rights, both spheres of law are complementary, not mutually exclusive', 80 (The nature of the general legal obligation imposed on State Parties to the Covenant, 26 May 2004, UN Doc. CCPR/C/21/Rev.1/Add.13, para. 11).

73 Schabas, '*Lex specialis*? Belt and suspenders?', 2007, 593.

and do not fundamentally contradict each other. In such situations, the *lex specialis* approach closely resembles the theory of complementarity, in the sense they both lead to the application of the most protective rule. Indeed, it is often the case that the more specialized rule will also be the most protective one. When two norms clearly contradict each other, however, one of the norms must prevail.[74] In this case, the applicable legal regime will be determined by reference to the *lex specialis* principle.

In relation to the issue at hand, that is, the protection of refugees and displaced persons in armed conflict, there does not appear to be any manifest conflict between the relevant norms. In fact, as the three branches of international law aim to protect human beings, they should definitely complement each other, in order to ensure that the best protection possible is afforded to displaced persons in the midst of an armed conflict.

The international protection of internally displaced persons

Internally displaced persons are defined as:

> persons or groups of persons who have been forced to flee or obliged to flee or to leave their homes of places of habitual residence, in particular as a result of, or in order to avoid the effects of armed conflict, situations of generalised violence, violations of human rights or natural or man-made disasters, and who have not crossed an internationally recognised state border.[75]

Until recently, IDPs, as a specific category of persons in need of protection, tended to be ignored by the international community. It was not until the early 1990s that the issue of the protection of internally displaced persons was placed on the agenda of the United Nations. In 1992, the UN Secretary-General appointed, at the request of the Commission on Human Rights, Mr Francis Deng as his Representative on Internally Displaced Persons,[76] whose first task was to examine existing international human rights, humanitarian and refugee law and standards and their applicability to the protection of and relief assistance to internally displaced persons.[77] Shortly afterwards, the Representative of the

[74] Droege, 'Elective affinities?', 524.

[75] UNCHR, 'Guiding Principles on Internal Displacement', Report of the Representative of the Secretary-General on Internally Displaced Persons, Mr Francis Deng, submitted pursuant to Commission Resolution 1997/39 (11 February 1998), E/CN.4/1998/53/Add.2, p. 2.

[76] The mandate of Mr Deng ended in June 2004. He was replaced in September 2004 by Professor Walter Kälin, who carried out the role until 2010, when it was taken over by Dr Chaloka Beyani in September of that year.

[77] UNCHR, 'Internally displaced persons', 5 March 1992, E/CN.4/RES/1992/73, para. 2.

UN Secretary-General on Internally Displaced Persons submitted a 'Comprehensive study on the human rights issues related to internally displaced persons' to the Commission.[78] Finally, after a long period of preparation and consultation with a team of international legal experts,[79] the Representative presented, in 1998, the 'Guiding Principles on Internal Displacement'[80] to the UN Commission on Human Rights, in response to an earlier request 'to develop an appropriate framework... for the protection of internally displaced persons'.[81] The Guiding Principles are neither a binding convention, nor a declaration adopted by the General Assembly after negotiations by Member States, but a set of non-binding principles,[82] intended to provide clear guidelines to governments, intergovernmental and non-governmental organizations (NGOs) and other actors in their dealings with IDPs.

The Guiding Principles are the outcome of a comprehensive two-part study, entitled 'Compilation and Analysis of Legal Norms',[83] which examined international human rights law, international humanitarian law and international refugee law, by analogy, and concluded that while existing law provided substantial protection for the rights of internally displaced persons, there were significant areas in which it failed to provide an adequate basis for their protection and assistance.[84] The Guiding Principles thus lay down relevant principles applicable to the internally displaced through the different phases of displacement, providing 'protection against arbitrary displacement, access to protection and assistance during displacement and guarantees during return or alternative settlement and reintegration'.[85]

Although not legally binding per se, the normative value of the Guiding Principles should not be underestimated. Indeed, the Guiding Principles

[78] UNCHR, 'Comprehensive study prepared by Mr Francis Deng on the human rights issues related to internally displaced persons, pursuant to Commission on Human Rights resolution 1992/73', 21 January 1993, E/CN.4/1993/35.

[79] Cohen, 'The Guiding Principles on Internal Displacement', 2004, 462–5.

[80] UNCHR, 'Guiding Principles on Internal Displacement', Report of the Representative of the Secretary-General on Internally Displaced Persons, Mr Francis Deng.

[81] UNCHR Res. 1996/52, 19 April 1996, E/CN.4/RES/1996/52.

[82] Kälin, 'How hard is soft law?', 2001.

[83] UNCHR, 'Compilation and Analysis of Legal Norms, Part I' (5 December 1995), E/CN.4/1996/52/Add.2; 'Compilation and Analysis of Legal Norms, Part II, Legal aspects relating to the protection against arbitrary displacement' (11 February 1998), E/CN.4/1998/53/Add.1.

[84] 'UNCHR, 'Guiding principles on Internal Displacement', Introductory note, para. 7.

[85] *Ibid.*, para. 9.

restate to a large extent existing principles of conventional and/or customary international law, particularly in so far as they are applied in situations of armed conflict.[86] In his last report as Representative of the Secretary-General on the human rights of internally displaced persons, Walter Kälin announced that he was 'pleased to report that the authority of the Guiding Principles has been consolidated at the international level since he assumed his mandate'.[87] Indeed, the Guiding Principles have been acknowledged by various UN bodies[88] and have generally been well received by the international community. In a 1999 Report, the UN Secretary-General recommended that, in situations of massive internal displacement, the Security Council encourage states to follow the legal guidance provided in the Guiding Principles.[89] In addition, the UN Human Rights Council has stated that it recognizes the Guiding Principles 'as an important international framework for the protection of internally displaced persons',[90] while the previous Commission on Human Rights and the UN General Assembly have acknowledged that 'the protection of internally displaced persons has been strengthened by identifying, reaffirming and consolidating specific standards for their protection, in particular through the Guiding Principles on Internal Displacement'.[91]

However, the most significant developments have taken place in Africa, making it the only region with two binding instruments specifically protecting internally displaced persons.[92] The Great Lakes Protocol on the Protection and Assistance to Internally Displaced Persons, which entered into force in June 1998, requires the eleven Member States of the Great Lakes region to 'adopt and implement the Guiding Principles as a regional framework for providing protection and assistance to internally displaced persons in the Great Lakes Region'.[93] Furthermore, on 23 October 2009, the

[86] Kälin, 'The Guiding Principles on internal displacement as international minimum standard and protection tool', 2005, 29.

[87] UN Human Rights Council (UNHRC), Report of Representative of the Secretary-General on the human rights of internally displaced persons, 5 January 2010, A/HRC/13/21, para. 11.

[88] Deng, 'The global challenge of internal displacement', 2001, 147.

[89] UNSC, Report of the Secretary-General to the Security Council on the protection of civilians in armed conflict, 8 September 1999, S/1999/957, Recommendation 7.

[90] UNHRC, 'Mandate of the Special Rapporteur on the Human Rights of Internally Displaced Persons', 23 June 2010, A/HRC/RES/14/6, para. 9.

[91] UNHRC, Resolution 2005/46, 24 April 2005, E/CN.4/RES/2005/46, preambular para. 5; UNGA Resolution 64/162, 'Protection and assistance to internally displaced persons', 17 March 2010, A/RES/64/162, preambular para. 10.

[92] UNHRC, 2010 Report of Representative of the Secretary-General on the human rights of internally displaced persons, para.12.

[93] International Conference on the Great Lakes Region (ICGLR), Protocol on the Protection and Assistance to Internally Displaced Persons, Art. 6(1).

African Union (AU) adopted the Convention for the Protection and Assistance of Internally Displaced Persons in Africa (Kampala Convention).[94] It is the first legally binding instrument imposing clear duties on states with regard to the protection and assistance of internally displaced persons. By ratifying the Convention, states undertake to prevent arbitrary displacement,[95] to provide protection and humanitarian assistance to internally displaced persons during displacement[96] and to seek lasting solutions to the problem of internal displacement.[97] The Convention also imposes obligations on members of armed groups to protect and assist IDPs in internal armed conflicts.[98] As of October 2011, the Convention has been signed by 31 of the 53 Member States of the AU, but has only been ratified by 11.[99] It needs fifteen ratifications to enter into force and thus become legally binding.

At the domestic level, significant efforts have been made by states to incorporate the Guiding Principles into their national legislation. In 2009, the Representative of the Secretary-General on IDPs reported that fifteen countries, including Iraq, Colombia, Uganda and Burundi had adopted policies or legislation specifically addressing internal displacement.[100] According to the Representative, '[t]here are some indications that the Guiding Principles are emerging as customary law, providing a binding interpretation of the international legal norms upon which they are based'.[101]

Conclusion

As demonstrated, international human rights, humanitarian law and refugee law apply concurrently in time of armed conflict to ensure that refugees and displaced persons benefit from the best protection possible from the scourge of war. The Guiding Principles on Internal Displacement, although not legally binding per se, also constitute a non-negligible source of protection for IDPs in armed conflicts.

94 African Union Convention for the Protection and Assistance of Internally Displaced Persons in Africa, Kampala, 22 October 2009.

95 *Ibid.*, Art. 4. 96 *Ibid.*, Art. 5. 97 *Ibid.*, Art. 11. 98 *Ibid.*, Art. 8.

99 IDMC, 'Making the Kampala Convention real: from paper to action', www.internal-displacement.org/kampala-convention/making-it-real (accessed 7 October 2011).

100 UNHRC, Report of Representative of the Secretary-General on the human rights of internally displaced persons, Walter Kälin, 9 February 2009, A/HRC/10/13, para. 12.

101 UNHRC, Report of Representative of the Secretary-General on the human rights of internally displaced persons, 5 January 2010, para. 11.

Nevertheless, international humanitarian law remains the main legal regime applicable in such situations. The issue of the protection of displaced persons in armed conflict has rarely been addressed, or in a rather cursory way, from the view of international humanitarian law. Yet, many issues arise that have been given too little consideration. Furthermore, the question of the protection of refugees and displaced persons enables one to draw valuable conclusions with regard to the state of international humanitarian law in particular, and international law in general. Consequently, this study will focus on aspects of this protection which relate to international humanitarian law specifically. Wherever possible, the analysis employed in this book will draw parallels with developments in other areas of international law, especially human rights protection. However, given the scope of this book, it is inevitable that human rights issues should only receive peripheral coverage and only to the extent that it informs the regime of protection in the *lex specialis* of humanitarian law.

1 The prohibition of forced displacement in international armed conflicts

Wars and armed conflicts are the main causes of displacement across the world. Conflict-related displacement may be triggered by a number of factors. First, displacement may be a 'normal' consequence of war. Many civilians will flee the general dangers of war resulting from confrontations between the belligerents and return to their place of residence once the hostilities have ended.[1] They may also be lawfully relocated or evacuated by one of the parties to a conflict for military or security reasons.[2] Nevertheless, in a 1992 report, the Representative of the Secretary-General on Internally Displaced Persons observed that, while population movements in time of war were inevitable, 'in some situations the number of persons forced to flee [was] multiplied as a result of excesses committed against the civilian population or military strategies which target the civilian population'.[3]

Forced displacement is often the consequence of systematic human rights abuses and violations of the laws of war on the part of a party to a conflict, whether a state's armed forces or insurgents. For instance, as a result of the 2008 conflict between Georgia and the Russian Federation, an estimated 10,000 to 15,000 were internally displaced within the

[1] For instance, most Lebanese and Israeli displaced by the conflict between Israel and Hezbollah were able to return to their homes before the end of 2006 (IDMC, *Internal Displacement*, 2007, p. 9).

[2] Civilians must be protected from the effects of attacks. Under Article 58 of Protocol I, parties to a conflict must remove the civilian population, individual civilians and civilian objects under their control from the vicinity of military objectives. Article 78 of Protocol I provides for the evacuation of children in certain circumstances. In addition, civilians may be evacuated to special safety zones, as envisaged by Articles 14 and 15 of the Fourth Geneva Convention and Articles 59 and 60 of Protocol I.

[3] UNCHR, 'Analytical report by the Secretary-General on internally displaced persons' (14 February 1992), para. 19.

Tskhinvali Region/South Ossetia, while 19,381 people, mainly ethnic Georgians, were displaced across the de facto border.[4] According to the Representative of the Secretary-General on the Human Rights of Internally Displaced Persons, much of the displacement was caused or followed by violations of international humanitarian law committed by the parties to the conflict, including the deliberate destruction and looting of ethnic Georgian villages, as well as the use of weapons in urban areas that were not accurate enough to discriminate between military and civilian targets.[5] International humanitarian law, the Fourth Geneva Convention in particular, endeavours to protect civilians in situations of armed conflict. As a fundamental principle of international humanitarian law, civilians enjoy general protection against dangers arising from military operations.[6] The warring parties therefore have an obligation to distinguish between civilians and combatants and civilian objects and military objectives at all times.[7] International humanitarian law prohibits attacks which target combatants and civilians indiscriminately, as well as direct attacks on civilians. Acts such as collective punishment,[8] pillage,[9] hostage-taking,[10] rape[11] or any other act aimed at terrorizing the civilian population[12] are also prohibited. Accordingly, most forced movements of population would be avoided if the belligerents duly respected these humanitarian rules.[13]

However, more than just an unfortunate consequence of the carelessness of belligerents, forced displacement is increasingly used as a tactic of war. Civilians are directly targeted and deliberately displaced by the belligerents, as part of a strategy to weaken the adversary.[14] Forced displacement is also often carried out as part of a wider 'ethnic cleansing'

[4] UNHRC, 'Report of the Representative of the Secretary-General on the Human Rights of Internally Displaced Persons, Walter Kälin, Follow-up to the report on the mission to Georgia', 14 January 2009, UN Doc. A/HRC/13/21/Add.3, para. 3.

[5] *Ibid.*, paras. 7–15. [6] Protocol I, Art. 51(1). [7] Protocol I, Art. 48.

[8] Geneva Convention IV, Art. 33(1); Protocol II, 4(2)(b).

[9] Geneva Convention IV, Art. 33(2); Protocol II, Art. 4(2)(g).

[10] Geneva Convention IV, Art. 34; Protocol II, Art. 4(2)(c).

[11] The Fourth Geneva Convention and the two Additional Protocols provide for the special protection of women, in particular against rape, forced prostitution and any other form of indecent assault (Art. 27; Protocol I, Art. 76 and Protocol II, Art. 4(2)(e)).

[12] Protocol I, Art. 51(2) prohibits 'acts or threats of violence the primary purpose of which is to spread terror among the civilian population', while Protocol II, Art. 4(2)(d) prohibits acts of terrorism in non-international armed conflicts.

[13] Bugnion, 'Réfugiés, personnes déplacées et droit international humanitaire', 281.

[14] IDMC, *Global Overview*, 2006, p. 17.

campaign.[15] Additionally, forced population movements in occupied territory can be immediately followed by the settlement of another population with close links to the agent of displacement. In this context, population transfers and settlement policies are used with the aim of altering the demographic composition of a territory.[16]

As noted, international human rights law applies at all times, including in situations of armed conflict. Although not expressly contained in any regional or universal human rights instrument, protection against arbitrary displacement may be inferred from a number of human rights provisions, notably the right to freedom of movement and choice of residence, as enshrined in Article 12(1) of the ICCPR.[17] Indeed, '[f]orced displacement is the denial of the exercise of freedom of movement and choice of residence, since it deprives a person of the choice of moving or not and of choosing where to reside'.[18] This was also recognized by the UN Sub-Commission on Prevention of Discrimination and Protection of Minorities, which stated, in a 1996 Resolution that:

> practices of forcible exile, mass expulsion and deportation, population transfer, forcible population exchange, unlawful forcible evacuation, eviction and forcible relocation, 'ethnic cleansing' and other forms of forcible displacement of populations within a country or across borders deprive the affected populations of their right to freedom of movement.[19]

In addition, provisions relating to privacy, including the protection from interference with one's home,[20] as well as the right to adequate housing,[21] also constitute barriers against arbitrary displacement.[22] However, these

15 During the conflicts in the former Yugoslavia, ethnic cleansing was practised systematically in areas of Bosnia and Herzegovina under Serb control. According to the Special Rapporteur of the Commission on Human Rights, '[t]he term ethnic cleansing refers to the elimination by the ethnic group exercising control over a given territory of members of other ethnic groups. A wide variety of methods are used to accomplish this end, including... transfer or relocation of populations by force' (UNGA, 'Report on the situation of human rights in the territory of the former Yugoslavia prepared by Mr Tadeusz Mazowiecki' (17 November 1992) UN Doc. A/47/666, para. 9).

16 See below Chapter 3.

17 Art. 12(1) provides that: 'Everyone lawfully within the territory of a State shall, within that territory, have the right to liberty of movement and freedom to choose his residence'. The right to freedom of movement and choice of residence is also contained in ACHR, Art. 22(1); Protocol No. 4 to ECHR, Art. 2(1) and African Charter, Art. 12(1).

18 UNCHR, 'Compilation and analysis of legal norms, Part II', para. 34.

19 UNCHR (Sub-Commission), Res. 1996/9 (1996) UN Doc. E/CN.4/SUB.2/RES/1996/9.

20 ICCPR, Art. 17(1); ACHR, Art. 11; ECHR, Art. 8.

21 ICESCR, Art. 11(1).

22 UNCHR, 'Compilation and analysis of legal norms, Part II', paras. 46, 50.

rights do not form part of the non-derogable core of human rights and may, as a result, be derogated from in times of public emergency.[23]

In contrast, international humanitarian law lays down non-derogable obligations, binding on all parties to an armed conflict. As well as seeking to shelter civilian populations from the effects of hostilities, international humanitarian law expressly prohibits the forced displacement of civilians in times of war. The prohibition of population transfers in belligerent occupation is the most comprehensive, as it combines a prohibition of forcible transfers of civilians both from and within occupied territory with a prohibition of transfer of the occupying power's own population into the territory.[24] International humanitarian law also proscribes the forced movement of civilians in non-international armed conflict, unless the security of civilians or imperative military reasons so demand.[25] Yet, there seems to be a legal gap in the existing protection regime, as international humanitarian law does not regulate the forced displacement of civilians in unoccupied territory during an international armed conflict.

The prohibition of deportation and forcible transfers in situations of occupation

Practices of forcible transfers and deportations of civilians in situations of occupation are expressly prohibited by the Fourth Geneva Convention. However, the interpretation of Article 49 is subject to contention. States often deny that a population transfer within the meaning of Article 49(1) of the Convention is taking place, arguing instead that they are carrying out a lawful evacuation of the civilian population, as envisaged in the second paragraph of the same provision. Furthermore, a number of uncertainties arise as to the exact scope and content of the prohibition of forced displacement under customary international law. Accordingly, the present chapter will attempt to address some of these uncertainties, starting with an overview of the state of the law as regards the practice of population transfer prior to the 1949 Geneva Conventions.

The prohibition of deportations and population transfers in pre-Geneva Conventions customary law

The first written rule prohibiting the forced displacement of civilians in armed conflict is to be found in Article 23 of the Lieber Code, according to which '[p]rivate citizens are no longer murdered, enslaved, or carried

[23] See above, Introduction. [24] See below Chapter 3. [25] See below Chapter 2.

off to distant parts'.[26] The Lieber Code represents the first codification of the laws of war. Although initially aimed at the US armed forces in the specific context of the American Civil War, the Code is widely regarded as the precursor of the 1899 and 1907 Hague Conventions.[27]

And, yet, the Hague Conventions make no reference to a similar prohibition of deportation or forcible transfer of civilians. However, the lack of explicit prohibition of deportations in the Hague Conventions should not be held as implicitly allowing such deportations. According to Georg Schwarzenberger, the prohibition of deportations was a 'self-understood rule' at the time of the Hague Peace Conferences of 1899 and 1907.[28] Its inclusion in the Hague Regulations was 'rejected as falling below the minimum standard of civilisation and, therefore, not requiring express prohibition'.[29] Similarly, Alfred-Maurice de Zayas describes the right of a population not to be expelled from its homeland as 'so fundamental that until after World War II it was not deemed necessary to codify it in a formal manner'.[30] Some authors have expressed doubts as to the existence of such a rule despite the silence of the Convention and of the *travaux préparatoires*.[31] Pictet however explains this silence by the fact that 'the practice of deporting persons was regarded at the beginning of this century as having fallen into abeyance'.[32]

It is nevertheless worth noting that implicit protection against deportation may be found in the provisions of the Hague Regulations relating to the duties of the occupying power. Indeed, deportation measures against the occupied population seem irreconcilable with Article 46, which provides for respect for family rights and the protection of property.[33] Bassiouni also argues that Articles 47 to 53 provide for other protections, which when read with Article 46, 'indicate by implication that civilian populations are to remain in place and not to be deported'.[34]

[26] Lieber, 'Instructions for the government of armies of the United States in the field' (1863), in Schindler and Toman (eds.), *The Laws of Armed Conflict*, 2004, p. 3.

[27] Schindler and Toman, *The Laws of Armed Conflict*, p. 3; Meron, 'Deportation of civilians as a war crime', 1993, p. 202.

[28] Schwarzenberger, *International Law as Applied by International Courts and Tribunals*, 1989, p. 228.

[29] *Ibid.*, p. 227. [30] de Zayas, 'Population, expulsion and transfer', 1997, 1062.

[31] Lapidoth, 'The expulsion of civilians from areas which came under Israeli control in 1967', 1990, 98.

[32] Pictet, *Commentary on the Geneva Conventions*, 1958, p. 279.

[33] Bassiouni, *Crimes against Humanity*, 1999, p. 302; Henckaerts, 'Deportation and transfer of civilians', 1993–4, 481; de Zayas, 'Mass population transfers', 1975, 212; Schwarzenberger, *International Law as Applied by International Courts and Tribunals*, p. 228.

[34] Bassiouni, *Crimes against Humanity*, p. 302.

In the case of mass deportations of civilians, they also constitute general penalties prohibited under Article 50 of the Regulations.[35]

Furthermore, the ICRC notes in its commentary on Article 49 that Articles 6(b) and 6(c) of the Charter of the Nuremberg International Military Tribunal (IMT),[36] its judgment and decisions by other courts support the view that the deportation of inhabitants of occupied territory is contrary to the laws and customs of war.[37] The Nuremberg Tribunal not only dealt with practices of deportations, but also the more general practice of 'Germanization' of occupied territories. Count 3J of the indictment held:

> In certain occupied territories purportedly annexed to Germany, the defendants methodically and pursuant to plan endeavoured to assimilate these territories politically, culturally, socially and economically into the German Reich. They endeavoured to obliterate the former national character of these territories. In pursuance of these plans, the defendants forcibly deported inhabitants who were predominantly non-German and replaced them by thousands of German colonists.[38]

In its judgment of 30 September 1946, the IMT stated that:

> Hitler discussed with Rosenberg, Goering, Keitel and others his plan for the exploitation of the Soviet population and territory, which included among other things the evacuation of the inhabitants of Crimea and its settlement by Germans.
>
> A somewhat similar fate was planned for Czechoslovakia by the defendant von Neurath, in August 1940; the intelligentsia were to be 'expelled', but the rest of the population was to be Germanised rather than expelled or exterminated, since there was a shortage of Germans to replace them.[39]

Consequently, the IMT found the accused guilty of the war crime and crime against humanity of deportations for slave labour or for other

[35] de Zayas, 'Mass population transfers', 212; Schwarzenberger, *International Law as Applied by International Courts and Tribunals*, p. 228.

[36] Agreement for the establishment of an International Military Tribunal for the prosecution and punishment of the major war criminals of the European Axis, signed in London on 8 August, 1945, 82 UNTS 279. Article 6(b) of the Charter defines 'deportation to slave labor or for any other purpose of civilian population of or in occupied territory' as a war crime, while Article 6(c) includes 'deportation and other inhumane acts committed against any civilian population before or during the war' among crimes against humanity.

[37] Pictet, *Commentary* (1958), p. 279, fn. 5.

[38] *Trial of the Major War Criminals before the International Military Tribunal*, 253–4 (Nuremberg edn, 1947), 57.

[39] *Judgment of the International Military Tribunal for the Trial of German Major War Criminals, Nuremberg, 30 September and 1 October 1946* (London: HMSO, 1946), p. 53.

purposes.[40] It also found some of the respondents guilty of attempting to 'Germanise' the occupied territories as a crime against humanity.[41] Moreover, the judgment held that by 1939, the war crimes defined in Article 6(b) of the Charter were already regarded as being declaratory of the laws and customs of war.[42] On 11 December 1946, the United Nations General Assembly unanimously adopted the 'Principles of international law recognized by the Charter of the Nuremberg Tribunal and the judgment of the Tribunal'.[43] Other war crimes tribunals also condemned the practice of deportations of civilians, most notably in the cases of *Milch*,[44] *Krupp*[45] and *Von Leeb (High Command* case).[46]

In light of the provisions of the Hague Regulations regarding the duties of the occupying power, the principles of the Nuremberg Charter and the jurisprudence of the Nuremberg Tribunal, it is clear that the deportation of civilians from occupied territory constituted, prior to the adoption of the 1949 Geneva Conventions, a violation of international customary law.[47]

Deportations, forcible transfers and evacuations in the 1949 Geneva Conventions

On account of the experience of the Second World War, particularly the deportation of millions of civilians from German-occupied territories for

40 *Ibid.*, p. 85 (Goering), p. 97 (Franck), p. 100 (Frick), p. 104 (Funk), p. 114 (von Schirach), p. 115 (Sauckel), p. 118 (Jodl), p. 121 (Seyss-Inquart), pp. 123–4 (Speer).

41 *Ibid.*, p. 95 (Rosenberg), p. 100 (Frick), pp. 125–6 (von Neurath), p. 129 (Bormann).

42 *Ibid.*, p. 65.

43 UNGA Res. 95(I) – Affirmation of the principles of international law recognized by the Charter of the Nürnberg Tribunal (11 December 1946), UN Doc. A/RES/(I). The Nuremberg principles were later formulated by the International Law Commission (ILC) and adopted by the UN General Assembly in Res. 488(V) – Formulation of the Nürnberg Principles (12 December 1950), UN Doc. A/RES/488(V). The ILC Report appears in (1950) II Yearbook of the ILC 374.

44 *United States of America* v. *Erhard Milch*, Trials of War Criminals before the Nuremberg Military Tribunals under Control Council Law no. 10, vol. 2 (1949) p. 790; (1947) 14 AD 299.

45 *United States of America* v. *Alfred Krupp and others*, *ibid.*, no. 10, vol. 9 (1950) p. 1430; (1948) 15 AD 620.

46 *United States of America* v. *Wilhelm von Leeb et al.* ('High Command Case'), *ibid.*, no. 10, vol. 11 (1950) p. 462, 603; (1948) 15 AD 376, 394. The United States Military tribunal held that: 'There is no international law that permits the deportation or the use of civilians against their will for other than on reasonable requisitions for the needs of the army, either within the area of the army or after deportation to rear areas or to the homeland of the occupying power.'

47 Meron, 'Deportation of civilians as a war crime', p. 218; de Zayas, 'Mass population transfers', 213–19.

the purpose of forced labour or extermination, the ICRC and the drafters of Geneva Conventions felt the need to clearly address the issue of population transfers in occupied territory. Accordingly, Article 49(1) of the Fourth Geneva Convention prohibits deportations and forcible transfers in and from occupied territory, while Article 49(2) allows for the evacuation of civilians 'if the security of the population or imperative military reasons so demand'.

Deportations and forcible transfers

In accordance with Article 49(1) of the Civilians Convention:

> Individual or mass forcible transfers, as well as deportations of protected persons from occupied territory to the territory of Occupying Power or to that of any other country, occupied or not, are prohibited, regardless of their motive.

Article 49(1) lays down a clear, absolute prohibition of deportations and forced transfers. However, it should be noted that this provision does not place a prohibition on transfers of all kinds. It only proscribes 'forced' or involuntary transfers of persons.[48] In this context, forced transfers are not limited to physical force, but may also include 'threat of force or coercion, such as that caused by fear of violence, duress, detention, psychological oppression or abuse of power against such person or persons or another person, or by taking advantage of a coercive environment'.[49]

All deportations or forcible transfers are illegal, irrespective of their motive or justification.[50] The prohibition is absolute and does not allow for derogations on grounds of military necessity. Alternatively, the existence of an illegal purpose such as slave labour is not required for a deportation or forcible transfer to be unlawful.[51] Similarly, the destination of the deportation or transfer is irrelevant for the assessment of the legality of the measure.[52] Article 49(1) expressly prohibits deportations 'to the territory of Occupying Power or to that of any other country, occupied or not'. As noted by the Appeals Chamber of the ICTY, in the *Krnojelac* case: '[t]he forced character of displacement and the forced uprooting

[48] Pictet, *Commentary* (1958), p. 278.

[49] *Prosecutor* v. *Krstic*, IT-98-3-T, Trial Judgment, 2 August 2001, para. 529. For a discussion on the involuntary nature of deportations and forcible transfers in the ICTY jurisprudence, see below Chapter 4.

[50] Geneva Convention IV, Art. 49(1).

[51] Arai-Takahashi, *The Law of Occupation*, 2009, p. 329.

[52] Henckaerts, 'Deportation and transfer of civilians', 472.

of the inhabitants of a territory entail the criminal responsibility of the perpetrator, not the destination to which these inhabitants are sent'.[53]

Furthermore, the prohibition of Article 49(1) encompasses both deportations from and forcible transfers within occupied territory. Although they both entail forced displacement, deportation and transfer are two distinct concepts:

> Whereas deportation implies expulsion from the national territory, the forcible transfer of population could occur wholly within the frontiers of one and the same State.[54]

Nevertheless, as observed by the ICTY, the distinction between deportation and forcible transfer 'has no bearing on the condemnation of such practices in international humanitarian law'.[55] Indeed, Article 49(1) is so constructed as to underline the distinction between 'individual or mass forcible transfers' within a territory on the one hand and 'deportations of protected persons from occupied territory' on the other hand,[56] and to stress that both are proscribed under international humanitarian law. This is clearly the interpretation adopted by the ICRC, which states that:

> Article 49 of the Fourth Convention prohibits *all forcible transfers*, as well as deportations of protected persons from occupied territory. [my italic][57]

Finally, Article 49(1) prohibits every forced transfer or deportation of civilians from occupied territories, notwithstanding the collective or individual character of the transfers. The issue has been discussed at length in the context of Israeli deportations of Palestinians from the West Bank and Gaza. Ever since the beginning of the occupation of the Palestinian Territories, Israel has been deporting Palestinians, alleged terrorists,

53 *Prosecutor* v. *Krnojelac*, IT-97-25-A, Appeals Judgment, 17 September 2003, para. 218.

54 ILC, *Draft Code of Crimes against the Peace of Security and Mankind*, 'Report of the International Law Commission on the work of its 48th Session' (6 May–26 July 1996), UN Doc. A/51/10, 100.

55 *Krstic*, Trial Judgment, para. 522. For a discussion on the difference between deportations and forcible transfers in the ICTY jurisprudence, see below Chapter 4.

56 As stressed by Henckaerts, if it was to be otherwise, there would have been a comma after deportations, so as to read: 'Individual or mass forcible transfers, as well as deportations, of protected persons from occupied territory' ('Deportation and transfer of civilians', 472, fn. 8).

57 Sandoz *et al.*, *Commentary on the Protocols*, p. 1000. The *Commentary* also adds in a footnote: 'In fact, by using the word "nevertheless", paragraph 2 . . . clearly shows that paragraph 1 also prohibits forcible transfers within occupied territory'.

political leaders and other 'subversive' individuals, on security grounds.[58] The Israeli Supreme Court has consistently affirmed the legality of the deportations and interpreted Article 49 as only prohibiting mass deportations, similar to those carried out in the Second World War, as opposed to individual deportations for reasons of security.[59]

This restrictive interpretation of Article 49(1) has been widely criticized. For the majority of the doctrine, the language of Article 49 is 'clear and categorical' and the prohibition it lays down must be construed as an absolute prohibition, of both collective and individual deportations.[60] It is undisputed that the drafting of the Geneva Conventions was heavily influenced by the atrocities committed during the Second World War and that Article 49 is a direct response to the mass deportations of Jewish or other civilians carried out by the Nazis. However, as clearly stated by Dinstein, the outlook of the Geneva Conventions is 'prospective and not retroactive', and the purpose of Article 49 is 'to ensure that, in the future, *any* deportation of protected persons from occupied territories [will] be unlawful'.[61]

Evacuation of protected persons

In accordance with Article 49(2) of the Fourth Geneva Convention:

> Nevertheless, the Occupying Power may undertake total or partial evacuation of a given area if the security of the population or imperative military reasons so demand. Such evacuations may not involve the displacement of protected persons outside the bounds of the occupied territory except when for material reasons it is impossible to avoid such displacement. Persons thus evacuated shall be transferred back to their homes as soon as hostilities in the area in question have ceased.

[58] Roberts, 'Prolonged military occupation', 1992, pp. 65–6; A. Lesch, 'Israeli deportation of Palestinians from the West Bank and the Gaza Strip, 1967–1978', *Journal of Palestine Studies*, 8 (1979), 101–31; B'Tselem, 'Deportation of Palestinians from the occupied territories and the mass deportation of December 1992' (June 1993), p. 4, www.btselem.org/English/Publications/Index.asp?TF=04 (accessed 4 May 2011).

[59] See for instance, HC 785/87, *Abd al Nasser al Aziz al Affo et al.* v. *IDF Commander of the West Bank* ('Affo' Judgment) (1987) 29 ILM (1990) 140, 152–5.

[60] Meron, *Human Rights and Humanitarian Norms as Customary Law*, 1989, p. 49, fn. 130; Dinstein, 'Deportations', 1993, 15; Kretzmer, *The Occupation of Justice*, 2002, p. 45; Dayanim, 'The Israeli Supreme Court and the deportations of Palestinians', 1994, 157–66; Henckaerts, 'Deportation and transfer of civilians', 471. This interpretation of Article 49(1) is also supported by the UN Security Council, which, in its Resolution 641(1989) of 30 August 1989, expressed grave concern over the deportation by Israel of five Palestinian civilians, and called upon Israel to ensure the safe and immediate return of those deported and 'to desist forthwith from deporting any other Palestinian civilians'.

[61] Dinstein, 'Deportations', 14.

Before proceeding to the analysis of the content and implications of this evacuation provision, it is necessary to first determine its relationship with the prohibition of deportation and forcible transfers, as contained in Article 49(1).

Evacuation: an exception to the prohibition of deportation?

Although often referred to as the exception to paragraph 1's basic rule,[62] evacuation for imperative military reasons or on grounds of civilian security is an altogether different concept from that of 'deportations and forcible transfers'.[63] As noted by the ICRC commentary, the prohibition of deportation and forcible transfers is 'absolute and allows of no exceptions'.[64] Evacuation is a separate rule and the prohibition of deportation remains non-derogable.[65] As explained by Dinstein:

> Security considerations are conceded as relevant in manifold contexts in the Geneva Convention – e.g., the second paragraph of Article 49 which pertains to evacuations – but they are conspicuously omitted from the first paragraph concerning deportations.[66]

Similarly, under the Statute of the ICC, 'the deportation or transfer of all or parts of the population of the occupied territory within or outside this territory' constitutes a war crime.[67] No reference is made to a possible exception for imperative military reasons. Accordingly, as rightly and clearly expressed by one commentator: '[d]eportations and forced transfers are always unlawful; evacuations may be permissible'.[68]

Unfortunately, this is not the position adopted by the ICRC in its study of customary international humanitarian law, which states, in Rule 129:

> Parties to an international armed conflict may not deport or forcibly transfer the civilian population of an occupied territory, in whole or in part, unless the security of the civilians involved or imperative military reasons so demand.[69]

[62] Pictet, *Commentary* (1958), p. 280; Henckaerts, 'Deportation and transfer of civilians', 473.

[63] Jacquemet, 'Cross-fertilization', 670. Jacquemet talks of a 'putative exception': 'But it is not a true exception, as that paragraph covers situations different from those stipulated in paragraph 1 . . . Evacuation for imperative military reasons is not the same act or the same concept as deportation.'

[64] Pictet, *Commentary* (1958), p. 279.

[65] Arai-Takahashi, *Law of Occupation*, pp. 343–4.

[66] Dinstein, 'Deportations', 19.

[67] ICC Statute, Art. 8(2)(b)(viii).

[68] Piotrowicz, 'Displacement and displaced persons', 2007, p. 342.

[69] Henckaerts and Doswald-Beck, *Customary International Humanitarian Law*, vol. 1, Rule 129, p. 457.

The wording of the Rule has been criticized as 'unfortunate',[70] because it potentially rationalizes a practice which is categorically prohibited under Article 49(1), 'regardless of [its] motive'.[71]

Evacuation of civilians on grounds of security or imperative military reasons
Article 49(2) envisages the possibility of evacuation of protected persons. However, in order to protect the interests of the population concerned, and to prevent abuses by the occupying power, Article 49 lays down a number of important safeguards.[72]

First of all, evacuation of civilians may only be carried out in two exceptional circumstances: 'if the security of the population or imperative military reasons so demand'. The first justification relates to the security of the civilian population. In fact, when read in conjunction with Article 58(a) of the 1977 Protocol I, Article 49(2) not only grants a right, but also imposes a duty on the occupying power to evacuate civilians from the vicinity of military objectives.[73] Thus, when taken in the interests of the civilian population, evacuation has a protective element which is totally absent from all types of deportation.[74]

In addition, evacuation is permitted when 'imperative military reasons so demand', for instance when the presence of protected persons in an area hampers military operations.[75] Military necessity represents, along with the principle of humanity, a core concept of international humanitarian law. It is indeed widely accepted that international humanitarian law is 'predicated on a subtle equilibrium between diametrically opposed impulses: military necessity and humanitarian considerations'.[76]

70 Piotrowicz, 'Displacement and displaced persons', p. 342.

71 Arai-Takahashi suggests that '[t]he more coherent view [would be] to highlight the non-derogable nature of the rule forbidding deportation and forcible transfer and to treat the evacuation as a separate rule that falls outside the definitional scope of the rule set forth in Article 49(1)' (*Law of Occupation*, p. 344).

72 Pictet, *Commentary* (1958), p. 280.

73 Protocol I, Art. 58 provides that: 'The Parties to the conflict shall, to the maximum extent feasible: Without prejudice to Article 49 of the Fourth Convention, endeavour to remove the civilian population, individual civilians and civilian objects under their control from the vicinity of military objectives.'

The duty to remove civilians and civilian objects from the vicinity of military objectives is a customary rule of international law. See Henckaerts and Doswald-Beck, *Customary International Humanitarian Law*, vol. 1, Rule 24, p. 74.

74 Schwarzenberger, *International Law as Applied by International Courts*, p. 232.

75 ICRC Commentary Geneva Convention IV, p. 280.

76 Dinstein, *The Conduct of Hostilities*, 2004, p. 16. See also Sandoz *et al.*, *Commentary on the Protocols*, pp. 392–3, para. 1389.

Article 49(2) expressly allows for evacuations of civilians when justified by 'imperative military reasons'. What constitutes a legitimate military reason, however, may be difficult to determine. In this regard, two decisions by war crimes tribunals are particularly relevant. During his trial before the United States Military Tribunal, German General Lothar Rendulic was accused of violating Article 23(g) of the 1907 Hague Regulations[77] by ordering scorched-earth tactics, as well as the evacuation of the entire population of the Norwegian province of Finnmark, during the retreat of his German troops.[78] Rendulic had argued that such tactics were justified by military necessity, as it seemed to be the only way to delay the advance of the Russian troops in pursuit of the Germans,[79] while the evacuations were motivated by concerns for the safety of the civilian population.[80] After noting that no loss of life directly resulted from the evacuation, the Tribunal concluded that:

> It is our considered opinion that the conditions, as they appeared to the defendant at the time were sufficient, upon which he could honestly conclude that urgent military necessity warranted the decision made. This being true, the defendant may have erred in the exercise of his judgment but he was guilty of no criminal act.[81]

Accordingly, the legality of an evacuation order based on military necessity must be assessed in light of the knowledge available to the military commander at the time, irrespective of the fact that a subsequent examination of the facts may show an absence of military necessity.

The second decision relevant to this discussion is the trial of Field Marshal Erich von Manstein before a British military tribunal. Von Manstein was charged with and convicted of 'the mass deportation and evacuation of civilian inhabitants' from the Ukraine in 1944.[82] Von Manstein had argued that the evacuations were justified by military necessity, in order to prevent espionage and 'to deprive the enemy of labour potential'.[83] The

[77] Art. 23(g) of the 1907 Hague Regulations provides that it is specifically forbidden '[t]o destroy or seize the enemy's property, unless such destruction or seizure be imperatively demanded by the necessities of war'.

[78] *United States of America* v. *Wilhelm List et al.* (the *Hostage* case) (1948) 15 AD 632, 647.

[79] *Ibid.*, 648.

[80] Bill, 'The Rendulic "rule"', 2009, 124. Bill quotes Rendulic's order to his troops: 'I request all officers concerned to carry out this evacuation in the sense of a relief action for the Norwegian population. Though it will be necessary here and there to be severe, all of us must attempt to save the Norwegians from Bolchevism and to keep them alive.'

[81] *Hostage* case, 649.

[82] *In re von Lewinski* (called von Manstein) (1949) 16 AD 509, 510.

[83] *Ibid.*, 521.

Tribunal however did not find it to be a sufficient reason for the deportation of the population from their homes and the destruction of their property.[84] Thus, both Alfred de Zayas and Jean-Marie Henckaerts infer from this decision that the defence of military necessity is restricted to 'situations where the army commanders judge that the safety of the civilian population requires that they be removed from the battle zone, and not when the same army commanders decide that military advantage would be gained by removing the population and scorching the earth behind them'.[85]

While it may be argued that the exception of military necessity lessens the protection against forced displacement and may be easily abused by the occupying power, it should be remembered that the absolute prohibition constitutes the basic rule and that the exception of necessity is subject to strict interpretation.[86] Forcible transfers of populations are presumed to be unlawful. Consequently, the burden is on the occupying power to prove that overriding military reasons make the evacuation *imperative*. Indeed, as noted in the commentary on the Convention, 'if it is not imperative, evacuation ceases to be legitimate'.[87] Furthermore, the ICTY held, in *Simić*, that 'in view of the drastic nature of a forced displacement of persons, recourse to such measures would only be lawful in the gravest of circumstances and only as measures of last resort'.[88]

[84] *Ibid.*, 522–3. After noting that the requirement in Article 23(g) of the Hague Regulations was 'imperative necessity', and not merely an 'advantage', the Tribunal held that: 'For a retreating army to leave devastation in its wake may afford many obvious disadvantages to the enemy and corresponding advantages to those in retreat. That fact alone, if the words in this article mean anything at all, cannot afford a justification.' However, with regard to the deportation of civilians, the Tribunal held that Article 23(g) was not applicable and that 'if [deportation] is to be defended at all, it must be upon some ground other than military necessity'. Consequently, the only valid justification for the forced evacuation of civilians would be the safety of the civilian population.

[85] de Zayas, 'Mass population transfers', 219; Henckaerts, 'Deportation and transfer of civilians', 475. However, for a slightly diverging view, see Bill, 'The Rendulic "rule"':

> Von Manstein and other cases may stand only for the principle that widespread and extensive evacuations, with little concern for the human needs of the evacuees, are too much to be supported by military necessity. But there may be less extreme evacuations, premised only on a military advantage anticipated and not on the safety of the population, which will not offend Article 49. In making this point I am hardly arguing for a wider use of such evacuations; I only point out that the law may not have yet advanced to the humanitarian stage suggested by other commentators. (150)

[86] Pellet, 'The destruction of Troy will not take place', 1992, p. 196.

[87] Pictet, *Commentary* (1958), p. 280.

[88] *Prosecutor* v. *Simić*, IT-95-9-T, Judgment, 17 October 2003, para. 125, fn. 218.

As a further safeguard, Article 49(2) stipulates that evacuations may not involve the displacement of protected persons outside the borders of the occupied territory, unless it is physically impossible to do otherwise.[89] Unlike deportations or forcible transfers, evacuation is a provisional measure.[90] Protected persons must therefore be brought back to their homes as soon as hostilities in the area have ended.

Treatment of displaced persons during evacuation

In an effort to mitigate the adverse effects of displacement, Article 49(3) provides that the occupying power should ensure, 'to the greatest practicable extent', that proper accommodation is provided to the evacuees and that the removals are effected 'in satisfactory conditions of hygiene, health, safety and nutrition, and that members of the same family are not separated'.[91] These conditions constitute minimum humanitarian standards against which to assess the legality of a transfer of population. In the *Krupp* case,[92] the US Military Tribunal at Nuremberg adopted, as the law applicable to deportation from occupied territory, the opinion by Judge Phillips in *Re Milch*, which laid down the conditions under which deportations of civilians became a war crime:

> The third and final condition under which deportation becomes illegal occurs whenever generally recognized standards of decency and humanity are disregarded. This flows from the principle that an otherwise permissible act becomes a crime when carried out in criminal manner.[93]

Consequently, an evacuation carried out in accordance with Article 49(2), i.e. for the security of civilians or imperative military reasons, may nonetheless be unlawful if it does not meet the requirements set out in paragraph 3.

Paragraph 3 places a duty of care on the occupying power 'undertaking such transfers or evacuations', but does this obligation extend to illegal transfers of civilians? The applicability of Article 49(3) to all situations of forced displacement, including those that are considered to be unlawful, is subject to debate. One writer argues that '[t]he distinction between lawful and unlawful displacement is inconsequential in terms of the kind

[89] Pictet, *Commentary* (1958), p. 280. [90] *Ibid.*

[91] Henckaerts and Doswald-Beck, *Customary International Humanitarian Law*, vol. 1, Rule 131, p. 463.

[92] *In re Krupp and others*, 1 AD 620, 626. [93] *In re Milch*, 14 AD 299, 302.

of treatment the civilian population should be afforded during their displacement. Regardless of the legality of their displacement, civilians are entitled to a minimum set of guarantees and protection.'[94] While nothing in Article 49(3) or the related state practice supports this argument,[95] the obligation of protection, even during unlawful displacement, may be derived from the general IHL principle of humane treatment,[96] the duty of the occupying power to ensure the provision of food and medical supplies for the occupied population,[97] including displaced persons, as well as the provisions of international human rights law, notably the right to food, clothing and housing, as enshrined in Article 11(1) of the ICESCR.[98]

The prohibition of deportations and forcible transfers as a norm of customary international law

As demonstrated earlier, the deportation of civilians and subsequent colonization of occupied territory was already prohibited under customary international law before the adoption of the Geneva Conventions. The question remains as to whether the prohibition of deportations and forcible transfers as enshrined in Article 49(1) also constitutes a norm of customary international law.

The Fourth Geneva Convention is both an extension and a codification of the international rules and practices governing the treatment of alien

94 Abebe, 'Displacement of civilians during armed conflict', 2009, 826; see also Gillard, 'The role of international humanitarian law for the protection of internally displaced persons', 2005, 41.

95 Piotrowicz, 'Displacement and displaced persons', p. 349. Most military manuals only refer to the obligation to provide basic necessities in situations of evacuation. For instance, the UK MoD's *Manual of the Law of Armed Conflict* provides that: 'An area may be totally or partially evacuated by the occupying power if . . . to the greatest extent practicable: (1) proper accommodation is provided, (2) movement takes place under satisfactory conditions of hygiene, health, safety and nutrition, and (3) members of the same family are not separated' (2004, para. 11.55).

96 Common Article 3 of the Geneva Conventions states that: 'Persons taking no active part in the hostilities, including members of armed forces who have laid down their arms and those placed hors de combat by sickness, wounds, detention, or any other cause, shall in all circumstances be treated humanely'; Article 75(1) Protocol I provides that 'Persons who are in the power of a Party to the conflict and who do not benefit from more favourable treatment under the Conventions or under this Protocol shall be treated humanely in all circumstances'. Similarly, in non-international armed conflicts, Article 4(1) Protocol II provides that: 'All persons who do not take a direct part or who have ceased to take part in hostilities, whether or not their liberty has been restricted . . . shall in all circumstances be treated humanely.'

97 Geneva Convention IV, Art. 55.

98 See below Chapter 6.

enemies in a belligerent country and the treatment of the inhabitants of occupied territory.[99] It comprises provisions that are 'no more than attempts to clarify existing rules of international customary law'[100] and other provisions that enlarge the legal duties of the parties to a conflict. It is generally considered that those provisions of the Convention which codify earlier rules are *declaratory* of customary international law and therefore binding on all parties to a conflict, whether or not they have ratified the Convention. On the other hand, the provisions which create new law and extend the duties of the belligerents are applicable only between contracting parties. These innovative Treaty provisions may progressively come to be accepted as generally applicable, thereby becoming *constitutive* of customary law.

There is an ongoing debate among legal scholars as to which provisions of the Fourth Convention are constitutive and which ones are declaratory in nature. Dinstein, for instance, maintains that the prohibition of deportations in Article 49 'incontrovertibly goes beyond customary international law'.[101] However, it is clear, from the analysis of pre-Geneva customary law, that the prohibition of mass deportation already existed before the Conventions and that Article 49(1) merely codifies this prohibition. This opinion is supported by Theodor Meron, who argues that:

> At least the central elements of Article 49(1), such as the absolute prohibitions of forcible mass and individual transfers and deportations of protected persons from occupied territories stated in Article 49(1), are declaratory of customary law even when the object and setting of the deportations differ from those underlying German World War II practices which led to the rules set forth in Article 49.[102]

As for individual deportations, Meron adds that although it is less clear that they were already prohibited in 1949, he believes that this prohibition has by now come to reflect customary law. The ICRC commentary on Article 49 also considers that the prohibition of deportation may be regarded today 'as having been embodied in international law'.[103]

[99] Yingling and Ginnane, 'The Geneva Conventions of 1949', 1952, 411.

[100] Schwarzenberger, *International Law as Applied by International Courts*, pp. 165–6. Schwarzenberger considers that these provisions comprise articles in Section I of Part III of the Convention, in which a number of requirements of the standard of civilization are codified, as well as the prohibition of the deportation of inhabitants of occupied territories in Article 49.

[101] Dinstein, 'Deportations', 13.

[102] Meron, *Human Rights and Humanitarian Norms*, p. 48.

[103] Pictet, *Commentary* (1958), p. 279.

In the *North Sea Continental Shelf* cases, the International Court of Justice laid down the requirements which had to be met for a treaty provision to be considered to have become a customary norm of international law:

Not only must the acts concerned amount to a settled practice, but they must also be such, or be carried out in such a way, as to be evidence of a belief that this practice is rendered obligatory by the existence of a rule of law requiring it. The need for such a belief, i.e., the existence of a subjective element, is implicit in the very notion of the *opinio juris sive necessitatis*. The States concerned must therefore feel that they are conforming to what amounts to a legal obligation.[104]

State practice shows a consistent condemnation of practices of deportation, forcible transfers and mass expulsion. In 1995 for instance, the Security Council adopted Resolution 1034, in which it condemned 'in the strongest possible terms' the violations of international humanitarian law and human rights committed in the territory of former Yugoslavia by Bosnian Serb and paramilitary forces, in particular the 'consistent pattern of... mass expulsions'.[105] In 1970, the UN General Assembly unanimously adopted a resolution entitled 'Basic principles for the protection of the civilian population in armed conflicts', which stated that: 'Civilian populations, or individual members thereof, should not be the object of... forcible transfers'.[106] In *Tadić*, the International Criminal Tribunal for former Yugoslavia held that the principles laid down in the resolution were 'declaratory of the principles of customary international law regarding the protection of civilian populations and property in armed conflicts'.[107]

Furthermore, the virtually universal condemnation of Israeli deportations of Palestinians from the occupied territories reflects *opinio juris* and further contributes to the formation of a customary norm of international law.[108] Indeed, the UN General Assembly has consistently denounced 'the evacuation, deportation, expulsion, displacement and transfer of Arab inhabitants of the occupied territories'.[109] The Security Council has also repeatedly expressed its opposition to the deportation of Palestinian

104 *North Sea Continental Shelf*, Judgment, ICJ Reports 1969, p. 3, para. 77.

105 UNSC Res. 1034 (21 December 1995) UN Doc. S/RES/1034, para. 2.

106 'Basic principles for the protection of the civilian population in armed conflicts', UNGA Res. 2675(XXV) (9 December 1970), para. 7.

107 *Prosecutor* v. *Tadić (Decision on the Defence Motion for the Interlocutory Appeal on Jurisdiction)*, IT-941, 2 October 1995, para. 112.

108 Meron, *Human Rights and Humanitarian Norms*, p. 49, fn. 131.

109 E.g. UNGA Res. 35/122 C (11 December 1980), Res. 40/161 D (16 December 1985), Res. 47/70 E (14 December 1992), Res. 47/172 (22 December 1992), Res. 48/41 C (10 December 1993).

civilians from the occupied territories.[110] The 2005 ICRC study on customary international humanitarian law has confirmed that the prohibition of all forcible transfers and deportations in situations of occupation is a norm of customary international law.[111]

IHL and states' own nationals: gaps in protection

Forced displacement of a state's own nationals in armed conflict

International humanitarian law is essentially rooted in a traditional conception of interstate armed conflicts. In 1949, based on the experiences of the Second World War, the drafters of the Fourth Geneva Convention sought to protect enemy nationals and inhabitants of occupied territory, as a category of victims of war in desperate need of protection. Consequently, under Article 4 of the Civilians Convention, persons protected by the Convention are those who find themselves, in case of a conflict or occupation, in the hands of a party to a conflict or occupying power of which they are not nationals.[112] Civilians considered as 'protected persons' benefit from the whole spectrum of protection, as established by the Fourth Geneva Convention. In contrast, and in accordance with the general principle of non-interference within a state's internal affairs,[113] international humanitarian law does not regulate the relations between a state and its own citizens.[114] A state's own nationals are thus excluded from the definition of 'protected persons'. International humanitarian law is indeed based on the premise that civilians do not need special protection from their own government in times of war.

This difference of regime is especially significant in relation to the issue of forced displacement. Civilians in occupied territory benefit from the protection of Article 49 of the Civilians Convention against 'individual or mass forcible transfers'. During an international armed conflict, while

110 UNSC Res. 468 (18 May 1980), Res. 469 (20 May 1980), Res. 484 (19 December 1980), Res. 607 (5 January 1988), Res. 608 (14 January 1988), Res. 636 (7 July 1989), Res. 641 (31 August 1989), Res. 681 (20 December 1990), Res. 694 (24 May 1991), Res. 726 (6 January 1992), Res. 799 (18 December 1992).

111 Henckaerts and Doswald-Beck, *Customary International Humanitarian Law*, vol. 1, Rule 129, p. 457.

112 Pictet, *Commentary* (1958), p. 46.

113 The principle of non-interference in the internal affairs of a state is enshrined in Article 2(7) of the Charter of the United Nations, 24 October 1945, 1 UNTS XVI: 'Nothing contained in the present Charter shall authorize the United Nations to intervene in matters which are essentially within the domestic jurisdiction of any State'.

114 Pictet, *Commentary* (1958), p. 46.

there is no explicit prohibition of forced displacement of enemy nationals, they are nonetheless protected against the arbitrariness of the Detaining Power.[115] In contrast, nationals of a belligerent fall outside the ambit of international humanitarian law. They may rely, as citizens of their country, on the protection of international and regional human rights law, which, as noted in the introductory chapter, continues to apply in time of war. Thus, where the protection offered by the laws of war is unavailable, such as in the present case of a state's own nationals, human rights law should, in principle, provide continuous protection.[116]

Protection against arbitrary displacement is implicitly contained in the right to freedom of movement and the choice of residence.[117] Furthermore, 'it is a firmly established rule of international law that a State may not expel or deport its nationals'.[118] This freedom from expulsion is a corollary of nationals' right to enter or return to their own country,[119] as provided for by Article 13(4) UDHR,[120] Article 12(4) of the ICCPR[121] and Article 12(2) of the African Charter on Human Rights and Peoples' Rights.[122] Additionally, the Universal Declaration prohibits arbitrary exile[123] and two regional instruments clearly lay down a prohibition of expulsion of nationals. Article 3 of Protocol 4 of the European Convention on Human Rights provides that:

> 1 No one shall be expelled, by means either of an individual or of a collective measure, from the territory of the State of which he is a national.
>
> 2 No one shall be deprived of the right to enter the territory of the State of which he is a national.[124]

[115] Geneva Convention IV, Arts. 35–46.

[116] Meron, *Humanization of International Law*, pp. 47–8; Greenwood, 'Rights at the frontier', p. 287.

[117] See above, Introduction to this Chapter.

[118] Sohn and Buergenthal, *The Movement of Persons across Borders*, 1992, p. 85.

[119] Henckaerts, *Mass Expulsion*, 1995, p. 79; Sohn and Buergenthal, *Movement of Persons across Borders*, p. 85; Dinstein, 'Deportations', 5.

[120] Universal Declaration on Human Rights (UDHR), UNGA Res. 217A (III) UN Doc. A/810, Art. 13(2): 'Everyone has the right to leave any country, including his own, and to return to his country'.

[121] ICCPR, Art. 12(4): 'No one shall be arbitrarily deprived of the right to enter his own country'.

[122] African Charter on Human Rights and Peoples' Rights, Art. 12(5): 'Every individual shall have the right to leave any country including his own, and to return to his country, This right may only be subject to restrictions, provided for by law for the protection of national security, law and order, public health or morality'.

[123] UDHR, Art. 9: 'No one shall be subjected to arbitrary arrest, detention or exile'.

[124] Protocol No. 4 to the Convention for the Protection of Human Rights and Fundamental Freedoms Securing Certain Rights and Freedoms Other than Those Already Included in

Similarly, Article 22(5) of the American Convention on Human Rights states that:

> No one shall be expelled from the territory of the State of which he is a national or be deprived of the right to enter it.

However, two caveats shall be noted. First, while the two above-mentioned regional instruments clearly and unconditionally prohibit expulsion of nationals, the prohibition laid down in the Universal Declaration and the ICCPR is limited to the *arbitrary* exile or expulsion of nationals.[125] However, Henckaerts notes that instances of non-arbitrary expulsion of a national are 'hardly conceivable except for the case of fraudulently naturalized aliens or persons having dual nationality'.[126]

Second, the ICCPR, the European Convention on Human Rights and the American Convention of Human Rights all contain a derogation clause, which enables a state party to derogate from certain rights 'in time of public emergency', subject to a number of strict conditions.[127] While each instrument contains a catalogue of human rights considered so fundamental that no derogation is ever allowed – the so-called 'non-derogable rights',[128] none of them includes freedom of movement or freedom from expulsion.[129] Thus, as noted by Meron, 'although in time of emergency the question of deportation is of particular importance, there is no prohibition of arbitrary deportations, even on a massive scale'.[130]

As a result, and provided that the state fulfils the strict conditions required for a derogation, nationals may be deprived of the protection offered by human rights law against arbitrary displacement and expulsion. On the other hand, Article 49 of the Civilians Convention, which expressly prohibits the deportation and forcible transfer of civilians, is not applicable to states' own nationals. The remaining question is therefore whether it is possible to derive a legal basis for the prohibition of forced displacement of a state's own nationals in other provisions of the Fourth Geneva Convention and the Protocol I.

As part of the civilian population, states' own nationals are protected by the rules regulating the conduct of hostilities, including the principle

the Convention and in the First Protocol, 16 September 1963, ETS No. 46, AJIL, 58 (1964), 334, Article 3.

125 Dinstein, 'Deportations', 6. 126 Henckaerts, *Mass Expulsion*, p. 81.

127 ICCPR, Art. 4(1), ECHR, Art. 15(1) and ACHR, Art. 27(1).

128 ICCPR, Art. 4(2), ECHR, Art. 15(2) and ACHR, Art. 27(2).

129 Dinstein, 'Deportations', 10.

130 T. Meron, *Human Rights Law-making in the United Nations* (Oxford: Oxford University Press, 1986), p. 91, cited in Dinstein, 'Deportations', 11.

of civilian immunity. Article 51(7) of the Protocol I prohibits the forced movement of civilians in order to attempt to shield military objectives from attacks or to shield military operations. Under Article 58, belligerents shall endeavour to remove the civilian population under their control from the vicinity of military objectives. In addition, Articles 14 and 15 of the Fourth Convention provide for the establishment of neutralized zones and other places of refuge for civilians to be evacuated to.[131] These are the only provisions of general application directly relevant to the issue of displacement of civilians in the territory of a party to a conflict. At the time of the drafting of the Convention, it seemed indeed inconceivable that belligerents would deliberately displace their own citizens.

Furthermore, Article 75 of the First Protocol lays down fundamental guarantees applicable to 'all persons who are in the power of a Party to the conflict who do not benefit from more favourable treatment' under the Conventions or the Protocol. The application of Article 75 to a belligerent's own nationals has been the subject of a long and heated debate since the ICRC first introduced Article 65 of the ICRC Draft, which expressly mentioned 'the Parties' own nationals'.[132] Most academic writers and commentators support the view that own nationals are entitled to the protection of Article 75, referred to, by Hans-Peter Gasser, as 'a humanitarian safety net'.[133] The applicability of Article 75 to own nationals was recognized by the Eritrea–Ethiopia Claims Commission, which held that:

> [Article 75] applies even to a Party's treatment of its own nationals. These guarantees distil basic human rights most important in wartime. Given their fundamental humanitarian nature and their correspondence with generally accepted human rights principles, the Commission views these rules as part of customary international humanitarian law.[134]

131 See below Chapter 7.

132 Bothe *et al.*, *New Rules for Victims of Armed Conflicts*, 1982, pp. 456–60. According to this commentary, when the representative of the ICRC introduced Article 65, he sought to justify the reference to parties' own nationals by 'the arbitrary manner in which a Party to the conflict might easily treat its own nationals should they pose a threat to its security'. This inclusion in the draft article faced strong opposition, especially from the USA and Australia, and it was therefore decided to remove all reference to specific categories of persons who would benefit from the protection of Article 75.

133 Gasser, 'Protection of the civilian population', 1995, p. 233. According to Mohammed El Kouhene: 'The principle of application of the fundamental guarantees of Article 75 to own nationals is incontestable; it is derived from both conventional and customary law' (*Les garanties fondamentales de la personne*, 1986, p. 19; my translation).

134 Eritrea–Ethiopia Claims Commission (EECC), Partial Award, Civilians Claims, *Eritrea's Claims 15, 16, 23 & 27–32 between The State of Eritrea and the Federal Democratic Republic of*

However, this provision is only applicable to own nationals if they are 'affected by a situation referred to in Article 1' of the First Protocol, namely an armed conflict. This requirement significantly reduces the scope of application of Article 75:

> It excludes all persons who are not exposed to the dangers resulting from the armed conflict and it excludes likewise acts of the Party in power not connected with the armed conflict, such as the normal administration of justice and purely internal measures to ensure the good order and discipline of their own armed forces.[135]

This restriction was essential to guarantee a consensus at the Diplomatic Conference.[136] Indeed, by limiting the application of Article 75 to own nationals who are connected with an international armed conflict, it leaves states with the satisfaction that their exclusive jurisdiction on internal matters is respected. Concerning a state's own nationals of enemy origin, it is fair to assume that they are affected by the armed conflict, as, like traitors and collaborators, they are perceived by the state as pledging allegiance to the enemy. They should therefore benefit from the fundamental guarantees enshrined in Article 75 of the First Protocol, in particular the guarantees of humane treatment and due process.

As the law stands today, these are the only guarantees from which a state's own nationals in an interstate armed conflict may benefit, under international humanitarian law. In terms of forced displacement, this protection is insufficient. There are a number of instances where uncertainty regarding the legal status of certain individuals enables states to take advantage of the situation and to deport them under false pretences. In addition to the fundamental guarantees of humane treatment and due process, international humanitarian law should explicitly prohibit the arbitrary forced displacement of all civilians on the territory of a party to an international armed conflict, particularly when motivated by reasons of ethnicity or origins. As a minimum, Article 75 of Protocol I should incorporate a paragraph on the prohibition of forced displacement, similar to that applicable in non-international armed conflict. Indeed, by prohibiting forced displacement 'for reasons connected with the conflict', Article 17 of Protocol II provides states with a welcome safeguard, as it ensures that judicially imposed extraditions, with no relation to

Ethiopia (17 December 2004), para. 30, www.pca-cpa.org/showpage.asp?pag_id=1151 (accessed 31 August 2011).

135 Bothe *et al.*, *New Rules for Victims of Armed Conflicts*, p. 459.

136 Sandoz *et al.*, *Commentary on the Protocols*, p. 868.

the conflict, remain within their exclusive domestic jurisdiction.[137] The reference, in Article 75, to persons 'affected by a situation referred to in Article 1', combined with an explicit prohibition of forced displacement 'for reasons connected with the conflict' would effectively protect affected persons, such as nationals of enemy origin, from arbitrary deportation, while ensuring that the state's domestic jurisdiction is respected.

Aside from the lack of specific protection from displacement for states' own nationals, the above discussion has highlighted important issues of general interest, related to the nature of international humanitarian law and its reliance on the nationality of the victim for its application.

International humanitarian law and the nationality issue

According to the *Encyclopedia of Public International Law*, the term 'nationality' indicates 'the existence of a legal tie between an individual and a State, by which the individual is under the personal jurisdiction of that State'.[138] Although a concept of nationality revolving entirely around the notion of the state seems fully adequate in terms of diplomatic protection, one cannot help but wonder about the adequacy of such a state-centric criterion for the applicability of international humanitarian law.

Redefining 'protected persons' in inter-ethnic armed conflicts

The traditional interstate conception of international humanitarian law has progressively evolved with the emergence of internal armed conflicts. Common Article 3 of the Geneva Conventions and the Protocol II, dedicated to non-international armed conflicts, regulate the relations between a state and its nationals and constitute a remarkable interference with the state's exclusive jurisdiction on domestic matters. In contrast, the definition of protected persons under the Fourth Geneva Convention reflects 'the traditional state-centric, reciprocity-based approach of the law of the war'.[139]

However, contemporary armed conflicts are becoming more and more complex and do not always fit in the traditional dichotomy between international and non-international armed conflicts. In an increasingly interdependent world, internal conflicts rarely remain matters of a purely domestic nature. Civil wars often entail economic, political or other consequences for neighbouring countries or allies of the state concerned, often prompting them to intervene in favour of one of the parties to the

[137] See below Chapter 2. [138] Randelzhoffer, 'Nationality', 1997, p. 502.
[139] Meron, *Humanization of International Law*, p. 34.

conflict, be it the legitimate government or the insurgents. In addition, armed conflicts are increasingly fought along ethnic or religious lines. In such conflicts, the nationality of the belligerents bears very little relevance, and a conflict which started out within the borders of a state may reach international proportions due to foreign intervention. International inter-ethnic conflicts are frequently associated with policies of ethnic cleansing, involving, among other means, the extensive displacement of civilian populations. Such was the case of the conflicts in former Yugoslavia, which the International Tribunal for former Yugoslavia held that they could be characterized 'at different times and places as either internal or international armed conflicts, or as a mixed internal–international armed conflict'.[140] As a result, aspects of 'internationalized' internal armed conflicts leave the realm of the law of internal armed conflicts to become regulated by the law of international armed conflicts.

The specificity of these inter-ethnic armed conflicts is that, in most cases, the victims share the same nationality as their abusers. As civilians in the hands of a power of which *they are nationals*, these victims fall outside the ambit of protection of the Civilians Convention. Accordingly, a belligerent could effectively displace or otherwise abuse fellow nationals belonging to a particular ethnic group, because they do not fit the definition of 'protected persons'. Such a result would be devastating for all civilians caught up in inter-ethnic armed conflicts and would be at odds with the very purpose of international humanitarian law, the protection of all victims of war.

The Yugoslav Tribunal has acknowledged the changing nature of armed conflicts and the inadequacy of the criterion of nationality for the applicability of international humanitarian law. Article 2 of the Statute of the Tribunal requires that grave breaches of the Fourth Geneva Convention may only be prosecuted when perpetrated against persons regarded as 'protected' under the Convention.[141] Accordingly, it had been argued before the Tribunal that Bosnian Serbs were of the same nationality as their Bosnian Muslim victims, who, as a result, could not be considered as 'protected persons' within the meaning of Article 4.[142]

140 *Tadić*, Jurisdiction Appeal, para. 73.

141 *Ibid.*, para. 81.

142 *Tadić*, Jurisdiction Appeal, paras. 578–606; *Prosecutor* v. *Balskić*, Judgment, Case IT-95-14-T (3 March 2000), para. 126; *Prosecutor* v. *Alekovski*, Appeals Judgment, Case IT-95-14/1-A (24 March 2000). In the *Čelebići* case, the defence argued, this time regarding Bosnian Serb victims, that 'the nationality of all the detainees was Bosnian, the same as that of the party to the conflict detaining them and, thus, they are outwith the ambit of Article 4 of Geneva Convention IV' (*Prosecutor* v. *Delalic, Mucic, Delic and Landzo* (*Čelebići camp*), Judgment, Case IT-96-21-T (16 November 1998), para. 240).

In its landmark *Tadić* judgment, the Appeals Chamber of the Yugoslav Tribunal rejected this argument. Having established that the Bosnian Serb armed forces, known as the Army of the Serbian Republic of Bosnia and Herzegovina/Republika Srpska (VRS), were to be regarded as de facto organs of the Federal Republic of Yugoslavia (FRY), the Appeals Chamber concluded that the conflict in Bosnia-Herzegovina constituted an international armed conflict at the relevant time.[143] The Appeals Chamber then considered whether, despite both perpetrators and victims being of the same nationality, the Bosnian Muslim victims could be regarded as 'protected persons' within the meaning of Article 4 of the Fourth Geneva Convention. Specifically referring to refugees in armed conflicts, the Tribunal held that, in contemporary international armed conflicts, substantial relations were more relevant than legal bonds of nationality:[144]

> While previously wars were primarily between well-established States, in modern inter-ethnic armed conflicts such as that in the former Yugoslavia, new States are often created during the conflict and ethnicity rather than nationality may become the grounds for allegiance . . . Under these conditions, the requirement of nationality is even less adequate to define protected persons . . . [A]llegiance to a Party to the conflict and, correspondingly, control by this Party over persons in a given territory, may be regarded as the crucial test.[145]

Consequently, the Appeals Chamber found that the Bosnian Muslim victims were 'protected persons', since they did not owe allegiance to nor receive diplomatic protection from the state (the FRY) on whose behalf the Bosnian Serb armed forces had been fighting.[146] This flexible interpretation of Article 4 of the Civilians Convention has since been confirmed in subsequent judgments. In the *Čelebići* case, the Appeals Chamber defended its position and maintained that the interpretation of the nationality requirement of Article 4 in the *Tadić* Appeals Judgment did not constitute 'a rewriting of the Geneva Convention IV or a "re-creation" of the law'.[147]

143 In its decision on merits, the Appeals Chamber explained that an armed conflict originally internal in character could 'become international (or, depending upon the circumstances, be international in character alongside an internal armed conflict) if (i) another State intervenes in that conflict through its troops, or alternatively if (ii) some of the participants in the internal armed conflict act on behalf of that other State'. Applying the 'overall control' test, the Appeals Chamber determined that Bosnian Serb armed forces were to be regarded as acting under the overall control and on behalf of the FRY. As a result, the armed conflict in Bosnia and Herzegovina between the Bosnian Serbs and the central authorities of Bosnia and Herzegovina was an international armed conflict (*Tadić*, IT-94-1-T, Appeal Chamber Judgment, 15 July 1999, paras. 84, 162).

144 *Ibid.*, paras. 165–6. 145 *Ibid.*, para. 166. 146 *Ibid.*, para. 169.

147 *Prosecutor* v. *Delalic, Mucic, Delic and Landzo* (*Čelebići camp*), Appeals Judgment, Case IT-96-21-A (20 February 2001), para. 73.

The acknowledgement, by the ICTY, that the protection afforded to civilians by the Fourth Convention is ill-adapted to the nature of modern armed conflicts is a significant step in the right direction of change. This decision by the ICTY to adopt a broad interpretation of 'protected persons' reflects a progressive move in all spheres of international humanitarian law towards a more comprehensive protection of victims of armed conflicts.[148] Nevertheless, this broad interpretation of the notion of 'protected persons', based on allegiance rather than nationality, raises doubts as to its scope of application. Is it strictly limited to inter-ethnic conflicts or does it extend to all types of international conflicts, including traditional interstate armed conflicts?[149] This question needs to be addressed in light of contemporary interstate armed conflicts, such as the Ethiopia–Eritrea conflict.

The nationality issue in relation to contemporary interstate armed conflicts: the Ethiopia–Eritrea case

The application of a broad notion of 'protected persons' to all types of international conflicts is very likely to face strong opposition from states.[150] Indeed, if allegiance to a party to a conflict became the relevant ground for protection, it would in effect mean that, in traditional international armed conflicts, individuals considered by most states as traitors would be entitled to the protection of the Convention.[151] It is very doubtful that such an outcome would be easily accepted by states.

However, nationality issues are rarely straightforward and allegiance to a country could be a good indicator, particularly when faced with nationals of enemy descent. There have been many cases of civilians deported, transferred or interned because of their enemy ancestry. This was the case during the Second World War, when over 110,000 Japanese-Americans were forcibly removed to 'War Relocation Centres' by Presidential Order 9066. More than two-thirds of those interned were American citizens.[152] Nowadays, nationals of enemy origin are still being singled out for deportation, especially in the case of newly separated countries, where civilians hold double-citizenship and nationality becomes a subject of contention. Such was the case when, during the armed conflict between Ethiopia and

148 See generally, Meron, *Humanization of International Law*, pp.1–89.

149 Quéguiner, 'Dix ans après la création du Tribunal pénal international pour l'ex-Yougoslavie', 2003, 302.

150 *Ibid.* 151 *Ibid.*, 303.

152 Asian-Nation, *Japanese-American Internment*, www.asian-nation.org/internment.shtml (accessed 1 November 2011).

Eritrea, thousands of Ethiopians of Eritrean origin were stripped of their Ethiopian citizenship and expelled from Ethiopia.[153]

In June 1998, shortly after the beginning of the war with its neighbour and former province, Eritrea, the Ethiopian government started to expel Eritreans and Ethiopians of Eritrean origin. It is estimated that about 75,000 people were forcibly expelled from Ethiopia during the war, which ended in December 2000.[154] Many of the people expelled possessed Eritrean nationality, but a substantial number of deportees had been born in Ethiopia when Eritrea was a part of that country, had lived in Ethiopia all their lives and had no other recognized citizenship than Ethiopian.[155] The Ethiopian authorities claimed that the expulsions were justified on grounds of national security and were only targeted at enemy foreigners. They argued that people of Eritrean origin who had registered to vote in the 1993 referendum on Eritrean independence had acquired Eritrean citizenship, thereby losing their Ethiopian nationality.[156] Eritrea, on the other hand, claimed that participation in the referendum did not have legal significance because 'Eritrea was not yet a State capable of conferring nationality'.[157] As a result, Ethiopia had wrongly deprived thousands of Ethiopian citizens of Eritrean origins of their nationality.[158]

On 17 December 2004, the Eritrea–Ethiopia Claims Commission, established pursuant to the December 2000 Peace Agreement, delivered a partial award on the issue.[159] In the Commission's opinion, those who participated in the 1993 referendum had indeed acquired Eritrean nationality,

[153] Similarly, the Eritrean government forcibly expelled or took part in the voluntary repatriation of around 70,000 Ethiopians. However, in this case, the nationality of the expellees was not an issue.

[154] HRW, 'The Horn of Africa war: mass expulsions and the nationality issue' (January 2003) HRW Index No. A1503, p. 5.

[155] *Ibid.*

[156] EECC, Partial Award, Civilians Claims, *Eritrea's Claims 15, 16, 23 and 27–32*, para. 43. Ethiopia's argument is based on Article 11 of the 1930 Ethiopian Nationality law, which provides that Ethiopian nationality is lost when a citizen acquires another nationality. Additionally, the 1992 Eritrean Nationality Proclamation (Proclamation No. 21/1992) provides that 'any person born to a parent of Eritrean origin in Eritrea or abroad is an Eritrean national by birth'. The Eritrean Referendum Proclamation defines persons qualified for the referendum as 'any person having Eritrean citizenship pursuant to Proclamation No. 21/1992 on the date of his application for registration and who was 18 years or older or would attain such age at any time during the registration period, and who further possessed an Identification Card issued by the Department of Internal Affairs'.

[157] EECC, Partial Award, Civilians Claims, *Eritrea's Claims 15, 16, 23 and 27–32*, para. 44.

[158] *Ibid.*, para. 39.

[159] EECC, Partial Award, Civilians Claims, *Eritrea's Claims 15, 16, 23 and 27–32*.

pursuant to Proclamation No. 21/1992.[160] At the same time, the Commission found that Ethiopia continued to regard them as its own nationals, due to the issuance of Ethiopian passports after the referendum and thus held that:

> Ethiopian nationals who acquired Eritrean nationality through qualifying to participate in the 1993 Referendum on Eritrean self-determination acquired dual nationality as citizens of both the States of Eritrea and Ethiopia.[161]

Consequently, the Claims Commission found that Ethiopia was entitled to deprive those dual nationals of their Ethiopian nationality if they were thought to pose a threat to its wartime security.[162] It thus concluded that Ethiopia could lawfully expel these persons as nationals of an enemy state, 'although it was bound to ensure them the protections required by Geneva Convention IV and other applicable international humanitarian law'.[163] Nevertheless, the Commission also found that Ethiopia had forcibly expelled some of its own nationals from rural areas, as well as family members of previous expellees, in violation of international law.[164]

The Claims Commission erred in its conclusion that the mere participation in the referendum on independence amounted to recognition of nationality. It should indeed have considered the rules on acquisition of nationality in case of partial state succession,[165] as well as the principle according to which nationality may not be conferred against the will of an individual, and concluded that Ethiopians of Eritrean origin having their habitual residence in Ethiopia still retained Ethiopian nationality and, as such, should not have been treated as enemy nationals. Instead, the Commission held that they were dual nationals, and that, one of their nationalities being that of the enemy, they were in 'an unusual and potentially difficult position'.[166]

160 The Commission held that it was not persuaded by Eritrea's argument that registration as an Eritrean national in order to participate in the 1993 Referendum was without important legal consequences: 'The governing body issuing those cards was not yet formally recognized as independent or as a member of the United Nations, but it exercised effective and independent control over a defined territory and a permanent population and carried on effective and substantial relations with the external world, particularly on economic matters. In all these respects, it reflected the characteristics of a State in international law' (*ibid*., para. 48).

161 *Ibid*., Award, para. 13, Finding on dual nationality, para. 37.

162 EECC, Partial Award, Civilians Claims, *Eritrea's Claims 15, 16, 23 and 27–32*, para. 72.

163 *Ibid*., para. 82.

164 *Ibid*., paras. 83–98.

165 For an in-depth discussion on acquisition of nationality in case of partial state succession, see Weis, *Nationality and Statelessness in International Law*, 1979, pp. 144–60.

166 EECC, Partial Award, Civilians Claims, *Eritrea's Claims 15, 16, 23 and 27–32*, para. 55.

Notwithstanding the Commission's findings on nationality, this case clearly demonstrates that international humanitarian law is ill-adapted to deal with issues arising from contemporary situations of armed conflicts. The international law of armed conflict is still based, for the most part, on a traditional notion of armed conflict between nation-states, just as it was in 1949. Although the 1977 Protocols attempt to convey a more accurate picture of the contemporary world, through the recognition of wars of national liberation and internal armed conflicts, new issues have arisen with the advent of newly independent countries. In particular, as shown in the Eritrea–Ethiopia case, the nationality of the victims of war in an interstate armed conflict may not be as easy to determine as it once was. Furthermore, although entirely reliant on the state-oriented concept of nationality for its applicability *ratione personae*, international humanitarian law does not provide any definition for it. Yet, a lack of clear definition often leads to abuse by governments.[167]

[167] Similarly, a lack of clear definition of 'conflicts not of international character' has been constantly taken advantage of by states involved in situations of internal violence. See below Chapter 2.

2 The prohibition of forced movement of civilians in non-international armed conflicts

According to the Internal Displacement Monitoring Centre, 'internal conflict is by far the most important factor generating displacement'.[1] In fact, some of the countries that produced the highest numbers of internally displaced persons in recent years, such as Sudan and Colombia,[2] are also plagued by some of the worst or protracted internal conflicts. In 2006, many IDP situations were generated by 'complex, sometimes internationalized, conflicts, involving elements of inter-communal violence and campaigns by governments or non-state actors directed against civilians', best exemplified by the violence in Chad, the Democratic Republic of Congo or Iraq.[3] To a lesser extent, civilians also flee across international borders and seek refuge in neighbouring countries.[4]

In this context, it seems pertinent to ponder why internal conflicts generate so much displacement. According to Pictet:

> Civil wars, in proportion, engender more suffering than international wars, because of the hatred and savagery which characterize them. Why is this? To be cynical about it, it might well be because we know so well the people we are fighting against and have our own reasons for detesting them.[5]

Civil wars divide the peoples of a country along ethnic, racial, religious or political lines and thus have a personal and intimate component that

1 IDMC, *Global Overview 2006*, p. 13.

2 According to the USCRI's refugee survey, as of 31 December 2005, there were more than 5.3 million IDPs in Sudan, while Colombia counted 2.9 million IDPs (USCRI, *World Refugee Survey 2006*, 2007, tables 9, 11).

3 IDMC, *Global Overview 2006*, p. 16.

4 For example, as of 31 December 2005, Sudan had generated 670,900 refugees, Myanmar 727,100, Burundi, 438,500 and Liberia, 219,800 (USCRI, *World Refugee Survey 2006*, tables 8, 11).

5 Pictet, *Development and Principles of International Humanitarian Law*, 1982, p. 44.

is lacking in interstate wars. As a result, the principal victims of such conflicts are civilians, who reportedly account for 90 per cent of casualties in internal wars.[6] Civilians often flee a general climate of insecurity caused by confrontations between government armed forces and rebels. Increasingly, civilians are being directly targeted and deliberately displaced by the belligerents. As part of counter-insurgency operations, civilians are regularly uprooted by their own governments or by army-backed paramilitary groups. On the other hand, they may be forced to flee as a result of targeted attacks by insurgents. Finally, displacement of a targeted ethnic group may be carried out in order to facilitate the domination of the area involved by another more favoured group.[7] Accordingly, forced displacement of civilians is no longer an unfortunate consequence of the conflict; it has become a deliberate strategy of war.

While some of the practices causing displacement, such as violence to life and person,[8] acts of terrorism,[9] pillage[10] and forced recruitment of children,[11] constitute in themselves violations of international humanitarian law, the practice of forced displacement is explicitly prohibited by Article 17 of Protocol II to the Geneva Conventions. Thus, provided that the state on whose territory the armed conflict is taking place has ratified the Protocol and the conflict meets the criteria laid down in Article 1,[12] government armed forces, paramilitaries and rebels all have a duty not to forcibly displace civilians.

The prohibition of forced movement of civilians under Article 17 of Protocol II

In 1949, in response to the deportation practices of the Second World War, the drafters of the Geneva Conventions felt the need to address the issue of forced movement of civilians in times of war. However, while Article 49 of the Civilians Convention explicitly deals with forced displacement in occupied territory, Common Article 3 is completely silent on this

[6] Cohen and Deng, *Masses in Flight*, p. 6.

[7] Bothe *et al.*, *New Rules for Victims of Armed Conflicts*, p. 691.

[8] Geneva Conventions, Common Art. 3(1)(a) and Protocol II, Art. 4 (2)(a).

[9] Protocol II, Art. 4 (2)(d). [10] Protocol II, Art. 4 (2)(g). [11] Protocol II, Art. 4 (3)(c).

[12] Protocol II, Art. 1(1): 'This Protocol . . . shall apply to all armed conflicts which . . . take place in the territory of a High Contracting Party between its armed forces and dissident armed forces or other organized armed groups which, under responsible command, exercise such control over a part of its territory as to enable them to carry out sustained and concerted military operations and to implement this Protocol.'

matter.[13] Until 1977, there was no explicit prohibition of displacement in internal armed conflict. Yet, the ICRC commentary notes, 'the problem is particularly acute in situations of non-international armed conflict in which there have been cases, for example, of the forced movement of ethnic groups and national groups opposed to the central government'.[14] As occurrences of transfers and deportations of civilians during civil wars increased in frequency, a codified prohibition of displacement in civil wars became very desirable indeed.

Article 17 of the Protocol II, which applies exclusively to non-international armed conflicts, provides that:

> 1 The displacement of the civilian population shall not be ordered for reasons related to the conflict unless the security of the civilians involved or imperative military reasons so demand. Should such displacements have to be carried out, all possible measures shall be taken in order that the civilian population may be received under satisfactory conditions of shelter, hygiene, health, safety and nutrition.
> 2 Civilians shall not be compelled to leave their own territory for reasons connected with the conflict.

The wording of this provision is inspired by the prohibition of forced displacement in situations of occupation, as contained in Article 49 of the Fourth Convention. Although most of the conclusions reached with regards to evacuations in the previous chapter are also applicable in internal armed conflicts, the two regimes are clearly distinct and contain important differences and specificities, thus justifying a separate analysis of the prohibition of forced displacement in internal armed conflicts. The first paragraph of Article 17 deals with displacement of civilians within the territory of a contracting party, while the second paragraph covers forced displacement outside this territory.[15]

Forced movement of civilians within the territory of a contracting party

The forced displacement of the civilian population 'for reasons related to the conflict' is prohibited. These last words were added to the original

[13] Common Article 3 nevertheless provides that persons not taking part in the hostilities shall be treated humanely at all times, and prohibits such measures as to constitute 'violence to life and person' and 'outrages upon personal dignity, in particular humiliating and degrading treatment'. It is clear that these minimum standards would certainly be violated by the mass displacement of civilians. See: Sandoz *et al.*, *Commentary on the Protocols*, p. 1472, fn. 1; de Zayas, 'Mass population transfers', 221.

[14] Sandoz *et al.*, *Commentary on the Protocols*, p. 1472.

[15] *Prosecutor* v. *Milošević*, Decision on motion for judgment of acquittal, IT-02-54, 16 June 2004, paras. 55–6.

ICRC draft, as the Committee felt that displacement may be necessary in certain cases of epidemic or natural disasters.[16] Such displacements are not related to the armed conflict, and therefore do not come within the scope of Article 17.

Lawful displacement of civilians in internal armed conflicts

Paragraph 1, which is based on Article 49(2) of the Fourth Geneva Convention, prohibits the forced movement of civilians, unless justified by security reasons or military imperatives. As explained in the *Handbook for Applying the Guiding Principles on Internal Displacement*, displacement is the exception and not the rule; consequently, the burden is on the warring party to make the case that population movements are justified.[17]

Security of civilian population

With reference to the exception of security of the civilian population, the ICRC commentary on the Protocols observes that '[i]t is self-evident that a displacement designed to prevent the population from being exposed to grave danger cannot be expressly prohibited'.[18]

It is certainly true that, in accordance with the principle of distinction between civilians and combatants, which is customary in both international and non-international armed conflicts,[19] a party to an internal conflict has the right, and indeed the duty, to evacuate civilians under its control from the vicinity of a military objective.[20] As a result, the movement, even forced, of civilians from the scene of intense fighting,

[16] OR vol. XV, 295, CDDH/215/Rev.1, para. 150.

[17] UN Office for the Coordination of Humanitarian Affairs (OCHA), *Handbook for Applying the Guiding Principles on Internal Displacement*, 1 November 1999, www.unhcr.org/cgi-bin/texis/vtx/refworld/rwmain?page=search&docid=3d52a6432 (accessed 22 November 2011), p. 16.

[18] Sandoz *et al.*, *Commentary on the Protocols*, p. 1472.

[19] Henckaerts and Doswald-Beck, *Customary International Humanitarian Law*, vol. 1, Rule 1, p. 8.

[20] *Ibid.*, Rule 24, p. 75. The ICRC study notes that, while Protocol II does not explicitly require parties to the conflict to take precautions against the effects of attacks, Article 13(1) provides that 'the civilian population and individual civilians shall enjoy general protection against the dangers arising from military operations'. It would be difficult for a party to comply with this obligation without removing the civilians from the vicinity of military objectives. Furthermore, the ICTY held in the *Kupreskić* case that the duty to remove civilians from the vicinity of military objectives contained in Article 58 Protocol I was now part of customary international law, because it specified and fleshed out general pre-existing norms (*Prosecutor* v. *Kupreskić*, Judgment (14 January 2000) Case No. IT-95-16-T). Thus, the ICRC study argues, the principle of distinction, which is customary in non-international armed conflicts, 'inherently requires respect for this rule'.

or from an area likely to be targeted by rebel attacks, is permitted, and required. During the 1974–7 international conference, the exceptions to the prohibition of forced displacement were criticized by the Norwegian delegation, which qualified the draft article as 'rather too weak' and feared that the exceptions 'might give rise to abuse'. In particular, the Norwegian delegate observed that:

> The security of civilians should not require their forced displacement, because if their security was genuinely threatened, civilians would be prepared to move of their own accord.[21]

Unfortunately, Norway's predictions became reality. Time and again, governments and rebel groups have used and abused the 'security of civilians' argument to justify their unlawful practices of forced displacement.

Burundi's *regroupement* policy is a typical example of forced relocation of a civilian population into camps under the guise of security concerns. The first wave of *regroupement* occurred between 1996 and 1998, when the Tutsi-dominated government forced at least 250,000 people into 50 camps scattered throughout the country.[22] The government had argued that the camps were a temporary measure necessary to protect the population from attacks by rebel groups.[23] As a result of a significant reduction in insurgent activity in most areas and strong international criticism, the camps were progressively dismantled in 1998.[24]

In September 1999, in response to ongoing attacks on Bujumbura by the Hutu rebel movement FNL (Forces Nationales pour la Libération), the Burundian authorities revived the *regroupement* policy. It is estimated that by early 2000, some 380,000 inhabitants of the surrounding Bujumbura rural region – over 81 per cent of the population – had been forcibly relocated into *regroupement* camps.[25] President Buyoya asserted that *regroupement* was not a policy of the government but rather a programme of

[21] OR vol. XIV, p. 229, CDDH/III/SR.25, para. 4.

[22] USCRI, 'Country Report: Burundi' (2000), web.archive.org/web/20010731092239/www.refugees.org/world/countryrpt/africa/2000/burundi.htm (accessed 12 July 2011).

[23] *Ibid.*; AI, 'Burundi – forced relocation; new patterns of human rights abuses' (15 July 1997), AI Index AFR 16/019/1997, p. 3.

[24] HRW, 'Burundi: emptying the hills – regroupment camps in Burundi' (1 July 2000) HRW Index No. A1204, www.hrw.org/legacy/reports/2000/burundi2 (accessed 22 November 2011).

[25] UNCHR, 'Report of the Representative of the Secretary-General on Internally Displaced Persons: profiles in displacement: forced relocation in Burundi' (6 March 2000) E/CN.4/2001/5/Add.1, p. 4.

operational measures dictated by security considerations.[26] The Burundian authorities claimed that the camps had one objective:

> To protect the civil population, who are often used by the rebels as human shields in the event of contact with units of the national army, and to protect people from being massacred by the rebels.[27]

In reality, it is doubtful that the *regroupements* were motivated by security considerations. According to several reports, during the round-ups, soldiers made it clear to the local population that any person remaining outside the camps would be considered to be linked to Hutu rebel groups and therefore a legitimate military target during counter-insurgency operations.[28] Human Rights Watch reported that soldiers sometimes shot and killed those who did not follow the orders quickly or completely enough.[29] In the following days, soldiers reportedly combed the hills and killed those who had stayed.[30] How could the Burundian government argue that the *regroupements* were justified for the security of the civilian population, when its armed forces went about killing the very population it sought to protect? It is clear that the *regroupements* were in fact meant to deprive the FNL of support from the local population.[31] Moreover, as noted by Casanovas, methods of war consisting in the internment of displaced persons, in order to consider all persons outside this zone as enemy combatants, are prohibited by international humanitarian law.[32]

The situation in the camps was very precarious. The residents lacked food, water and shelter, and the levels of malnutrition and disease were high. A study of mortality in the *regroupement* camps concluded that twice as many people died from disease and war-related deaths in the camps as would have died had they stayed in their own homes.[33] There have been numerous reports of abuses committed by Tutsi-dominated armed forces against the displaced people.[34] In light of these considerations, it could be

26 *Ibid.*; See also UNSC, 'Statement by the government of Burundi on protected sites issued at Bujumbura on 17 January 2000', S/2000/33: 'The Government reaffirms that the regrouping of people in protected sites is not connected with any policy designed to coerce them in any way whatsoever' (3).

27 *Ibid.*, 2. 28 AI, 'Burundi – forced relocation', p. 1; HRW, 'Emptying the hills'.

29 HRW, 'Emptying the hills'. 30 AI, 'Burundi – Forced relocation', p. 1

31 HRW, 'Emptying the hills'.

32 Casanovas, 'La protection internationale des réfugiés et des personnes déplacées dans les conflits armés', 2003, 54.

33 HRW, 'Emptying the hills'.

34 HRW, 'Burundi: government forcibly displaces civilians' (4 June 2002), http://hrw.org/english/docs/2002/06/04/burund4018.htm (accessed 22 November 2011).

argued that, rather than protecting the civilian population, these camps actually reduced the security of their residents. Finally, the security argument is difficult to sustain when the hundreds of thousands of civilians interned in those camps were mostly Hutu. It appears evident that the *regroupements* were ethnically targeted and that, as a result, the forced displacement of Hutu civilians into camps constituted a form of 'ethnic cleansing'.[35] The international community exerted strong pressure on the Burundian government to close the camps.[36] The *regroupement* camps were eventually dismantled in 2000. For several years after that, and despite official denials, forced *regroupements* of populations were still alleged to be taking place.[37]

Imperative military reasons

Forced displacement of civilians may also be ordered if 'imperative military reasons so demand'. According to the ICRC commentary, each situation of potential displacement of civilians should be scrutinized most carefully, as the adjective 'imperative' reduces to a minimum cases in which displacement may be ordered.[38] The commentary adds:

> Clearly, imperative military reasons cannot be justified by political motives. For example, it would be prohibited to move a population in order to exercise more effective control over a dissident ethnic group.[39]

35 Cohen and Deng, *Masses in Flight*, p. 41.

36 On 12 November 1999, the President of the Security Council issued a statement on behalf on the Council, calling on the government of Burundi 'to halt the policy of forced regroupment and to allow the affected people to return to their homes, with full and unhindered humanitarian access throughout the process' (UNSC, 'Statement by the President of Security Council' (12 November 1999), S/PRST/1999/32). In addition, in January 2000, the UN Inter-Agency Standing Committee (IASC) issued a policy statement on Burundi, stressing the illegality of the *regroupement*: 'Policy on forced relocation ("*regroupement*") in Burundi' (19 January 2000); the EU issued a statement calling upon 'the Burundi Government to call a halt to the policy of forced removals and to *allow* the people to return to their property as quickly as possible' (Declaration by the presidency on behalf of the European Union on the forced removals in Burundi (8 October 1999), www.consilium.europa.eu/ueDocs/cms_Data/docs/pressData/en/cfsp/ACFA0.htm (accessed 12 July 2011)).

37 According to HRW and the ICG, in April–May 2002, Burundian armed forces regrouped more than 30,000 civilians into 'protection sites' in Ruyigi province: HRW, 'Burundi: government forcibly displaces civilians' (4 June 2002), http://hrw.org/english/docs/2002/06/04/burund4018.htm (accessed 12 July 2011); ICG, 'Réfugies et déplacés Burundais: construire d'urgence un consensus sur le rapatriement et la réinstallation' (2 December 2003), www.crisisgroup.org/fr/regions/afrique/afrique-centrale/burundi/B017-refugees-and-internally-displaced-in-burundi-the-urgent-need-for-a-consensus.aspx (accessed 12 July 2011).

38 Sandoz et al., *Commentary on the Protocols*, pp. 1472–3.

39 *Ibid.*

Similarly, the forced gathering of thousands of civilians into camps for the sole purpose of depriving rebel groups of local support is unjustified under international humanitarian law.

In Colombia, displacement is a consequence of the long-lasting internal armed conflict and political violence that have been tearing Colombia apart for over forty years.[40] Forced movement of civilians has been consistently used by all actors in the conflict, as a way to 'settle their scores'.[41] Areas are 'cleansed' of the real or perceived support base of the opposing side and repopulated with the armed group's own supporters. In addition, Colombian revolutionary group FARC has reportedly forced the displacement of thousands of civilians as a delaying tactic against the paramilitaries.[42] In this case, it is clear that the displacement of civilians was not the consequence of fighting between two adversaries but, rather, a deliberate strategy of warfare. However, forced movement of civilians may only be ordered in exceptional circumstances, for *imperative* military reasons. It may not be used as a method of war, in order to acquire a military advantage. Moreover, as civilians were forcibly displaced to hinder the advance of the paramilitary groups, it is assumed that they found themselves under attack once their path crossed that of the paramilitaries. Therefore, the FARC's perceived military imperative outweighed considerations relative to the security of civilians. It is evident from the wording of Article 49(2) of the Fourth Convention and Article 17(1) of the Second Protocol that the prohibition of forced displacement of civilians is the norm and that evacuation for security or military reason is the exception. Articles 49(2) and 17(1) are humanitarian provisions laid down for the benefit of the civilian population. Thus, in the context of forced displacement, and in the case of incompatibility between the two, the security of the civilian population should be deemed to prevail over the military reason.[43]

Both exceptions to the prohibition of displacement may be easily abused by the belligerents. For this reason, justifications given for the movement

40 The conflict in Colombia has pitted left-wing guerrilla groups – particularly the Revolutionary Armed Forces of Colombia (FARC) and the National Liberation Army (ELN) – against the government's forces and paramilitary groups, organized under an umbrella organization known as AUC (Autodefensas Unidas de Colombia – United Self-Defence Groups of Colombia).

41 UNCHR, 'Report of the Representative of the Secretary-General on internally displaced persons: profiles in displacement: follow-up mission to Colombia' (11 January 2000) E/CN.4/2000/83/Add.1, para. 2.

42 HRW, 'War without quarter – Colombia and international humanitarian law' (October 1998) HRW Index No. 187–7.

43 See above Chapter 1.

of civilians must always be the subject of a rigorous assessment. Furthermore, when displacement does occur, it must meet the strict requirements of shelter, hygiene, health, safety and nutrition.

Conditions of displacement

In case of displacement, the authorities in charge have a responsibility to 'ensure that all feasible alternatives have been explored in order to avoid displacement altogether'.[44] In a situation of armed conflict, such alternatives could entail, for instance, diverting the conflict from certain areas, or the establishment of safe corridors for the delivery of food to communities cut off by the conflict.[45]

Should displacement nevertheless occur for reasons of civilian security or military imperatives, 'all measures shall be taken to minimize displacement and its adverse effects'.[46] In particular, the civilian population 'shall be received under satisfactory conditions of shelter, hygiene, health, safety and nutrition'.[47] Protocol II also requires that 'all appropriate steps shall be taken to facilitate the reunion of families temporarily separated'. The conditions under which displacement is actually carried out constitute an essential element for the determination of the lawfulness of the displacement. If it doesn't meet the requirements set out in Article 17(1), displacement becomes unlawful, even though it may have been justified by security reasons or military imperatives.[48] Furthermore, displacement of civilians should last no longer than required by the circumstances. According to the handbook on the Guiding Principles, this means that solutions to displacement should be explored and implemented as soon as possible.[49]

In Burundi, the authorities failed to comply with their obligations to provide adequate assistance and protection to the population displaced into *regroupement* camps. Many reports have deplored the humanitarian conditions in the camps. Human Rights Watch observed that Burundian authorities provided no food, no water and no building materials for newly arrived camp residents, and said nothing about how long they would be required to live there.[50] Refugees International expressed concern at the deplorable health conditions in the camps, which had become a breeding ground for communicable diseases, such as cholera, dysentery

[44] 'Guiding Principles on Internal Displacement', Principle 7.
[45] OCHA, *Handbook for Applying the Guiding Principles*, pp. 17–18.
[46] 'Guiding Principles on Internal Displacement', Principle 7.
[47] Protocol II, Art. 17(1). [48] See above Chapter 1.
[49] OCHA, *Handbook for Applying the Guiding Principles*, p. 17.
[50] HRW, 'Emptying the hills'.

and other bronchial and upper respiratory conditions.[51] According to the UN Inter-Agency Standing Committee (IASC), the impact of these measures on the affected population was disastrous. It noted that the government failed to make provision for food, water and shelter for those relocated to the sites and that 'the government's claim that it was the responsibility of the international community to assist the affected people was unacceptable, and was rejected'.[52]

The above arguments relating to lawful situations of displacement in internal armed conflict are where the similarities between Article 17 and Article 49 end. There remain many controversies as to the exact scope of the provision governing forced movement of civilians in non-international armed conflicts.

'Ordering' the displacement of civilians

It has been argued that Article 17(1) prohibits the order to displace the civilian population, rather than the act of displacement itself.[53] Indeed, Article 17(1), contrary to Article 49(1) Geneva Convention IV, expressly provides that '[t]he displacement of the civilian population shall not be *ordered*'. Similarly, the ICRC study on customary IHL states, in Rule 129, that: 'Parties to a non-international armed conflict may not *order* the displacement of the civilian population.'[54] In addition, Article 8(2)(e)(viii) of the ICC Statute, which is based on Article 17(1), states 'Ordering the displacement of the civilian population for reasons related to the conflict, unless the security of the civilians involved or imperative military reasons so demand' was a war crime in non-international armed conflict. Element 1 of the *Elements of Crimes* requires that '[t]he perpetrator ordered a displacement of a civilian population'.[55]

Such an order has been interpreted as meaning either an official governmental order directly addressed to the civilian population or an order

51 Refugees International, 'Burundi: regroupment camp conditions rapidly deteriorating' (1 March 2000), http://reliefweb.int/node/60271 (accessed 31 October 2011)

52 IASC, 'Policy on forced relocation ("*regroupement*") in Burundi'.

53 Piotrowicz, 'Displacement and displaced persons', p. 347; Carey, 'Is prevention through accountability possible?', 1999, 26; Roch, 'Forced displacement in the former Yugoslavia', 1995, 17; *Prosecutor* v. *Gotovina, Cermak and Markač*, Defendant Ante Gotovina's Preliminary motion challenging jurisdiction pursuant to Rule 72(A)(i) of the Rules of procedure and evidence, IT-06-90-PT, 18 January 2007, para. 8.

54 Henckaerts and Doswald-Beck, *Customary International Humanitarian Law*, vol. 1, Rule 129, p. 457; (my italic).

55 Report of the Preparatory Commission for the International Criminal Court, Finalised Draft Text of the Elements of the Crime (6 July 2000), UN Doc. PCNICC/2000/INF/3/Add.2, 46.

to displace the population given within the chain of command of a state or of an armed group.[56] The first case covers situations where civilians are displaced by their own government as part of counter-insurgency operations, in an attempt to '[dry] up the sea in which guerrilla fish swim'.[57] This practice consists of relocating the civilian population in camps or other designated areas, in order to deprive rebel forces of the support of the local population. Civilians are then often gathered in camps for internally displaced persons, in deplorable living conditions.[58] An alternative interpretation requires the order to have been given within a chain of command, thus covering cases of indirect forced displacement, such as the mistreatment of civilians so as to 'encourage' them to leave, provided that they were ordered by a superior to soldiers or insurgents under their command.[59] Although in line with the literal meaning of Article 17(1), both interpretations have been rejected by Jan Willms as contrary to the object and purpose of Protocol II to 'ensure a better protection for the victims of... armed conflicts'.[60] Indeed, as noted by Willms, '[t]he protection of civilians would be seriously compromised if forced displacement were only illegal pursuant to an order. This holds true especially where a whole campaign is being conducted to displace the civilian population.'[61]

Forced displacement may take many forms, including the direct forced relocation of civilians, 'voluntary' resettlements in other parts of the territory, or indirect coerced movement, as a result of systematic human rights abuses.[62] Such forced movements, although part of a general policy directed at a specific civilian population, need not necessarily derive from a clear order. During the 1999 Kosovo conflict, for instance, forces

[56] Willms, 'Without order, anything goes?', 2009, 551–4.

[57] Bothe *et al.*, *New Rules for Victims of Armed Conflicts*, p. 691.

[58] On 2 October 2002, in response to increasing attacks by the Lord's Resistance Army in northern Uganda, the government of Uganda ordered thousands of civilians in the Gula, Kitguma and Pader districts (Acholiland) to move into 'protected villages'. By the end of 2002, there were more than 800,000 IDPs in northern Uganda, or approximately 70 per cent of the population of Acholiland (HRW, 'Abducted and abused: renewed conflict in northern Uganda' (July 2003) HRW Index No. A1512, 4).

[59] Willms, 'Without order, anything goes?', 552. This interpretation is based on the context of Article 17. Indeed, Article 17(2) provides that 'civilians shall not be compelled to leave their own territory'. According to Willms, '[t]he compelling of civilians is possible by indirect means; the term clearly does not require an order. If State representatives had wanted to draft an unambiguous provision not requiring an order, they would have done so by also using "compel" in Article 17(1), which deals with the forced displacement of the civilian population from their territory.'

[60] Willms, 'Without order, anything goes?', 551, 553, quoting the preamble to Protocol II.

[61] *Ibid.*, 552.

[62] Roch, 'Forced displacement in the former Yugoslavia', 6.

of the former Republic of Yugoslavia and Serbia were accused of forcibly expelling and internally displacing hundreds of thousands of Kosovo Albanians from their homes across the entire province of Kosovo. The indictment of Slobodan Milošević charged the former Serbian president with deportation and forcible transfer as crimes against humanity and stated that:

> To facilitate these expulsions and displacements, forces of the FRY and Serbia intentionally created an atmosphere of fear and oppression through the use of force, threats of force, and acts of violence.[63]

It is argued that Article 17(1) Protocol II prohibits the act of forced displacement, irrespective of whether an order to this effect was given or not. Indeed, 'if ordering of displacement is prohibited, this seems to imply that the act of forced displacement is prohibited too'.[64] The term 'order' was not discussed at the 1974–7 international conference.[65] In fact, the delegations present merely referred to a general 'prohibition of forced displacement . . . in internal conflicts'.[66] However, the Switzerland delegation mentioned the situations where 'the Parties to the conflict were obliged to order displacements',[67] namely 'when the security of civilians or imperative military reasons so demand', or even for reasons unrelated to the conflict. It could therefore be argued that the term 'order' relates to displacement for the security of civilians or imperative military reasons, which may indeed only be carried out following an order, either directly to the civilian population or within the chain of command. Thus, Article 17(1) contrasts unlawful forced displacement with other situations of displacement of civilians which have been lawfully ordered. In addition, it could also be argued that the word 'order' places the emphasis on the military commander ordering the displacement and on the fact that the order in itself constitutes a breach of international humanitarian law, even if not carried out.[68]

While Article 17(1) refers to the 'ordering' of displacement, subsequent condemnations by UN organs of displacement practices carried out in internal armed conflicts do not appear to have considered whether such practices resulted from an actual order.[69] Similarly, more general

63 *Prosecutor* v. *Milošević et al.*, Second Amended Indictment (Kosovo), IT-02-54, 16 October 2001, para. 55.

64 Willms, 'Without order, anything goes?', 554.

65 *Ibid.*, 550.

66 OR vol. XIV, p. 226, CDDH/III/SR.24, para. 58.

67 *Ibid.*, para. 53.

68 Piotrowicz, 'Displacement and displaced persons', p. 347.

69 For instance, in a resolution on the Sudan, the UNSC condemned 'all acts of violence and violations of human rights and international humanitarian law by all parties to the

resolutions on the protection of civilians in armed conflict refer to the 'prohibition of the forcible displacement of civilians in situations of armed conflict', with no differentiation between international and non-international armed conflicts and no mention of the need for a displacement to have been carried out as a result of an express order in internal armed conflict.[70] In addition, while a small number of states have used the formulation of Article 17(1) in their national legislation or military manuals,[71] the majority of them seems to have abandoned any reference to an order.[72]

The International Criminal Tribunal for the Former Yugoslavia (ICTY) has considered charges of deportation and forcible transfer as crimes against humanity committed in internal armed conflicts on a number of occasions.[73] In most cases, it has discussed the issue under the heading 'forcible displacement', an umbrella term encompassing both deportation and forcible transfer.[74] The jurisprudence of the ICTY has indeed consistently held that the *actus reus* of 'forcible displacement' is '(a) the displacement of persons by expulsion or other coercive acts, (b) from an area in which they are lawfully present, (c) without grounds permitted under international law'.[75] The only distinction between deportation and forcible transfer lies in the fact that deportations are carried out across borders, while forcible transfers occur within national boundaries.[76] The ICTY has never argued that Article 17 Protocol II distinguishes between

crisis, in particular by the Janjaweed, including... forced displacements' (Res. (2004), 30 July 2004, UN Doc. S/RES/1556/2004). See also UNGA Res. 50/93, 22 December 1995, para. 2.

70 In its 1970 resolution on basic principles for the protection of civilian populations in armed conflicts, the UNGA affirmed that '[c]ivilian populations, or individual members thereof, should not be the object of... forcible transfers' (Res. 2675 (XXV), 9 December 1970, para. 7).

71 For instance, the UK *Manual of the Law of Armed Conflict* provides that: 'It is prohibited to order the displacement of the civilian population for reasons related to the conflict, unless the security of the civilians involved or imperative military reasons so demand' (para. 15.14).

72 Willms, 'Without order, anything goes?', 557. While New Zealand's *Military Manual* (1992) merely states that: 'It is forbidden to displace the civilian population for reasons connected with the conflict', Colombia's *Basic Military Manual* (1995) drops the requirement of an order and instead provides that it is prohibited to 'oblige civilian persons to move because of the conflict, except if security or imperative military reasons so demand' (ICRC Customary International Humanitarian Law Database, www.icrc.org/customary-ihl/eng/docs/v2 (accessed 19 July 2011)).

73 See below Chapter 4.

74 *Prosecutor* v. *Šainović et al.*, Trial Judgment, IT-05-87, 26 February 2009, para. 164.

75 *Ibid.* 76 See below Chapter 4.

internal displacement, which must result from an order (Article 17(1)), and external displacement, where civilians may simply have been 'compelled' to leave (Article 17(2)). Thus, the existence of an order of displacement does not appear to constitute an element of forcible transfer, at least in so far as it constitutes a crime against humanity. The forced displacement of civilians in internal armed conflicts has never been addressed by an international tribunal with respect to war crimes.[77] Consequently, a decision of the ICC on this very issue is much needed.

In conclusion, it is argued that forcible displacements, whether they result from an order or the more insidious coercion of civilians to leave, are prohibited in non-international armed conflict. If it weren't the case, most parties would be in a position to avoid their responsibilities by deliberately creating a climate of terror,[78] leaving the civilian population with no other choice but to leave and then claiming that no order was ever given.[79] However, it is essential to emphasize that the prohibition of displacement, in occupation as in internal conflicts, is on the 'forced' displacement of civilians and should be differentiated from the voluntary displacement of civilians, fleeing the general dangers of war.

Forced movement of civilians outside 'their own territory'

While most of those uprooted by civil wars seek safety within their own country, a substantial number flee across international borders, into neighbouring countries. For instance, at the end of 2005, some 693,632 Sudanese refugees had fled the conflict in Sudan, mostly to Uganda and Chad.[80] Most of them had been forced to flee as a direct result of attacks

[77] *Ibid.*

[78] See, for instance, *Milošević*, Second Kosovo Indictment, para. 57:

> In addition to the deliberate destruction of property owned by Kosovo Albanian civilians, forces of the FRY and Serbia committed widespread or systematic acts of brutality and violence against Kosovo Albanian civilians in order to perpetuate the climate of fear, create chaos and a pervading fear for life. Forces of the FRY and Serbia went from village to village and, in the towns and cities, from area to area, threatening and expelling the Kosovo Albanian population. Kosovo Albanians were frequently intimidated, assaulted or killed in public view to enforce the departure of their families and neighbors. Many Kosovo Albanians who were not directly forcibly expelled from their communities fled as a result of the climate of terror created by the widespread or systematic beatings, harassment, sexual assaults, unlawful arrests, killings, shelling and looting carried out across the province.

[79] Willms, 'Without order, anything goes?', 564.

[80] *2005 UNHCR Statistical Yearbook*, Sudan, www.unhcr.org/4641bec40.html (accessed 25 November 2011).

by government-backed militia, the Janjaweed and/or government forces, in the Darfur region.[81]

Article 17 of Protocol II not only prohibits the forced displacement of civilians within their own country, but also states that 'civilians shall not be compelled to leave their own territory for reasons connected with the conflict'. The prohibition of forced movement of civilians outside their territory is absolute. However, the wording of the provision is somewhat ambiguous. Two points shall be made, first, regarding the extent of 'their own territory', and, second, with reference to the 'reasons connected with the conflict'.

Uncertainty as to the extent of 'their own territory'

The terms of Article 17(2) are rather ambiguous and what constitutes 'their own territory' is unclear. Does it refer to the national territory of a country, the civilians' own territory, or the territory under the control of armed forces?[82] According to the ICRC commentary, 'it is clear that there was never any doubt in anyone's mind that the phrase was intended to refer to the whole of the territory of a country'.[83] Yet, the adopted Article 17 has dropped the adjective 'national' and only refers to 'their own territory'.

> In fact, this formula appears to be better suited to all the possible cases which might arise in a situation covered by Protocol II, and to take into account, in particular, situations where the insurgent party is in control of an extensive part of the territory.[84]

Thus, in this case, insurgents should not compel civilians to leave *the area under their authority*.[85] This interpretation of Article 17(2) coincides with the prohibition of forced displacement from occupied territory under Article 49(1) of the Fourth Convention. In virtue of Article 1(1) Protocol II, which defines the material field of application of Protocol II, one of the criteria for the application of the Protocol is that insurgents must 'exercise such control over a part of its territory as to enable to carry out sustained and concerted military operations and to implement this protocol'. This criterion is closely related to the requirement of effective occupation for the application of the law of belligerent occupation. Thus, in a situation

81 International Commission of Inquiry on Darfur, 'Report to the United Nations Secretary-General' (25 January 2005), 85, www.un.org/News/dh/sudan/com_inq_darfur.pdf (accessed 3 November 2011).
82 Hulme, 'Armed conflict and the displaced', 103.
83 Sandoz *et al.*, *Commentary on the Protocols*, 1474. 84 *Ibid.* 85 *Ibid.*

of civil war within the meaning of Article 1, the status of the insurgent armed group in control of a territory may be similar to that of a de facto occupying power. In the context of forced displacement, both Article 17(1) of Protocol II and Article 49(2) of the Civilians Convention provide for the evacuation of civilians 'if the security of civilians or imperative military reasons so demand'. Additionally, Article 49(1) lays down an absolute prohibition on deportations of civilians from occupied territory. If one draws a parallel between both provisions, it seems reasonable to conclude that Article 17(2) lays down an absolute prohibition of forced displacement of civilians outside the territory under rebel control. The reference to 'their own territory' would thus aim to place an emphasis on the insurgents', as well as the government's, obligation not to compel civilians to leave the territory under their control.

However, this would effectively mean that forced displacement of civilians within a state is absolutely prohibited in certain circumstances only, depending on who the agent of displacement is. In any case, this interpretation only applies to large-scale civil wars within the meaning of Article 1 of Protocol II. Most internal armed conflicts however fall short of the criteria laid down in Article 1. Consequently, it is safe to assume that a customary prohibition of forced displacement in non-international armed conflicts, if such a rule exists,[86] would undoubtedly involve the absolute prohibition of displacement outside *national* territory, rather than the territory under the control of a belligerent.

Absolute prohibition of displacement 'for reasons connected with the conflict'

Like Article 49(1), on which it is based, the prohibition of deportations in internal armed conflict is absolute and allows for no exception, whether for the security of civilians or for imperative military reasons. It covers measures taken against civilians, either individually or collectively.[87] The expulsion of groups of civilians outside a territory by government armed forces or armed groups because of military operations is thus prohibited,[88] as is the expulsion of a group of civilians because of their affiliation to an ethnic group or their alleged support to one of the parties to the conflict.

The prohibition of forced displacement in paragraph 2 however only applies to deportations ordered 'for reasons connected with the conflict'. This qualification, added by the Third Committee, reflects a concern that the article should not interfere with judicial systems which use exile

[86] See below pp. 65–71. [87] Sandoz *et al.*, *Commentary on the Protocols*, p. 1474. [88] *Ibid.*

as a penalty or with normal extradition proceedings.[89] The draft article adopted by Committee III thus included an exception referring to judicially imposed exile, which was then deleted in Article 17, for the sake of simplification.[90] Accordingly, if a measure of deportation is ordered as a consequence of the conflict, it constitutes a forced movement covered by Article 17.[91] However, if the deportation follows a conviction with no relation to the conflict, it falls outside the ambit of the article and remains within the realm of a state's exclusive jurisdiction on domestic matters.

Despite several ambiguities, the prohibition of forced displacement in non-international armed conflicts is well established under Article 17 of Protocol II. However, the extent of the displacement crisis in internal armed conflicts is in stark contrast to the number of conflicts in which the Protocol has actually been applicable. Some of the countries most affected by internal displacement, for instance the Sudan, Nepal and Angola, have not ratified the Second Protocol and are not bound by its provisions. In contrast, Colombia is a party to the Protocol, but none of the parties to the conflict accepts its applicability. The Protocol's high threshold means that it is only applicable in large-scale civil wars of great intensity.[92] Thus, the essential question remains whether the prohibition of forced displacement contained in the Protocol constitutes a customary norm of international humanitarian law, binding on all parties to a non-international armed conflict, irrespective of the state of ratification of the Protocol or of whether the conflict meets the threshold of Article 1.

The prohibition of forced displacement in non-international armed conflicts under customary international law

Before proceeding to the examination of the prohibition of forced movement of civilians in non-international armed conflicts as a customary norm of international law, it is first necessary to reflect on the customary status of Protocol II and on customary rules governing internal conflicts in general.

89 Bothe *et al.*, *New Rules for Victims of Armed Conflicts*, p. 693; OR vol. XV, p. 295, CDDH/215/Rev.1, para. 150.

90 Bothe *et al.*, *New Rules for Victims of Armed Conflicts*, p. 693; Sandoz *et al.*, *Commentary on the Protocols*, p. 1474.

91 Sandoz *et al.*, *Commentary on the Protocols*, p. 1474.

92 Cassese, 'Civil war and international law', 2008, p. 122.

Customary rules of international humanitarian law governing internal armed conflicts

As stated by Theodor Meron, the question of the customary character of the rules applicable in non-international armed conflicts is important for several reasons.[93] First, as the first instrument entirely dedicated to non-international armed conflicts, Protocol II contains twenty-eight articles, which develop and elaborate the law applicable to these conflicts. However, contrary to the Geneva Conventions, it has not gained universal acceptance.[94] It is therefore important to establish which provisions of the Protocol are part of customary international law and thus binding on non-parties. Furthermore, with the exception of Article 13, Protocol II does not address the conduct of hostilities in internal armed conflicts. The identification of customary rules in this respect is thus equally important for all state parties.[95] Finally, customary rules of international law governing non-international armed conflicts are binding on all parties to such conflicts, irrespective of questions of applicability of the Protocol for insurgents. Meron observes that:

> The cruelty of internal armed conflicts, the frequent lack of regard for the principles of humanity by the parties to such conflicts, and, except for Common Article 3 and the essential core of non-derogable human rights, the uncertainty as to the binding rules governing internal armed conflicts, all make the identification and the development of applicable customary rules urgent and compelling.[96]

It is generally agreed that certain principles and rules governing the conduct of hostilities are applicable to large-scale internal armed conflicts, i.e. conflicts which present the characteristics of intensity, duration and magnitude of the Spanish Civil War.[97] As regards Common Article 3, the International Court of Justice declared, in its *Nicaragua* Judgment, that it

[93] Meron, *Human Rights and Humanitarian Norms*, pp. 71–2.

[94] As of July 2011, 166 states were parties to Protocol II. See ICRC Treaty database, www.icrc.org/ihl (accessed 19 July 2011).

[95] Meron, *Human Rights and Humanitarian Norms*, p. 72. [96] *Ibid.*

[97] Cassese, 'The Geneva Protocols and customary international law', 1984, 112. The Spanish Civil War reached such magnitude as to acquire features of an international armed conflict. As a result, the parties to the conflict and other European states affirmed that general rules on the protection of civilians were applicable to this conflict. These rules have become part of customary international law, provided the internal armed conflict presents the same characteristics as the Spanish Civil War, which, incidentally, are laid down in Article 1 of Protocol II. In *Tadić*, the ICTY confirmed that these rules aimed at protecting the civilian population from the hostilities were the first rules to emerge as customary norms of international law, 'at least in those internal conflicts that constituted large-scale civil wars' (Jurisdiction Appeal, para. 100).

constituted a 'minimum yardstick' in the event of non-international as well as international armed conflicts and represented 'essential requirements of humanity'.[98] The rules laid down in Common Article 3 are thus binding upon any state and any insurgent group, party to a non-international armed conflict.

During the drafting of the Second Protocol however, states were reluctant to accept the existence of rules of customary law governing internal armed conflicts.[99] This is evidenced by the noticeable difference of language between the Martens Clause contained in the preamble to Protocol II and that in Article 1(2) of the First Protocol.[100] Indeed, while the latter refers to 'the principles of international law derived from established custom, from the principles of humanity and from the dictates of public conscience', the preamble to Protocol II merely provides that 'the human person remains under the protection of the principles of humanity and the dictates of public conscience'. According to Bothe *et al.*:

> This is justified by the fact that the attempt to establish rules for a non-international conflict only goes back to 1949 and that the application of common Art. 3 in the practice of States has not developed in such a way that one could speak of 'established custom' regarding non-international conflicts.[101]

Nevertheless, many commentators have argued that Protocol II contains 'a basic core of human rights, some of which have already been recognised as customary in human rights instruments and should also be considered as such when stated in instruments of humanitarian law'.[102] This opinion is supported by the ICRC commentary, which states that:

> Protocol II contains virtually all the irreducible rights of the Covenant on Civil and Political Rights . . . These rights are based on rules of universal validity to which States can be held, even in the absence of any treaty obligation or any explicit commitment on their part.[103]

Many states have upheld the view of a customary 'basic core' of Protocol II. Indeed, during a workshop on customary law and Protocols I and II,

98 *Military and paramilitary activities in and against Nicaragua*, para. 218.
99 Meron, *Human Rights and Humanitarian Norms*, p. 72; Moir, *Law of Internal Armed Conflict*, p. 133.
100 Moir, *Law of Internal Armed Conflict*, p. 133; Greenwood, 'Customary law status of the 1977 Geneva Protocols', 1991, p. 112.
101 Bothe *et al.*, *New Rules for Victims of Armed Conflicts*, p. 620.
102 Meron, *Human Rights and Humanitarian Norms*, p. 73.
103 Sandoz *et al.*, *Commentary on the Protocols*, p. 1340.

Michael J. Matheson, Deputy Legal Adviser to the United States Department of State, observed that:

> the basic core of Protocol II is, of course, reflected in Common Article 3 of the 1949 Geneva Conventions, and therefore is, and should be, a part of generally accepted customary law. This specifically includes its prohibitions on violence towards persons taking no active part in hostilities, hostage taking, degrading treatment, and punishment without due process.[104]

Greenwood acknowledges that 'in places Protocol II does no more than restate principles already contained in common Article 3', while in other provisions, such as Article 4(1) and (2) and Article 6(2), the Protocol does 'no more than cloak the bare bones of Article 3 with a moderate amount of flesh'. These provisions thus undoubtedly constitute norms of customary international law. Nevertheless, he adds, it is difficult 'to avoid the conclusion that most of Protocol II has to be regarded as confined to treaty law in the absence of more substantial State practice evidencing an acceptance of its provisions into customary law'.[105]

The jurisprudence of the ICTY has been instrumental in the development of the international humanitarian law regulating non-international armed conflicts. In *Tadić (Appeal on Jurisdiction)*, the Appeals Chamber thus confirmed that Common Article 3 to the Four Geneva Conventions and Article 19 of the Hague Convention on the Protection of Cultural Property in the Event of an Armed Conflict were part of customary law, and held that:

> Many provisions of the [Protocol II] can now be regarded as declaratory of existing rules or as having crystallized emerging rules of customary law or else as having been strongly instrumental in their evolution as general principles.[106]

After an examination of state practice, including the Spanish Civil War and the Biafra conflict in Nigeria, as well as resolutions of the UN General Assembly and the reaction and statements from states to certain conflicts, the Appeals Chamber concluded that customary rules had developed to govern internal strife, particularly with regard to the conduct of hostilities.[107] Nevertheless, the Tribunal crucially observed that the

104 Remarks of Michael J. Matheson on the US position on the relation of customary international law to the 1977 Protocols, in Dupuis *et al.*, 'American Red Cross Conference on international humanitarian law', 1987, 430–1.

105 Greenwood, 'Customary law status of the Geneva Protocols', p. 113.

106 *Tadić*, Jurisdiction Appeal, paras. 98 and 117.

107 'These rules ... cover such areas as protection of civilians from hostilities, in particular from indiscriminate attacks, protection of civilian objects, in particular cultural

emergence of general rules on internal armed conflicts did not imply that internal strife was regulated by general international law in all its aspects, and noted two particular limitations:

> (1) only a number of rules and principles governing international armed conflicts have gradually been extended to apply to internal conflicts; and (ii) this extension has not taken place in the form of a full and mechanical transplant of those rules to internal conflicts; rather, the general essence of those rules, and not the detailed regulation they may contain, has become applicable to internal conflicts.[108]

In conclusion, it is clear that those provisions of the Second Protocol that merely restate or elaborate on Common Article 3 are part of customary international law. Additionally, those provisions which create new law depend on state practice and *opinio juris* in order to become part and parcel of customary international law. The question of the customary status of the Article 17 of the Protocol thus remains to be addressed.

The prohibition of forced movement of civilians in internal armed conflicts as a customary norm of international humanitarian law

It is generally considered that a substantial number of provisions of Protocol II, such as, for instance, the protection of medical and religious personnel,[109] the protection of objects indispensable to the survival of the civilian population,[110] and the protection of works and installations containing dangerous forces[111] mark a clear departure from customary rules.[112] Article 17 on the prohibition of forced movement of civilians is one of those innovative provisions. Concerning the legal force of this category of provisions, Cassese notes:

> The opposition of a conspicuous group of States to the Protocol precludes the conclusion that these provisions reflect a general consent going beyond their contractual nature. Consequently, they will only become binding on those States which ratify the Protocol.[113]

This opinion is shared by many commentators. During the workshop on customary law and the 1977 Protocols, Commander Fenrick argued that Article 17 was 'linked somewhat tenuously to the humane treatment provision of common article 3 and much more clearly to article 49 of the

property, protection of all those who do not (or no longer) take active part in hostilities, as well as prohibition of means of warfare proscribed in international armed conflicts and bans of certain methods of conducting hostilities' (*ibid.*, para. 127).

108 *Ibid.*, para. 126. 109 Protocol II, Art. 9.

110 Protocol II, Art. 14. 111 Protocol II, Art. 15.

112 Cassese, 'Geneva Protocols and customary international law', 110. 113 *Ibid.*

fourth Geneva Convention'.[114] He therefore suggested that this provision constituted 'new law'.

At the time of the drafting of the Protocols, customary international humanitarian law governing internal armed conflicts was very limited, and primarily involved rules relating to the conduct of hostilities and minimum standards of humanity. It is very doubtful that the prohibition of forced movement of civilians was regarded in any way as a customary norm of international humanitarian law. As a consequence of its innovative nature, Article 17 of Protocol II was only binding on states party to the Protocol. The question however remains as to the possible evolution of this conventional rule into a norm of customary law over the past thirty years.

According to the 2005 ICRC study on customary international humanitarian law, the prohibition of displacement of civilians is a norm of customary international law, applicable in both international and non-international armed conflicts.[115] In this respect, the study found evidence of state practice in military manuals which are applicable, or have been applied, in non-international armed conflicts,[116] the national legislation of states,[117] as well as official statements and reported practice in the context of non-international armed conflicts.[118] The UN Security

114 Remarks of Commander W. J. Fenrick, in Dupuis *et al.*, 'American Red Cross Conference on international humanitarian law', 473.

115 Henckaerts and Doswald-Beck, *Customary International Humanitarian Law*, vol. 1, Rule 129, p. 457.

116 For instance, Colombia's *Basic Military Manual* states that it is prohibited to 'oblige civilian persons to move because of the conflict, except if security or imperative military reasons so demand' (Henckaerts and Doswald-Beck, *Customary International Humanitarian Law*, vol. 2, §44); the *Military Instructions* of the Philippines provide that emphasis should be placed on allowing the civilian population to remain in their homes, on the basis that large-scale movement of civilians creates logistical and strategic difficulties for the military (*ibid.*, §56).

117 According to Colombia's Law on Internally Displaced Persons, Colombians have the right not to be forcibly displaced, while Colombia's Penal Code punishes 'anyone who, during an armed conflict, without military justification, deports, expels or carries out a forced transfer or displacement of the civilian population from its own territory' (*ibid.*, §§83–4). Sudan is not a party to Protocol II. Nevertheless, Article 153(2) of its Armed Forces Act 2007 provides that: 'Subject to provisions of the Criminal Act of 1991, shall be punished with imprisonment for a term not exceeding ten years, whoever commits, within the framework of a methodical direct and widespread attack, directed against civilians, any of the following acts . . . (b) transfer, or forcefully deport the populace [from] their areas, without a justification required by security of the population or persistent military necessity' (ICRC, Customary International Humanitarian Law Database, www.icrc.org/customary-ihl/eng/docs/v2) (accessed 19 July 2011).

118 In 1997, in a letter addressed to the Secretary-General and the President of the Security Council, the Permanent Representative of Afghanistan to the United Nations referred

Council,[119] the General Assembly[120] and the Commission on Human Rights[121] have all condemned practices of forced displacement of civilians and ethnic cleansing in internal armed conflicts, on more than one occasion.

The prohibition of forced displacement of civilians in internal armed conflicts is now firmly established, both in conventional and customary international humanitarian law, and is binding on all parties to an internal armed conflict, state and non-state actors. Nevertheless, forced displacement of civilians remains a common feature of internal wars. Forced displacement is consistently used by all parties to the conflict, as a way to assert their power and maintain their hold over the local population and territory. In conflicts with a strong ethnic element, forced removal of the population can be used as part of a general 'ethnic cleansing' policy. The problem does not lie with the lack of legal standards but with the lack of respect for the rules, which is inherently linked to the internal nature of the conflict. While the lack of ratification of Protocol II and inadequate enforcement mechanisms in non-international armed conflicts may explain part of the problem, an equally important issue relates to the applicability *ratione materiae* of international humanitarian law. Indeed, many instances of forced displacement are carried out in situations qualified by the state concerned as 'internal disturbances', and are thus excluded from the ambit of international humanitarian law.

to 'the heinous policy of coercive eviction and mass deportation' by the Talibans of more than 60,000 civilians from the province of Parwan to the capital, Kabul, as a crime against humanity (S/1997/54); according to the ICRC study, the Report on the practice of France states that France especially censures the forcible displacement of the civilian population, when carried out in both international and non-international armed conflicts (Henckaerts and Doswald-Beck, *Customary International Humanitarian Law*, vol. 2, §171) and the Report on US Practice states that 'Article 17 of Protocol II reflects general US policy on displacement in internal armed conflicts' (*ibid.*, §191).

119 The UNSC has adopted several resolutions condemning the forcible displacements of civilians and the practice of ethnic cleansing in the former Yugoslavia, see: Res. 752 (15 May 1992), Res. 819 (16 April 1993) and Res. 1019 (9 November 1995); see also general condemnation of forced displacement in armed conflict, UNSC Res. 1674 (28 April 2006).

120 E.g. UNGA Res. 55/116 'Situation of human rights in the Sudan' (4 December 2000): The General Assembly expresses its deep concern at 'the impact of the current armed conflict . . . and the continuing serious violations of human rights and international humanitarian law by all parties, in particular . . . (ii) the occurrence, within the framework of the conflict in Southern Sudan, of cases of . . . forced displacement of population'.

121 E.g. condemnation by the Commission on Human Rights of acts of forcible displacement in Burundi (E/CN.4/RES/1997/77), the Democratic Republic of the Congo (E/CN.4/RES/2004/84), the Sudan (E/CN.4/RES/2002/16).

Forced displacement in situations of internal disturbances and tensions

According to the ICRC, internal disturbances involve 'situations in which there is no non-international armed conflict as such, but there exists a confrontation within the country, which is characterized by a certain seriousness or duration and which involves acts of violence'.[122] Such situations do not amount to an armed conflict and are expressly excluded from the scope of Protocol II[123] and international humanitarian law in general. Accordingly, many situations of internal violence, which would otherwise qualify as non-international armed conflicts, at least within the meaning of Common Article 3, are often characterized by the government concerned as 'internal disturbances'. State authorities indeed have a tendency to deny that an armed conflict is taking place on their territory, in an effort to free themselves from the limitations imposed by international humanitarian law.[124] As observed by Richard Baxter, '[t]he first line of defense against international humanitarian law is to deny that it applies at all'.[125]

In the absence of an impartial body to authoritatively characterize the conflict, denial of the applicability of international humanitarian law is fairly common.[126] Common Article 3, which does not define 'armed conflicts not of an international character', indeed leaves a wide margin

[122] Conference of Government Experts, document submitted by the ICRC, Title V, *Protection of victims of non-international armed conflicts* (1971), 79, cited in ICRC, 'ICRC protection and assistance activities in situations not covered by international humanitarian law' (1988) 28 IRRC 9, 12.

[123] Protocol II, Art. 1(2): 'This Protocol shall not apply to situations of internal disturbances and tensions, such as riots, isolated and sporadic acts of violence and other acts of a similar nature, as not being armed conflicts.'

[124] For instance, the Colombian government has consistently denied the existence of an armed conflict in Colombia, instead referring to the violence that has displaced over 3 million Colombians, as 'terrorist activities' (Refugees International, 'Colombia cannot deny internal armed conflict' (24 January 2005), http://reliefweb.int/node/164332 (accessed 3 November 2011)). Similarly, since 1999, the Russian authorities have denied that an internal armed conflict was taking place in Chechnya, thus preventing the application of international humanitarian law. 'As a result, Additional Protocol II of 1977 to the Geneva Conventions was intentionally not applied to protect the local populations' (Russian NGO shadow report on the observance of the Convention against Torture and other Cruel, Inhuman or Degrading Treatment or Punishment by the Russian Federation for the period from 2001 to 2006 (November 2006), www.demos-center.ru/images/out.pdf (accessed 3 November 2011).

[125] R. Baxter, 'Some existing problems of humanitarian law', in *The Concept of International Armed Conflict: Further Outlook*, 1, 2 (proceedings of the international symposium on humanitarian law, Brussels 1974), cited in Meron, *Human Rights in Internal Strife*, 1987, p. 43.

[126] Meron, *Humanization of International Law*, pp. 30–1.

for governments to contest its applicability.[127] Additionally, the threshold of application of Protocol II is so high that it limits the application of the Protocol to 'situations at or near the level of full-scale civil war'.[128] As a result, Protocol II has very rarely been applied in practice. According to the UN Secretary-General:

> admitting the application of the Protocol is seen as conferring international legitimacy on opposition forces . . . and/or implicit admission on the Government's part of its lack of effective control in the country.[129]

In contrast, by characterizing a situation as an internal disturbance, governments ensure that it remains within their domestic jurisdiction, leaving them free to act as they wish in their repression of dissidents.[130] A situation of serious internal tension characteristically involves specific types of human rights violations, such as mass arrests, large-scale measures restricting personal freedom, including administrative detention and assigned residence, and probably ill-treatment, torture or inhuman conditions of detention.[131] Many are forced to flee as a result of human rights violations or due to a government's repression campaign against dissidents or agitators.

In situations of internal violence that fall short of armed conflict, individuals may only rely on human rights law for their protection. Yet, as previously noted, existing human rights, such as the freedom of movement and residence, are phrased in general terms and do not contain an explicit prohibition of forced displacement.[132] Moreover, these rights are not absolute and may be subject to restrictions and derogations in time of 'public emergency'. Consequently, states may argue that the existence of public emergency justifies derogation from the right to freedom of movement, while at the same time denying the armed character of the internal conflict, thus refusing the applicability of Common Article 3 and Protocol II. As stated by Meron:

> The combined effect of derogations from the normally applicable human rights and of the inapplicability of humanitarian law results in denial of elementary protections to denizens of states involved in internal conflicts.[133]

[127] UNCHR, 'Minimum humanitarian standards: analytical report of the Secretary-General' (5 January 1998) E/CN.4/1998/87, para. 74.

[128] *Ibid.*, para. 79. [129] *Ibid.*

[130] Casanovas, 'La protection internationale des réfugiés et personnes déplacées', 59.

[131] ICRC, 'ICRC protection and assistance activities', 13.

[132] Kälin and Goldman, 'Legal framework', in Cohen and Deng, *Masses in Flight*, p. 78. See above Chapter 1.

[133] Meron, 'On the inadequate reach of humanitarian and human rights law', 1983, 603.

To remedy this lacuna in the law, Meron drafted his 'Draft Model Declaration on Internal Strife', which contained an 'irreducible and non-derogable core of human and humanitarian norms that must be applied in situations of internal strife and violence'.[134] In December 1990, an expert meeting convened in Turku/Åbo, Finland, and adopted, on the basis of this draft, a Declaration of Minimum Humanitarian Standards.[135] The Declaration reaffirms 'minimum humanitarian standards which are applicable in all situations, including internal violence, disturbances, tensions and public emergency, and which cannot be derogated from under any circumstances'.[136] This instrument should thus be particularly useful 'in all situations of internal violence, and in the gray zone between war and peace'.[137] Among the standards included in the Declaration is the prohibition of forced displacement of civilians. Article 7 declares that:

> The displacement of the population or parts thereof shall not be ordered unless their safety or imperative security reasons so demand . . .
>
> No persons shall be compelled to leave their own territory.

The Declaration was considered by the Sub-Commission on the Prevention of Discrimination and the Protection of Minorities, which then transmitted the text of the Declaration to the Commission on Human Rights 'with a view to its further elaboration and eventual adoption'.[138] In Resolution 1995/29, the Commission recognized 'the need to address principles applicable to situations of internal and related violence, disturbance, tension and public emergency, in a manner consistent with international law and the Charter of the United Nations'. The matter has remained on the agenda of the United Nations ever since. The UN Secretary-General regularly submits an analytical report on the issue of 'fundamental standards of humanity'.[139] Additionally, the process of identifying minimum standards applicable at all times has been discussed by governments, independent experts and non-governmental organizations (NGOs).[140] The

[134] Meron, 'Draft model declaration on internal strife', 1988, 60.

[135] Declaration of Minimum Humanitarian Standards, in UNCHR, 'Report of the Sub-Commission on Prevention of Discrimination and Protection of Minorities on its 46th Session' (1995) E/CN.4/1995/116.

[136] *Ibid.*, Art. 1.

[137] Eide *et al.*, 'Combating lawlessness in grey zone conflicts', 1995, 216–17.

[138] UNCHR, 'Minimum humanitarian standards', para. 11.

[139] E/CN.4/1998/87; E/CN.4/1999/92; E/CN.4/2000/94; E/CN.4/2001/91; E/CN.4/2002/103; E/CN.4/2004/90; E/CN.4/2006/87.

[140] UNCHR, 'Fundamental standards of humanity: Report of the Secretary-General' (12 January 2001) E/CN.4/2001/91, para. 5; see for instance Report of the international

general conclusion resulting from these consultations and the Secretary-General reports is that 'there are no evident substantive legal gaps in the protection of individuals in situations of internal violence'. According to the UN Secretary-General:

> while there is no apparent need to develop new standards, there is a need to secure practical respect for international human rights and humanitarian law in all circumstances and by all actors. The process should thus aim at strengthening the practical protection through the clarification of uncertainties in the application of existing standards in situations, which present a challenge to their effective implementation.[141]

As for international humanitarian law, it is clear that the rigid characterization of armed conflicts on which it is based does not reflect the reality of contemporary conflicts and poses a significant problem in terms of protection of civilians. In practice, the line between internal disturbances and internal armed conflict is often blurred. The confusion created by the different legal regimes is easily abused by governments, to the sole detriment of the civilian population. Alternatively, a situation of violence may consecutively be characterized as internal tension, non-international armed conflict and internationalized armed conflict, in a very short period of time.[142] In this case, it may be difficult, for the actors involved in the conflict, to determine the legal regime applicable.

Unfortunately, it appears evident that no state would agree to the inclusion of internal disturbances within the ambit of international humanitarian law. It would be deemed to constitute an unacceptable intrusion

workshop on minimum humanitarian standards, Cape Town (27–29 September 1996), in UNCHR, 'Minimum humanitarian standards: Report of Secretary-General' (28 January 1997) E/CN.4/1997/77/Add.1; Report of the expert meeting on fundamental standards of humanity, Stockholm (22–24 February 2000) in UNCHR, 'Letter dated 30 March 2000 from the head of the delegation of Sweden', E/CN.4/2000/145.

141 UNCHR, 'Fundamental standards of humanity: Report of the Secretary-General' (3 March 2006) E/CN.4/2006/87, para. 3.

142 For instance, the second war in the DRC, which started in August 1998, is a complex mixture of internal conflicts within the Congo, between the Congolese government and various rebel factions, and interstate armed conflicts which, at times, have involved as many as six states in the Congolese territory. See International Crisis Group, 'Congo at war – a briefing on the internal and external players in the Central African conflict' (17 November 1998) www.unhcr.org/refworld/docid/3ae6a6ce20.html (accessed 3 November 2011). Despite numerous peace agreements, the fighting continues, particularly in the resource-rich Kivu region. On 19 December 2005, the ICJ held that Uganda had violated the sovereignty and territorial integrity of the DRC and was an occupying power in the region of Ituri (*Case concerning armed activities on the territory of the Congo (Democratic Republic of the Congo* v. *Uganda)* Judgment, ICJ Reports 2005, p. 168, paras. 165, 178 and 345).

into the sphere of their domestic affairs. It is nevertheless essential that at least the humanitarian provisions of Common Article 3 and Protocol II apply in situations of internal disturbances and be respected by all actors. Should it be otherwise, the difference of protection for civilians in borderline situations would be unfair and contrary to the purposes of international humanitarian law.

3 Case study: Israeli settlements, the Separation Wall and displacement of civilians in the Occupied Palestinian Territory

Introduction: the practice of population transfer in situations of armed conflict

Population transfer is a common feature of armed conflict and, more specifically, of belligerent occupation. According to the 1993 UN report 'The human rights dimensions of population transfers', one of the principal devices used by an occupying power to extend control over a territory is to implant its own reliable population into the territory.[1] Eventually, the occupying power will allege that humanitarian concerns compel it to remain in the territory to extend its protection to the implanted civilian population.[2] The occupying authorities may also invoke territorial or ideological claims to justify the presence of their own civilians in the occupied territory. Settlement policies are usually coupled with the forced displacement of the original population, who may either become internally displaced within their own country, or become refugees across international borders.[3]

Occupying powers often resort to practices of population transfer in order to create facts on the ground, in a way that will irreversibly affect the situation in the occupied territory and play in their favour in case of future peace settlements. In addition, the UN 'population transfer' report observes that:

[1] UNCHR (Sub-Commission), 'The human rights dimensions of population transfer, including the implantation of settlers, Preliminary report prepared by Mr A. S. Al-Khasawneh and Mr R. Hatano' (6 July 1993) UN Doc. E/CN.4/Sub.2/1993/17, para. 35.

[2] *Ibid.*

[3] Meindersma, 'Population transfers in conflict situations', 1994, 38.

Population transfer has been conducted with the effect or purpose of altering the demographic composition of a territory in accordance with policy objectives or prevailing ideology, particularly when that ideology or policy asserts the dominance of a certain group over another.[4]

There are numerous instances of population transfer, including the Chinese policy of settling large numbers of ethnic Chinese in Tibet, following the occupation of the territory in 1951,[5] and the continuous arrival of Turkish settlers in northern Cyprus, ever since the invasion of Cyprus by Turkey in 1974 and the following partition of the island.[6] Contemporary international armed conflicts have not been spared by population transfers. Following the 1990 Iraqi invasion of Kuwait, the Iraqi authorities expelled Kuwaiti nationals from various areas of Kuwait and replaced them with Iraqi families brought in from Iraq, in order to establish their presence and create a fait accompli.[7] Furthermore, the second half of the twentieth century saw the rise of crueller, deadlier armed conflicts. Parties have increasingly been fighting along ethnic lines, and conflicts which started out as internal have become internationalized. With the emergence of inter-ethnic conflicts, forced displacements have become the primary aim, as opposed to the tragic consequence, of the war. The conflict in former Yugoslavia brought to light the appalling practice of 'ethnic cleansing', which entailed the forced removal of members of an ethnic group from designated territories and their subsequent

[4] UNCHR, Preliminary report on population transfer, para. 17.

[5] A. de Zayas, 'Ethnic cleansing: applicable norms, emerging jurisprudence, implementable remedies', www.alfreddezayas.com/Chapbooks/Ethn_clean.shtml (accessed 26 October 2011).

[6] Council of Europe (Committee on Migration, Refugees and Demography), 'Colonisation by Turkish settlers of the occupied parts of Cyprus', Report of the Rapporteur (2 May 2003) Doc. 9799, para. 32. The report was then endorsed by the Parliamentary Assembly of the Council of Europe in Recommendation 1608 (2003). See also A. de Zayas, 'The Annan Plan and the implantation of Turkish settlers in the occupied territory of Cyprus' (24 July 2005), www.alfreddezayas.com/Articles/cyprussettlers.shtml (accessed 26 October 2011).

[7] In a letter addressed to the Secretary-General, the Permanent Representative of Kuwait to the UN also added that the Iraqi authorities had forcibly taken over some homes which were in the process of construction by the public housing authority of the Kuwaiti Ministry of Housing and installed Iraqi immigrants. According to the Kuwaiti Representative, the object of these crimes was 'to bring about a comprehensive alteration of the demographic structure of Kuwait' (S/21843). The Security Council condemned the forced departure of Kuwaitis and the relocation of Iraqi population in Kuwait in Resolutions 674 of 29 October 1990 and 677 of 28 November 1990.

repopulation by members of a different ethnic group, for the purpose of creating an ethnically homogeneous territory.[8]

The 1949 Geneva Conventions expressly forbid the forced displacement of civilians and subsequent resettlement of the occupying power's own population in occupied territory.[9] Nevertheless, the exact content of the protection is subject to dispute, and diverging interpretations abound. The practice of population transfer is indeed one of the most controversial and debated issues, particularly with regard to the establishment of the settlements in occupied territory. In order to address these issues properly and thoroughly, this chapter will consist of a case study on one of the most notorious instances of population transfers: the continuing implantation of Israeli settlements into Occupied Palestinian Territory (OPT).

According to the BADIL Resource Center, 'Palestinian refugees and internally displaced persons (IDPs) are the largest and longest-standing case of displaced persons in the world today.'[10] At the end of 2008, there were an estimated 6.6 million Palestinian refugees and 427,000 internally displaced Palestinians, representing 67 per cent of the entire Palestinian population worldwide.[11] The majority of Palestinian refugees and IDPs were displaced as a result of the first Arab–Israeli war in 1948 and following the occupation of the West Bank, including East Jerusalem and the Gaza Strip in 1967.[12] Nowadays, internal displacement in the OPT has been the result of Israeli actions and policies, including military operations, house demolitions and land confiscation, in connection with a global settlement policy, which is being consolidated by the construction

[8] Meindersma, 'Population transfers in conflict situations', 37. For a detailed study on population transfers in the former Yugoslavia, see Meindersma, 'Population exchanges: international law and state practice – part 2', 1997.

[9] Geneva Convention IV, Art. 49(6).

[10] BADIL Resource Center for Palestinian Residency and Refugee Rights, *Survey of Palestinian Refugees and Internally Displaced Persons 2008–2009* (December 2009), www.badil.org/index.php?product_id=119&page=shop.product_details&category_id=2&flypage=garden_flypage.tpl&option=com_virtuemart&Itemid=4&vmcchk=1&Itemid=4 (accessed 20 May 2011), p. ix.

[11] *Ibid.*, pp. 56–7.

[12] *Ibid.* The so-called '1948 refugees' were displaced in the context of the 1948 Arab–Israeli War and the creation of the State of Israel and constitute the largest group of refugees (5.7 million). The second category of refugees comprises approximately 955,247 '1967 refugees', i.e. Palestinians who were displaced as a result of the 1967 Arab–Israeli War. In addition, Palestinian IDPs include approximately 335,000 Palestinians displaced from 1947 to 1949, who have remained in the area that became the State of Israel in 1948 and their descendants ('1948 IDPs'), and around 129,000 Palestinians displaced in the OPT since 1967.

of the Separation Wall in the West Bank.[13] The first part of this study will focus on the Israeli settlement policy, its implications for the Palestinian people, and the legal issues arising from such practice. Subsequently, the recent Advisory Opinion of the ICJ on the Separation Wall[14] will provide an unprecedented opportunity to examine the legality of settlements in a more general context.

Israeli settlements and displacement of Palestinian civilians

Israeli settlement policy in the OPT

Ever since the end of the Six-Day War in 1967 and the resulting occupation of part of the Palestinian Territory, Israel has been pursuing a policy of implantation of settlements in the West Bank, the Gaza Strip and occupied East Jerusalem. Israel aims, with the settlements, to create facts on the grounds that will predetermine the outcome of any negotiations by making Israeli withdrawal from the Palestinian territories politically unfeasible.[15] It has been argued that Israel hopes to prevent the emergence of a Palestinian state by breaking up the territorial contiguity of the OPT.[16] Every Israeli government since 1967 has actively pursued a policy of settlements in the OPT, though for differing reasons and through various means. Initially, government policy roughly followed the Alon Plan, which focused on security concerns and distinguished between areas densely populated by Palestinians, which would eventually be returned to Jordan, and strategic areas, which would remain under Israeli control.[17] However, from 1974, the right-wing religious movement Gush Emunim started applying pressure on the Israeli government to establish as many Jewish settlements as possible throughout 'the Land of Israel'.[18] When the

13 BADIL Resource Centre for Palestinian Residency and Refugee Rights and the Norwegian Refugee Council/Internal Displacement Monitoring Centre, *Displaced by the Wall – Pilot study on forced displacement caused by the construction of the West Bank Wall and its associated regime in the Occupied Palestinian Territories* (September 2006), www.internal-displacement.org/8025708F004BE3B1/%28httpInfoFiles%29/D03CD0BE11176177C12571F5003523AD/$file/displaced%20by%20wall.pdf (accessed 20 May 2011), p. 15.

14 *Legal Consequences of the Construction of a Wall in the Occupied Palestinian Territory*, Advisory Opinion, ICJ Reports 2004, 136.

15 Kretzmer, *Occupation of Justice*, p. 75.

16 UNCHR, 'Question of the violation of human rights in the Occupied Arab Territories, including Palestine, Report of the Special Rapporteur John Dugard' (6 March 2002) UN Doc. E/CN.4/2002/32, para. 24.

17 Kretzmer, *Occupation of Justice*, p. 75.

18 B'Tselem, 'Land grab – Israel's settlement policy in the West Bank' (May 2002), p. 14, www.btselem.org/Download/200205_Land_Grab_Eng.pdf (accessed 10 May 2011).

right-wing Likud Party came to power in 1977, it shared the same ideological and political ideas and thus undertook to accelerate the settlement programme and consolidate Israel's hold on Palestine. Settlement activities continued under each new government and throughout the negotiations of the Oslo Accord, and have been gaining in strength ever since.[19] In 2007, there were over 450,000 settlers living in 149 settlements in the West Bank, including East Jerusalem.[20] Approximately 57 per cent of the total settler population in the West Bank lived within a 10-kilometre radius of the old city of Jerusalem.

Displacement of civilians as a result of the settlements

The settlements have had disastrous consequences for the Palestinian people. Their freedom of movement has been seriously affected by the bypass roads linking the settlements to Israel and the numerous Israeli checkpoints and roadblocks. In 2001, it was estimated that some 900,000 Palestinians, or 30 per cent of the population of the occupied territories, were negatively affected by Israeli restrictions on freedom of movement.[21] Furthermore, there have been ongoing tensions between the Palestinians and the Israeli settlers. Settlers have reportedly committed numerous acts of violence against Palestinians and destroyed Palestinian agricultural land and property.[22] In the first ten months of 2008, the UN Office for the Coordination of Humanitarian Affairs (OCHA) recorded 290 settler-related incidents targeting Palestinians and their property, which resulted in 131 Palestinian deaths or injuries.[23] In 2007, Israeli human rights organizations B'Tselem and the Association for Civil Rights in Israel reported that settler violence, imposed curfews and the closing of shops and

[19] *Ibid.*

[20] OCHA, 'The humanitarian impact on Palestinians of Israeli settlements and other infrastructure in the West Bank' (July 2007), p. 12, www.ochaopt.org/documents/TheHumanitarianImpactOfIsraeliInfrastructureTheWestBank_ch1.pdf (accessed 14 April 2012).

[21] UNCHR, 'Question of the violation of Human Rights in the Occupied Arab Territories, including Palestine – update to the mission report of the Special Rapporteur Giorgio Giacomelli' (21 March 2001) E/C.N.4/2001/30, para. 36.

[22] UNCHR, 'Question of the violation of human rights in the Occupied Arab Territories' (6 March 2002), para. 25; Al-Haq, 'Waiting for justice: Al-Haq's 25th Anniversary Report' (2005), http://asp.alhaq.org/zalhaq/site/books/files/Annual%20Report%20Combo.pdf (accessed 18 May 2011).

[23] OCHA Special Focus, 'Unprotected: Israeli settler violence against Palestinians and their property' (December 2008), 1, www.ochaopt.org/documents/ocha_opt_settler_vilonce_special_focus_2008_12_18.pdf (accessed 13 May 2011).

businesses in the city centre of Hebron had led to the mass departure of Palestinians.[24]

The implantation of Israeli settlements in the OPT is closely connected to the displacement of Palestinians. In 1979, a Security Council Commission[25] addressed the consequences of the Israeli settlement policy on the local population and concluded that there was a correlation between the establishment of the settlements and the displacement of the Arab population.[26] It also reported that the Arab inhabitants still living in the territories, particularly the West Bank and Jerusalem, were subjected to continuous pressure to emigrate in order to make room for new settlers who, by contrast, were encouraged to come to the area.[27] The Commission thus concluded that the settlement policy was causing 'profound and irreversible changes of a geographical and demographic nature' in the occupied territories.[28]

Thirty years later, house demolitions and forced evictions, revocation of residency rights, confiscation of land and the construction of colonies and related infrastructures are still the main causes of internal displacement in the OPT since 1967.[29] At the end of 2008, the estimated number of internally displaced persons in the OPT reached 129,000.[30] While it is clear that the Israeli settlements in the OPT have adversely impacted on

[24] B'Tselem and the Association for Civil Rights in Israel, 'Ghost town: Israel's separation policy and forced eviction of Palestinians from the Center of Hebron' (May 2007) www.btselem.org/english/publications/summaries/200705_hebron.asp (accessed 13 May 2011); see also B'Tselem, 'Hebron, Area H-2: Settlements cause mass departure of Palestinians' (August 2003), www.btselem.org/Download/200308_Hebron_Area_H2_Eng.pdf (accessed 13 May 2011).

[25] The Commission was established by the Security Council in Resolution 446 (1979) to 'examine the situation relating to settlements in the Arab territories occupied since 1967, including Jerusalem'.

[26] UNSC, 'Report of the Security Council Commission established under Resolution 446 (1979)' S/13450 (12 July 1979), paras. 221–6. The Commission reported that since 1967, when the settlement policy started, the Arab population had been reduced by 32 per cent in Jerusalem and the West Bank. As to the Golan Heights, the Syrian authorities stated that 134,000 inhabitants had been expelled leaving only 8,000 (i.e. 6 per cent of the local population) in the occupied Golan Heights. The report added: 'The Commission is convinced that in the implementation of its policy of settlements, Israel has resorted to methods – often coercive and sometimes more subtle – which included the control of water resources, the seizure of private properties, the destruction of houses and the banishment of persons, and has shown disregard for basic human rights, including the right of the refugees to return to their homeland' (para. 222).

[27] *Ibid.*, para. 223. [28] *Ibid.*, para. 226.

[29] BADIL, *Survey of Palestinian Refugees and Internally Displaced Persons 2008–9*, p. 2.

[30] *Ibid.*, p. 57. This figure includes 37,000 Palestinian refugees who suffered subsequent secondary forced displacement inside the OPT.

the local Palestinian population, the legal status of these settlements under international law is widely controversial.

The debate over the legality of the settlements in the OPT

The prohibition of transfer of the occupying power's own population in international law

By virtue of Article 49(6) of the Civilians Convention:

> The Occupying Power shall not deport or transfer parts of its own civilian population into the territory it occupies.

According to the ICRC commentary, Article 49(6) was 'intended to prevent a practice adopted during the Second World War by certain Powers, which transferred portions of their own population to occupied territory for political and racial reasons or in order, as they claimed, to colonize those territories'.[31] The exact scope of the prohibition is subject to contention. However, it is clear that the prohibition of population transfer, including the implantation of settlers into occupied territory, is absolute. Article 49(6) does not envisage situations where population transfer would be permitted for the security of civilian population or imperative military reasons.

The prohibition of population transfers may also be derived from a fundamental principle of the law of belligerent occupation, namely, the prohibition of permanent changes in occupied territory. International law imposes a general ban on the acquisition of a territory by force.[32] The annexation of a conquered territory is therefore prohibited by international law. Intrinsically linked with the prohibition of annexation is the basic rule that occupation does not confer sovereignty over the occupied territory. As a result, the occupying power only exercises temporary de facto authority.[33] It follows from this that all measures taken by the occupying power should affect only the administration of the territory.[34] The occupier must administer the territory, not only for his own military purposes, but also, as far as possible, for the public benefit of the

[31] Pictet, *Commentary* (1958), p. 282. [32] UN Charter, Art. 2(4).

[33] This principle is clearly expressed in Article 43 of the Hague Regulations, which states: 'The authority of the legitimate power having *in fact* passed into the hands of the occupant, the latter shall take all the measures in his power to restore, and ensure, as far as possible, public order and safety, while respecting, unless absolutely prevented, the laws in force in the country' [my italic].

[34] Gasser, 'Protection of the civilian population', p. 242.

inhabitants.[35] It has a duty to preserve a status quo in the territory and must refrain from creating permanent changes in the occupied territory. Accordingly, any movement of population, whether in or out of the occupied territory, which affects the population in such a way as to dramatically alter the demographic composition of this territory, must be regarded as a permanent change contrary to the fundamental principles of the law of belligerent occupation.

Furthermore, practices of population transfer clearly constitute breaches of international human rights law, including the right to freedom of movement, the principle of non-discrimination and the right of self-determination.[36] The right to self-determination is widely regarded as a customary rule of international law.[37] In addition, the ICJ has held that the right of peoples to self-determination was 'one of the essential principles of contemporary international law' and acknowledged its *erga omnes* character.[38] By virtue of this right, all peoples have the right to 'freely determine their political status and freely pursue their economic, social and cultural development'.[39] At the root of self-determination, is the right to exist as a people. Consequently, the forced movement of a people from its homeland and its dispersion around the world would necessarily constitute a violation of their right to self-determination.[40] In addition, as stated by the ICJ, the application of the right of self-determination requires a free and genuine expression of the will of the peoples concerned.[41] However, the expression of the will of the peoples may be undermined by the massive implantation of settlers in a specified territory.[42]

The UN Security Council has repeatedly condemned attempts to alter the demographic composition of an occupied territory. For instance, in 1992, it called upon all parties 'to ensure that forcible expulsions of persons from the area where they live and any attempt to change the ethnic composition of the population anywhere in the former Socialist Republic

35 Oppenheim, *International Law*, 1952, pp. 433–4.

36 Meindersma, 'Population transfers in conflict situations', 60–72.

37 Canadian Supreme Court, *Reference Re Secession of Quebec* 37 ILM 1342 (1998), para. 114.

38 *East Timor (Portugal v. Australia)*, Judgment, ICJ Reports 1995, 90, para. 29.

39 *Declaration on the Granting of Independence to Colonial Countries and Peoples*, UNGA 1514 (XV) of 14 December 1960, UN Doc. A/4684 (1961); *Declaration on Principles of International Law concerning Friendly Relations and Co-operation among States in Accordance with the Charter of the United Nations*, UNGA Res. 2625 (XXV) of 24 October 1970, UN Doc. A/5217 (1970).

40 Meindersma, 'Population transfers in conflict situations', 64.

41 *Western Sahara*, Advisory Opinion, ICJ Reports 1975, 12, para. 55.

42 UNCHR, Preliminary report on population transfers, para. 36.

of Yugoslavia, cease immediately'.[43] In his 1997 final report on human rights and population transfers, the Special Rapporteur proposed a draft declaration for adoption by the Commission on Human Rights, which provided that:

> The settlement, by transfer or inducement, by the Occupying Power of parts of its own civilian population into the territory it occupied or by the Power exercising de facto control over a disputed territory is unlawful.[44]

It further stated that:

> Practices and policies having the purpose or effect of changing the demographic composition of the region in which a national, ethnic, linguistic, or other minority or an indigenous population is residing, whether by deportation, displacement, and/or the implantation of settlers, or a combination thereof, are unlawful.[45]

In light of the above considerations, and after careful examination of state practice, the ICRC found that the prohibition of transfers of populations into occupied territory was a customary rule of international law, applicable in international armed conflict.[46]

Israel's position on the legality of the settlements

Population transfers in occupied territory are prohibited under both Article 49 of the Fourth Geneva Convention and customary international law. The legal status of the Israeli settlements should therefore be relatively straightforward, and yet they have been the subject of a heated debate for over forty years, not least due to Israel's refusal to recognize the de jure applicability of the Fourth Geneva Convention to the OPT.[47] Israel's

[43] UNSC Res. 752 (15 May 1992) UN Doc. S/RES/752, para. 6; see also UNSC Res. 677 (28 November 1990), in which the Security Council condemns 'the attempts by Iraq to alter the demographic composition of Kuwait'.

[44] UNCHR, 'Human rights and population transfer – final report of the Special Rapporteur, Mr Al-Khasawneh' (27 June 1997) E/CN.4/Sub.2/1997/23, Annex II, Draft declaration on population transfer and the implantation of settlers, Art. 5.

[45] *Ibid.*, Art. 6.

[46] Henckaerts and Doswald-Beck, *Customary International Humanitarian Law*, vol. 1, Rule 130, p. 462.

[47] Israel's position is based on a 'missing reversioner' theory, first advanced by Professor Yehuda Blum, in 'The missing reversioner', 1968, 279. According to this theory, neither Jordan nor Egypt were 'legitimate sovereigns' in the West Bank and the Gaza Strip in 1967; these territories thus cannot be considered as 'the territory of a High Contracting Party' within the meaning of Article 2 of the Geneva Conventions. Israel has nevertheless declared its intention to respect de facto the 'humanitarian provisions' of the Convention in the occupied territories. However, it has never clarified which provisions of the Fourth Geneva Convention it regards as 'humanitarian'.

legal position has been criticized by most legal scholars[48] and has enjoyed very limited support outside its borders.[49] The UN Security Council,[50] the General Assembly[51] and the International Committee of the Red Cross[52] have consistently reaffirmed the applicability of the law of belligerent occupation, including the Fourth Convention, to the OPT.

As observed by Professors Brownlie and Goodwin-Gill, the Fourth Geneva Convention is not concerned with origins of conflict or the status of territory.[53] Article 2, which defines the scope of application of the Convention, indeed clearly stipulates that:

> The Convention shall . . . apply to *all cases of partial or total occupation* of the territory of a High Contracting Party, even if the said occupation meets with no armed resistance. [my italic]

In addition, Article 1 calls for respect of the Convention 'in all circumstances' and Article 4 provides that inhabitants of the occupied territory

48 Dinstein dismissed the 'missing reversioner' theory as 'based on dubious legal grounds' ('Belligerent occupation and human rights', 1978, 107). See also Brownlie and Goodwin-Gill, 'The protection afforded by international humanitarian law to the indigenous population of the West Bank and the Gaza Strip', 2003; Meron, 'West Bank and Gaza', 1978, 108–19; Roberts, 'Prolonged military occupation', pp. 43–9.

49 The de jure applicability of the Civilians Convention has in fact been recognized by most states, including the USA. In 1978, the US legal adviser indeed observed that: '[the principles of belligerent occupation] appear applicable whether or not Jordan or Egypt possessed legitimate sovereign rights in respect of those territories. Protecting the reversionary interest of an ousted sovereign is not their sole or essential purpose; the paramount purposes are protecting the civilian population of an occupied territory and reserving permanent territorial changes, if any, until the settlement of the conflict' ('Letter by Herbert J. Hansell, Legal Adviser of the US Department of State, 21 April 1978' (1978) *Digest of US Practice Intl. L.*, 1578).

50 E.g. UNSC Res. 446 (22 March 1979), in which the Security Council 'affirms the applicability of the Fourth Geneva Convention and calls upon Israel, as the Occupying Power, to abide scrupulously by the Geneva Conventions'.

51 E.g. UNGA Res. 35/122A (11 December 1980), in which the General Assembly 'reaffirms that the Geneva Convention relative to the protection of civilian persons in time of war, of 12 August 1949, is applicable to Palestinian and other Arab territories occupied by Israel since 1967, including Jerusalem'.

52 ICRC (Official Statement) 'Conference of the High Contracting Parties to the Fourth Geneva Convention' (5 December 2001): 'In accordance with a number of resolutions adopted by the United Nations General Assembly and Security Council and by the International Conference of the Red Cross and the Red Crescent, which reflect the view of the international community, the ICRC has always affirmed the de jure applicability of the Fourth Geneva Convention to the territories occupied since 1967 by the State of Israel, including Jerusalem' (www.icrc.org/web/eng/siteeng0.nsf/htmlall/5fldpj?opendocument#2 (accessed 17 May 2011)).

53 Brownlie and Goodwin-Gill, 'Protection afforded by international humanitarian law to the indigenous population of the West Bank and the Gaza Strip', para. 66.

shall be 'protected persons'.[54] There is therefore no doubt that the Fourth Geneva Convention applies to the whole of the OPT and that Israel, as the occupying power, has rights and duties towards the Palestinian population of the West Bank, the Gaza Strip and East Jerusalem. In particular, Article 49 of the Convention, which remains applicable in case of prolonged occupation,[55] expressly prohibits the forced displacement of Palestinians by the Israeli authorities, as well as the transfer of Israeli civilians, including the implantation of settlers, into the OPT. Israel has consistently argued that, despite the alleged inapplicability of the Fourth Convention, the implantation of settlements has complied with Article 49 of the Convention. In addition, Israel has also alleged that the requisition of Palestinian private lands for the establishment of settlements has been in conformity with its obligations under the 1907 Hague Regulations.

Requisition and destruction of property for security reasons

The establishment of Israeli settlements in the OPT has required the expropriation and destruction of many Palestinian private properties. However, the law of belligerent occupation attaches great importance to private and public property in occupied territory. Article 53 of the Fourth Geneva Convention prohibits the destruction, by the occupying power, of all property, real or personal, whether it is the private property of protected persons, state property, that of the public authorities or of social or cooperative organizations, except where such destruction is rendered absolutely necessary by military operations.[56] Moreover, under Article 46 of the Hague Regulations, private property cannot be confiscated.

Between 1967 and 1979, Israel's main justification for the expropriations and destructions of Palestinian properties was based on Article 52 of the Hague Regulations.[57] Israel alleged that it was justified in requisitioning privately owned Palestinian land, due to security considerations. During this period, almost 47,000 dunums of private land were requisitioned, most of which were intended for the establishment of

[54] *Ibid.*; see also Letter by the Legal Adviser of the US Department of State.

[55] In case of prolonged occupation, i.e. more than one year after the general close of military operations, Article 6 Geneva Convention IV stipulates that 'the Occupying Power shall be bound, for the duration of the occupation, to the extent that such power exercises the functions of government in such territory', by the humanitarian provisions of the Convention, including Article 49.

[56] Pictet, *Commentary* (1958), p. 301.

[57] Hague Regulations, Art. 52: 'Requisitions in kind and services shall not be demanded from municipalities or inhabitants except for the needs of the army of occupation.'

settlements.[58] Many Palestinians whose lands were being requisitioned 'for military needs' petitioned the Israeli Supreme Court against these measures. At first, the Court accepted the Israeli view and held that the requisitions of privately owned land and the establishment of civilian settlements thereupon actually served military and security needs and were therefore lawful, as long as they were temporary.[59]

It is very doubtful that the establishment of civilian settlements can be justified 'for the needs of the army of occupation'. Even if the settlements were really implanted for security reasons, doubts have been raised as to whether the settlements contribute to national security or whether they in fact undermine it.[60] Indeed, the presence of settlers is a major cause of tension in the area, and the settlers themselves are often at the origin of friction with the Palestinians.[61] In view of the mutual hostility between Palestinians and settlers, it would be difficult for Israel to maintain that the settlements are necessary to its national security.

Israel's policy of land confiscation stopped in 1979, following a landmark judgment by the Israeli Supreme Court, in the *Elon Moreh* case.[62] The case concerned the establishment of a civilian settlement at Elon Moreh, adjacent to the town of Nablus, on land privately owned by Arab residents.[63] Israel claimed that the establishment of the settlement in the area was required for security reasons. However, as opposed to previous cases, the Court also heard the arguments of settlers at the Elon Moreh site, who joined as respondents. The settlers rejected the argument that the settlement was being built on grounds of security, relying instead on

58 B'Tselem, 'Land grab', p. 48. Note that 1 dunum = ¼ acre or 1,000 m^2.

59 See the *Beth El* case, in which the Court found that Jewish settlements in occupied territories served actual and real security needs:

> It is indisputable that in occupied areas the existence of settlements – albeit 'civilian' – of citizens of the Occupying Power contributes greatly to the security in that area and assists the army in fulfilling its task. One need not be a military and defence expert to understand that terrorist elements operate with greater ease in an area solely inhabited by a population that is indifferent or sympathizes with the enemy, than in an area in which one also finds people likely to observe the latter and report any suspicious movement to the authorities. Terrorists will not be granted a hideout, assistance or supplies by such people. (HC 606/78, *Suleiman Tawfiq Oyyeb and others* v. *Minister of Defence and others* (*Beth El* case), 15 March 1979, repr. in (1985) II *Palestine Yearbook of International Law*, 134)

60 Roberts, 'Prolonged military occupation', 67.

61 Karp Report on the investigation of suspicious or criminal activity by Jewish settlers in the West Bank, repr. in (1984) I *Palestine Yearbook of International Law*, 185.

62 HCJ 390/79, *Dweikat et al.* v. *Government of Israel et al.* 3 October 1979, translated in (1984) I *Palestine Yearbook of International Law*, 134.

63 *Ibid.*, 135.

ideological and religious claims.[64] The petitioners submitted an affidavit by a former army chief of staff, Lieutenant-General (Reserves) Bar-Lev, who also contested the security argument.[65] In light of the evidence before it, the Court had no choice but to conclude that the decision to establish a settlement at Elon Moreh was based primarily on political, rather than military considerations and that the settlement was intended to be permanent.[66] The Court therefore declared the requisition order illegal.

Use of public land for the establishment of the Israeli settlements

Following the *Elon Moreh* debacle, Israel had to find other ways to requisition land for the establishment of settlements in the OPT, mostly through the controversial manipulation of a 1858 Ottoman Land law, which applied in the West Bank at the time of occupation and enabled Israel to take possession of lands proclaimed as 'State land'.[67] With this method, approximately 40 per cent of the West Bank was declared state land[68] and consequently requisitioned by Israel, on the basis of Article 55 of the Hague Regulations, which provides that:

> The Occupying State shall be regarded only as administrator and usufructuary of public buildings, real estate, forests, and agricultural estates belonging to the hostile State, and situated in the occupied country. It must safeguard the capital of these properties, and administer them in accordance with the rules of usufruct.

According to Israel's Ministry of Foreign Affairs, 'there is a positive duty which obliges the authority to take possession of public property in order to safeguard it pending final determination as to the status of the territory concerned'.[69] By asserting that the establishment of settlements is part of its obligations to temporarily administer Palestinian public property, Israel adopts a very broad interpretation of Article 55. As usufructuary, Israel has a right to enjoy the fruits of Palestinian public property, land

64 *Ibid.*, 141. 65 *Ibid.*, 138.

66 *Ibid.*, 150: 'the decision to establish a permanent settlement intended from the outset to remain in its place forever – even beyond the duration of the military government which was established in Judea and Samaria – encounters a legal obstacle which is insurmountable, because the military government cannot create in its area facts for its military needs which are designed *ab initio* to exist even after the end of the military rule in that area, when the fate of the area after the termination of military rule is still not known'.

67 B'Tselem, 'Land grab', p. 51. 68 *Ibid.*

69 Israel MFA, 'Israel's settlements – their conformity with international law' (December 1996), www.mfa.gov.il/MFA/Government/Law/Legal Issues and Rulings/ISRAEL-S SETTLEMENTS - CONFORMITY WITH INTERNATION (accessed 17 May 2011).

and natural resources, such as water and oil, provided it doesn't alter the nature or substance of this property. In exercising its powers, the occupant may only create permanent changes in the occupied territory required by its own military needs or in the interests of the local population. Most of all, the occupant must not exercise its authority in order to further its own interests, or to meet the needs of its own population.[70] In this context, it is difficult to see how the construction of permanent settlements can be viewed as mere administration of Palestinian lands and enjoyment of their fruits. Indeed, the destruction of houses and olive trees, the irreversible alteration of the landscape, and the exodus of Palestinians from their lands are in complete contradiction to the rules of usufruct and the principles of the law of belligerent occupation, and therefore invalidate the Israeli argument.

Settlements in compliance with Article 49(6) of the Fourth Geneva Convention

While it rejects the de jure applicability of the Fourth Geneva Convention to the OPT, Israel has always maintained that its settlement policy nevertheless conforms to Article 49(6) of the Convention. The Israeli position is summarized as follows by Israel's Ministry of Foreign Affairs:

> The provisions of the Geneva Convention regarding forced population transfer to occupied sovereign territory cannot be viewed as prohibiting the voluntary return of individuals to the towns and villages from which they, or their ancestors, had been ousted . . . It should be emphasised that the movement of individuals to the territory is entirely voluntary, while the settlements themselves are not intended to displace Arab inhabitants, nor do they do so in practice.[71]

It should be pointed out that Israel's position has never been articulated in any proceedings, be it before the Israeli High Court or any other judicial body. The Israeli High Court has always refused to address the legality of settlements under the Fourth Geneva Convention. According to the Court, Article 49 does not reflect customary international law and may therefore not be relied upon before Israeli courts.[72] In addition, the Israeli government refused to participate in the proceedings before the ICJ in

[70] Cassese, 'Powers and duties of an occupant in relation to land and natural resources', 1992, p. 420.

[71] Israel MFA, 'Israeli settlements and international law' (May 2001), www.mfa.gov.il/MFA/Peace+Process/Guide+to+the+Peace+Process/Israeli+Settlements+and+International+Law.htm (accessed 17 May 2011).

[72] HC 698/80, *Kawasme et al.* v. *Minister of Defence et al.* (1980), 35(1) *Piskei Din* 617, English summary in (1981) 11 IYHR, 349, 350.

the *Legal Consequences of the Construction of a Wall in the Occupied Palestinian Territory*, which addressed for the first time the question of the legality of the Israeli settlements. The Israeli arguments, based on statements by the Ministry of Foreign Affairs and opinions of Israeli academic writers, will nevertheless be analysed below.

Article 49(6) only prohibits forcible transfers

Israel's main argument is based on an alleged distinction between 'forcible transfers' of people and the 'voluntary' movement of individuals into occupied territory. Indeed, the Israeli Ministry of Foreign Affairs maintains that Article 49(6) 'was intended to deal with forced transfers of population like those which took place in Czechoslovakia, Poland and Hungary before and during the war'.[73] This argument is supported by Professor Yoram Dinstein, who contends that such voluntary settlements, if not carried out on behalf of the occupant's government and in an institutional fashion, are not 'necessarily illegitimate'.[74] However, it should be pointed out that, as opposed to the first paragraph of Article 49, which expressly prohibits 'forcible transfers' of population, there is no reference in paragraph 6 to any notion of force. Indeed, the provision only stipulates that the 'Occupying Power *shall not deport or transfer* parts of its own population into the territories it occupies' (my italic). It can therefore be argued that the word 'forcible' was intentionally omitted from the text of paragraph 6, thereby reinforcing the idea that, voluntary or not, all transfers of population into an occupied territory are prohibited under international humanitarian law.

Moreover, it is commonly agreed that even if voluntary movement into occupied territory was compatible with Article 49(6), Israel's settlement activity would not fit this definition.[75] Indeed, Israel's actions have contributed greatly, in one way or another, to the establishment and expansion of settlements in the occupied territories. Throughout the years, successive Israeli governments have offered various financial benefits and incentives to encourage Israelis to move to the OPT.[76] Such incentives include generous tax benefits, government housing subsidies, as well as

[73] Israel MFA, 'Israel's settlements – their conformity with international law'.
[74] Dinstein, 'Belligerent occupation and human rights', 124.
[75] Meindersma, 'Population transfers in conflict situations', 51; Roberts, 'Prolonged military occupation', p. 67; Benvenisti, *The International Law of Occupation*, 1993, p. 140.
[76] B'Tselem, 'By hook and by crook: Israeli settlement policy in the West Bank' (July 2010), 37–47, www.btselem.org/Download/201007_By_Hook_and_by_Crook_Eng.pdf (accessed 17 May 2011).

subsidized loans and grants for settlers to buy their houses.[77] These financial inducements are clear evidence of the Israeli government's implication in the settlements activity in the occupied territories, at variance with the Israeli claim that 'the movement of individuals to the territory is entirely voluntary'.

Many states hold the view that such an involvement is in contravention to the provisions of Article 49(6). In 1978, the US Legal Adviser of the Department of State stated that paragraph 6:

> seems clearly to reach such involvements of the occupying Power as determining the location of settlements, making land available and financing of settlements, as well as other kinds of assistance and participation in their creation. And the paragraph appears applicable whether or not harm is done by a particular transfer.[78]

This position is shared by the Palestine Liberation Organization (PLO), who argue that:

> [Article 49(6)] also sought to cover not only forcible transfers but also the case where the occupying power positively encourages settlement of its own people in the territory under occupation. If ever there was a case that fitted precisely the prohibition in the sixth paragraph of article 49, this must be the Israeli policy on colonies.[79]

Moreover, the 'transfer, *directly or indirectly*, by the Occupying Power of parts of its own population into the territory it occupies' (my italic) constitutes a war crime under the ICC Statute. The addition of the words 'directly or indirectly' marks a departure from the wording of Article 85(4)(a) of the Protocol I, from which Article 8(2)(b)(viii) is derived. According to a commentary on the Statute, the inclusion of 'indirect' in the article seems to indicate that the population of the occupying power need not necessarily be physically forced or otherwise compelled and that acts of inducement or facilitation may also fall under this war crime.[80] In 2002, the Office of the Legal Adviser to the Israeli Ministry of Foreign Affairs stated that, while Israel fully supported 'the goals of the Court and its desire to ensure

[77] OCHA, The humanitarian impact on Palestinians of Israeli settlements 2007, pp. 32–3; S. Hever, 'The economy of occupation, part 2: the settlements – economic cost to Israel' (July 2005), 7–8, Alternative Information Center, www.alternativenews.org/images/stories/downloads/socioeconomic_bulletin_02.pdf (accessed 17 May 2011).

[78] Letter of the US Legal Adviser of the Department of State concerning the legality of Israeli settlements in the occupied territories, 1577.

[79] PLO (Negotiations Affairs Department), 'Israeli colonies and international law', www.nad-plo.org/etemplate.php?id=264 (accessed 1 November 2011).

[80] Dörmann, *Elements of War Crimes*, 2002, p. 211.

that no perpetrator of heinous crimes goes unpunished', it had concerns that the Court would be subjected to political pressures and that its impartiality would be compromised.[81] Israel's main concern lay in the inclusion of the war crime of transfer of population into occupied territory:

> This particular offence represents neither a grave breach of the Fourth Geneva Convention, nor does it reflect customary international law. The inclusion of this offence, under the pressure of the Arab States, and the addition of the phrase 'directly or indirectly', is clearly intended to try to use the court to force the issue of Israeli settlements without the need for negotiation as agreed between the sides.[82]

As a result, Israel refused to ratify the ICC Statute and expressly stated its intention not to become a party to the Treaty.[83]

Finally, the Israeli claim that the settlements comply with Article 49(6) should be analysed with regard to the intended beneficiaries of the provision. Israeli academic writer Julius Stone claimed that one of the aims of the prohibition in Article 49(6) was 'to protect the inhabitants of the occupant's own metropolitan territory from genocidal or other inhuman acts of the occupant's government'.[84] In this regard, he added:

> Ignoring the overall purpose of Article 49, which would *inter alia* protect the population of the State of Israel from being removed against their will into occupied territory, it is now sought to be interpreted so as to impose on the Israel government a duty to prevent any Jewish individual from voluntarily taking residence in that area. For not even the most blinkered adversary of Israel could suggest that the individual Jews who (for example) are members of Gush Emunim groups, are being in some way forced to settle in Judea and Samaria (the West Bank)![85]

81 Israel MFA (Office of the Legal Adviser), 'Israel and the International Criminal Court' (June 2002) www.mfa.gov.il/MFA/MFAArchive/2000_2009/2002/6/Israel and the International Criminal Court (accessed 17 May 2011).

82 *Ibid.*

83 On 28 August 2002, the UN Secretary-General, as depository, received a letter from the government of Israel, stating: 'In connection with the Rome Statute of the International Criminal Court... Israel does not intend to become a party to the treaty. Accordingly, Israel has no legal obligations arising from its signature on 31 December 2000. Israel requests that its intention not to become a party, as expressed in this letter, be reflected in the depository's status lists relating to this treaty' (American Non-Governmental Organizations Coalition for the International Criminal Court (AMICC), Ratifications and Declarations, www.amicc.org/icc_ratifications.html (accessed 17 May 2011).

84 Stone, 'Discourse 2: Jewish settlements in Judea and Samaria', in *Israel and Palestine: Assault on the Law of Nations*, 1981, p. 180.

85 *Ibid.*

However, as rightly noted by Christa Meindersma, a discussion on the prohibition of population transfers into occupied territory should consider not only the voluntary movement of the settlers, but also and most importantly, 'the voluntariness on the part of the recipient population'.[86] Indeed the 'voluntary migration' argument completely overlooks the fact that it is the inhabitants of the occupied territory, and not the occupying power's own population, who are 'protected persons' under the Fourth Geneva Convention.[87] As nationals of the occupying power, Israeli settlers do not come within the meaning of Article 4 of the Convention. In addition, the drafters of the Convention adopted Article 49(6) with the clear intention of protecting the occupied population from colonization by the occupying power.[88] The fact that the Israeli government did not force its own citizens to move into the OPT is beside the point. The only significant matter is the fact that Israeli civilians came and settled on Palestinian land. That the movement of Israeli settlers on their land was voluntary is entirely irrelevant for the Palestinians. The harm caused to their land and their livelihood by the implantation of settlements remains the same.

The settlements are not intended to displace civilians

The Israeli Ministry of Foreign Affairs has argued that 'the settlements themselves are not intended to displace Arab inhabitants, nor do they do so in practice'.[89] First of all, it should be recalled that the Israeli settlements do, in fact, create displacement. The land expropriations and house demolitions involved in the construction of settlements, the violence resulting from the difficult cohabitation between Palestinians and settlers and the scarcity of resources all contributed to Palestinians having to leave their place of residence. In addition, this argument is irrelevant under Article 49(6). Indeed, this provision does not mention a motive for a transfer of population to take place and nothing in the commentary seems to suggest a possible limitation of the application of the article to a situation where the civilian population is displaced.[90] According to the US Legal Adviser, forced displacement is dealt with separately in the Convention and paragraph 6 would be redundant if limited to cases of displacement.[91] Displaced or not, Palestinians in occupied territories are still deeply affected by the Jewish settlements.

86 Meindersma, 'Population transfers in conflict situations', 52.

87 Benvenisti, *International Law of Occupation*, p. 140.

88 Pictet, *Commentary* (1958), p. 282.

89 Israel MFA, 'Israeli settlements and international law'.

90 Mallison and Mallison, 'Israeli settlements in the occupied territories', 1989–9, 119.

91 Letter of the US Legal Adviser of the Department of State concerning the legality of Israeli settlements in the occupied territories, 1577.

Displacement is only one of several consequences of settlements, whose global objective is to alter the demographic composition of an occupied territory and create facts on the grounds. Accordingly, the purpose of Article 49(6) is not only to prevent population transfers, but more generally to preclude the occupying power from altering the demographic composition of the occupied territory, irrespective of whether or not displacements occur as a result.

Historical and ideological claims

Israel has also claimed that the existence of Jewish settlements in the OPT is a continuation of a long-standing Jewish presence.[92] Historical claims such as this one are generally encountered in the context of *jus ad bellum*, when states use or threaten to use force in order to take a territory that they consider rightfully theirs.[93] In this case, they argue that the prohibition against force as contained in Article 2(4) of the UN Charter does not apply, as the use of force is merely intended to recover part of their territory unlawfully occupied by another state. This argument was invoked by India in relation to Goa in 1961 and by Argentina in 1982, when it intended to 'recover' the Falkland Islands.[94] Similarly, Iraq attempted to justify its invasion of Kuwait on 2 August 1990 by claiming that Kuwait was historically part of Iraq and that it had only been separated as a result of British colonialism.[95] However, as rightly noted by Schachter, given the considerable number of territorial disputes throughout the world, if such a claim were accepted, it would considerably reduce the scope of the prohibition of the use of force. In fact, the international community has never recognized territorial claims as an acceptable exception to the prohibition of use of force.[96]

Likewise, just as territorial claims are rejected in the context of *jus ad bellum*, historical or ideological claims to a territory cannot be accepted in *jus in bello*. The recognition of transfers of population into occupied territory as a continuation of long-standing presence in that territory would not only be open to abuse but would also set a dangerous precedent, in contravention to the most basic principles of belligerent occupation. Moreover, this argument is once again irrelevant under Article 49(6) of the Fourth Convention, which makes no mention of a possible historical claim in support of the legality of settlements. Any historical or ideological claim

[92] Israel MFA, 'Israel's settlements – their conformity with international law'.

[93] Schachter, *International Law in Theory and Practice*, 1991, pp. 116–17. [94] *Ibid.*

[95] Greenwood, 'New world order or old?', 1992, 156.

[96] *Ibid.*; see, for instance, UNSC Res. 662 (9 August 1990) declaring the annexation of Kuwait by Iraq as 'null and void'.

that Israel or the Jewish people may have over the Palestinian territory has no legal validity under international humanitarian law.

Agreements between Israel and the PLO do not prohibit settlements

Finally, Israel asserts that the bilateral agreements between Israel and the Palestinians, namely the Oslo Accords,[97] contain no prohibition on the building or expansion of settlements. Article V(3) of the Declaration of Principles in particular provides that the issue of settlements is among a number of issues to be negotiated in the permanent status negotiations. Accordingly, Israel claims that there is no restriction on settlement activity during the interim period.[98] However, Article XXXI(7) of the Interim Agreement clearly states that:

> Neither side shall initiate or take any step that will change the status of the West Bank and the Gaza Strip pending the outcome of the permanent status negotiations.

Watson thus argues that, while the Oslo Accords do not outlaw existing settlements, they impose serious restrictions on the creation of new settlements, especially in the West Bank and Gaza Strip.[99] Furthermore, the Fourth Geneva Convention expressly prohibits agreements between the parties to a conflict if they deprive protected persons from the protection of the Convention. As a general rule, Article 7 of the Convention states that 'no special agreements shall adversely affect the situation of protected persons, as defined by the present convention, nor restrict the rights which it confers upon them'. Article 47 reaffirms the applicability of this rule in occupied territory:

> Protected persons who are in Occupied Territory shall not be deprived, in any case or in any manner whatsoever, of the benefits of the present Convention . . . by any agreement concluded between the authorities of the Occupied Territories and the Occupying Power.

There is no doubt that most Israeli settlements in the occupied territories have been established in violation of the rights of the Palestinian population. Therefore, agreements between Israel and the Palestinians which

97 Declaration of Principles on Interim Self-Government Arrangements, Israel–Palestine Liberation Organization (13 September 1993), 32 ILM 1525 (1993); the Israeli–Palestinian Interim Agreement on the West Bank and the Gaza Strip, Israel–PLO (28 September 1995), 36 ILM 551 (1997).

98 Israel MFA, 'Israel's settlements – their conformity with international law'.

99 Watson, *The Oslo Accords*, 2000, p. 136.

would allow settlements in the OPT, or simply tolerate them pending a settlement of the conflict, violate the Fourth Geneva Convention.

International condemnation of the Israeli settlement policy

The international community as a whole has repeatedly and consistently condemned the Israeli settlement policy. The UN Security Council,[100] the General Assembly[101] and the Commission on Human Rights[102] have all denounced the settlements as contrary to international law. In 1979, the UN Security Council adopted a resolution of major importance, which has defined the UN position on the Israeli settlements ever since. In resolution 446, the Security Council determined that Israel's policy and practices of settlements had no legal validity and called on Israel, as the occupying power:

[100] UNSC Res. 446 (22 March 1979), Res. 452 (20 July 1979), Res. 465 (1 March 1980) and Res. 476 (30 June 1980). However, since 1980, any attempt by the Security Council to adopt a resolution condemning Israeli settlements has been consistently hampered by the US veto. See vetoed draft resolutions S/15895 of 2 August 1983, S/1995/394 of 17 May 1995, S/1997/199 of 7 March 1997 and S/1997/241 of 21 March 1997. More recently, the Obama administration made its first use of the US veto power by rejecting Draft Resolution S/2011/24. The proposed resolution, which was drafted by the Arab Group and adopted by fourteen members of the Security Council, including the UK and France, clearly condemned 'the continuation of settlement activities by Israel, the occupying Power, in the Occupied Palestinian Territory, including East Jerusalem, and of all other measures aimed at altering the demographic composition, character and status of the Territory, in violation of international humanitarian law and relevant resolutions' (E. Pilkington, 'US vetoes UN condemnation of Israeli settlements', *Guardian*, 19 February 2011, www.guardian.co.uk/world/2011/feb/19/us-veto-israel-settlement (accessed 17 May 2011).

[101] E.g. UNGA Res. 34/90 B (12 December 1979), Res. 36/147 C (16 December 1981), Res. 37/88 C (9 December 1982), Res. 38/79 D (15 December 1983). In addition, every year since 1997, the General Assembly adopts a resolution entitled 'Israeli settlements in the occupied Palestinian territory, including Jerusalem and the occupied Syrian Golan': e.g. UNGA Res. 52/66 (10 December 1997), Res. 56/61 (10 December 2001), Res. 59/123 (10 December 2004) and Res. 60/106 (8 December 2005), which states that: 'Israeli settlements in the Palestinian territory, including East Jerusalem, and in the occupied Syrian Golan are illegal and an obstacle to Peace and economic and social development.'

[102] E.g. UNCHR Res. 2005/6 (22 April 2005), which expresses grave concern at: 'the continuing Israeli settlements and related activities, in violation of international law, including the expansion of settlements, the expropriation of land, the demolition of houses, the confiscation and destruction of property, the expulsion of Palestinians and the bypass roads, which change the physical character and demographic composition of the occupied territories . . . and constitute a violation of the [Fourth Geneva Convention], and in particular article 49 of that Convention; settlements are a major obstacle to the establishment of a just and comprehensive peace and the creation of an independent, viable, sovereign and democratic Palestinian State.'

to abide scrupulously by the 1949 Fourth Geneva Convention, to rescind its previous measures and to desist from taking any action which would result in changing the legal status and geographical nature and materially affecting the demographic composition of the Arab territories occupied since 1967, including Jerusalem, and, in particular, not to transfer parts of its own civilian population into the occupied Arab territories.[103]

In 2001, the International Committee of the Red Cross expressed 'growing concern about the consequences in humanitarian terms of the establishment of Israeli settlements in the occupied territories, in violation of the Fourth Geneva Convention',[104] while the Conference of the high contracting parties to the Fourth Geneva Convention reaffirmed the illegality of the settlements.[105] Many states have also been critical of the Israeli settlement policy. The European Council has called on Israel to halt its settlement activities on several occasions.[106] Arab states have adamantly condemned the Israeli settlements,[107] while the PLO has denounced Israeli colonization policies and practices as violations of international humanitarian law and principles of international law.[108] Even Israel's strongest ally, the US government, has expressed its opposition to the Israeli settlements in the OPT. The US position was defined in 1978 by the Legal Adviser to the Department of State:

103 UNSC Res. 446 (22 March 1979) UN Doc. S/RES/446.

104 ICRC (Official Statement) 'Conference of the High Contracting Parties to the Fourth Geneva Convention' (5 December 2001).

105 ICRC (Declaration) 'Conference of the High Contracting Parties to the Fourth Geneva Convention' (5 December 2001): 'The participating High Contracting Parties call upon the Occupying Power to fully and effectively respect the Fourth Geneva Convention in the Occupied Palestinian Territory, including East Jerusalem, and to refrain from perpetrating any violation of the Convention. They reaffirm the illegality of the settlements in the said territories and of the extension thereof' (para. 12).

106 European Council, 'EU Presidency Conclusions, Annex IV: Declaration on the Middle East Process' (16 and 17 June 2005), EU Doc. 10255/05: 'The European Council also stresses for a halt to Israeli settlement activities in the Palestinian Territories. This implies a complete cessation of construction of dwellings and new infrastructures such as bypass roads. The European Council also calls for the abolition of financial and tax incentives, and of direct and indirect subsidies, and the withdrawal of exemption benefiting the settlements and their inhabitants. The European Council urges Israel to dismantle illicit settlement outposts. Settlement policy is an obstacle to peace and it threatens to make any solution based on the coexistence of two States physically impossible' (point 6).

107 As reflected in UN votes, and letters of Permanent Representatives to the UNSC.

108 PLO, 'Israeli colonies and international law'.

While Israel may undertake, in the occupied territories, actions necessary to meet its military needs and to provide for orderly government during the occupation ... the establishment of the civilian settlements in those territories is inconsistent with international law.[109]

However, the US official stance has been relatively inconsistent ever since. The initial US position on the illegality of the Israeli settlements was expressly based on the Fourth Geneva Convention, until President Reagan declared in 1981 that the settlements were 'not illegal'.[110] Subsequently, recent US administrations have all declined to address the legal issue of the Israel settlements, although they have opposed them on the basis that they constitute an obstacle to peace in the Middle East.[111]

On 30 April 2003, the Quartet, consisting of representatives of the United States, the European Union, the Russian Federation and the United Nations, presented the government of Israel and the Palestinian authority with a 'road map' for peace in the Middle East.[112] The road map laid down clear, reciprocal obligations upon both parties with the ultimate goal of ending the Israeli–Palestinian conflict by 2005, through the creation of an independent Palestinian state, alongside a strong and secure State of Israel. Among the obligations set out for Israel, the Quartet called on Israel to freeze all settlement activities (including natural growth settlements.

Despite almost universal condemnation by the international community, settlement expansion in the Palestinian territories has continued unabated throughout the years. Israeli measures associated with the construction of these settlements, including construction of bypass roads, land confiscation and demolition of houses, have had a disastrous effect on Palestinians, in the West Bank and East Jerusalem in particular. One of the most drastic measures has been the construction, since 2002, of the Separation Wall in the West Bank, which has consolidated the situation created by the settlements and added to the plight of the Palestinian people. In July 2004, the ICJ issued an Advisory Opinion stating that the

[109] Letter by Herbert J. Hansell, Legal Adviser of the US Department of State, 1578.

[110] Neff, 'Settlements in US policy', 1994, 53–4.

[111] CMEP and Foundation for Middle East Peace, 'Statements on American policy toward settlements by US Government Officials, 1968–2009', www.fmep.org/analysis/analysis/israeli-settlements-in-the-occupied-territories (accessed 17 May 2011).

[112] UNSC, Letter dated 7 May 2003 from the Secretary-General addressed to the President of the Security Council – Annex 'A performance-based road map to a permanent two-state solution to the Israeli–Palestinian conflict', S/2003/529. The road map was then endorsed by the Security Council in Res. 1515 (19 November 2003).

construction of the Wall in the OPT violated international law. The implications of the Advisory Opinion in relation to the Israeli settlements and the prohibition of population transfers and forced displacement in general will be analysed below.

The ICJ, the Separation Wall and the settlements

The Separation Wall and internal displacement of Palestinians

In response to continuing terrorist attacks on Israeli soil, the government of Israel decided, in April 2002, to build a 'Separation Fence'[113] for the purpose of controlling Palestinian entry into the territory of Israel and preventing further acts of terrorism. 'At times, it takes the form of an eight-metre-high concrete wall, at other times it takes the form of a barrier some 60–100 metres wide with buffer zones protected by barbed wire and trenches and patrol roads on either side of an electric fence.'[114] Once completed, the Barrier will be 707 km long.[115]

Only 15 per cent of the Barrier's length runs along the 1949 armistice line between Israel and Jordan (also known as the 'Green Line').[116] The remaining path of the Barrier departs from the Green Line and cuts into the West Bank so as to incorporate Israeli settlements.[117] According to an OCHA report, eighty West Bank Israeli settlements, comprising over 85 per cent of the total Israeli settler population in the West Bank (including East Jerusalem), will lie between the Barrier and the Green Line.[118] The

113 Also referred to as the 'Anti-terrorist Fence' by its supporters, and known as the 'Annexation Wall' or the 'Apartheid Wall' by its opponents. The rest of the international community, including the UN, commonly refer to the Separation Wall/Fence/Barrier.

114 UNCHR, 'Report of the Special Rapporteur on the situation of human rights in the Palestinian territories' (27 February 2004), E/CN.4/2004/6/Add.1, para. 8.

115 OCHA, 'West Bank barrier route projections' (July 2010) www.ochaopt.org/documents/ocha_opt_route_projection_july_2010.pdf (accessed 17 May 2011).

116 *Ibid.*

117 In the north of the West Bank, the route of the Barrier deviates up to 22 km from the Green Line to incorporate the Ari'el settlement. In addition, adjacent to Jerusalem, the planned Barrier route will encircle the Ma'ale Adumin settlement group and will extend 14 km into the West Bank (i.e. 45 per cent) across its width (OCHA, 'Preliminary analysis of the humanitarian implications of the April 2006 Barrier projections' (July 2006), www.humanitarianinfo.org/opt/docs/UN/OCHA/OCHABarrierProj_6jul06.pdf (accessed 20 May 2011), 3).

118 OCHA, 'Six years after the International Court of Justice Advisory Opinion: the impact of the Barrier on health' (July 2010), www.ochaopt.org/documents/ocha_opt_special_focus_july_2010_english.pdf (accessed 17 May 2011).

area between the Barrier and the Green Line is designated as a 'Closed zone' or 'Seam zone' and will, when completed, incorporate 9.4 per cent of the West Bank.[119] Approximately 33,000 West Bank Palestinians will be located in the 'Closed zone', in addition to the majority of the 250,000 residents of East Jerusalem.[120]

According to a UN report, the Separation Barrier will be responsible for a whole 'new generation of displaced persons'.[121] In 2005, house demolitions and land confiscation by the government of Israel in connection with the construction of the Barrier were the main cause of internal displacement.[122] A Palestinian survey undertaken in May 2005 on the impact of the Wall indicated that 2,448 households were already displaced from the localities that the Wall passed through.[123]

Local inhabitants are said to be deeply concerned at the possibility of increased uprooting and displacement as a result of harsher living conditions, including high levels of social and economic marginalization, property demolitions and protracted access restrictions in threatened villages.[124] According to the ICRC, the lives of Palestinians have been dramatically affected, due to restrictions on freedom of movement and access to jobs, health facilities, schools, land and family members.[125] Palestinians on either side of the Wall are affected by these restrictions. Palestinians living in the 'Closed zone' need a 'permanent resident permit' in order to remain in the zone. However, health and education services are generally located on the other side of the Barrier and residents of the 'Closed zone' need to pass through specifically designated gates to access their

119 OCHA, 'West Bank barrier route projections' (July 2010). 120 *Ibid.*

121 UNCHR, 'Report of the Special Rapporteur on the situation of human rights in the Palestinian territories' (17 January 2006), E/CN.4/2006/29, para. 20.

122 IDMC, 'Palestinian territories – West Bank Wall main cause of new displacement amid worsening humanitarian situation' (21 June 2006), 4, www.internal-displacement.org/8025708F004BE3B1/%28httpInfoFiles%29/B373C6CCA0474439C125719400383504/$file/Palestinian%20Territories%20-June%202006.pdf (accessed 17 May 2011).

123 Palestinian Central Bureau of Statistics, 'Survey on the impact of the Expansion and Annexation Wall on the socio-economic conditions of the Palestinians localities which the wall passes through, June 2005' (September 2005), www.pcbs.gov.ps/Portals/_pcbs/PressRelease/Socioeconomic_June_e.pdf (accessed 17 May 2011).

124 Written Statement submitted by Palestine to the International Court of Justice in relation to the request for Advisory Opinion on the legal consequences of the construction of a wall in the Occupied Palestinian Territory, 125.

125 ICRC (press release), 'Israel/occupied and autonomous Palestinian territories: West Bank Barrier causes serious humanitarian and legal problems' (18 February 2004) http://reliefweb.int/sites/reliefweb.int/files/reliefweb_pdf/node-142541.pdf (accessed 17 May 2011).

schools, health care facilities and workplaces.[126] Palestinians on the east side of the Barrier have often been cut off from their farms, land and water resources, and require a special 'visitor' permit to cross the Wall and enter the area.[127] However, at least 40 per cent of applications for permits are rejected and the process of application has been described as 'humiliating'.[128] All these restrictions and hardships have compelled many Palestinians to leave the closed areas, abandon their land and relocate to the Palestinian side of the Barrier.

The ICJ Advisory Opinion on Legal Consequences of the Construction of a Wall in the Occupied Palestinian Territory

Events leading to the request for an Advisory Opinion

On 9 October 2003, in a letter addressed to the President of the Security Council, the Permanent Representative of the Syrian Arab Republic, acting in his capacity as Chairman of the Arab Group and on behalf of the State Members of the League of Arab States, requested an immediate meeting of the Security Council to consider the 'grave and ongoing Israeli violations of international law, including international humanitarian law, and to take the necessary measures in this regard'.[129] The letter also included a draft resolution, which was considered by the Council on 14 October 2003, under Agenda item 'The situation in the Middle East, including the Palestine question'. The Security Council meetings provided the parties concerned with a forum for discussion in which to put forward their position on the construction of the Separation Wall and to discuss the root of the problem, namely the construction of Israeli settlements in the OPT.

The Permanent Observer of Palestine declared that the establishment of the 'expansionist wall of conquest' complemented Israeli settlements activities and was illegal under international law and international humanitarian law.[130] In his reply, the Israeli representative explained at

[126] OCHA and UNRWA, 'The humanitarian impact of the Barrier: four years after the Advisory Opinion of the International Court of Justice' (July 2008), www.ochaopt.org/documents/Barrier_Report_July_2008.pdf (accessed 17 May 2011).

[127] *Ibid.*

[128] UNCHR, Report of the Special Rapporteur on the situation of human rights in the Palestinian territories 2006, para. 17.

[129] Letter dated 9 October 2003 from the Permanent Representative of the Syrian Arab Republic to the United Nations addressed to the President of the Security Council, S/2003/973.

[130] 4841st meeting of the Security Council, 14 October 2003, 10:30 a.m., S/PV.4841, 5.

length the reasons why Israel felt compelled to build the 'security fence'. He indicated that the fence was a temporary security measure and that it was 'one of the most effective non-violent methods of preventing the passage of terrorists and their armaments from the terrorist factories in the heart of Palestinian cities to the heart of civilian areas in Israel'.[131] He also drew attention to the fact that the fence had no political significance and that it was not intended to change the status of the land.[132]

The Representative of Malaysia, speaking on behalf of the Non-Aligned Movement, declared himself to be 'extremely concerned at the implications and long-term effect of Israel's continued settlement policies and the construction of the wall in the occupied Palestinian territory',[133] while the European Union expressed its strong opposition to the construction by Israel of a separation wall in the West Bank and called on Israel to freeze all settlement activities.[134] The draft resolution submitted for consideration was put to a vote but once again failed to be adopted, due to the negative vote of a permanent member of the Security Council.[135]

On 15 October 2003, the Chairman of the Arab Group requested the resumption of the Tenth Emergency Special Session of the General Assembly 'in light of the inability of the Security Council to fulfil its responsibility for the maintenance of international peace and security due to the exercise by one of its permanent members of the veto, in order to address the grave issue of Israel's expansionist wall in the Occupied Palestinian Territory, including East Jerusalem'.[136] The Tenth Emergency Special Session of the General Assembly[137] thus reconvened on 20 October 2003 and

131 *Ibid.*, 8. 132 *Ibid.*, 10.

133 Statement by the Representative of Malaysia, on behalf of the Non-Aligned Movement (*ibid.*, 25).

134 Statement by the Ambassador of Italy, on behalf of the EU (*ibid.*, 42).

135 There were 10 votes in favour, 1 against and 4 abstentions. In his statement, the US representative explained his negative vote, not because he considered the Separation Barrier or the Israeli settlements to be legal, but because the draft resolution was unbalanced and did not condemn terrorism in explicit terms (UNSC, 4842nd meeting, 14 October 2003, 10:45 p.m., S/PV.4842, 2).

136 Letter dated 15 October 2003 from the Permanent Representative of the Syrian Arab Republic to the United Nations addressed to the President of the General Assembly (A/ES-10/242).

137 UNGA Res. 377A(V) (3 November 1950), entitled 'Uniting for Peace', provides that:

> if the Security Council, because of lack of unanimity of the permanent members, fails to exercise its primary responsibility for the maintenance of international peace and security in any case where there appears to be a threat to the peace, breach of the peace, or act of aggression, the General Assembly shall consider the matter immediately with a view to making appropriate recommendations to

adopted resolution ES-10/13, by which it demanded that 'Israel stop and reverse the construction of the wall in the Occupied Palestinian Territory, including in and around East Jerusalem, which is in departure of the Armistice Line of 1949 and is in contradiction to relevant provisions of international law' and requested the UN Secretary-General to report on compliance with the resolution within one month.[138]

The report of the Secretary-General, released on 24 November 2003, confirmed the non-compliance by Israel with the demands of resolution ES-10/13.[139] In light of the report, the General Assembly adopted resolution ES-10/14, requesting the ICJ, pursuant to Article 65 of the Statute of the Court, to urgently render an Advisory Opinion on the following question:

> What are the legal consequences arising from the construction of the wall being built by Israel, the occupying Power, in the Occupied Palestinian Territory, including in and around East Jerusalem, as described in the report of the Secretary-General, considering the rules and principles of international law, including the Fourth Geneva Convention of 1949, and relevant Security Council and General Assembly resolutions?[140]

The Court received forty-nine written statements, the majority of them arguing that the construction of the wall violated international law. Many states also urged the Court to deny jurisdiction or to decline to answer the question posed by the General Assembly. The United Kingdom, for instance, requested the Court to exercise its discretion and to decline to

> Members for collective measures, including in the case of a breach of the peace or act of aggression the use of armed force when necessary, to maintain or restore international peace and security. If not in session at the time, the General Assembly may meet in emergency special session within twenty-four hours of the request therefore. Such emergency special session shall be called if requested by the Security Council on the vote of any seven members, or by a majority of Members of the United Nations.

In 1997, after the Security Council failed on two occasions to adopt a resolution condemning the construction of a new settlement in Jebel Abu Gneim, in occupied East Jerusalem, due to a negative vote by the USA, the General Assembly, acting pursuant to Res. 377A(V), convened its Tenth Emergency Special Session, under the title 'Illegal Israeli actions in occupied East Jerusalem and the rest of the occupied territory'. The 10th Emergency Special Session has since been reconvened on several occasions.

138 UNGA Res. ES-10/13 (21 October 2003) paras. 1, 3 (144 in favour, 4 against and 12 abstentions).

139 UNGA, 'Report of the Secretary-General prepared pursuant to General Assembly Resolution ES-10/13' (24 November 2003), A/ES-10/248.

140 UNGA Res. ES-10/14 (8 December 2003) (90 in favour, 8 against, 74 abstentions).

answer the question, as, it argued, an Advisory Opinion on this matter 'would be likely to hinder, rather than assist, the peace process'.[141]

On 9 July 2004, the ICJ nevertheless rendered the Advisory Opinion, *Legal Consequences of the Construction of a Wall in the Occupied Palestinian Territory*. The Court ruled, by fourteen votes to one, that:

> The construction of the wall being built by Israel, the occupying Power, in the Occupied Palestinian Territory, including in and around East Jerusalem, and its associated regime, are contrary to international law.[142]

The Advisory Opinion

In the first part of the Opinion, the Court dealt with questions of jurisdiction and judicial propriety. The Court ruled that it had jurisdiction to give the Advisory Opinion requested by resolution ES-10/14,[143] and refused to use its discretionary power to decline to give that opinion.[144]

The Court then addressed the question put to it by the General Assembly. After a brief clarification of the terms of the question,[145] the Court proceeded to an analysis of the status of the territory concerned[146] and a

141 Written statement of the United Kingdom of Great Britain and Northern Ireland (January 2004), para.1.6. The UK had previously voted in favour of Resolution ES-10/13 which demanded that Israel stopped and reversed the construction of the Wall. However, the UK stressed in its statement that it believed that the most important priority in the Middle East was the achievement of a negotiated settlement based upon the road map drawn up by the Quartet (*ibid*., para. 1.5).

142 *Legal Consequences of the Construction of a Wall*, para. 3A of the dispositif.

143 *Ibid*., paras. 24–42. The Court rejected the arguments that the General Assembly had acted *ultra vires* under the Charter when it requested an Advisory Opinion on the legal consequences of the construction of the wall in the OPT (paras. 24–8) and that the request violated Res. 377 A(V) (paras. 29–35). The Court also held that the issue of the construction of the Separation Wall was a 'legal question' within the meaning of Article 96(1) of the UN Charter (paras. 36–41).

144 *Ibid*., paras. 43–65 According to the Court's jurisprudence, only 'compelling reasons' should lead the Court to refuse to give an opinion (para. 44). The Court thus examined each of the arguments put forward as to why it should not exercise its jurisdiction (paras. 46–64) and concluded that there was no compelling reason for it to use its discretionary power not to give an opinion on the question asked by the General Assembly (para. 65).

145 The Court noted that different terms were being employed to describe the 'wall', either by Israel ('fence') or by the Secretary-General ('barrier') but that none of them were accurate. It thus decided to use the terminology employed by the General Assembly and to refer to the 'wall'. The Court also noted that some parts of the Wall were being built, or planned to be built, on the territory of Israel itself, and that it was not called upon to examine the legal consequences arising from the construction of those parts of the Wall (*ibid*., para. 67).

146 The Court concluded that: 'The territories situated between the Green Line and the former eastern boundary of Palestine under the Mandate were occupied by Israel in

description of the works already constructed or in the course of construction. The Court then determined the rules and principles of international law relevant in assessing the legality of the measures taken by Israel, and ruled that both the Hague Regulations and the Fourth Geneva Convention, as well as certain human rights instruments were applicable to the OPT.[147]

Next, the Court addressed the question of whether the construction of the Wall violated those rules and principles. In this regard, the Court noted that the Wall's route had been traced in such a way as to include Israeli settlements within the 'Closed Area' and that the settlements had been themselves established in breach of international law.[148] The Court also found that the construction of the Wall posed a risk of further alterations to the demographic composition of the OPT by contributing to the departure of Palestinians from certain areas.[149] The Court thus concluded that the construction of the Wall severely impeded the exercise by the Palestinian people of their right to self-determination, and was therefore a breach of Israel's obligation to respect that right.[150]

The Court also observed that the construction of the Wall had led to the destruction or requisition of properties under conditions which contravened the requirements of Articles 46 and 52 of the Hague Regulations and Article 53 of the Fourth Geneva Convention.[151] Concerning the military necessity exception contained in Article 53, the Court was 'not convinced that the destructions carried out contrary to the prohibition in Article 53 of the Fourth Geneva Convention were rendered absolutely necessary by military operations'.[152] The Court found that the construction of the Wall impeded the liberty of movement of the inhabitants of the OPT, as well as their right to work, to health, to education and to an adequate standard of living. Finally, the construction of the Wall, by contributing to the alteration of the demographic composition of OPT, contravened Article 49 paragraph 6 of the Fourth Geneva Convention.[153] The Court thus held:

1967 during the armed conflict between Israel and Jordan. Under customary international law, these were therefore occupied territories in which Israel had the status of occupying Power. Subsequent events in these territories . . . have done nothing to alter this situation. All these territories (including East Jerusalem) remain occupied territories and Israel had continued to have the status of occupying Power' (*ibid.*, para.78).

[147] *Ibid.*, paras. 86–113. [148] *Ibid.*, paras. 119–20. [149] *Ibid.*, para. 122. [150] *Ibid.*
[151] *Ibid.*, para. 132. [152] *Ibid.*, para.135. [153] *Ibid.*, paras. 133–4.

> The wall, along the route chosen, and its associated regime gravely infringe a number of rights of Palestinians residing in the territory occupied by Israel, and the infringements resulting from that route cannot be justified by military exigencies or by the requirements of national security or public order. The construction of such a wall accordingly constitutes breaches by Israel of various of its obligations under the applicable international humanitarian law and human rights instruments.[154]

In addition, the Court rejected Israel's claim that the construction of the Wall was consistent with the right of self-defence enshrined in Article 51 of the UN Charter, simply concluding that Article 51 had no relevance in this case.[155] The Court also stated that Israel could not rely on a state of necessity which would preclude the wrongfulness of the construction of the Wall.[156]

Having concluded that, by the construction of the Wall in the OPT, Israel had violated various international law obligations, the Court then examined the consequences of those violations. First, Israel has an obligation to put an end to the violation of its international obligations flowing from the construction of the Wall in OPT[157] and to make reparation for the damage suffered.[158] Furthermore, all states are under an obligation not to recognize the illegal situation resulting from the construction of the Wall in the OPT, and not to render aid or assistance in maintaining the situation created by such construction. In addition, 'all the States parties to the Geneva Convention . . . are under an obligation, while respecting the United Nations Charter and international law, to ensure compliance by Israel with international humanitarian law as embodied in that Convention'.[159] Finally, the United Nations, and especially the General Assembly and the Security Council, should consider what further action is required to bring to an end the illegal situation resulting from the construction of the Wall.[160]

The issue under consideration is whether the principles of international humanitarian law on the prohibition of population transfer are applicable to the Israeli policy and practices of settlements and, more recently, the construction of the Separation Wall in the OPT. The following section will therefore examine the relevant findings of the Advisory Opinion and assess the implications of the ruling on the general prohibition of settlements and population transfers in occupied territory.

154 *Ibid.*, para. 137. 155 *Ibid.*, para. 139. 156 *Ibid.*, para. 140. 157 *Ibid.*, para. 151.
158 *Ibid.*, paras. 152–3. 159 *Ibid.*, para. 159. 160 *Ibid.*, para. 160.

The legality of the settlements in light of the ICJ ruling

The main criticism of the Court's ruling has related to the reasoning, or lack thereof, used by the Court to reach its conclusions. In general, while agreeing with most of the Court's conclusions, many have felt that the ICJ had missed an opportunity to clearly address some issues of international law.[161] Indeed, as underlined by Judge Higgins in her separate opinion:

> It might have been expected that an Advisory Opinion would have contained a detailed analysis, by reference to the texts, the voluminous academic literature and the facts at the Court's disposal... Such an approach would have followed the tradition of using Advisory Opinions as an opportunity to elaborate and develop international law.[162]

In Ardi Imseis's view, the Court's unwillingness to offer exhaustive and compelling reasons for its conclusions 'will undoubtedly cast a cloud over its findings, particularly for those of us who held greater expectations of what the Court might have achieved'.[163] The reasoning behind the Court's conclusions is especially weak on questions of international humanitarian law in general, and on the illegality of the settlements in particular. The Court merely stated that the Israeli settlements in the OPT had been established in breach of international law.[164] Two questions thus remain: first, was the reasoning used in reaching this conclusion sufficiently adequate? Second, how does the illegality of the Israeli settlements affect the illegality of the Separation Wall?

161 Kretzmer, 'The Advisory Opinion', 2005, 88.

162 Separate Opinion of Judge Higgins, para. 23. Other criticisms of the Advisory Opinion concerned the Court's lack of fact analysis and the poor explanation, if any, of its findings. In his declaration, Judge Buergenthal explained that he voted against the Court's findings on the merits because it 'did not have before it the requisite factual bases for its sweeping findings' and should have therefore declined to hear the case. In his view, without an in-depth examination of the nature of cross-Green Line terrorist attacks and their impact on Israel and its population, the findings made by the Court were 'not legally well founded': 'In my view, the humanitarian needs of the Palestinian people would have been better served had the Court taken these considerations into account, for that would have given the Opinion the credibility I believe it lacks' (paras. 1 and 3).

163 Imseis, 'Critical reflections', 2005, 103.

164 *Legal Consequences of the Construction of a Wall*, para. 120 The Court was unanimous on this finding, as even Judge Buergenthal, who had voted against the Court's findings, stated in his declaration: 'I agree that this provision [Art. 49, para. 6] applies to the Israeli settlements in the West Bank and that their existence violates Article 49, paragraph 6' (para. 9).

On the illegality of the settlements in occupied territory

The Court rejected Israel's argument that Article 49(6) allowed for voluntary migration of individuals into occupied territory. Instead, it confirmed that the prohibition contained in Article 49(6) concerned both forcible and voluntary transfers of population into occupied territory:

> That provision prohibits not only deportations or forced transfers of population such as those carried out during the Second World War, but also any measures taken by an occupying Power in order to organize or encourage transfers of parts of its own population into the occupied territory.[165]

While this proposition is undoubtedly true, it is regrettable that the Court did not offer a more detailed reasoning on such an important issue. The Court merely stated that since 1977, Israel had 'conducted a policy and developed practices involving the establishment of settlements in the Occupied Palestinian Territories' in violation of Article 49(6) and that three resolutions of the Security Council had condemned these policies and practices.[166] However, the Court did not provide any explanation as to how it came to the conclusion that *all* transfers of population into occupied territory were prohibited under Article 49(6).

Given the controversial character of the settlements and the debatable interpretation by Israel of Article 49(6), the Court missed an opportunity to offer an authoritative interpretation of the provision. Indeed, it is clear, upon reading Article 49 as a whole, that paragraph 6 prohibits all forms of transfers of civilians, as opposed to paragraph 1, which only relates to 'forcible transfers'. In addition, the Court did not think it necessary to describe the measures taken by Israel in order to encourage settlements in the OPT, thus casting doubts over which specific measures would constitute, in the eyes of the ICJ, unlawful transfer of population. The Court should have taken time to explain how it had reached the conclusion that the mere organization or encouragement of transfer, in addition to direct transfer of population into occupied territory, constituted a violation of Article 49(6) of the Convention. Furthermore, and this is of primary importance, the Court should have clarified that 'protected persons' within the meaning of Article 4 of the Fourth Geneva Convention are the Palestinian people and not the population of Israel. Finally, the Court made no mention of other arguments put forward by Israel, such as its historical and ideological claims of a 'Greater State of Israel' or

[165] *Legal Consequences of the Construction of a Wall*, para. 120. [166] *Ibid.*, paras. 120–1.

the argument that settlements are not intended to displace Palestinians. As noted earlier, none of these arguments can justify the settlement of populations into an occupied territory, under both international law and international humanitarian law. By reaching such a general conclusion, the Court failed to properly address the issue of the illegality of settlements and therefore deliver a strong message on the Israeli settlements in the OPT.

On the relationship between the illegality of the settlements and the illegality of the Separation Wall

Notwithstanding the Court's findings on the legality of settlements, doubts have been expressed over the relevance of the issue with regards to the legality of the Wall. Some critics have even argued that the question of the legality of the settlements should not have been addressed.[167]

It is undeniable that the route of the Wall was established to incorporate the settlements.[168] Consequently, the questions of the legality of the settlements and that of the Wall are inevitably interconnected, and the Court was right to address the issue of settlements in its Advisory Opinion. However, although the ICJ held that the Israeli settlements were established in violation of Article 49(6), it failed to provide any explanation as to why such violation would result in the illegality of the Wall.[169] It seems that the Court considered that the unlawfulness of the settlements under Article 49(6) directly affected the legality of the Wall, but the lack of explanation in this regard is rather disappointing. Additionally, it may be argued that the presence of settlements in the OPT, coupled with the route of the Separation Wall, significantly alter the demographic composition of the territory and prejudge the future frontier between Israel and Palestine, thus amounting to de facto annexation. These issues, establishing a link between the settlements and the Wall, will be examined below.

[167] Ruth Lapidoth, for instance, contends that the ICJ has dealt with matters that are not directly relevant to the issue, including the legality of the settlements. She argues that since the Court ruled that all the segments of the fence situated in the OPT were illegal, without making a distinction among its various segments (e.g. those that protect Israel proper and those that protect settlements) the discussion of the legality of the settlements was not necessary, and thus only an *obiter dictum* ('The Advisory Opinion and the Jewish settlements', 2005, 293–4).

[168] UNCHR, 'Report of the Special Rapporteur on the situation of human rights in the Palestinian territories' (7 December 2004) E/CN.4/2005/29: 'Settlements in East Jerusalem and the West Bank are the principal beneficiaries of the wall and it is estimated that approximately half of the 400,000 settler population will be incorporated on the Israeli side of the wall' (para. 24).

[169] Kretzmer, 'Advisory Opinion', 91.

Construction of a wall for the protection of unlawful settlements

The Court observed that the route of the Wall included within the 'Closed Area' some 80 per cent of the settlers living in the OPT and that it was apparent that 'the wall's sinuous route [had] been traced in such a way as to include within that area the great majority of the Israeli settlements'.[170] In light of these considerations, the ICJ held that:

> The route chosen for the wall gives expression *in loco* to the illegal measures taken by Israel with regard to Jerusalem and the settlements.[171]

This finding is yet another example of the Court's lack of reasoning on such an important issue. In the Court's view, the fact that the route of the Wall was designed to incorporate the unlawful settlements rendered the Separation Wall automatically unlawful under Article 49(6). What is the legal basis behind this finding? The Court does not develop the point any further.

It has been argued that the illegality of the settlements, which the Wall seeks to protect, entails *ipso facto* the illegality of the Wall.[172] The issue here stems from the fact that the Jewish settlements have been established in contravention of the law of belligerent occupation and Article 49(6) of the Fourth Convention in particular. The settlements being unlawful, any action undertaken to legitimize and strengthen this situation should therefore be illegal. This does not necessarily mean that Israel is prevented from taking any measure to protect the Israeli settlements. Indeed, as acknowledged by the ICJ, Israel has the obligation, under human rights law, to protect all individuals present in the OPT, including Israeli settlers.[173] In addition, the Oslo Accords clearly state that, until a resolution on the final status of the settlements, Israel carries 'the responsibility for overall security of Israelis and Settlements, for the purpose of safeguarding their internal security and public order, and will have all the powers to take the steps necessary to meet this responsibility'.[174]

170 *Legal Consequences of the Construction of a Wall*, para. 119.

171 *Ibid.*, para. 122. 172 Declaration of Judge Buergenthal, para. 9.

173 *Legal Consequences of the Construction of a Wall*, paras. 106–13; see Shany, 'Head against the Wall?', 2004, 366; similarly, Kretzmer argues that: 'a theory that posits that the fact that civilians are living in an illegal settlement should prevent a party to the conflict from taking any measures to protect them would seem to contradict fundamental notions of international humanitarian law' ('Advisory Opinion', 93).

174 Israeli–Palestinian Interim Agreement, Article XII. On the legal status of the Oslo Accords and their relevance in the context of the Wall Advisory Opinion, see Watson, 'The "Wall" decisions', 2005, 22–4.

However, when considering security measures, Israel must bear in mind that the settlements have been established in breach of international humanitarian law and that it has an obligation to put an end to it. Therefore, any long-term measure, such as the construction of a separation wall, which consolidates a situation considered illegal under international law, is unlawful.

This theory is supported by the UN Special Rapporteur, John Dugard, who stressed in his 2004 report that 'the illegal nature of settlements makes it impossible to justify the penetration of the Wall into Palestinian territory as a lawful or legitimate security measure to protect settlements'.[175] The issue was also brought to the attention of the ICJ during the proceedings. As Palestine noted, in its written statement:

> The settlements being unlawful, there can be no legal right to protect them by diverting the course of the Wall away from the Green Line.[176]

These arguments are based on a general principle of international law – *ex injuria jus non oritur* – according to which 'an illegal act cannot produce legal rights'.[177] Although the issue was explicitly raised, the Court did not address it. Instead, it made a sweeping statement on the illegality of the Wall derived from the illegality of the settlements. It could have simply stated that the fact that the Wall was designed to protect unlawful settlements rendered it illegal *ipso facto* and that there was therefore no need to examine security concerns.[178]

The Court could also have tackled the issue in relation to the question of a state of necessity. Having concluded that the construction of the Wall constituted breaches of international humanitarian law and human rights instruments, the Court indeed went on to consider whether Israel could rely on a state of necessity which would preclude the wrongfulness of the construction of the Wall.[179] The Court relied on the

[175] UNCHR, 2004 Report of the Special Rapporteur on the situation of human rights in the Palestinian territories, para. 26.

[176] Written statement for Palestine, para. 467; see also Written statement for the League of Arab States, para. 9.17.

[177] Separate Opinion of Judge Elaraby, para. 3.1.

[178] Oral statement for Palestine, para. 12; see also Shany, 'Capacities and inadequacies', 2005, 220, fn. 17.

[179] *Legal Consequences of the Construction of a Wall*, para. 140. According to the ILC Commentary on the Draft Articles on Responsibility of States for Internationally Wrongful Acts: 'The term "necessity" ("état de nécéssité") is used to denote those exceptional cases where the only way a state can safeguard an essential interest threatened by a grave and imminent peril is, for the time being, not to perform some

Gabčíkovo-Nagymaros Project jurisprudence, in which it held that the state of necessity was 'a ground recognized by customary international law for precluding the wrongfulness of an act not in conformity with an international obligation' and observed that such ground could only be accepted 'on an exceptional basis' and 'under strictly defined conditions'.[180] One of these conditions required that the act being challenged be 'the only way for the State to safeguard an essential interest against a grave and imminent peril'.

The Court thus held:

> In the light of the material before it, the Court is not convinced that the construction of the wall along the route chosen was the only means to safeguard the interests of Israel against the peril which it has invoked as justification for that construction.[181]

The Court overlooked the principle that 'necessity may not be relied on if the responsible State has contributed to the situation of necessity', as expressed in Article 25(2)(b) of the Draft Articles on Responsibility of States for Internationally Wrongful Acts.[182] Even if there were a state of necessity related to the security of Israeli settlers in the OPT, Israel could not rely upon that state of necessity because it had created it itself.[183] Consequently, the construction of unlawful settlements in the OPT should preclude the invocation of a state of necessity in order to protect them.[184]

Although the ICJ reached the right conclusion as regards the illegality of the settlements and the subsequent illegality of the Separation Wall, the lack of fact-based analysis and detailed legal reasoning are regrettable. Yet, as demonstrated above, the legal arguments were plenty. In addition, the illegality of the Separation Wall does not only derive from the violation of Article 49(6) per se. The basis for the illegality of the Wall may also be found in a more general principle of the law of belligerent occupation, linked to the establishment of settlements and population transfers: the prohibition of permanent changes in occupied territory.

other international obligation of lesser weight or urgency' (ILC, 'Report of the International Law Commission on the work of its 48th Session' (6 May–26 July 1996), UN Doc. A/51/10, 194).

180 *Gabčíkovo-Nagymaros Project (Hungary/Slovakia)*, Judgment, ICJ Reports 1997, p. 7, para. 51.

181 *Legal Consequences of the Construction of a Wall*, para. 140.

182 Draft Articles on Responsibility of States for Internationally Wrongful Acts, (2001) II *Yearbook of the International Law Commission*, 31, 80.

183 *Gabčíkovo-Nagymaros Project*, para. 57.

184 Shany, 'Head against the Wall?', 364.

Alteration of the demographic composition of the Palestinian territory

Both the settlements and the Separation Wall dramatically alter the demographic composition of the Palestinian territories, thereby creating unlawful permanent changes. The establishment of settlements in the OPT is invariably accompanied by the departure of Palestinians, amounting to a de facto expulsion of Palestinians, in violation of Article 49(1) of the Civilians Convention. The combination of the two creates a substantial change in the demographic structure of the Palestinian territory, contrary to international humanitarian law.

The effect of settlements on the demography of Palestine was acknowledged by the UN Security Council when it determined, in 1980:

> that all measures taken by Israel to change the physical character, demographic composition, institutional structure or status of the Palestinian or other Arab territories occupied since 1967, including Jerusalem, or any part thereof have no legal validity.[185]

As regards the Separation Barrier, its effect on the demographic composition of the Palestinian territories is undeniable. As underlined by Palestine in its written statement:

> Faced with a choice of remaining in a walled-off town, perhaps requiring residence permits, perhaps needing permission for daily crossings of the Wall for work or education or medical care, and moving elsewhere, it is unsurprising that there is increasing evidence of widespread displacement of the population of the Occupied Palestinian Territory, including East Jerusalem, from areas outside the Wall.[186]

According to the League of Arab States, 'it is the practical effect, if not the intended result of the wall that the population in the areas cut off by that barrier move away because of the unbearable living conditions'.[187] Similarly, the UN Special Rapporteur argues that one of the unofficial purposes of the Wall, along with the incorporation of settlers within Israel and the seizure of Palestinian land, is 'to compel Palestinian residents in the so-called "Seam Zone" between the Wall and the Green Line and those residents adjacent to the Wall, but separated from their lands by the Wall, to leave their homes and start a new life elsewhere in the West Bank, by making life intolerable for them'.[188]

185 UNSC Res. 465 (1 March 1980) UN Doc. S/RES/465.
186 Written Statement of Palestine, para. 480.
187 Written Statement of the League of Arab States, para. 9.14.
188 UNCHR, 'Report of the Special Rapporteur on the situation of human rights in the Palestinian Territories' (December 2004), p. 35.

The ICJ recognized, in the Advisory Opinion, that the settlements and the Separation Barrier unlawfully alter the demographic composition of the OT:

> in the view of the Court, since a significant number of Palestinians have already been compelled by the construction of the wall and its associated regime to depart from certain areas, a process that will continue as more of the wall is built, that construction, coupled with the establishment of the Israeli settlements . . . is tending to alter the demographic composition of the Occupied Territories.[189]

The Court concluded that by doing so, the construction of the Wall and its associated regime contravened Article 49(6) of the Fourth Geneva Convention and the Security Council resolutions.[190] While this is certainly true, it may have been appropriate for the Court to add that, as far as the displacement of Palestinians is concerned, the construction of the Wall and its associated regime also violated Article 49(1), which prohibits 'individual or mass forcible transfers' in occupied territory. Yet, the Court only mentions the displacement of civilians as an element of the prohibition of demographic changes in occupied territory, as opposed to a prohibition per se.

De facto annexation of Palestinian land

The government of Israel has consistently maintained that the Wall is a temporary measure, whose sole purpose is to prevent terrorism. During a meeting at the General Assembly on 8 December 2003, the Israeli Permanent Representative to the United Nations indeed underlined the temporary, non-political nature of the Wall:

> As soon as the terror ends, the fence will no longer be necessary. The fence is not a border and has no political significance. It does not change the legal status of the territory in any way.[191]

Nevertheless, it is an undeniable fact that the immediate beneficiaries of the Wall are the settlers.[192] Indeed, the route of the Barrier departing from the Green Line was manifestly planned in order to incorporate 56 settlements containing some 170,000 settlers on the Israeli side of the Wall,[193] resulting in 'some 10 per cent of Palestinian land being included

[189] *Legal Consequences of the Construction of a Wall*, paras. 122, 133. [190] *Ibid.*, para. 134.

[191] A/ES-10/PV.23, 6; *Legal Consequences of the Construction of a Wall*, para. 116.

[192] UNCHR, 'Report of the Special Rapporteur on the situation of human rights in the Palestinian territories' (8 September 2003) E/CN.4/2004/6, para. 12.

[193] B'Tselem, 'Under the guise of security: routing the Separation Barrier to enable the expansion of Israeli settlements in the West Bank' (December 2005), www.btselem.org/Download/200512_Under_the_Guise_of_Security_Eng.pdf (accessed 20 May 2011).

in Israel'.[194] In fact, this intrusion into the West Bank has been construed on many occasions as de facto annexation. In his 2006 report, Special Rapporteur John Dugard established a direct link between the settlements in the West Bank and the route of the Wall, and noted:

> Like the settlements it seeks to protect, the Wall is manifestly intended to create facts on the ground. It may lack an act of annexation, as occurred in the case of East Jerusalem and the Golan Heights. But its effect is the same: annexation.[195]

A number of states have expressed doubts about the alleged temporary nature and security purpose of the Wall,[196] while others have more openly condemned Israel's 'expansionist policy'.[197] Furthermore, the General Assembly has stated, in resolution ES-10/13 of 21 October 2003, that:

> the route marked out for the wall under construction by Israel, the occupying Power, in the Occupied Palestinian Territory, including in and around East Jerusalem, could prejudge future negotiations and make the two-State solution physically impossible to implement and would cause further humanitarian hardship to the Palestinians.

During the proceedings before the ICJ, several states expressed concerns towards Israel's de facto annexation of Palestinian territory.[198] In the course of the oral pleadings, the Court heard a statement by Mr Vaughan Lowe, on behalf of Palestine:

> The wall is changing the status of the Occupied Palestinian Territory. It is, entirely foreseeably, causing demographic and other changes in the Occupied Palestinian Territory that will eliminate the possibility of the Palestinian people effectively exercising their right to self-determination, and this is tantamount to de facto annexation of territory.[199]

194 UNCHR, 2006 Report of the Special Rapporteur on the situation of human rights in the Palestinian territories, para. 14.

195 *Ibid.*

196 During a meeting at the Security Council, on 14 October 2003, the French representative stated that: 'This will be a permanent structure that will permanently change geographic and demographic data. The building of the wall can only encourage the development of settlements and aggravate the already serious problems that these are causing' (S/PV.4841, 18).

197 Statement of the Representative of the Islamic Republic of Iran (S/PV.4841, 27); see also Statement of the Representative of Malaysia, on behalf of the Non-Aligned Movement (S/PV.4841, 26).

198 See Written Statement of Palestine, para. 481; Written Statement of the League of Arab States, para. 9.19; Written Statement of the Government of the Republic of South Africa, paras. 12–23.

199 ICJ – Verbatim Record of public sitting held on Monday 23 February 2004 at 10:00 a.m., Oral statement for Palestine, 53.

After noting the assurances given by Israel that the construction of the Wall did not amount to annexation and that the Wall was a temporary measure, the ICJ held:

> The Court considers that the construction of the wall and its associated regime create a 'fait accompli' on the ground that could well become permanent, in which case, and notwithstanding the formal characterization of the wall by Israel, it would be tantamount to de facto annexation.[200]

The Court has thus focused on the permanency of the Wall, rather than its implied purpose. This may be explained by the fact that the Court lacked the evidentiary basis to declare that the construction of the Wall constituted an outright act of annexation.[201] Consequently, only if it acquired a permanent character would the construction of the Wall amount to de facto annexation.[202] In principle, this finding seems reasonable. However, a more thorough examination by the Court of each segment of the Wall that encroaches upon Palestinian territory in order to incorporate Israeli settlements would have enabled it to make a more reasoned judgment in relation to a potential act of de facto annexation.[203]

With this Advisory Opinion, the ICJ had the opportunity to address for the first time the issue of the illegality of the settlements in the Palestinian territories, and to render an unequivocal decision on the subject. While the conclusions of the Court are to be welcomed in most respects, the lack of reasoning behind the findings will inevitably affect the outcome of the opinion.

The aftermath of the ICJ ruling

Beit Sourik and the implications of the ICJ ruling for Israel

On 30 June 2004, the Israeli High Court of Justice rendered its own decision on the legality of a 40-kilometre section of the Wall, in *Beit Sourik*

200 *Legal Consequences of the Construction of a Wall*, para. 121.
201 Kretzmer, 'Advisory Opinion', 92.
202 Judge Higgins agrees with the Court's findings that 'the wall does not at the present time constitute, *per se*, a de facto annexation' (Separate Opinion of Judge Higgins, para. 31). Judge Koroma, on the other hand, is of the opinion that 'the construction of the wall has involved the annexation of parts of the occupied territory by Israel . . . contrary to the fundamental international law principles of non-acquisition of territory by force' (Separate Opinion of Judge Koroma, para. 2). Judge Elaraby argues that the Court's finding should have been incorporated in the dispositif with an affirmation that the OPT could not be annexed (Separate Opinion of Judge Elaraby, para. 2.5).
203 Kretzmer, 'Advisory Opinion', 94.

Village Council v. *Israel*.[204] While the Israeli Court clearly stated that the purpose of the Separation Fence could not be to draw a political border, it came to the conclusion that the Fence was in fact motivated by security concerns.[205] It held that Israel was entitled, under the law of belligerent occupation, 'to take possession of individual land in order to erect the separation fence upon it on the condition that this is necessitated by military needs'.[206] However, the Court also stated that security considerations were not enough to justify the construction of the Wall in Palestinian territory and that security powers had to be 'properly balanced against the rights, needs, and interests of the local population'.[207] The Court thus applied the principle of proportionality to its examination of the legality of the Fence. In this respect, the key question was: 'whether the Separation Fence route . . . injures the local inhabitants to the extent that there is no proper proportion between this injury and the security benefit of the fence'.[208] The High Court, while validating orders for some parts of the Wall, held that most of the Barrier's route imposed disproportionate hardships on Palestinians and had to be re-examined.

The ICJ Advisory Opinion and the *Beit Sourik* decision share a few common grounds, but these are far outweighed by the differences between them.[209] Indeed, where the ICJ reached broad, sweeping conclusions on the illegality of the Wall, the Israeli Court, applying a three-part proportionality test on each segment of the Wall, found that some, but not all of them violated international law.[210] The Israeli Court's decision, if not the more convincing in terms of its findings, is surely the more satisfying in terms of fact analysis and reasoning. However, the Israeli Court failed to address the issue of the legality of settlements in occupied territory, a nonetheless important factor in the determination of the legality of the Separation Wall.[211] In addition, as opposed to the High Court of Justice's decision, which is binding on Israel, the international court's opinion, 'advisory' in essence, has no binding effect. The government of Israel thus announced that it would not follow the ICJ's ruling but would abide

[204] HCJ 2056/04, *Beit Sourik Village Council* v. *Government of Israel and the Commander of IDF Forces in the West Bank* (30 June 2004). The petition, filed by the residents of villages north-west of Jerusalem, argued that the military orders of seizure of their land were illegal in light of Israeli administrative law and the principles of public international law (paras. 9–11).

[205] *Ibid.*, paras. 27–8. [206] *Ibid.*, para. 32. [207] *Ibid.*, para. 34.

[208] *Ibid.*, para. 44. [209] Watson, '"Wall" decisions', 24.

[210] *Ibid.* [211] Shany, 'Head against the Wall?', 366.

by the High Court's decision.[212] In August 2004 the Israeli High Court however instructed the Israeli government to produce a statement assessing the implications of the Advisory Opinion.[213]

The Israeli Cabinet approved a revised route of the Wall in February 2005 and once again in April 2006.[214] Stretching a total of 707 km, the revised Barrier route now incorporates about 9.4 per cent of the West Bank and East Jerusalem, as opposed to the initial 12.7 per cent.[215] However, as noted by the Association for Civil Rights in Israel, although the new route reduces to some degree the scope of human rights violations resulting from the Barrier, it still significantly infringes on the human rights of the Palestinians residing in the vicinity.[216] In addition, while the new route of the Wall follows more closely the Green Line in the locality of the Hebron hills, it penetrates more deeply into Palestinian territory further north to include settlements in the Gush Etzion Bloc near Bethlehem.[217] It is also clear that the construction of the Wall enables the continuing expansion of settlement activity in the closed zone,[218] with complete disregard of the ICJ's ruling.

The government of Israel eventually replied to the request of the High Court of Justice to assess the implications of the ICJ Advisory Opinion. In a statement presented to the Israeli Court on 23 February 2005, the government of Israel declared:

> It is the position of the State of Israel that the factual background before the Court when it wrote the Advisory Opinion was lacking, inexact and now irrelevant in a manner that precludes its conclusions that the entire route of the fence within

212 A. Benn, S. Shamir and Y. Yoaz, 'Israel firmly rejects ICJ fence ruling', *Haaretz* (11 July 2004), www.haaretz.com/hasen/pages/ShArt. jhtml?itemNo=449729&contrassID=2&subContrassID=1&sbSubContrassID=0&listSrc=Y (accessed 23 May 2011).

213 UNCHR, 2004 Report of the Special Rapporteur on the situation of human rights in the Palestinian territories, para. 38.

214 Since 2002, the Israeli Cabinet has approved four routes of the Wall, in 2003, 2004, 2005 and 2006. See OCHA, 'Six years after the International Court of Justice Advisory Opinion: the impact of the Barrier on health' (July 2010), fn. 2. The latest route, revised and approved on 30 April 2006, is available on the Israeli MoD, at: www.securityfence.mod.gov.il/pages/eng/route.htm (accessed 24 May 2011).

215 OCHA, 'West Bank barrier route projections' (July 2010).

216 A. Pinchuk, 'The responses in Israel to the ICJ Advisory Opinion on the legal consequences of the construction of a wall in the Occupied Palestinian Territory' (8–9 March 2005), Geneva, United Nations Office, p. 12, http://unispal.un.org/UNISPAL.NSF/0/321BFD8CAB197930852574B8006D8A7D (accessed 28 November 2011).

217 UNCHR, 2006 Report of the Special Rapporteur on the situation of human rights in the Palestinian Territories, para. 14.

218 *Ibid.*, paras. 22–8.

the West Bank was in violation of international law from having any application upon the cases before the High Court of Justice. These cases should be decided based upon the factual and normative bases that have been developed by Israel's Supreme Court as exemplified in the Beit Sourik case.[219]

The Israeli High Court of Justice has backed the government's opinion in subsequent decisions, including the *Alfei Menashe* case,[220] in which the Israeli Court dismissed the ICJ's Advisory Opinion, for being based upon insufficient factual basis, particularly in respect of security considerations for the construction of the Wall.[221] Instead, the Israeli Court vowed to continue to examine each of the segments of the Fence, as they are brought for its decision, and to ask itself, 'regarding each and every segment, whether it represents a proportional balance between security–military need and the rights of the local population'.[222]

Reaction of the international community to the Advisory Opinion

Shortly after the issuance of the Court's Advisory Opinion, the tenth emergency session of the General Assembly reconvened. On 20 July 2004, the General Assembly adopted Resolution ES-10/15, which acknowledged the Advisory Opinion of the ICJ and demanded that Israel comply with its legal obligations.[223] The resolution also requested the Secretary-General to establish a register of damage relating to the construction of the Wall. Statements made during the session reflect the states' individual reactions to the Advisory Opinion. Most states expressed their support for the opinion's findings regarding the illegality of the Separation Wall. The representative of the Netherlands, speaking on behalf of the European Union, stated that: 'the Advisory Opinion largely [coincided] with the European Union's position on the legality of the barrier built by Israel on the Palestinian side of the Green Line'.[224] With the exception of Israel, no state

219 Israeli MFA, 'Unofficial summary of State of Israel's response regarding the Security Fence', 28 February 2005, www.mfa.gov.il/MFA/Government/Law/Legal+Issues+and+Rulings/Summary+of+Israels+Response+regarding+the+Security+Fence+28-Feb-2005.htm (accessed 23 May 2011).

220 HCJ 7957/04 – *Mara'abe* v. *Prime Minister of Israel* (15 September 2005), ruling available at: www.diakonia.se/sa/node.asp?node=861 (accessed 23 May 2011).

221 *Ibid.*, para. 74: 'the ICJ's conclusion, based upon a factual basis different than the one before us, is not *res judicata*, and does not obligate the Supreme Court of Israel to rule that each and every segment of the fence violates international law.'

222 *Ibid.*

223 UNGA Res. ES-10/15 (20 July 2004) A/RES/ES-10/15 (150 in favour, 6 against, 10 abstentions and 25 non-voting).

224 GAOR, 10th Emergency Special Session, 27th meeting (20 July 2004) A/ES-10/PV.27, 8. However, the EU expressed reservations on certain paragraphs of the Advisory Opinion:

which voted against the resolution or abstained from voting criticized the Court's conclusion on the illegality of construction of the Wall.[225] The USA's main concerns related to the content of the resolution, which was unbalanced and would 'politicize the Court's non-binding opinion'.[226] As regards the Advisory Opinion itself, the representative of the United States expressed concerns regarding the Court's conclusion on the right to self-defence,[227] but did not question the findings on the illegality of the Wall.

While a resolution by the General Assembly welcoming the Advisory Opinion was to be expected, a resolution by the Security Council any time soon is very unlikely, due to the strong probability of a US veto. Neither the General Assembly, nor the Security Council has considered the opinion since.[228]

What next?

In parallel with the construction of the Wall, the then Israeli Prime Minister Ariel Sharon announced, in 2004, a unilateral 'Disengagement Plan' to evacuate all the settlements in the Gaza Strip and four settlements in the northern part of the West Bank.[229] The disengagement thus concerned a

'We recognize Israel's security concerns and its right to act in self-defence. The European Union reconfirms its deep conviction that the Quartet road map . . . remains the basis for reaching a peaceful settlement. It calls on all sides to refrain from further escalation and to take the steps required to begin the implementation map.'

225 M. Hmoud, 'The significance of the Advisory Opinion rendered by the International Court of Justice on the legal consequences of the construction of a wall in the Occupied Palestinian Territory' (UN International Meeting on the Question of Palestine, p. 40).

226 A/ES-10/PV.27, 4.

227 In this regard, the US Representative stated that: '[The opinion] seems to say that the inherent right of self-defence, Article 51 of the United Nations Charter does not apply when a state is attacked by terrorist organizations. That seems to be directly at odds with the Security Council's resolutions adopted after 11 September 2001, which confirm the right of self-defence in the face of a terrorist threat.' For a discussion on the ICJ's findings on the right of self-defence, see R. Wedgwood, 'The ICJ Advisory Opinion on the Israeli security fence and the limits of self-defence', AJIL, 99 (2005), 52; S. D. Murphy, 'Self-defence and the Israeli Wall Advisory Opinion: an *ipse dixit* from the ICJ', AJIL, 99 (2005), 62.

228 UN (press release) 'UN experts mark anniversary of ICJ "Wall opinion" – call on Israel to halt the construction of the Wall' (4 August 2005) HR/05/092.

229 General outline of the Disengagement Plan available at: www.mfa.gov.il/MFA/Peace+Process/Reference+Documents/Disengagement+Plan+-+General+Outline.htm (accessed 23 May 2011); full text of the revised Disengagement Plan available at: www.mfa.gov.il/MFA/Peace+Process/Reference+Documents/Revised+Disengagement+Plan+6-June-2004.htm (accessed 23 May 2011).

mere 2 per cent of the total settler population living in the OPT.[230] Evacuation of Gaza started in August 2005 and was completed on 12 September 2005. In a letter addressed to the then US President George W. Bush, Sharon explained that the Disengagement Plan was designed 'to improve security for Israel and stabilize [its] political and economic situation'.[231] On the other hand, the general outline of the Disengagement Plan explicitly states that:

> in the West Bank, there are areas which will be part of the State of Israel, including cities, towns and villages, security areas and installations, and other places of special interest to Israel.[232]

The possibility of a future incorporation of part of the West Bank into the State of Israel upon negotiations of the permanent status agreement was also acknowledged by the US president:

> In light of new realities on the ground, including already existing major Israeli populations centers, it is unrealistic to expect that the outcome of final status negotiations will be a full and complete return to the armistice lines of 1949, and all previous efforts to negotiate a two-state solution have reached the same conclusion. It is realistic to expect that any final status agreement will only be achieved on the basis of mutually agreed changes that reflect these realities.[233]

It should nevertheless be pointed out that while such letters may be politically hugely significant, 'they carry no legal weight, and can certainly not compromise Palestinian rights under international humanitarian law',[234] which are protected by Articles 7 and 8 of the Fourth Geneva Convention.

On 25 November 2009, the Israeli government announced a 10-month moratorium on settlement construction in the West Bank.[235] However, the UN Special Rapporteur noted a number of caveats, most notably the

[230] Al-Haq, 'Waiting for justice', 143.

[231] Letter from PM Ariel Sharon to US President George W. Bush (14 April 2004), www.mfa.gov.il/MFA/Peace+Process/Reference+Documents/Exchange+of+letters+Sharon-Bush+14-Apr-2004.htm (accessed 23 May 2011).

[232] General outline of the Disengagement Plan.

[233] Letter from President Bush to PM Sharon (14 April 2004), http://georgewbush-whitehouse.archives.gov/news/releases/2004/04/20040414-3.html (accessed 24 May 2011).

[234] UNGA, 'Report of the Special Rapporteur on the situation of human rights in the Palestinian territories occupied by Israel since 1967' (25 August 2008), A/63/326, para. 29.

[235] MFA, Statement by PM Netanyahu on the Cabinet decision to suspend new construction in Judea and Samaria (25 November 2009), www.mfa.gov.il/MFA/Government/Speeches+by+Israeli+leaders/2009/Statement+by+PM_Netanyahu_suspend_new_construction_Judea_Samaria_25-Nov-2009.htm (accessed 24 May 2011).

fact that the freeze did not apply to East Jerusalem, considered as an integral part of Israel, and allowed for the construction of housing units and other buildings that had started before the freeze.[236] Furthermore, the moratorium did not stop settlement construction altogether, but merely slowed the pace of expansion in some part of the West Bank, only for the settlement activity to resume, following the end of the freeze, on 26 September 2010.[237] Meanwhile, the construction of the Separation Wall in the West Bank is still progressing. As of July 2010, 434 km (i.e. 61.4 per cent) of the Barrier had been completed and 60 km (i.e. 8.4 per cent) was under construction.[238]

Conclusion

Israel's policy and practices of settlements and the construction of the Separation Wall in the West Bank clearly show that, while the prohibition of population transfers in situations of occupation is clearly established, implementation and enforcement of international humanitarian are most problematic. Notwithstanding Israel's controversial interpretation of Article 49(6), there seems to be a fundamental lack of will on the part of the international community to ensure respect for the provisions of the Geneva Conventions, in accordance with Common Article 1.[239] Despite an ICJ Advisory Opinion declaring both the settlements and the Separation Wall to be illegal, the international community has failed to act. The disengagement from Gaza resulted in a reinforcement of Israel's position in the West Bank, while a self-imposed moratorium on settlement activity consisted of a rather partial and limited freeze and was never properly implemented. Both measures have aroused suspicions that these measures were carried out, not as a result of Israel's newfound concern for international law, but as a way of diverting attention away from the permanent establishment of settlements in the West Bank and

[236] UNGA, 'Report of the Special Rapporteur on the situation of human rights in the Palestinian territories occupied by Israel since 1967' (30 August 2010), A/65/331, para. 12.

[237] UNHRC, 'Report of the Special Rapporteur on the situation of human rights in the Palestinian territories occupied by Israel since 1967' (10 January 2011) A/HRC/16/72, para. 14.

[238] OCHA, 'West Bank barrier route projections' (July 2010).

[239] Art. 1 Common to the four Geneva Conventions states that 'The High Contracting Parties undertake to respect and ensure respect for the present Convention in all circumstances.'

the ongoing construction of the Separation Wall, thereby consolidating Israel's hold on part of the Palestinian territory.

In spite of the evident unlawfulness of population transfers, there is, regarding the Middle East situation in particular, an overbearing ideological component that threatens to render any contrary legal argument devoid of force and meaningfulness.[240] In such cases, population transfers become deeply rooted in the conflict and international humanitarian law gradually loses its relevance.

240 Henckaerts, 'Deportation and transfer of civilians', 518.

4 Forced displacement as an international crime

Population transfers in international instruments

Deportations and forcible transfers are prohibited as war crimes and crimes against humanity in numerous international criminal instruments.

Article 147 of the Fourth Geneva Convention defines the 'unlawful deportation or transfer . . . of a protected person' as a grave breach of the Convention.[1] Protocol I, which further expands the definition of grave breaches, clearly states that grave breaches of the Conventions and the Protocol 'shall be regarded as war crimes'.[2] Among other acts, Article 85(4) defines as grave breaches of the Protocol, 'when committed wilfully and in violation of the Conventions or the Protocol':

> (a) the transfer by the Occupying Power of parts of its own civilian population into the territory it occupied, or the deportation or transfer of all or parts of the population of the occupied territory within or outside this territory, in violation of Article 49 of the Fourth Convention.

The protection against population transfers into occupied territory is thus significantly improved. Indeed, this practice, which was initially a mere breach of the Geneva Convention, now constitutes a grave breach 'because

[1] Grave breaches of the Geneva Conventions represent some of the most serious violations of IHL. Such violations must therefore be subject to criminal punishment. For this purpose, the Geneva Conventions impose three separate obligations on states on the basis of mandatory universal jurisdiction: the duty to enact special criminal legislation for the prosecution of war criminals; the duty to search for persons alleged to have committed breaches of the Convention; and the duty to bring such persons before its own courts, or to hand them over for trial to another high contracting party concerned. See Arts. 49 Geneva Convention (I), 50 Geneva Convention (II), 129 Geneva Convention (II), 146 Geneva Convention (IV).

[2] Protocol I, Art. 85(5).

of the possible consequences for the population of the territory concerned from a humanitarian point of view'.[3]

Additionally, under the 1998 Statute of the ICC, 'the transfer, directly or indirectly, by the Occupying Power of parts of its own civilian population into the territory it occupies, or the deportation or transfer of all or parts of the population of the occupied territory within or outside this territory' constitutes a war crime in international armed conflict,[4] while '[o]rdering the displacement of the civilian population for reasons related to the conflict, unless the security of the civilians involved or imperative military reasons so demand' constitutes a war crime in non-international armed conflict.[5] The International Law Commission's 1996 Draft Code of Crimes against the Peace of Security and Mankind defines 'unlawful deportation or transfer or unlawful confinement of protected persons' as a war crime under Article 20(a)(vii).[6] Article 20(c)(i) also condemns 'the transfer by the Occupying Power of parts of its own population into the territory it occupies' as a war crime. In its 1991 commentary, the International Law Commission observed that:

> It is a crime to establish settlers in an occupied territory and to change the demographic composition of an occupied territory... Establishing settlers in an occupied territory constitutes a particularly serious misuse of power, especially since such an act could involve the disguised intent to annex the territory. Changes to the demographic composition of an occupied territory seemed to the Commission to be such a serious act it could echo the seriousness of genocide.[7]

As well as constituting a war crime, the deportation of civilians is explicitly proscribed as a crime against humanity under Article 5(d) of the ICTY Statute, Article 3(d) of the ICTR Statute, Article 2(d) of the Statute of the Special Court of Sierra Leone (SCSL),[8] Section 5.1(d) of UNTAET Regulation 2000/15 on the establishment of the Cambodian Extraordinary

[3] Sandoz *et al.*, *Commentary on the Protocols*, p. 1000.

[4] ICC Statute, Art. 8(2)(b)(viii). [5] ICC Statute, Art. 8(2)(e)(viii).

[6] ILC, 'Draft Code of Crimes against the Peace and Security of Mankind: Titles of texts of articles on Draft Code of Crimes against the Peace and Security of Mankind adopted by the International Law Commission at its forty-eighth session' (1996), UN Doc. A/CN.4/L.532, 8.

[7] ILC, 'Draft Code of Crimes against the Peace of Security and Mankind: Report of the International Law Commission on the work of its 43rd Session' (29 April–19 July 1991) UN Doc. A/46/10, 271.

[8] Statute of Special Court for Sierra Leone, 16 January 2002, appended to a letter dated 6 March 2002 from the Secretary-General addressed to the President of the Security Council, UN Doc. S/2002/246.

Courts[9] and Article 7(1)(d) of the ICC Statute. Article 7(2)(d) of the ICC Statute defines 'Deportation or forcible transfer of population' as 'forced displacement of the persons concerned by expulsion or other coercive acts from the area in which they are lawfully present, without grounds permitted under international law'.

There have been numerous prosecutions of deportations and forcible transfers of civilians before the ICTY. In addition, several former Khmer Rouge leaders have been charged by the Extraordinary Chambers in the Courts of Cambodia (ECCC) with 'unlawful deportation or transfer' as a grave breach of the Geneva Conventions, as well as deportation and forcible transfer as crimes against humanity, and are currently awaiting trial.[10]

On 4 March 2009, the Pre-Trial Chamber of the ICC issued an Arrest Warrant for the Sudanese President, Omar Al-Bashir, for his alleged criminal responsibility for, among other crimes, forcible transfer as a crime against humanity, within the meaning of Article 7(1)(d) of the ICC Statute.[11] Similarly, the Sudanese Minister of Humanitarian Affairs, Ahmad Harun, as well as the alleged top commander of the Militia/Janjaweed, Ali Kushayb, are both the subjects of arrest warrants for the commission of war crimes and crimes against humanity, among them the forcible transfer of civilians in the Darfur region.[12] All suspects are still at large. Charges have yet to be brought against an individual on grounds of unlawful transfer of parts of the occupying power's own population into occupied territory.

The jurisprudence of the ICTY has made an invaluable contribution to the development and clarification of the crimes of deportation and forcible transfer. A detailed analysis of the ICTY jurisprudence will therefore be the subject of the following paragraph, before moving on to the issue of population transfers as war crimes in internal armed conflicts.

9 UN Transitional Administration in East Timor (UNTAET), Regulation 2000/15, On the Establishment of Panels with Exclusive Jurisdiction over Serious Criminal Offences, 6 June 2000, UNTAET/REG/2000/15.

10 Nuon Chea, Provisional detention order, 19 September 2007, para. 1; Leng Sary, Provisional detention order, 14 November 2007, para. 2; Leng Thirith, Provisional detention order, 14 November 2007, para. 2; Khieu Samphan, Provisional detention order, 19 November 2007, para. 2.

11 *Prosecutor* v. *Omar Al-Bashir*, Warrant of arrest for Omar Hassan Ahmad Al-Bashir, ICC-02/05-01/09, 4 March 2009, p. 7.

12 *Prosecutor* v. *Ahmad Harun and Ali Kushayb*, Warrant of arrest for Ahmad Harun, ICC-02/05-01/07, 27 April 2007; *The Prosecutor* v. *Ahmad Harun and Ali Kushayb*, Warrant of arrest for Ali Kushayb, ICC-02/05-01/07, 27 April 2007.

Deportations and forcible transfers in the jurisprudence of the ICTY

The conflicts that tore the former Socialist Federal Republic of Yugoslavia apart during most of the 1990s were characterized by widespread human rights abuses and the displacement of civilian populations, in some cases as part of an ethnic-cleansing campaign.[13] In Bosnia and Herzegovina, ethnic cleansing was practised systematically by Serbs in order to expel Muslims and Croats from areas under their control.[14] Between April 1992 and July 1995, '[t]housands of civilians were unlawfully expelled or deported to other places inside and outside the Republic of Bosnia and Herzegovina' and 'the result of these expulsions was the partial or total elimination of Muslims and Bosnian Croats in some of Bosnian Serb-held regions of Bosnia and Herzegovina'.[15] Serb populations were also the victims of ethnic cleansing in certain parts of Bosnia and Herzegovina under the control of the Bosnian government or under Bosnian Croat control.[16] Furthermore, in 1993 UN Special Rapporteur Tadeusz Mazowiecki reported allegations of arbitrary executions and 'ethnic cleansing' by Croatian government forces in the Medak 'pocket', predominantly populated by Croatian Serbs.[17]

The International Criminal Tribunal for the Former Yugoslavia was created in 1993 by the UN Security Council, pursuant to Resolution 808 of 22 February 1993 and Resolution 827 of 25 May 1993,[18] to prosecute persons responsible for serious violations of international humanitarian law committed in the territory of the former Yugoslavia since 1991. It has jurisdiction over grave breaches of the Geneva Conventions, other serious

13 Bassiouni, *The Law of the International Criminal Tribunal for the Former Yugoslavia*, 1996, p. 48.

14 UNGA, 'Report on the situation of human rights in the territory of the former Yugoslavia prepared by Mr Tadeusz Mazowiecki' (17 November 1992), UN Doc. A/47/666, para. 19.

15 *Prosecutor* v. *Karadžić and Mladić*, Review of the indictments pursuant to Rule 61 of the Rules of procedure and evidence, IT-95-5-R61 and IT-95-18-R61, 11 July 1996, para. 16.

16 However, Mazowiecki notes, the number of Croat and Muslim refugees fleeing areas of Bosnia and Herzegovina under Serbian control was three to four times greater than the number of Serbian refugees and displaced persons from Bosnia and Herzegovina (UNGA, 'Report on the situation of human rights in the territory of the former Yugoslavia', para. 12).

17 UNCHR, 'Fifth periodic report on the situation of human rights in the territory of the former Yugoslavia submitted by Mr Tadeusz Mazowiecki' (17 November 1993), UN Doc. E/CN.4/1994/47, para. 100. According to UNHCR statistics, as of October 1993, there were an estimated 254,000 Serbian displaced persons and refugees from and within Croatia (para. 99).

18 UNSC Res. 808 (1993), UN Doc. S/RES/808, UNSC Res. 827 (1993), UN Doc. S/RES/827.

violations of the laws and customs of war, crimes against humanity and genocide.[19] Over the years, the ICTY has had the opportunity to address the issue of forced displacement on numerous occasions and has developed an important jurisprudence in this regard.[20]

The bulk of the Tribunal's cases relating to forced displacement has been concerned with charges of crimes against humanity. Although the ICTY Statute only refers to 'deportation' as a crime against humanity, the jurisprudence of the ICTY has established a distinction between deportation under Article 5(d) of the Statute and other inhumane acts (forcible transfer) under Article 5(i) of the Statute.[21] At other times, the Tribunal has also found that the forcible transfer of civilians could constitute persecution as a crime against humanity, within the meaning of Article 5(h) of the Statute.[22] The *Naletilić* Judgment is the only decision of the Yugoslav Tribunal dealing with the charge of unlawful transfer of civilians under Article 2(g) of the Statute as a grave breach of the Geneva Conventions.[23]

Finally, the ICTY has considered deportation and forcible transfer in relation to charges of genocide. In 1995, former Serb leader Radovan Karadžić and Bosnian Serb military commander Ratko Mladić were jointly indicted on counts of grave breaches of the Geneva Conventions of 1949, violations of the laws and customs of war, genocide and crimes against humanity for crimes committed against Bosnian Muslims and Bosnian Croats in Bosnia and Herzegovina.[24] Initially, they were charged

[19] ICTY Statute, Arts. 2–5. [20] Gillard, 'Role of international humanitarian law', 43.

[21] *Prosecutor* v. *Stakić*, Trial Judgment, IT-97-24, 31 July 2003, para. 671; *Prosecutor* v. *Krstić*, Trial Judgment, IT-98-33, 2 August 2001, para. 519.

[22] *Prosecutor* v. *Blagojević*, Trial Judgment, IT-02-60-T, 17 January 2005, para. 579.

[23] *Prosecutor* v. *Naletilić and Martinović*, Trial Judgment IT-98-34-T, 31 March 2003, para. 513. In *Simić*, the defendants were charged under Art. 2(g) ICTY with the crime of 'unlawful deportation or transfer' as a grave breach of the Geneva Conventions of 1949 (Count 3). However, the Trial Chamber dismissed the charges due to the fact that the prosecution had failed to plead in the Fifth Amended Indictment the existence of an international armed conflict in the area during the relevant period (paras. 104–20). In addition the Serbian President, Slobodan Milošević, was charged with 'unlawful deportation or transfer' under Art. 2(g) of the Statute, for the forcible transfer and deportation of thousands of Bosnian Muslim, Bosnian Croat and other non-Serb civilians to locations outside of Serb-held territories (Bosnia-Herzegovina indictment), as well as the deportation or forcible transfer of at least 170,000 Croat and other non-Serb civilians (Croatia indictment). However, he died in custody in March 2006.

[24] *Prosecutor* v. *Radovan Karadžić and Ratko Mladić*, Indictment 'Bosnia and Herzegovina', IT-95-5-I, 24 July 1995; *Prosecutor* v. *Radovan Karadžić and Ratko Mladić*, Indictment 'Srebrenica', IT-95-5-18, 16 November 1995.

with 'unlawful deportation and transfer of civilians' as a crime against humanity.[25] However, in its review of the indictment pursuant to Rule 61, the Trial Chamber stated that deportation could also constitute 'serious bodily or mental harm' done to the members of a group under a count of genocide.[26] The Tribunal thus invited the Prosecutor 'to consider broadening the scope of the characterization of genocide to include other criminal acts listed in the first indictment than those committed in the detention camps'.[27] Accordingly, in addition to deportation and inhumane acts (forcible transfer) as crimes against humanity, Karadžić and Mladić are indicted on a count of genocide for crimes committed to eliminate the Bosnian Muslims in Srebrenica.[28] Radovan Karadžić was arrested by the Serbian authorities on 21 July 2008 and transferred to The Hague a week later.[29] His trial commenced on 26 October 2009 and is still ongoing. Similarly, after almost twenty years spent escaping Justice, Ratko Mladić was finally arrested in Serbia on 26 May 2011.[30] He is currently awaiting trial.

The definition of the crimes of 'deportation' and 'forcible transfer' in the ICTY jurisprudence

As noted, an act of deportation or forcible transfer may be classified as a war crime or a crime against humanity, or both, and may even constitute

[25] *Prosecutor* v. *Radovan Karadžić and Ratko Mladić*, Indictment 'Bosnia and Herzegovina', IT-95-5-I, 24 July 1995, para. 19.

[26] *Prosecutor* v. *Karadžić and Mladić*, Review of the indictments, IT-95-5/18/I, 16 November 1995, para. 93.

[27] *Ibid.*, para. 95.

[28] Karadžić and Mladić are accused of having participated in a joint criminal enterprise to eliminate the Bosnian Muslims in Srebrenica by killing the men and boys of Srebrenica and forcibly removing the women, young children and some elderly men from Srebrenica. Both accused intended to destroy the Bosnian Muslims in Srebrenica as part of the Bosnian Muslim national, ethnical and/or religious group. During the siege of the Srebrenica enclave, Bosnian Serb forces are accused of having committed, under the command of Karadžić and Mladić, a number of crimes against Bosnian Muslims, including: 'causing serious bodily or mental harm to thousands of female and male members of the Bosnian Muslims of Srebrenica, including but not limited to the separation of men and boys from their families and the forcible removal of the women, young children and some elderly men from the enclave' (*Prosecutor* v. *Mladić*, Prosecution's Second Amended Indictment, IT-95-5/18-I, 1 June 2011, paras., 40–6; *Prosecutor* v. *Karadžić*, Third Amended Indictment, IT-95-5/18-I, 27 February 2009, paras. 41–7).

[29] ICTY, 'Tribunal welcomes arrest of Radovan Karadžić', press release, 21 July 2008, www.icty.org/sid/9952 (accessed 8 July 2011).

[30] ICTY, 'Tribunal welcomes arrest of Ratko Mladić', press release, 26 May 2011, www.icty.org/sid/10671 (accessed 8 July 2011).

genocide, if the required intent is present. The material element, or *actus reus*, of the grave breach of 'unlawful deportation or transfer' and the crimes against humanity of deportation and forcible transfer is essentially the same.[31] However, these crimes differ in many other respects.[32]

First of all, crimes against humanity, unlike grave breaches, which are perpetrated against persons or property regarded as 'protected' by the Geneva Conventions,[33] may be committed against *any* civilians, including the perpetrator's own nationals.[34] In addition, while it is now widely accepted that war crimes can be committed in both international and non-international armed conflict,[35] grave breaches of the Geneva Conventions remain only applicable to armed conflicts of an international character.[36] Crimes against humanity, on the other hand, may be committed both in time of peace and in time of war.[37] Furthermore, what clearly distinguishes a crime against humanity from an ordinary crime or a war crime is the requirement that it must have been committed in the context of a 'widespread or systematic attack directed against any civilian population'.[38]

With regard to the mental element of the crime, the *mens rea* of the grave breach of 'unlawful deportation or transfer' consists in the intent to deport or transfer the persons concerned.[39] As for the *mens rea* of deportation and forcible transfer as a crime against humanity, not only must the perpetrator intend to forcibly displace civilians, but he must also knowingly participate in a widespread or systematic attack against a civilian population.[40] Such acts may also amount to genocide, if perpetrated

31 Mettraux, *The Ad Hoc Tribunals*, 2005, p. 83; Frulli, 'Are crimes against humanity more serious than war crimes?', 2001, 333.

32 Frulli, 'Are crimes against humanity more serious than war crimes?', 333.

33 *Prosecutor* v. *Dusko Tadić* (*Decision on the Defence Motion for the Interlocutory Appeal on Jurisdiction*), IT-94-A, ICTY, 2 October 1995, para. 81.

34 *Kunarac*, Trial Judgment, IT-96-23&23/1, 22 February 2001, para. 423.

35 *Tadić*, Jurisdiction Appeal, para. 89; La Haye, *War Crimes in Internal Armed Conflicts*, 2008; Moir, 'Grave breaches', 2009, 763–87.

36 *Tadić*, Jurisdiction Appeal, para. 84.

37 *Ibid.*, para. 141.

38 Mettraux, *Ad Hoc Tribunals*, p. 155. As explained by the Trial Chamber of the ICTR: 'The concept of "widespread" may be defined as massive, frequent, large scale action, carried out collectively with considerable seriousness and directed against a multiplicity of victims. The concept of "systematic" may be defined as thoroughly organised and following a regular pattern on the basis of a common policy involving substantial public or private resources' (*Prosecutor* v. *Jean-Paul Akayesu*, ICTR-96-4-T, Trial Judgment, 2 September 1998, para. 580).

39 *Prosecutor* v. *Stakić*, IT-97-24-A, Appeal Judgment, 22 March 2006, paras. 304–7.

40 *Prosecutor* v. *Blaškić*, Trial Judgment, IT-95-14, 3 March 2000, para. 244.

'with intent to destroy, in whole or in part, a national, ethnical, racial or religious group'.[41]

While the *chapeau* requirements of each category of crime clearly differ, the definition of deportation or forcible transfer as a crime against humanity is virtually identical to the definition of 'unlawful deportation and transfer' as a grave breach of the Geneva Convention.[42]

Distinction between deportation and forcible transfer as crimes against humanity: the cross-border element

The ICTY has held that deportation and forcible transfer both entail the 'forced displacement of persons from the area in which they are lawfully present, without grounds permitted under international law'.[43] However, while the crime of deportation requires the displacement of civilians across national borders, forcible transfer takes place within national boundaries.[44] In *Prosecutor* v. *Stakić*, the Appeals Chamber held that the crime of deportation required the displacement of individuals across a de jure state border and accepted that under certain circumstances displacement across a de facto border may be sufficient to amount to deportation.[45] However, it rejected the Trial Chamber's earlier finding that the crime of deportation encompassed 'forced population displacement both across internationally recognised borders and de facto boundaries, such as the constantly changing frontlines',[46] on the grounds that a front line does not constitute a border.[47]

While the Appeals Chamber rejected the prosecution of forced displacement across front lines as a crime against humanity of deportation, it

41 ICC Statute, Art. 6; ICTY, Art. 4; ICTR Statute, Art. 2. The Trial Chamber of the ICTR noted in the *Akayesu* case that: 'Genocide is distinct from other crimes inasmuch as it embodies a special intent or *dolus specialis*. Special intent of a crime is the specific intention, required as a constitutive element of the crime, which demands that the perpetrator clearly seeks to produce the act charged. Thus, the special intent in the crime of genocide lies in "the intent to destroy, in whole or in part, a national, ethnical, racial or religious group, as such"' (para. 498).

42 Mettraux, *Ad Hoc Tribunals*, p. 180. However, as noted in the following paragraph, the Trial Chamber has recently adopted a different position with regard to the elements of deportation and forcible transfer and the relationship between war crimes and crimes against humanity (see below pp. 137–45).

43 *Prosecutor* v. *Krnojelac*, Trial Judgment, IT-97-25, 15 March 2002, para. 474; *Prosecutor* v. *Gotovina et al.*, Trial Judgment, IT-06-90, 15 April 2011, para. 1738.

44 *Krnojelac*, Trial Judgment, para. 474.

45 *Prosecutor* v. *Stakić*, Appeal Judgment, IT-97-24, 22 March 2006, paras. 278, 300.

46 *Prosecutor* v. *Stakić*, Trial Judgment, IT-97-24, 31 July 2003, para. 679.

47 *Stakić*, Appeal Judgment, para. 301.

recognized that such acts could nevertheless constitute 'other inhumane acts' pursuant to Article 5(i) of the Statute.[48] The jurisprudence of the Tribunal has indeed identified practices of forced displacement within or between national borders as constituting a form of inhumane treatment under Article 5(i) of the ICTY Statute.[49] The Trial Chamber noted in *Krstić* that forced displacement was by definition 'a traumatic experience, which [involved] abandoning one's home, losing property and being displaced under duress to another location' and thus amounted to an inhumane act as a crime against humanity.[50]

As noted by the Yugoslav Tribunal, Article 5(i) is a residual clause, which applies to acts that do not fall within any of the other sub-clauses of Article 5 of the Statute, but are sufficiently similar in gravity to the other enumerated crimes.[51] The Appeals Chamber of the ICTY has rejected concerns as to a possible violation of the principle of legality,[52] and held that the crime of 'other inhumane acts' formed part of customary law and that its function as a residual category was widely accepted.[53] Indeed, in *Prosecutor* v. *Kupreskić*, the Tribunal held that Article 5(i) was:

> [d]eliberately designed as a residual category, as it was felt undesirable for this category to be exhaustively enumerated. An exhaustive categorization would merely create opportunities for evasion of the letter of the prohibition.[54]

Drawing upon provisions of international human rights and humanitarian law, the Tribunal was able to identify 'a set of basic rights appertaining to human beings, the infringement of which may amount, depending on

48 *Ibid.*, para. 317.

49 *Prosecutor* v. *Krstić*, Trial Judgment, IT-98-33, 2 August 2001, paras. 521–3.

50 *Ibid.*, paras. 523, 532.

51 *Naletilić*, Trial Judgment, para. 247. For instance, the ICTY has dealt with charges of 'other inhumane acts' as injuries (*Prosecutor* v. *Kordić and Čerkez*, Appeal Judgment, IT-95-14/2-A, 14 December 2003, para. 117), attempted murder (*Prosecutor* v. *Vasiljerić*, Trial Judgment, IT-98-32, 29 November 2002, para. 234) and 'coordinated and protracted campaign of sniping, artillery, and mortar attacks upon civilian areas and the civilian population of Sarajevo, resulting in the suffering and injury of civilians' (*Prosecutor* v. *Galić*, Trial Judgment, IT-98-29, 5 December 2003, para. 151).

52 The charge of forcible transfer as 'other inhumane acts' had previously been dismissed by the Trial Chamber, on the grounds that '[t]he crime of "other inhumane acts" subsumes a potentially broad range of criminal behaviour and may well be considered to lack sufficient clarity, precision and definiteness', which would be contrary to the fundamental principle of legality (*nullum crimen sine lege*) (*Stakić*, Trial Judgment, para. 719, quoting the *Stakić* decision on Rule 98*bis* Motion for Judgment of Acquittal, para. 131).

53 *Stakić*, Appeal Judgment, para. 315.

54 *Prosecutor* v. *Kupreskić*, Trial Judgment, IT-95-16, 14 January 2000, para. 563.

the accompanying circumstances, to a crime against humanity'.[55] Thus, the Tribunal held that the expression 'other inhumane acts' 'undoubtedly embrace[d] the forcible transfer of groups of civilians'.[56]

An act of forcible displacement which, in addition to the general *chapeau* elements of crimes against humanity, meets the specific requirements for 'inhumane acts',[57] will be classified as such and will see its perpetrator convicted of a crime against humanity.

By way of conclusion, it is important to note that the qualification of an act of forcible displacement as 'deportation', a crime against humanity, or as 'forcible transfer', an inhumane act, although important from a legal point of view, does not entail any significant consequences for the victim. As noted by the Trial Chamber in *Milošević Rule 98bis* decision, 'the values protected by both crimes are substantially the same, namely the "right of the victim to stay in his or her home and community and the right not to be deprived of his or her property by being forcibly displaced to another location"'.[58] Thus, it concluded that:

> In terms of these values, there is no detriment to a victim if the crime of deportation is confined to transfer across borders, because if it is established that he has not been so transferred, then he is protected by the prohibition against forcible transfer, which applies to involuntary movements within national borders. In other words, the values so properly identified by the Trial Chamber in *Prosecutor* v. *Simić* of a right to remain in one's home and community are protected irrespective of whether deportation only takes place if there is transfer across borders.

The forcible character of the deportation or transfer

Another essential element of the definition of deportation and forcible transfer as an international crime is the involuntary nature of the

55 *Ibid.*, para. 566. 56 *Ibid.*

57 In *Krnojelac*, the Tribunal identified three requirements for an act to constitute an 'inhumane act' as a crime against humanity under Article 5(i) of the ICTY Statute: (a) the occurrence of an act or omission of similar seriousness to the other enumerated acts under the Article; (b) the act or omission causes serious mental or physical suffering or injury or constitutes a serious attack on human dignity; and (c) the act or omission is performed deliberately by the accused or a person or persons for whose acts or omissions he bears criminal responsibility (*Krnojelac*, Trial Judgment, para. 130). These elements also apply to 'cruel treatment', a serious violation of the laws and customs of war under Article 3 of the ICTY Statute; as well as 'inhuman treatment', a grave breach of the Geneva Conventions under Article 2(b) of the ICTY Statute.

58 *Prosecutor* v. *Slobodan Milošević*, Decision on Motion for Judgment of Acquittal, IT-02-54-T, 16 June 2004 [*Milošević*, Rule 98*bis* decision], para. 69, citing the Trial Chamber's ruling in *Prosecutor* v. *Simić*, Trial Judgment, IT-95-9, 17 October 2003, para. 130.

displacement.[59] Indeed, as stated by the Trial Chamber in the *Naletilić* case, transfers motivated by an individual's own genuine wish to leave are lawful.[60] The Yugoslav Tribunal has adopted a broad definition of 'forcible' transfers, holding that 'the term "forcible" is not limited to physical force, but may also include the threat of force or coercion, such as that caused by fear of violence, duress, detention, psychological oppression or abuse of power against such person or persons or another person, or by taking advantage of a coercive environment'.[61]

The determination of the intention and consent of the person concerned is therefore of paramount importance in order to ascertain the voluntary nature of the displacement. As noted by the Appeals Chamber, 'it is the absence of genuine choice that makes displacement unlawful'.[62] Similarly, 'an apparent consent induced by force or threat of force should not be considered to be real consent'.[63] Consequently, when assessing whether the displacement of a person was truly voluntary, it is necessary to place it into context and to take into account the situation and atmosphere prevailing at the time.[64] Concerning agreements on 'exchange' of populations between two military commanders or other representatives of the parties in a conflict, the Trial Chamber has clearly stated that '[m]ilitary commanders or political leaders cannot consent on behalf of the individual'.[65]

Accordingly, 'what matters is the personal consent or wish of an individual, as opposed to collective consent as a group, or a consent expressed by official authorities, in relation to an individual person, or a group of persons'.[66]

59 *Milošević*, Rule 98*bis* decision, para. 70; *Krnojelac*, Trial Judgment, para. 475.

60 *Naletilić*, para. 519.

61 *Krstić*, Trial Judgment, para. 529, quoting 'Report of the Preparatory Commission for the International Criminal Court, Finalised Draft Text of the Elements of the Crime' (6 July 2000) UN Doc. PCNICC/2000/INF/3/Add.2, 11, fn. 12; see also *Stakić*, Appeal Judgment, para. 281; *Simić*, Trial Judgment, para. 125; *Krnojelac* Trial Judgment, para. 475.

62 *Prosecutor* v. *Krnojelac*, Appeal Judgment, IT-97-25, 17 September 2003, para. 229.

63 *Simíc*, Trial Judgment, para. 125; *Krnojelac* Trial Judgment, para. 475, fn. 1435.

64 *Krnojelac*, Appeal Judgment, para. 229; *Simić*, Trial Judgment, para. 126.

65 *Naletilić*, Trial Judgment, paras. 522–3. The defence had argued that the transfer of around 450 Bosnian Muslim women, children and elderly from the village of Sovići to a territory under control of the Bosnian Armed Forces was conducted following an agreement between the Chief of Staff of the Croatian Defence Council (HVO) and the commander of the Bosnian Armed Forces. The Chamber held that it was not satisfied that any such agreement on exchange was negotiated.

66 *Simić*, Trial Judgment, para. 128.

The intent of the perpetrator

As for the *mens rea* for the crimes of deportation and forcible transfer, the Yugoslav Tribunal requires evidence of an intent to transfer the victim from his home or community.[67]

> it must be established that the perpetrator either directly intended that the victim would leave or that it was reasonably foreseeable that this would occur as a consequence of his action. If, as a matter of fact, the result of the removal of the victim is the crossing of a national border then the crime of deportation is committed; if there is no such crossing, the crime is forcible transfer.[68]

The jurisprudence is more divided, however, on whether the requirement is that of intent to *permanently* displace the victims.[69] While several judgments have entered convictions for deportation without making any findings on an intent to deport permanently,[70] others have held that the crimes of deportation and forcible transfer required an intent to have the victims permanently removed.[71] In reaching this conclusion, the Trial Chamber has relied on the ICRC commentary on Article 49 of Fourth Geneva Convention, which states that: '[u]nlike deportation or forcible transfer, evacuation is a provisional measure'. The Chamber has thus explained that deportations and forcible transfers are not 'by their nature provisional, which implies an intent that the transferred persons should not return'.[72] In relation to the forced movement of Bosnian Muslim civilians from the village Sovići, the Trial Chamber noted, in the *Naletilić* case, that no attempts had been made to return the displaced persons at the end of hostilities, and that, in fact, most of their houses had been torched, thereby demonstrating an intent that the persons be permanently displaced.[73]

This interpretation of Article 49 was recently rejected by the Appeals Chamber, which chose to follow the text of Article 49 rather than its commentary and concluded that: 'deportation does not require an intent that the deportees should not return'.[74] Although the Trial Chamber erred

67 *Milošević*, Rule 98*bis* decision, para. 78.
68 *Ibid.*
69 *Stakić*, Appeals Judgment, paras. 304–7.
70 *Ibid.*, para. 304, citing *Milošević*, Rule 98*bis* decision, para. 78; *Krnojelac*, Appeal Judgment, paras. 209–25; *Krstić*, Trial Judgment, paras. 519–32.
71 *Naletilić*, Trial Judgment, para. 520. See also *Simić*, Trial Judgment, para. 134 and *Stakić*, Trial Judgment, para. 686 fn. 1386.
72 *Naletilić*, Trial Judgment, para. 520 fn. 1362.
73 *Ibid.*, para. 526.
74 *Stakić*, Appeals Judgment, para. 306.

when it reached a contrary conclusion, this error proved harmless in this case because it had found that the Appellant intended to permanently displace the deportees.[75] The Appeals Chamber nevertheless held that, in future cases, 'Trial Chambers will not require proof of intent to permanently displace deportees.'[76]

The relationship between the crime against humanity of deportation and 'deportation or forcible transfer' as a war crime: the Gotovina *jurisprudence*

On 4 August 1995, Croatian forces launched 'Operation Storm', a military offensive undertaken with the objective to retake western Slovenia and the southern Krajina region of Croatia from Serbian control. The operation involved artillery attacks on a number of towns, mostly inhabited by ethnic Serb civilians, and led to the displacement of some 200,000 Croatian Serbs, including the entire Croatian Serb Army.[77] In the aftermath of the operation, Croatian forces were reported to have murdered, tortured and forcibly expelled Croatian Serb civilians who had remained in the area.[78]

Three senior Croatian Commanders, Ante Gotovina, Ivan Cermak and Mladen Markač, were indicted by the ICTY for a number of crimes committed during 'Operation Storm'. The accused were charged with deportation and inhumane acts (forcible transfer) as crimes against humanity and as underlying acts of the crime against humanity of persecution. The Joinder Indictment held that:

> From at least July 1995 to November 1995, Gotovina, Cermak and Markac... participated in a joint criminal enterprise, the common purpose being the permanent removal of the Serb population from the Krajina region by force, fear or threat of force, persecution, forced displacement, transfer and deportation, appropriation of property or other means.[79]

The *Gotovina* defence challenged the Tribunal's jurisdiction on the ground that the alleged acts took place during the conduct of hostilities, prior to restoration of Croatian authority over the Krajina region, and therefore

[75] *Ibid.* [76] *Ibid.*

[77] AI, 'Operation "Storm" – still no justice ten years on' (4 August 2005), AI Index: EUR 64/002/2005.

[78] *Ibid.*

[79] *Prosecutor* v. *Gotovina, Cermak and Markač*, Joinder Indictment, IT-06-90-PT, 6 March 2007, para. 12.

could not constitute 'deportation and forcible transfer' as crimes against humanity.[80] Indeed, the indictment clearly explains that '[t]he orchestrated campaign to drive the Serbs from the Krajina region began before the major military operation commenced on 4 August 1995, largely by the use of propaganda, disinformation and psychological warfare.'[81] The Serbian population, 'filled with panic and fear', were encouraged to leave the area, ahead of an imminent Croatian attack.[82] Croatian forces then proceeded to shell civilian areas, enter civilian Serb settlements at night and threaten those civilians who had not already fled, with gunfire and other intimidation. The defendant argued that these alleged acts 'relate solely to the ruses of war or conduct of hostilities prior to or during Operation Storm, and not to the deportations of civilians from the territory under the authority of Croatian forces'.[83] Thus, Gotovina alleged that there was no legal basis to apply deportation to situations other than occupations and that, 'by improperly expanding the scope of the crime of "deportation and forcible transfer" under customary law to cover alleged conduct of hostilities violations against persons in territories not under the authority of Croatian forces', the *nullum crimen sine lege* principle had been violated.[84]

Accordingly, the question presented to the Tribunal was whether, in armed conflict, the elements of deportation *qua* crime against humanity were identical to the corresponding war crime.[85] On 19 March 2007, the Pre-Trial Chamber answered in the negative and decided that 'occupation' was not an element of deportation as a crime against humanity under Article 5 of the Statute.[86]

In its judgment on merits, the Trial Chamber considered that the fear of violence and duress caused by the shelling of the towns of Benkovac, Gračac, Knin, and Obrovac in the Krajina region on 4 and 5 August 1995 created an environment in which those present had no choice but to leave. Consequently, the Trial Chamber found that the shelling

[80] *Prosecutor* v. *Gotovina, Cermak and Markač*, Defendant Ante Gotovina's Preliminary motion challenging jurisdiction pursuant to Rule 72(A)(i) of the Rules of procedure and evidence, IT-06-90-PT, 18 January 2007, paras. 10–18.

[81] *Gotovina et al.*, Joinder Indictment, para. 29. [82] *Ibid.*

[83] *Gotovina*, preliminary motion challenging jurisdiction, para. 12.

[84] *Ibid.*, paras. 13, 17.

[85] Akhavan, 'Reconciling crimes against humanity with the laws of war', 2008, 31.

[86] *Prosecutor* v. *Gotovina et al.*, Decision on several motions challenging jurisdiction, IT-06-90-PT, 19 March 2007, paras. 47–57.

amounted to the forcible displacement of civilians.[87] The Chamber further found that crimes, including murder, plunder, destruction, inhumane acts and detention, committed by members of Croatian military forces and Special Police after 5 August 1995 caused duress and fear of violence in their victims and those who witnessed them.[88] The Trial Chamber concluded that the forcible displacement of Krajina Serbs by means of unlawful attacks against civilians and civilian objects and by the commission of other crimes constituted deportation as a crime against humanity.[89]

The *Gotovina* ruling is hugely significant because it recognizes for the first time that, unlike the war crime of 'unlawful deportation or transfer', deportation as a crime against humanity is not limited to situations of occupation, but also applies to forced displacement resulting from the conduct of hostilities.[90]

The Tribunal's reasoning was twofold. First, it determined that war crimes did not necessarily constitute the *lex specialis* in relation to crimes against humanity committed in armed conflict, and that, as a result, the elements of crimes against humanity did not have to be interpreted in light of the laws of war. Second, the Tribunal declared that forced displacement of civilians during combat operations could amount to a crime against humanity. It has been argued that, by doing so, the Trial Chamber unduly challenged the traditional distinction between Hague law, related to the conduct of hostilities, and Geneva law, concerned with the protection of war victims in the hands of a party to the conflict.[91] Each issue will be analysed in turn.

The relationship between war crimes and crimes against humanity

As a preliminary matter, the Trial Chamber first addressed the defence argument that war crimes constituted the *lex specialis* in relation to the elements of crimes against humanity. As noted by the Chamber, the *Gotovina* defence 'consistently and repeatedly attempts to apply constructs of the laws and customs of war (war crimes) to charges of crimes against humanity'.[92] With regard to the issue at hand, the defence claimed that, when committed in armed conflict, the *actus reus* of 'deportation' and

[87] *Gotovina et al.*, Trial Judgment, paras. 1745–6.
[88] *Ibid.*, para. 1756. [89] *Ibid.*, para. 1763.
[90] Akhavan, 'Reconciling crimes against humanity with the laws of war', 23.
[91] *Ibid.*, 22.
[92] *Gotovina*, Decision on several motions challenging jurisdiction, para. 24.

'forcible transfer' as crimes against humanity should be interpreted in light of Article 49(1) of the Fourth Geneva Convention and Article 17(1) of Protocol II. In the past, the Trial Chamber had indeed held that Article 49 had 'no application in the absence of a state of occupation'.[93] Accordingly, the defence argued that:

> Both the crime of 'deportation and forcible transfer' in an international armed conflict, and the crime of 'forced movement of civilians' in an internal armed conflict, apply only to persons in territories actually placed under the authority of a party to the conflict. Thus, the Prosecutor can only invoke this crime with respect to persons situated in the 'Krajina' *after* it was placed under Croatian authority and not prior to or during Operation Storm as alleged in the Joinder Indictment.[94]

Although acknowledging that 'the rules of international humanitarian law serve, in times of armed conflict, as *lex specialis* in respect of the interpretation of the limits of prohibitions contained in instruments safeguarding the respect for human rights', the Tribunal nevertheless argued that 'any reference to the *lex specialis* principle with regard to war crimes and crimes against humanity in the context of the jurisdiction of the Tribunal, necessarily differs from this situation'.[95] Referring to the ICTY Statute, it added that:

> The inclusion of separate Articles governing crimes against humanity and war crimes is clearly not a matter of coincidence, but indicates that these two regimes exist separately and independently. Furthermore, while crimes against humanity under Article 5 of the Statute must be linked to the existence of an armed conflict, these crimes are not dependent upon the application of the 'laws and customs of war' enumerated separately under Article 3.[96]

The Tribunal concluded that 'the Gotovina Defence contention regarding war crimes as the *lex specialis* in relation to the elements of crimes against humanity [was] entirely unsupported and . . . based upon a misunderstanding of the co-existence of and relationship between war crimes and crimes against humanity in the jurisprudence of the Tribunal'.[97]

This ruling, however, appears to be in contradiction with an earlier ruling of the Trial Chamber. In the *Kupreskić* case, the Chamber held that 'murder as a crime against humanity requires proof of elements that murder as a war crime does not require (the offence must be part of a systematic or widespread attack on the civilian population)'.[98] The Trial

[93] *Naletilić*, Trial Judgment, para. 210.
[94] *Gotovina*, preliminary motion challenging jurisdiction, para. 15.
[95] *Gotovina*, Decision on several motions challenging jurisdiction, para. 24.
[96] *Ibid.*, para. 26. [97] *Ibid.*, para. 28. [98] *Kupreskić*, Trial Judgment, para. 701.

Chamber therefore concluded that: '[t]he prohibition of murder as a crime against humanity is *lex specialis* in relation to the prohibition of murder as a war crime'.[99] However, the Tribunal also held that 'the Trial Chamber may convict the Accused of violating the prohibition of murder as a crime against humanity only if it finds that the requirements of murder under both Article 3 [laws and customs of war] and under Article 5 are proved',[100] thereby clearly contradicting the *Gotovina* ruling that crimes under Article 5 'are not dependent upon the application of the "laws and customs of war" enumerated separately under Article 3'.

In relation to the crimes of deportation and forcible transfer, the Trial Chamber referred to the Appeals Chamber ruling in the *Stakić* case, which defined the *actus reus* of the crime of deportation as 'the forced displacement of persons by expulsion or other forms of coercion from the area in which they are lawfully present, across a de jure border or, in certain circumstances, a de facto border, without grounds permitted under international law', and concluded that 'nothing in the jurisprudence of the Tribunal supports the Defence contention that "occupation" is an element of the crime of deportation'.[101]

However, in reaching this conclusion, the Trial Chamber took no notice of the fact that the Appeals Chamber in *Stakić* referred to Article 49 of the Fourth Geneva Convention as 'the underlying instrument prohibiting deportation',[102] or that the Trial Chamber had held in *Krnojelac* that:

> Deportation is clearly prohibited under international humanitarian law. While some instruments prohibit deportation as a war crime, it is also prohibited specifically as a crime against humanity, and it is enumerated as such under the ICTY Statute . . . The content of the underlying offence, however, does not differ whether perpetrated as a war crime or as crime against humanity.[103]

Forced displacement during combat operations as a crime against humanity: an unwarranted attack on the Hague–Geneva law distinction?

The Trial Chamber also rejected the defence argument that the victims of deportation must be in the hands of a party to the conflict. Recalling

[99] *Ibid.*
[100] *Kupreskić*, Trial Judgment, para. 704. Akhavan, 'Reconciling crimes against humanity with the laws of war', 29.
[101] *Gotovina*, Decision on several motions challenging jurisdiction, para. 55.
[102] *Stakić*, Appeals Judgment, para. 306.
[103] *Krnojelac*, Trial Judgment, para. 473, as quoted by Akhavan, 'Reconciling crimes against humanity with the laws of war', 32.

that crimes against humanity had to be 'directed against any civilian population', the Chamber concluded that the Article 5 of the Statute therefore applied to 'any' civilian population, 'including one within the borders of the state of the perpetrator. There is no additional requirement in the jurisprudence that the civilian be in power of the party to the conflict.'[104] This specific point of the Tribunal's ruling has been qualified as 'problematic' by Professor Akhavan:

> The Chamber is clearly confusing the distinction between protection of civilians in occupied territory as distinct from combat situations, with the nationality of such civilians. The reference to 'any' civilian population is merely a relic of Article 6(b) of the Nürnberg Charter, which extended crimes against humanity to all victims irrespective of their nationality. It has no bearing whatsoever on the distinction between the Geneva Law and the Hague Law. Civilians in occupied territories and combat situations may possess the same nationality but be subject to different legal régimes within humanitarian law.[105]

That the reference in Article 5 to 'any' civilian population was meant to encompass all atrocities committed against civilians, including abuse by a state against its own civilians is uncontested. However, the issue in this case is not so much the existence or not of a situation of occupation, or the nationality of the civilians displaced, but, rather, that the alleged deportations and forcible transfers took place during actual combat operations, which are traditionally governed, not by the Geneva law, but by the Hague law. The prohibition of deportation and forcible transfer, as contained in Article 49 of the Civilians Convention, clearly belongs to Geneva law, as it seeks to protect civilians in the hands of an occupying power. However, by asserting that the crime of deportation can result from the conduct of hostilities, the Trial Chamber effectively places the prohibition of deportation and forcible transfer within the ambit of the Hague law. Professor Akhavan has criticized this interpretation of the crime of deportation *qua* crimes against humanity as undermining 'the viability of this otherwise unimpeachable norm of international law by effectively criminalizing the unfortunate consequences of military operations'.[106] Indeed, he claims, 'a lawful attack that complies with Hague Law principles of distinction and proportionality may still qualify as deportation *qua* crimes against humanity if a military commander simply knew that it would result in the displacement of civilians'.[107]

[104] *Gotovina*, Decision on several motions challenging jurisdiction, para. 56.
[105] Akhavan, 'Reconciling crimes against humanity with the laws of war', 33.
[106] *Ibid.*, 23. [107] *Ibid.*

Two points should be made in response to this argument. First, the separation between Hague law and Geneva law is not watertight.[108] A number of rules indeed belong to both the Hague and Geneva law. In fact, according to François Bugnion, the rules making up these two currents complement one another and have been grouped together under two different labels for the sake of convenience, rather than legality.[109] In addition, the 1977 Protocols, which reaffirm and develop the Geneva Conventions, also incorporate several elements of the Hague law, thereby effectively bringing the two currents ever closer, for an increased protection of the victims of war. The convergence of the two branches has also been acknowledged by the ICJ, which held, in its 1996 *Nuclear Weapons* Advisory Opinion, that:

> These two branches of the law applicable in armed conflict have become so closely interrelated that they are considered to have gradually formed one single complex system, known today as international humanitarian law. The provisions of the Additional Protocols of 1977 give expression and attest to the unity and complexity of that law.[110]

Second, it should be stressed that the Tribunal did not rule that the incidental flight of civilians as a result of the lawful conduct of hostilities in Croatia amounted to a crime against humanity. On the contrary, the displacement of civilians was triggered by a series of unlawful actions committed by the Croatian forces.

It has been argued that, for crimes against humanity committed during combat, such as murder or inhumane acts, proof of an unlawful attack constitutes a prerequisite for other offences related to shelling or sniping. As explained by W. J. Fenrick, '[w]here the crime base consists of shelling or sniping incidents in a combat environment, it is essential to prove that death, injury or damage was caused by an unlawful attack, that is, one directed against civilians or civilian objects or one directed against a military objective which may be expected to cause disproportionate incidental losses, before moving on to determine whether the additional elements necessary to establish the commission of other offences have also been established'.[111] If the attack was not unlawful, then the resultant death, injury or damage will not be considered as unlawful. Any other outcome would lead to the unsatisfactory situation where incidental civilian

[108] Bugnion, 'Droit de Genève et droit de La Haye', 2001, 909. [109] *Ibid.*

[110] *Legality of the Threat or Use of Nuclear Weapons*, 226, para. 75.

[111] Fenrick, 'Crimes in combat: the relationship between crimes against humanity and war crimes', 2004, 11.

casualties resulting from a lawful attack on legitimate military objectives would amount to a crime against humanity under Article 5 and lawful combat would, in effect, become impossible.[112] According to Fenrick:

> The unlawful attack foundation is essential to the assessment of legality even if there is no unlawful attack charge relating to a particular combat related incident. We cannot avoid the issue by simply avoiding the charge. Quite clearly there can be incidents in which it is so clear that the attack is directed against civilians that one can proceed with a persecution count or a war crime or crime against humanity count of murder. Even in such circumstances, however, it is essential that the prosecutor and the chamber take into account the unlawful attack elements, at least implicitly, before coming to the conclusion that counts charged have been proven.[113]

A similar reasoning appears to have been applied by the Trial Chamber in relation to charges of deportation and forcible transfer as a result of shelling or sniping attacks. In *Gotovina*, the Chamber found that the Croatian forces deliberately targeted civilian areas in the towns of Benkovac, Gračac, Knin and Obrovac in the Krajina region, and treated the towns themselves as targets for artillery fire. As such, the shelling of these four towns constituted an unlawful attack on civilian and civilian objects.[114] The Chamber then found that the artillery attack instilled great fear in those present in the towns and that this fear was 'the primary and direct cause of their departure'.[115]

112 *Galić*, Trial Judgment, para. 144. The accused was charged with crimes against humanity resulting from the unlawful acts committed by forces under his command, including murders and inhumane acts committed as a direct result of unlawful attacks on the civilian population by sniping and shelling. The Trial Chamber noted that:

> The Prosecution submits that, in the context of an armed conflict, the determination that an attack is unlawful in light of treaty and customary international law with respect to the principles of distinction and proportionality is critical in determining whether the general requirements of Article 5 have been met. Otherwise, according to the Prosecution, unintended civilian casualties resulting from a lawful attack on legitimate military objectives would amount to a crime against humanity under Article 5 and lawful combat would, in effect, become impossible. It therefore submits that an accused may be found guilty of a crime against humanity if he launches an unlawful attack against persons taking no active part in the hostilities when the general requirements of Article 5 have been established. The Trial Chamber accepts that when considering the general requirements of Article 5, the body of laws of war plays an important part in the assessment of the legality of the acts committed in the course of an armed conflict and whether the population may be said to have been targeted as such.

113 Fenrick, 'Crimes in combat', 12.

114 *Gotovina*, Trial Judgment, paras. 1743, 1892–1947.

115 *Ibid.*, paras. 1743–4.

After stating that the shelling amounted to the forcible displacement of civilians, the Trial Chamber then proceeded to determine whether the Croatian Army and Special Police forces who shelled these four towns did so with the intent to forcibly displace persons from the towns.[116] It concluded that the fact that the attacks deliberately targeted civilian areas and were carried out with the intention to discriminate against Krajina Serbs on political, racial, or religious grounds clearly showed intent to forcibly remove Serb civilians from the area.

Consequently, it should be stressed that, contrary to Professor Akhavan's characterization of the *Gotovina* ruling as a 'legal utopia that criminalizes incidental suffering in war',[117] the Trial Chamber of the ICTY made clear that the displacement of Krajina Serbs did not result from lawful combat operations, but from deliberate attacks, carried out with the clear intention to forcibly remove all Serb civilians in the area, as part of a widespread and systematic attack directed against the Croatian Serb civilian population. The fact that there were no charges for 'unlawful attacks' as violations of the laws and customs of war under Article 3 of the Statute is irrelevant and should not prevent the prosecution of offences deriving from such unlawful attacks. Gotovina filed notice of appeal on 17 May 2011. As noted, the Trial Chamber's ruling is innovative. It remains to be seen whether the Appeals Chamber will uphold it.

Can population transfers constitute war crimes in internal armed conflict?

As previously noted, forced displacement of civilians is one of the main features of civil wars. However, while the illegality of such acts has been clearly established, their criminalization is rather more uncertain. So far, no individual has ever been indicted on charges of war crime for the deportation or forcible transfer of civilians carried out in an internal armed conflict. In this regard, two questions should be asked: first, does international humanitarian law governing non-international armed conflicts provide for individual criminal responsibility? Second, does the deportation or forcible transfer of civilians constitute a war crime in internal armed conflicts?

116 *Ibid.*, paras. 1745, 1746.

117 Akhavan, 'Reconciling crimes against humanity with the laws of war', 36.

Individual criminal responsibility for war crimes committed in internal armed conflicts

The development of international humanitarian law, particularly as regards those rules governing internal conflicts, has historically been dominated by fears of intrusion on state sovereignty.[118] From the states' point of view, international humanitarian law indeed constitutes an undesirable limitation on state sovereignty, which imposes restraints on their ability to wage war. When it comes to internal armed conflicts, states are even more reluctant to limit their discretion, particularly in situations where their very existence, or identity, may be at stake.[119] Thus, in 1949, concerns for state sovereignty were very much at the forefront of the negotiations relative to the Geneva Conventions.[120] Although states had agreed on the introduction of a provision specifically applicable in situations of non-international armed conflict, they were nonetheless reluctant to attach it with universal jurisdiction and criminalize its violation under international law.[121] As a result, violations of Common Article 3 were not included in the 'grave breaches' provision of the Geneva Conventions. Similarly, Protocol II contains no provision on grave breaches and does not provide for individual criminal responsibility for violations of its norms.

Thus, until the beginning of the 1990s and the creation of the ad hoc international tribunals, it was generally thought that international humanitarian law applicable to non-international armed conflicts did not provide for individual criminal responsibility[122] and that war crimes were therefore limited to international armed conflicts.[123] The Final Report of the Commission of Experts on war crimes in the former Yugoslavia, for instance, clearly states that: 'there does not appear to be a customary international law applicable to internal armed conflicts which includes the concept of war crimes'.[124]

However, the general level of brutality involved in internal armed conflicts and, in particular, the large-scale massacres of civilians perpetuated

118 Meron, 'International criminalization of internal atrocities', 1995, 554; Robinson and von Hebel, 'War crimes in internal conflicts', 1992, 193.

119 Cassese, 'Civil war and international law', p. 110.

120 Lopez, 'Uncivil wars', 1994, 929.

121 *Tadić*, Jurisdiction Appeal, para. 80.

122 Plattner, 'Penal repression', 1990, 414.

123 La Haye, *War Crimes in Internal Armed Conflicts*, p. 131; Meron, 'International criminalization of internal atrocities', 559.

124 Final Report of the Commission of Experts established pursuant to SC Resolution 780, 27 May 1992, UN Doc. S/1994/674, para. 52.

in Rwanda between April and July 1994 have contributed to a radical transformation of IHL applicable to internal armed conflicts and the criminal responsibility of those responsible for its violation. There was indeed a growing sense of unease within the international community at the possibility that such atrocities could be left unpunished, for the sole reason that they were committed during an internal, rather than international, armed conflict. As clearly expressed by Theodor Meron:

> There is no moral justification, and no truly persuasive legal reason for treating perpetrators of atrocities in internal conflicts more leniently than those engaged in international wars.[125]

Thus, the Statute of the ICTR, adopted by the UN Security Council in 1994,[126] clearly recognizes criminal responsibility for violations of Common Article 3 and Protocol II, to which Rwanda is a party.[127] In its report to the Security Council, the UN Secretary-General stated that: 'Article 4 of the statute . . . includes violations of Additional Protocol II, which, as a whole, has not yet been universally recognized as part of customary international law, and for the first time criminalizes common article 3 of the four Geneva Conventions.'[128]

The Statute of the ICTY, on the other hand, does not explicitly provide for individual criminal responsibility for violations of IHL committed in internal armed conflicts. The Appeals Chamber of the ICTY nevertheless held, in *Tadić*, that violations of the laws and customs of war entailed individual criminal responsibility, regardless of whether they were committed in internal or international armed conflicts.[129] It stated that:

> customary international law imposes criminal liability for serious violations of common Article 3, as supplemented by other general principles and rules on the protection of victims of internal armed conflict, and for breaching certain fundamental principles and rules regarding means and methods of combat in civil strife.[130]

Therefore, individual criminal responsibility attaches not only to violations of Common Article 3 and Protocol II, but also to violations of other customary rules of international humanitarian law applicable to

[125] Meron, 'International criminalization of internal atrocities', 561.
[126] UNSC Resolution 955(1994) of 8 November 1994, Annex, UN Doc. S/RES/955(1994).
[127] ICTR Statute, Art. 4.
[128] UNSC, 'Report of the Secretary-General pursuant to paragraph 5 of the Security Council Resolution 955 (1994)', 13 February 1995, UN Doc. S/1995/134, para. 12.
[129] *Tadić*, Jurisdiction Appeal, para. 129. [130] *Ibid.*, para. 134.

non-international armed conflicts.[131] The *Tadić* decision has been described as 'the main catalyst in the evolution of the applicable law and the concept of criminality in internal armed conflicts'.[132] This holding was later confirmed by the Trial Chamber in its judgment on merits,[133] as well as in the *Čelebići* case,[134] and by the ICTR in the *Akayesu* case.[135]

Finally, the Statute of the ICC expressly grants jurisdiction to the Court over serious violations of Common Article 3[136] and other serious violations of the laws and customs applicable in armed conflicts not of an international character.[137] The inclusion of war crimes committed in internal conflicts in the ICC Statute was a controversial issue throughout the negotiations, but was largely influenced by the jurisprudence of the ICTY and the Statute of the ICTR, which expressly related to internal armed conflicts.[138]

Now that the existence of a principle of individual criminal responsibility for war crimes in internal armed conflicts has been established, the question remains as to whether the 'unlawful transfer' of civilians constitutes a war crime when committed within the context of a non-international armed conflict.

Forced displacement as a war crime in internal armed conflicts

There are two possible ways for a forcible transfer of population to constitute a war crime in internal armed conflict: (a) as a violation of the laws and customs of war under Article 3 ICTY and Article 4 ICTR; (b) as a war crime explicitly prohibited by the ICC Statute (Art. 8(2)(b)(viii)).

Unlawful transfer as a 'violation of the laws and customs of war'

Article 3 of the ICTY Statute grants the Tribunal power to prosecute persons violating the laws and customs. The Tribunal held that Article 3 was intended to refer to all violations of international humanitarian law, provided that they did not already fall under other provisions of the ICTY Statute dealing with genocide, crime against humanity or grave breaches

131 Moir, 'Grave breaches', 767–8.

132 La Haye, *War Crimes in Internal Armed Conflicts*, p. 132.

133 *Prosecutor* v. *Tadić*, Trial Judgment, IT-94-1-T, 7 May 1997, para. 613.

134 *Prosecutor* v. *Delalic, Mucic, Delic and Landzo* (*Čelebići camp*), Judgment, Case IT-96-21-T (16 November 1998), para. 308.

135 *Akayesu*, Trial Judgment, para. 615.

136 ICC Statute, Art. 8(2)(c).

137 ICC Statute, Art. 8(2)(e).

138 Robinson and von Hebel, 'War crimes in internal conflicts', 198–9.

of the Geneva Conventions.[139] The Appeals Chamber of the ICTY concluded that:

> Article 3 functions as a residual clause designed to ensure that no serious violation of international humanitarian law is taken away from the jurisdiction of the International Tribunal. Article 3 aims to make such jurisdiction watertight and inescapable.[140]

Accordingly, violations of Common Article 3 and other customary rules governing internal armed conflicts, including those contained in Protocol II, are included in Article 3 of the ICTY Statute.[141] Similarly, the ICTR noted in *Akayesu* that, in accordance with Article 4 of the Statute, the Tribunal had the power to prosecute persons committing or ordering to be committed *serious violations* of Common Article 3 and Protocol II.[142]

The Yugoslav Tribunal has recognized a number of prohibited acts as violations of the laws and customs under Article 3 of the Statute, including torture, cruel treatment, wilful killing and murder, pursuant to Common Article 3(1)(a) of the Geneva Conventions.[143] In addition, the Tribunal has also determined that certain acts committed in non-international armed conflicts constituted violations of the laws and customs of war, as recognized by Protocol II.[144] With regard to war crimes committed during the Rwandan Civil War, the first conviction for serious violations of Common Article 3 and Protocol II at the ICTR only dates back to 2003.[145] In 2005, Laurent Semanza was found guilty on appeal of serious violations of Common Article 3 and of Protocol II, pursuant to Article 4 of the ICTR Statute.[146]

It is clear that both violations of Common Article 3 and violations of the customary rules of Protocol II are regarded as serious violations of laws and customs of war, engaging the individual criminal responsibility of the perpetrators of those violations. However, as far as the war crime of unlawful transfer of civilians in internal armed conflict is concerned,

139 *Tadić*, Jurisdiction Appeal, para. 88. 140 *Ibid.*, para. 91. 141 *Ibid.*, para. 89.

142 *Akayesu*, Trial Judgment, para. 616.

143 *Krnojelac*, Trial Judgment, para. 128; *Prosecutor* v. *Strugar*, Trial Judgment, IT-01-42-PT, 31 January 2005, para. 260.

144 In the *Galić* and *Milošević* cases, for instance, both accused were charged with 'unlawfully inflicting terror upon civilians', and unlawful attacks on civilians, violations of the laws or customs of war pursuant to Article 3 of the Statute, Article 51 of the First Protocol and Article 13 of the Second Protocol (*Prosecutor* v. *Galić*, Indictment, IT-98-29-I, 26 March 1999; *Prosecutor* v. *Dragomir Milošević*, Amended Indictment, IT-98-29/1-PT, 18 December 2006).

145 Mettraux, *Ad Hoc Tribunals*, p. 28, fn. 17.

146 *Prosecutor* v. *Semanza*, Appeal Judgment, ICTR-9720-A, 20 May 2005, para. 371.

there has not yet been a decision on the matter. Thus, the question remains as to whether the forced movement of civilians in internal armed conflicts constitutes a violation of the laws and customs of war in accordance with Article 3 of the ICTY Statute and Article 4 of the ICTR Statute.

According to the Appeals Chamber of the ICTY, for a criminal conduct to constitute a 'serious violation of the laws and customs of war', it must meet, in addition to the *chapeau* requirements of war crimes,[147] the following criteria:

(i) the violation must constitute an infringement of a rule of international humanitarian law;
(ii) the rule must be customary in nature or, if it belongs to treaty law, the required conditions must be met;
(iii) the violation must be 'serious', that is to say, it must constitute a breach of a rule protecting important values, and the breach must involve grave consequences for the victim;
(iv) the violation of the rule must entail, under customary or conventional law, the individual criminal responsibility of the person breaching the rule.[148]

Each of these criteria will be analysed in turn in relation to the practice of forced displacement of civilians in internal armed conflict, in order to determine whether each could constitute a 'serious violation of the laws and customs of war' subject to prosecution by the ICTY under Article 3 of its Statute.

First, the prohibition of forced movement of civilians is clearly a rule of international humanitarian law, as stated in Article 17 of Protocol II. Second, the prohibition of forced displacement must either be customary in nature or, if conventional, be contained in a treaty to which the state concerned is a party. All the belligerents to the conflicts in the former Yugoslavia were parties to the Geneva Conventions and Protocols I and II.[149] Similarly, Rwanda is party to Protocol II. Consequently, all parties to the conflict were bound by the rules of Protocol II and, specifically, Article 17. Nevertheless, many states involved in civil wars have not ratified Protocol II and are therefore not bound by its conventional provisions. Notwithstanding the state of ratification of the Protocol, the prohibition

[147] The ICTY jurisprudence has identified two jurisdictional, or *chapeau*, requirements of war crimes: (a) there must be an armed conflict; and (b) a nexus must exist between the alleged offence and the armed conflict (*Kunarac et al.*, Trial Judgment, para. 402).

[148] *Tadić*, Jurisdiction Appeal, paras. 94–5.

[149] UNSC, *Final report of the Commission of Experts established pursuant to Security Council Resolution 780(1992)*, 27 May 1994, UN Doc. S/1994/674, Annex, para. 125.

of forced movement of civilians in non-international armed conflicts is a customary rule of international humanitarian law.[150] Consequently, the second condition is met.

The third condition requires that the violation constitute a breach of a rule protecting important values and involve grave consequences for the victim. The act of forcibly displacing civilians from their homes or residences incontrovertibly goes against the values and basic principles of international humanitarian law.[151] In addition, the devastating impact of displacement in terms of access to food, health care and education, family life and working life is well documented.[152]

Finally, the violation of the prohibition of forced displacement must entail, under customary or conventional law, the individual criminal responsibility of the person breaching the rule. When assessing whether this condition was met as regards the prohibition of direct attacks on civilians in the *Galić* case, the Trial Chamber of the ICTY referred to the intention of the state parties to the First Protocol, the 1992 London Programme of Action on Humanitarian issues signed between the parties to the conflict in Bosnia and Herzegovina,[153] as well as national criminal codes, and concluded that serious violations of the principle prohibiting attacks on civilians incurred individual criminal responsibility under the laws of war.[154] A similar reasoning can be applied by analogy to the prohibition of forced displacement of civilians. The deportation of civilians has long been recognized as a war crime within the context of international armed conflicts.[155] In addition, the national legislation of many states recognizes the forced displacement of civilians as a criminal offence, irrespective of whether it has been committed within

150 See above Chapter 2.

151 In a resolution entitled 'Basic principles for the protection of civilian populations in armed conflict', the UN General Assembly affirmed that 'Civilian populations, or individual members thereof, should not be the object of reprisals, forcible transfers or other assaults on their integrity' (Res. 2675(XXV) of 1970, UN Doc. A/8028 (1970), para. 7).

152 See below Chapter 6.

153 'Programme of Action on Humanitarian Issues Agreed between the Co-Chairmen to the Conference and the Parties to the Conflict', London, 27 August 1992. This Declaration states that: 'all parties to the conflict are bound to comply with their obligations under International Humanitarian Law and in particular the Geneva Conventions of 1949 and the Additional Protocols thereto, and that persons who commit or order the commission of grave breaches are individually responsible.'

154 *Galić*, Trial Judgment, para. 28.

155 Nuremberg Charter, Art. 6(b); Geneva Convention (IV), Art. 147; ICTY Statute, Art. 2(g); ICC Statute, Art. 8(2)(a)(vii).

the context of an international or internal armed conflict.[156] Finally, Article 8(2)(e)(viii) of the ICC Statute recognizes the forcible transfer of civilians in non-international armed conflicts as a war crime. It therefore seems reasonable to conclude that the violation of the prohibition of forced displacement in non-international armed conflicts engages individual criminal responsibility under international humanitarian law. Accordingly, the prohibition of forced displacement meets all four of the *Tadić* criteria and its violation could constitute a violation of the laws and customs of war.

Furthermore, irrespective of the fact that forced displacement constitutes a violation of the laws and customs of war per se, it has been argued that the unlawful transfer of civilians could amount to cruel treatment, as a residual prohibition contained in the proscription of 'violence to life and person, in particular . . . cruel treatment' in Common Article 3(1)(a).[157] The ICTY has indeed developed an important jurisprudence in relation to forcible transfers of civilians as 'other inhumane acts', pursuant to Article 5(i) of the Statute.[158] By analogy, one could therefore argue that the unlawful transfer of civilians may also constitute cruel treatment within the meaning of Common Article 3(1)(a), a serious violation of the laws and customs of war under Article 3 ICTY Statute and Article 4 ICTR Statute.

Forced displacement of civilians as war crime under the ICC Statute

Furthermore, the forcible transfer of civilians in internal armed conflicts is expressly recognized as a war crime in the ICC Statute. Article 8(2)(e)(viii) defines as a serious violation of the laws and customs applicable in armed conflicts not of an international character: 'Ordering the displacement of the civilian population for reasons related to the conflict, unless the security of the civilians involved or imperative military reasons so demand'. This provision is directly derived from Article 17(1) of Protocol II.[159] War

156 See ICRC Customary International Humanitarian Law Database, vol. 2 Practice, www.icrc.org/customary-ihl/eng/docs/v2_rul_rule129 (accessed 26 November 2011).

157 Dingwall, 'Unlawful confinement as a war crime', 2004, 142. Dingwall's analysis of the prohibition of 'violence to life and person, in particular . . . cruel treatment' in Common Article 3(1)(a) relates to the specific crime of 'unlawful confinement' but can be applied, by analogy, to the war crime of 'unlawful deportation and forcible transfer'.

158 See above pp. 132–4.

159 According to a commentary on the ICC Statute, cross-boundary displacements contained in Article 17(2) of the Protocol are also included in Article 8(2)(e)(viii) ICC (Zimmermann, 'War crimes', 2008, p. 498).

crimes in the ICC Statute are generally considered as part of customary international law.[160]

Although element 1 of the *Elements of Crimes* adopted with regard to Article 8(2)(e)(viii) requires that '[t]he perpetrator ordered a displacement of a civilian population', it should be noted that violation of the provision cannot be solely committed by the person actually ordering the displacement, but also by anybody carrying out the displacement and whose individual criminal responsibility is engaged by virtue of Article 25 of the Statute.[161] In addition, while Article 8(2)(e)(viii) refers to 'the civilian population', implying that only the forced displacement of a minimum number of civilians is prohibited,[162] element 1 refers to the displacement of '*a* civilian population'. According to the *Elements of Crimes* commentary, the term 'a population' clarifies that the perpetrator does not need to order the displacement of the whole civilian population.[163]

Only acts which are directly aimed at removing a civilian population from an area come within the definition of Article 8(2)(e)(viii).[164] Thus, acts which are only indirectly aimed at the removal of civilians, such as the intentional starvation of the civilian population in order to force them to leave an area, are not included.[165] Finally, an order to transfer a civilian population does not constitute a war crime if it is justified by the security of the civilian population or by imperative military reasons, or if it is unconnected with the armed conflict.

Conclusion

There has so far been no prosecution for deportation or forcible transfer as a war crime committed in internal armed conflict, despite the widely reported cases of forced displacement of civilians, particularly during the conflicts in Kosovo[166] and Darfur. Milošević was indicted for deportation and inhumane acts (forcible transfer) as crimes against humanity,

160 However, the opposite is not necessarily true and not all violations of IHL considered as war crimes under customary international law are included in the ICC Statute. For instance, the ICC Statute contains no rules relating to the prohibition of certain means and methods of warfare in internal warfare, and thus remains behind customary international law (Werle, *Principles of International Criminal Law*, 2005, p. 285).

161 Zimmermann, 'War crimes 2(c)–(f)', p. 497; Dörmann, *Elements of War Crimes*, p. 472.

162 Zimmermann, 'War crimes 2(c)–(f)', p. 497.

163 Dörmann, *Elements of War Crimes*, pp. 472–3.

164 Zimmermann, 'War crimes 2(c)–(f)', p. 497. 165 *Ibid.*

166 Carey, 'Is prevention through accountability possible?', 243–88.

pursuant to Article 5(d) and (i) of the ICTY Statute,[167] while the arrest warrants issued in relation to the situation in Darfur all concerned charges of forcible transfer as a crime against humanity.[168]

Yet, deportations and forcible transfers in internal armed conflict may be prosecuted as 'serious violations of the laws and customs of war' or as cruel treatment under Common Article 3(1)(a) of the Geneva Conventions, and, unlike grave breaches or crimes against humanity, do not require any evidence of 'protected person' status or of scale and planning.[169] They also constitute a war crime under Article 8(2)(e)(viii) of the ICC Statute.

One may only assume that the ongoing controversy relating to individual criminal responsibility for violations of international humanitarian law committed in internal armed conflicts, as well as the evidentiary difficulties involved in establishing the commission of a war crime in such situations have led the Prosecutor to err on the side of caution. Another factor which may explain the lack of prosecution of war crimes in internal armed conflict is that, if it can be demonstrated that the alleged conduct committed within the context of an internal armed conflict was part of a widespread and systematic practice directed at the civilian population, the Prosecutor may decide to charge the individual concerned with the more serious crimes against humanity,[170] as was the case for the forcible displacement of civilians in Darfur.

In addition, even though the ICC Statute expressly provides for the prosecution of unlawful transfers in non-international armed conflicts, it is the policy of the ICC Prosecutor to concentrate upon the most large-scale and most representative crimes.[171] Indeed, Article 8(1) of the ICC Statute provides that the Court shall have jurisdiction in respect of 'war crimes in particular when committed as part of a plan or policy or as part of a large scale commission of such crimes'. While this does not constitute an element of crime, the Prosecutor believes that it provides 'Statute guidance that the Court is intended to focus on situations meeting these

167 *Milošević*, Second Amended Indictment, paras. 62, 63.

168 Warrant of arrest for Omar Hassan Ahmad Al-Bashir, p. 7.

169 Dingwall, 'Unlawful confinement as a war crime', 140.

170 For a discussion on the comparative gravity of war crimes and crimes against humanity, see *Prosecutor* v. *Erdemović*, Joint separate opinion of Judges McDonald and Vohrah, paras. 20–7.

171 Sassòli, 'Implementation of international humanitarian law', 2007, 54; see also Letter from the Chief Prosecutor of the ICC, Concerning the Situation in Iraq, 9 February 2006, www.icc-cpi.int/NR/rdonlyres/04D143C8-19FB-466C-AB77-4CDB2FDEBEF7/143682/OTP_letter_to_senders_re_Iraq_9_February_2006.pdf (accessed 28 November 2011).

requirements'.[172] Furthermore, in accordance with Article 17(1) of the ICC Statute, the Court may decline the exercise of jurisdiction on grounds of insufficient gravity. In February 2006, the Pre-Trial Chamber I of the ICC held that, in order to satisfy this 'gravity' threshold, 'the conduct which is the subject of a case must be either systematic (pattern of incidents) or large-scale' and 'due consideration must be given to the social alarm such conduct may have caused in the international community'.[173] Many instances of forced displacement of civilians carried out in civil wars may fall short of these strict requirements. This should not minimize the importance and the devastating impact that such displacements have on the populations affected. Perpetrators of such unlawful practices should not escape punishment for the mere reason that a large-scale and systematic conduct could not be demonstrated.

172 Letter of the ICC Prosecutor re Iraq, p. 8.
173 *Prosecutor* v. *Dyilo*, Decision Concerning Pre-Trial Chamber I's Decision of 10 February 2006 and the Incorporation of Documents into the Record of Mr Thomas Lubanga Dyilo, ICC-01/04-01/06, 24 February 2006, para. 46.

5 The protection of refugees under international humanitarian law

Introduction: refugee protection in armed conflict – concurrent application of legal regimes

International humanitarian law primarily seeks to prevent the displacement of civilians both through the elaboration of rules of protection for all civilians and the express prohibition of forced displacement in armed conflict. As such, international humanitarian law protects civilians from becoming refugees or internally displaced persons in the first place.[1] Nevertheless, forced displacement still occurs on a massive scale, often as a consequence of human rights and humanitarian law violations carried out by the belligerents during an armed conflict. While most people fleeing violence choose or are forced to remain within their own country in refugee-like conditions, others will seek refuge across international borders. In some cases, their host country will in turn become engulfed in an armed conflict and refugees will once again become victims of war.

International humanitarian law and international refugee law share a similar goal: the protection of persons in the hands of a state of which they are not nationals.[2] While international humanitarian law is mainly concerned with the protection of enemy nationals in the hands of a party to an armed conflict, international refugee law seeks to protect individuals who have sought refuge from persecution on the territory of a third country. However, the two bodies of law do not operate in isolation from each other and are, in fact, closely interconnected. International humanitarian law and international refugee law may indeed apply successively, when violations of the laws of war force individuals to flee and seek refuge

[1] Bugnion, 'Refugees, displaced persons and international humanitarian law', 2004, 1407.

[2] Brett and Lester, 'Refugee law and international humanitarian law', 2001, 713.

in a neighbouring or third country.[3] Article 1A(2) of the 1951 Refugee Convention defines a 'refugee' as any person who has a 'well-founded fear of being persecuted for reasons of race, religion, nationality, membership of a particular social group or political opinion' and is outside his or her country of origin. In contrast, notes the UNHCR, '[p]ersons compelled to leave their country of origin as a result of international or national armed conflicts are not normally considered refugees under the 1951 Convention or 1967 Protocol'.[4] However, there is a growing recognition, in refugee jurisprudence[5] and literature,[6] that individuals fleeing civil wars and armed conflicts may nevertheless qualify as Convention refugees if they can prove that they were subjected to, or at serious risk of, persecution for a Convention reason, as opposed to the general dangers of war. When assessing persecutory harm in situations of armed conflict, reference should be made to the relevant norms of international humanitarian law, particularly the rules governing the conduct of hostilities and the principle of civilian immunity.[7] Thus, in the context of a civil war, violations of Common Article 3 or Protocol II or threats thereof will constitute persecution if it can be demonstrated that they were motivated by the race, religion, nationality, social group or political opinion of the victims.[8] Similarly, military operations directed at a particular group of

[3] Jacquemet, 'Cross-fertilization', 652.

[4] UNHCR, *Handbook on Procedures and Criteria for Determining Refugee Status*, UN Doc. HCR/IP/4/Eng/REV.1, January 1992, para. 164. However, in response to the mass influx of refugees and asylum seekers arriving in Europe from the former Yugoslavia in the 1990s, EU Members decided to offer 'temporary protection' to persons fleeing areas of armed conflict and systematic or generalized violations of human rights. See Council Directive 2001/55/EC on Minimum standards for giving temporary protection, in the event of a mass influx of displaced persons and on measures promoting a balance of efforts between Member States in receiving such persons and bearing the consequences thereof, 21 July 2001.

[5] In *Salibian* v. *Minister of Employment and Immigration*, the Canadian Federal Court of Appeal declared that: 'a civil war situation does not pose an obstacle to a claim provided the fear is not a fear felt by all citizens indiscriminately because of the civil war but a fear felt by the applicant himself, by a group with which he is associated or, at the very least, by all citizens because of a risk of persecution based on one of the reasons in the definition' (*Vahe Salibian* v. *Minister of Employment and Immigration*, Canada: Federal Court, 24 May 1990, available at: www.unhcr.org/refworld/docid/3ae6b7100.html (accessed 6 September 2011)). See also Canadian Immigration and Refugee Board, *Guideline 1: Civilian non-combatants fearing persecution in civil war situations*, 7 March 1996, www.irb.gc.ca/eng/brdcom/references/pol/guidir/Pages/civil.aspx#II (accessed 6 September 2011).

[6] Hathaway, *The Law of Refugee Status*, 1991, pp. 185–8; Jacquemet, 'Cross-fertilization', 666; Goodwin-Gill and McAdam, *The Refugee in International Law*, 2007, pp. 126–31.

[7] Storey and Wallace, 'War and peace in refugee law jurisprudence', 2001, 349.

[8] Bayefski and Fitzpatrick, *Human Rights and Forced Displacement*, 2000, p. 6.

civilians, in violation of the fundamental principle of distinction, will be regarded as persecution if their target is a group of persons *hors de combat* who share certain racial, religious or political characteristics.[9]

International humanitarian law and international refugee law will also apply concurrently, when refugees find themselves in the hands of a party to an armed conflict.[10] As civilian refugees in a situation of armed conflict, they may claim protection under both branches of international law.[11] Indeed, as refugees, they benefit from the continuing protection of international refugee law, which applies at all times, even in time of armed conflict. Furthermore, as the legal regime specifically applicable within the context of an armed conflict, international humanitarian law will extend its protection to refugees who find themselves on the territory of a party to an armed conflict, namely refugees who fled conflict or persecution in their home country and settled on the territory of a state subsequently embroiled in an armed conflict – whether an international armed conflict against their home country[12] or another state altogether,[13] or a civil war[14] – or refugees who fled war in their country to find refuge, albeit temporary and precarious, in a country also engaged in an armed conflict. In contrast, refugees who fled to a neutral or non-belligerent state are excluded from the scope of protection of international humanitarian law.[15]

As long as they do not actively participate in the hostilities, refugees are protected as civilians by international humanitarian law.[16] They enjoy

9 Kälin, 'Flight in times of war', 641–2.

10 Jacquemet, 'Cross-fertilization', 652.

11 *Ibid.*

12 For instance, Iranian refugees of Kurdish origin were interned in the Al-Tash camp in Iraq during the Iran–Iraq War. Krill, 'The ICRC's policy on refugees and IDPs', 2001, 615.

13 For instance, Palestinian refugees, who settled in Iraq, became the victims of physical attacks and abuse by local Iraqis, following the US-led invasion of Iraq and the subsequent fall of Saddam Hussein. See below pp. 172–3.

14 For instance, Rwandan refugees, who fled the civil war in Rwanda and sought refuge in Zaire and Burundi, have subsequently been embroiled in local inter-ethnic conflicts in their host territories. See UNCHR, 'Report on the situation of human rights in Rwanda', 20 January 1997, UN Doc. E/CN.4/1997/61, para. 136.

15 Bugnion, 'Refugees, displaced persons and international humanitarian law', 1409. However, Bugnion notes that refugees who flee to neutral states may nevertheless benefit from certain provisions of international humanitarian law, such as the principle of civilian immunity and the protection against attacks, particularly in refugee camps (see below Chapter 7), as well as provisions relating to the tracing of missing persons, family news and the reunification of families separated by the war (see below Chapter 6).

16 In the context of the present study, 'refugees' shall be understood as civilians, i.e. persons who do not take a direct part in hostilities. Thus, 'refugee warriors' engaged in armed operations against their country of origin or within their state of asylum do not

a general protection against the dangers of war and must be humanely treated at all times. In addition, a few provisions of international humanitarian law are specifically aimed at protecting refugees in international armed conflict. The Fourth Geneva Convention indeed lays down explicit rules concerning the relationship between refugees and their host state on the one hand, and between refugees and their country of origin on the other hand.[17] The specific protection afforded to refugees was subsequently extended by Protocol I to the Geneva Conventions.

This chapter endeavours to examine the protection afforded to civilian refugees caught up in armed conflict. As a preliminary matter, an exploration of the various applicability issues arising from the definition of 'protected persons' in relation to refugees is necessary. The remainder of the chapter will then examine the protection afforded by international humanitarian law to refugees in international armed conflict, with particular reference to the plight of 'enemy' refugees on the territory of a party to a conflict and the predicament of refugees when the occupying power is their country of origin. Finally, the principle of *non-refoulement* in international humanitarian law will be examined, particularly as it relates to other branches of international law.

Refugee protection under international humanitarian law

Are refugees protected as 'protected persons' under Article 4 of the Fourth Geneva Convention?

As non-nationals in the hands of a party to an international conflict, refugees should, in principle, benefit from the status of 'protected persons' under Article 4 of Geneva Convention IV.[18] However, the second paragraph of Article 4 states that:

> Nationals of a State which is not bound by the Convention are not protected by it. Nationals of a neutral State who find themselves in the territory of a belligerent State, and nationals of a co-belligerent State, shall not be regarded as protected persons while the State of which they are nationals has normal diplomatic representation in the State in whose hands they are.

come within the ambit of this study. In addition, genuine refugees who join the armed forces of their host state, or inversely, prisoners of war who seek refugee protection at the end of the war are excluded from the scope of this study.

17 Sandoz *et al.*, *Commentary on the Protocols*, p. 846.

18 Geneva Convention IV, Art. 4(1) defines 'protected persons' as 'those who, at a given moment and in any manner whatsoever, find themselves, in case of a conflict or occupation, in the hands of a Party to the conflict or Occupying Power *of which they are not nationals*' [my italic].

Accordingly, refugee nationals of an enemy state on the territory of a belligerent are entitled, as 'protected persons', to the full protection of the Fourth Geneva Convention. In contrast, refugees who are nationals of a neutral or co-belligerent state which has 'normal diplomatic representation' in the state in which they find themselves will not be protected by the Fourth Convention. The same applies to refugee nationals of a non-contracting state, although, admittedly, the risk of it occurring is somewhat limited, given the quasi-universality enjoyed by the Geneva Conventions. Similarly, refugee nationals of a state allied to the occupying power will not benefit from the protection of the Convention, if diplomatic relations exist between the two countries. More importantly, refugees may find themselves in a potentially dangerous situation if their state of origin – the state from which they have fled – occupies their state of refuge following an armed conflict. Indeed, as the Fourth Geneva Convention seeks primarily to protect civilians from arbitrary treatment on the part of the enemy, a state's own nationals are excluded from the scope of the Convention.

The above situations clearly demonstrate that a protection based on a formal link of nationality is inadequate, as it does not take into account the situation of individuals who do not enjoy the protection of their own state.[19] At the time that the Geneva Conventions were adopted, some speakers already remarked that the term 'nationals' did not cover all cases, in particular where people had fled from their country and no longer considered themselves as nationals of that country.[20] In the case of refugees, allegiance to a host country would seem more relevant as a criterion than their formal nationality. Yet, the Fourth Geneva Convention only acknowledges this issue in two very specific situations.[21] Refugees had to wait until 1977 to see their status as 'war victims' finally recognized.

Expansion of the protection of refugees under Protocol I

The UNHCR, supported by the ICRC, had expressed concerns that the provisions of the Fourth Geneva Convention were insufficient in respect of the protection of refugees, who should be granted a status equally valid with respect to all parties to the conflict, including their state of origin.[22] During the 1974–7 Diplomatic Conference, the ICRC proposed the introduction of an article intended to deal with some of the

[19] Sandoz *et al.*, *Commentary on the Protocols*, p. 848.

[20] *Ibid.* [21] Geneva Convention IV, Arts. 44 and 70(2).

[22] ICRC, *Draft Additional Protocol to the Geneva Convention of August 12, 1949, Commentary*, 1972 Report, vol. 1, p. 80, para. 3.125.

Convention's omissions.[23] The draft article was adopted, without much debate, as Article 73 of Protocol I:

> Persons who, before the beginning of hostilities, were considered as stateless persons or refugees under the relevant international instruments accepted by the Parties concerned or under the national legislation of the State of refuge or State of residence shall be protected persons within the meaning of Parts I and III of the Fourth Convention, in all circumstances and without any adverse distinction.

Article 73 eliminates the restrictions contained in Article 4(2) of the Fourth Convention. Refugees are protected whether or not diplomatic representation exists between two countries. The fact that they have been recognized as refugees outweighs any consideration based on their nationality or their country of origin. However, in order to benefit from the protection afforded to protected persons under Parts I and III of the Civilians Convention, two criteria must be fulfilled.

First, they must have been considered as refugees 'under the relevant international instruments' or 'under the national legislation of the State of refuge or State of residence'. The 'relevant international instruments' include in particular the 1951 Convention Relating to the Status of Refugees and its 1967 Protocol, as well as regional instruments, such as the OAU Convention and the Cartagena Declaration, and any other instrument containing a definition of refugees.[24] In addition, these instruments must have been 'accepted by the Parties concerned'. This last requirement was added following a proposed amendment by the Soviet Union, which expressed concern at the possibility that states which had not accepted these instruments may find themselves indirectly bound by them on the basis of the Protocol.[25]

Second, refugees must have been considered as such 'before the beginning of hostilities'. The extension of the protection offered by Article 73 thus only applies to refugees who have fled from persecution or threat of persecution, rather than persons displaced by the conflict itself.[26] It seems that many states opposed granting protection to persons who fled during an armed conflict, as they feared it might encourage acts of desertion and treason.[27] Some countries expressed their disappointment with respect to this situation during the Diplomatic Conference.

[23] For the discussions leading to Article 73, see Official Records vol. 3, p. 287; vol. 4, p. 246; vol. 15, p. 12.
[24] Sandoz *et al.*, *Commentary on the Protocols*, p. 849.
[25] *Ibid.*; Official Records, vol. 15, p. 12. [26] Sandoz *et al.*, *Commentary on the Protocols*, p. 850.
[27] Obradovic, 'La protection des réfugiés dans les conflits armés internationaux', p. 147.

Syria in particular deplored the fact that the protection afforded by this provision hadn't been extended to persons forced to abandon their home due to hostilities, and who should in fact benefit from priority treatment.[28] There are indeed many valid reasons for individuals to flee their country; accordingly, such a wholesale rejection of wartime refugees is based on an arbitrary and unnecessary distinction, in direct contradiction to the humanitarian principles of protection of the Geneva Conventions.

Varying levels of protection for refugees caught up in armed conflict

The protection which a refugee is entitled to in armed conflict will therefore depend on a number of factors, including the state of ratification of relevant international humanitarian and refugee law instruments by the parties to the conflict, the time of arrival of the individual in the state of refuge, the nationality of the refugee, and finally, the qualification of the conflict.

The refugee in the hands of a state party to Protocol I

If a refugee finds him/herself on the territory or in the hands of a state party to the First Protocol, then Article 73 of the Protocol becomes automatically applicable, provided that the individual was recognized as a refugee 'under the relevant international instruments' or the legislation of the state or asylum before the beginning of hostilities. By virtue of Article 73, refugees 'shall be protected persons within the meaning of Parts I and III of the Fourth Convention' and will benefit from the protection provided by more than 120 articles devoted to 'protected persons',[29] in addition to that of Part II, which already applies to them as part of the civilian population. Refugees are protected by the Geneva Conventions irrespective of their nationality and regardless of the party into whose power they have fallen.[30] Nationals of a neutral or co-belligerent country which has diplomatic relations with their state of refuge, as well as nationals of a state not bound by the Convention, now benefit from the protection afforded by the Fourth Convention.[31] In a situation of belligerent occupation, refugees are considered as 'protected persons', even if the occupying power is their state of origin. Furthermore, the recognition of refugees as 'protected persons' could engage competent organizations, such as the International Committee of the Red Cross and the United Nations High

[28] Official Records, vol. 6, p. 246.
[29] Patrnogic, 'Protection of refugees in armed conflicts', 8.
[30] Pictet, *Commentary* (1958), p. 854.
[31] Krill, 'ICRC action in aid of refugees', 333.

Commissioner for Refugees, in concrete humanitarian actions relating to the protection of refugees in armed conflicts.[32]

The refugee in the hands of a power not party to Protocol I

If, on the other hand, the refugee is in the hands of a power not party to the First Protocol, Article 73 will not apply. In this case, the extent of the protection afforded by IHL to the refugee will depend on their nationality and whether they can be considered as 'protected persons' within the meaning of Article 4 of the Fourth Geneva Convention. Refugee nationals of a state not bound by the Convention, refugee nationals of a neutral or co-belligerent state with diplomatic representation in their state of refuge, as well as refugee nationals of the occupying power or of a co-belligerent state with normal diplomatic relations with the occupying state, will only benefit from the specific protection of Article 44 or Article 70(2) of the Fourth Convention, as well as the general protection afforded to the civilian population, certain norms of customary international law regarding the treatment of civilians in time of war, the fundamental guarantees of Article 75 of Protocol I and relevant rules of international refugee law.[33]

However, as noted earlier, a protection solely dependent on the nationality of the victim is no longer adequate in contemporary armed conflicts.[34] Thus, the Yugoslav Tribunal, referring to the specific case of refugees in armed conflicts, acknowledged that, as early as 1949, the legal bond of nationality was not regarded as crucial and that 'the lack of both allegiance to a State and diplomatic protection by this State was regarded as more important than the formal link of nationality'.[35] It further held that:

> Article 4 of Geneva Convention IV, if interpreted in the light of its object and purpose, is directed to the protection of civilians to the maximum extent possible. It therefore does not make its applicability dependent on formal bonds and purely legal relations. Its primary purpose is to ensure the safeguards afforded by the Convention to those civilians who do not enjoy the diplomatic protection, and correlatively are not subject to the allegiance and control, of the State in whose hands they may find themselves. In granting its protection, Article 4 intends to look to the substance of relations, not to their legal characterisation as such.[36]

Accordingly, all civilians who do not owe allegiance to, or receive diplomatic protection from, their state of nationality should be regarded as

[32] Patrnogic, 'Protection of refugees in armed conflicts', 8.
[33] Sandoz *et al.*, *Commentary on the Protocols*, p. 850. [34] See above Chapter 1.
[35] *Tadić*, Appeals Judgment, paras. 164–5. [36] *Ibid.*, paras. 166, 168.

'protected persons' within the meaning of Article 4 of the Fourth Geneva Convention. The jurisprudence of the ICTY may be applied, by analogy, to refugees in the hands of a belligerent not party to the First Protocol, and for whom Article 73 would otherwise not have been applicable.[37] There is a persuasive argument for paying due regard to the 'substance of relations' between a refugee and the detaining or occupying power, rather than the formal bond of nationality and the existence or not of diplomatic relations between two countries. Such considerations would indeed better reflect the reality of the situation and maximize the protection of refugees and other war victims in need of protection. However, it remains to be seen whether the 'substance of relations' doctrine could really be implemented in practice, particularly in conflicts which do not necessarily meet the specific characteristics of the conflicts in the former Yugoslavia.[38]

The refugee in a non-international armed conflict

Apart from Article 17 of Protocol II, which seeks to prevent civilians from becoming refugees or internally displaced persons, neither Common Article 3 of the Geneva Conventions nor Protocol II addresses the issue of refugees in non-international armed conflicts. Yet, there are countless instances of refugees caught up in civil wars. While people fleeing armed conflict and violence increasingly remain within their own country, others will flee across international borders, and seek asylum in neighbouring countries. However, mass refugee flows impose a huge pressure on host countries and create regional instability. Conflicts often spill across borders, as refugees become the source of conflict within or between countries.[39] Thus, refugees fleeing the perils of war often find themselves on the territory of a country itself involved in an armed conflict. As noted by Weiner, conflicts within the Horn of Africa, for example, are closely related to each other, as were the wars and refugee flows between El Salvador and Nicaragua.[40] In some cases, refugees, caught up between two civil wars, will find themselves being pushed back and forth from one country to the other, as they attempt to escape violence. For many, it involves a choice between a dangerous situation and a slightly less perilous one, as it has for many refugees in the West Africa region.[41]

[37] Wills, 'The obligations due to former "protected persons"', 2010, 127–8.

[38] See above Chapter 1.

[39] Weiner, 'Bad neighbors, bad neighborhoods', 25–6. [40] *Ibid.*, 26.

[41] HRW, 'Trapped between two wars: violence against civilians in western Côte d'Ivoire' (5 August 2003), HRW Index No. A1514.

Refugees in the territory of a country embroiled in a civil war should, in principle, benefit from the protection of international humanitarian law applicable in non-international armed conflicts, human rights law, international refugee law and national asylum laws. The issue arises when refugees find themselves in rebel-controlled territory. In this case, they will be dependent for their protection, not on the government of their host state, but on the armed group concerned. However, while the rules of international humanitarian law are widely accepted as binding on all actors of the conflict – state and non-state actors alike, the binding force of human rights law and refugee law on non-state actors is more controversial.[42] Accordingly, 'the obligation of non-governmental armed groups to respect the rights of refugees is . . . based on international humanitarian law and not on refugee law'.[43] It is therefore essential that humanitarian law effectively protects refugees in all situations that may arise during an internal armed conflict, whether in the hands of state or non-state actors.

Provided they are not directly participating in hostilities,[44] refugees in non-international armed conflicts are protected as civilians and, as such, benefit from the fundamental guarantees of humane treatment, as set out in Common Article 3 of the Geneva Conventions and elaborated in Article 4 of Protocol II. Thus, refugees 'shall in all circumstances be treated humanely, without any adverse distinction founded on race, colour, religion, or faith, sex, birth or wealth, or any other similar criteria'. In particular, they shall not be subjected to acts of violence, torture and other cruel treatments. The prohibition of collective punishment in Article 4(2)(b) of Protocol II is also relevant for refugees, as it prohibits the imposition of a punishment on an entire group of persons for acts that they have not personally committed.

Having set out the legal framework, it now remains to be seen whether international humanitarian law sufficiently provides for the protection needs of refugees caught up in armed conflict.

The protection of refugees on the territory of a party to an armed conflict

By virtue of the combined application of Article 4 of the Civilians Convention and Article 73 of Protocol I, refugees in the territory of a belligerent

[42] See above, Introduction. [43] Jacquemet, 'Cross-fertilization', 657.
[44] See below Chapter 7, for a definition of 'direct participation in hostilities'.

are entitled to the protection of Part III, Sections I and II of the Fourth Convention,[45] irrespective of their nationality.[46] Of particular relevance for refugees is Article 27 of the Fourth Convention, which enunciates the principles of humane treatment and non-discrimination towards 'protected persons'.

Refugees as aliens on the territory of a party to an international armed conflict

During the drafting of the Fourth Geneva Convention, one of the main concerns was to protect enemy aliens on the territory of a party to a conflict from the arbitrariness of the detaining power. During the two World Wars, civilians of enemy nationality were indeed often rounded up, interned and prevented from leaving the territory.[47] The drafters of the Convention thus sought to prevent future belligerents from interning, or taking any measures of control in their regards, on the sole basis of their nationality. The provisions of Section II of the Civilians Convention thus regulate the situation of 'Aliens in the Territory of a Party to the Conflict' and are particularly relevant for refugees who find themselves on the territory of an 'enemy' state.

Refugees who wish to leave the country, at the outset of, or during, a conflict, shall be entitled to do so, unless their departure is contrary to the interest of the state.[48] Should they wish to remain or should they be detained by their country of asylum, their situation shall continue to be regulated by the provisions concerning aliens in time of peace,[49] in this case, the national asylum legislation and applicable provisions of international refugee law. Article 7 of the 1951 Refugee Convention, in particular, provides that an asylum state shall accord to refugees the same treatment as it accords to aliens generally. Nevertheless, Article 9 enables state parties, 'in time of war or other grave and exceptional circumstances', to withhold or suspend rights from persons whose refugee status has yet to be confirmed by the state and who pose a clear risk to the national security of the host state. As explained by Hathaway:

45 Part III of the Fourth Convention regulates the status and treatment of protected persons. Section I comprises provisions common to the territories of the parties to the conflict and to occupied territories. Section II specifically addresses the situation of aliens in the territory of a party to a conflict, and Section III is entirely dedicated to the protection of civilians in occupied territories.

46 Provided that the state concerned has ratified Protocol I and the refugees meet the two criteria set out in Article 73.

47 Pictet, *Commentary* (1958), p. 232.

48 Geneva Convention IV, Art. 38.

49 *Ibid.*

a refugee poses a risk to the host state's national security if his or her presence or actions give rise to an objectionable, real possibility of directly or indirectly inflicted substantial harm to the host state's most basic interests, including the risk of an armed attack on its territory or its citizens, or the destruction of its democratic institutions.[50]

It is important to note, however, that Article 9 is only applicable in truly exceptional circumstances and in relation to individuals whose refugee status is still pending. In addition, the measures are by definition provisional, and should be discontinued once refugee status is confirmed.[51] Aside from this very specific case, the Refugee Convention does not allow states to suspend or derogate from Convention rights, even in time of emergency.[52]

In time of war, aliens of enemy nationality are often viewed with acute suspicion, and the state in whose hands they are may have recourse to measures of control and security if it deems it 'necessary as a result of the war'.[53] Such measures may involve the internment of all enemy nationals or their placement into assigned residence 'if the security of the State makes it absolutely necessary'.[54] The Red Cross commentary however observes that what constitutes an activity prejudicial to the internal or external security of the state is left 'very largely' to governments.[55] Such activity may entail subversive activity from inside the territory or direct assistance to the enemy power, as well as acts of espionage or sabotage.[56]

Protection of refugees against arbitrary treatment

International law does not object to measures of control against enemy aliens, as it presumes that enemy nationals will be inclined to help their country because of their allegiance.[57] Yet in the case of refugees, even if their nationality defines them as the enemy, they relinquished all links with their state of origin when they fled persecution and sought refuge

[50] Hathaway, *Rights of Refugees*, p. 266. [51] *Ibid.*, pp. 260–70. [52] *Ibid.*, p. 261.

[53] Geneva Convention, Art. 27(4). For instance, following the Iraqi invasion of Kuwait in August 1990, the Home Office imposed restrictions on all Iraqi nationals in the UK, and 176 Iraqi students considered to be security risks were placed in detention in Pentonville prison. In addition, all Iraqis were required to register with the police. From January 1991, Iraqi passport holders were barred from entering the country or extending their stay. However, Stefanie Grant notes that 'Instead of assuming emergency powers, the Home Secretary relied on the Immigration Act 1971 to equip himself with extensive powers of detention, restriction, deportation, refusal of entry and police registration' ('A just treatment for enemy aliens', 1991, 305).

[54] Geneva Convention, Art. 42. [55] Pictet, *Commentary* (1958), p. 257.

[56] *Ibid.*, p. 258. [57] Cohn, 'Legal aspects of internment', 1941, 206.

in another state. Therefore, Kempner notes, 'although they are "enemies" by origin, speech, and culture, they are often admirers of the enemy State in which they live'.[58] Their allegiance lies with their state of asylum, rather than with their state of origin. The issue of the treatment of enemy refugees first came to light during the Second World War, when large numbers of refugees escaped persecution from Nazi Germany. Their allegiance to their state of refuge was so great that certain countries decided to differentiate between real enemy aliens and 'friendly aliens who are technically enemies'.[59] The drafters of the Geneva Conventions, on the initiative of the State of Israel, addressed this issue and adopted Article 44, which crystallized the existing practice: [60]

In applying the measures of control mentioned in the present Convention, the Detaining Power shall not treat as enemy aliens exclusively on the basis of their nationality *de jure* of an enemy State, refugees who do not, in fact, enjoy the protection of any Government.

The Convention recognizes the fact that refugees are victims of their country of origin and cannot be treated as enemies based solely on their nationality. Article 44 thus invites belligerents to take into consideration 'a whole set of circumstances', other than the nationality of the person.[61] As correctly stressed by Kempner:

it is more important to inquire into the fundamental spiritual loyalties of a person rather than the formal facts concerning his national origin and previous residence.[62]

However, this provision does not constitute an absolute right to exemption from security measures.[63] As explained by the third Committee in its report, the object of the Article is to *recommend* to the states that they should not automatically consider as enemies those refugees who are not protected by their government, and also not to take account only of the legal citizenship of such refugees.[64] Refugees may still be interned, if it is determined that their political convictions and activities represent a danger to the security of the state.[65] Thus, a great deal is left to the

[58] Kempner, 'The enemy alien problem', 1940, 444. [59] *Ibid.*, 445.
[60] For the discussions leading up to Article 44, see Final Record, vol. 2-A, 660, 758, 826; vol. 2-B, 411; vol. 3, 128.
[61] Pictet, *Commentary* (1958), p. 264. [62] Kempner, 'The enemy alien problem', 458.
[63] Pictet, *Commentary* (1958), p. 264.
[64] Report of Committee III to the Plenary Assembly of the Diplomatic Conference of Geneva, vol. 2A, 826.
[65] Pictet, *Commentary* (1958), pp. 264–5.

discretion of the detaining power as regards the treatment of refugees on its territory.

It should also be pointed out that, contrary to Article 73 of the First Protocol, Article 44 does not make any distinction between refugees recognized as such before the beginning of hostilities and those recognized during the hostilities.[66] Consequently, Article 44 is the only provision of international humanitarian law which protects refugees displaced by war from arbitrary treatment.

Article 44 of the Civilians Convention served as a precedent for a related provision in the 1951 Refugee Convention, on account that if this rule was to be applied in time of war, a similar rule should *a fortiori* be applied in time of peace.[67] Accordingly, Article 8 of the Convention Related to the Status of Refugees states that:

> With regard to exceptional measures which may be taken against the person, property or interests of nationals of a foreign State, the Contracting States shall not apply such measures to a refugee who is formally a national of the said State solely on account of such nationality. Contracting States which, under their legislation, are prevented from applying the general principle expressed in this article, shall, in appropriate cases, grant exemptions in favour of such refugees.

In this context, 'exceptional measures' taken against enemy nationals shall be understood to comprise such measures as internment, sequestration of property, and blocking of assets.[68] During the negotiations, concerns were expressed by certain countries as to the possibility of 'fifth-columnists', i.e. enemy aliens pretending to be refugees, infiltrating the territory.[69] However, as stressed by the representatives of Denmark and Belgium, this provision applies to refugees already in the country and regarding whom enquiries have already been made.[70] Indeed, persons considered as refugees within the meaning of the 1951 Refugee Convention, and hence within the meaning of Article 73 of the First Protocol to the 1949 Geneva Conventions, have gone through the asylum procedure and been found to be in genuine need of protection. This, in itself, should constitute a sufficient guarantee for the state of refuge as to its national security. As a result, bona fide refugees on the territory of an enemy state should, in principle, be exempted from the imposition of measures of control directed at other enemy nationals.

66 Patrnogic, 'Protection of refugees in armed conflicts', 8.

67 Weis, *The Refugee Convention*, 1995, p. 60.

68 *Ibid.*

69 See reservations made by the UK representative at the 2nd session of the ad hoc Committee (*ibid.*, 61).

70 *Ibid.*, p. 63.

In conclusion, international humanitarian law recognizes that the plight of refugees on the territory of a party to an international armed conflict needs to be addressed. However, until 1977, the protection afforded to these refugees was rather limited, and only concerned refugees of enemy nationality. Thus, Article 73 of the First Protocol is a significant improvement, as it provides that all refugees on the territory of a belligerent at the outset of the hostilities shall be treated as 'protected persons' and thus be entitled to the full protection of international humanitarian law. Two problems nonetheless persist. First, this new protection regime still excludes certain categories of refugees, namely the nationals of a neutral or a co-belligerent state on the territory of a state that has not ratified the Protocol and those who have sought refuge on the territory of a belligerent after the beginning of hostilities. This situation thus creates a dual-protection system between refugees, which will only add to the existing confusion. The second question relates to the protection of refugees against arbitrary treatment based on their de jure enemy nationality. Obradovic argues that the refugee is sufficiently protected against the arbitrariness of the detaining power: 'the worst that can happen to him is to be treated like any enemy alien, with all the rights provided for by the Convention'.[71] On the other hand, during the 1974–7 Diplomatic Conference, the representative for the UNHCR stressed that, although mitigating the refugee's difficulty, Article 44 only covered measures of control and did not apply to other matters dealt with in Parts I and III of the Convention,[72] thus leaving a gap in the protection of refugees in armed conflict. In this regard, Pictet expresses the hope that in the absence of more detailed rules, the article will be applied 'in the broadest humanitarian spirit, in order that the maximum use may be made of the resources it offers for the protection of refugees'.[73]

The protection of refugees in armed conflict provides further evidence that international humanitarian law places too much emphasis on nationality as a criterion for protection. Refugees in armed conflict should indeed be recognized and protected as such, as a category of victims of war in urgent need of protection.

The protection of refugees in occupied territory

International humanitarian law acknowledges the precarious situation of refugees in time of war, particularly when they find themselves on the

[71] Obradovic, 'La protection des réfugiés dans les conflits armés internationaux', pp. 153–4 (my translation).

[72] Official Records, vol. 15, 16.

[73] Pictet, *Commentary* (1958), p. 265.

territory of an 'enemy' state. Furthermore, the situation of refugees may deteriorate, as their state of asylum becomes occupied by the very state they sought to escape.

The refugee in the hands of an occupying power

As third country nationals with no particular link to the conflict, refugees do not necessarily constitute a threat to the occupying power,[74] and are to be treated accordingly, as any foreigner in occupied territory. The occupying power also has the duty to respect the laws in force in the occupied territory before the occupation began, including national asylum laws, and must ensure that the obligations taken up by the occupied state towards refugees are respected. Furthermore, as inhabitants of occupied territory, refugees come within the ambit of Article 4 of the Civilians Convention and benefit from the protection of Articles 27–34 and 47–78 of the Convention, which protect the whole civilian population in occupied territory from the arbitrariness of the occupying power.

In accordance with Article 48 of the Convention, 'protected persons who are not nationals of the Power whose territory is occupied may avail themselves of the right to leave the territory'. This provision applies specifically to aliens in occupied territory, 'that is nationals of belligerent and neutral countries, but not the nationals of the occupied country or of the occupying Power and its allies'.[75] By extension, this provision thus applies to refugees in occupied territory. The right to leave the occupied territory is subject to the conditions of Article 35 of the Convention. In particular, the occupying power is entitled to refuse the departure of concerned protected persons if it is contrary to its national interests. Like aliens on the territory of a belligerent, protected persons in occupied territory have the right to appeal to a court or administrative board and to ask for a protecting power to intervene.[76] However, by definition, refugees do not, in fact, enjoy the protection of any government.[77] It is thus very unlikely that a protecting power would intervene in their favour. Furthermore, because of their precarious status, refugees may find that they have nowhere else to go and elect to remain in the territory.

In any case, refugees may not be forcibly transferred within, or deported from, occupied territory. It is indeed evident that Article 49, which prohibits forced displacement in occupied territory, also applies to refugees and ensures that they and other displaced persons do not become

[74] Obradovic, 'La protection des réfugiés dans les conflits armés internationaux', p. 151.

[75] Pictet, *Commentary* (1958), p. 276. [76] *Ibid.*, p. 277.

[77] Geneva Convention IV, Art. 44.

victims of multiple displacements. If they choose, or are made to remain in occupied territory, refugees must be treated with the same consideration by the occupant, without any adverse distinction based, in particular, on race, religion or political opinion.[78] They shall not be arrested, prosecuted or convicted by the occupying power for acts committed or for opinions expressed before the occupation, with the exception of breaches of the laws and customs of war.[79] In addition, the property of refugees is protected from destruction, except where such destruction is rendered absolutely necessary by military operations.[80]

The situation of a refugee in the hands of an occupying power should be relatively straightforward, so long as the latter is not the refugee's state of origin. However, as recently illustrated in Iraq, refugees in occupied territory may find themselves in a very vulnerable situation, even when they are nationals of a neutral state. In 2003, Human Rights Watch and Amnesty International documented attacks against, and forced evictions of, refugees and third country nationals by Iraqis in the immediate aftermath of the fall of the government of Saddam Hussein.[81] Particularly targeted were Palestinian refugees, who became subject to physical attacks and abuse by Iraqis, resentful of their government's perceived preferential treatment of Palestinians.[82]

> According to the Baghdad Office of the Palestine Liberation Organization (PLO), between April 9 and May 7, 2003, some 344 Palestinian families comprising 1,612 individuals were either expelled or were forced to leave their homes in Baghdad.[83]

Thousands of Palestinians, as well as Iranian Kurdish refugees, who also came under attack, were forced to leave their houses and to become displaced once again. Many sought refuge in Jordan. However, Jordan rapidly closed its borders to these communities, forcing them to remain inside no man's land between the Iraqi and Jordanian border. By 20 April 2003, at least 1,000 Palestinians and Iranian Kurdish refugees were in no man's land.[84] Following international pressure, the Jordanian authorities agreed to let in some 550 Palestinians but refused entry to the Iranian Kurds, who were forced to remain in no man's land until 2005.

[78] *Ibid.*, Art. 27. [79] *Ibid.*, Art. 70(1). [80] *Ibid.*, Art. 53.

[81] HRW, 'Flight from Iraq: attacks on refugees and other foreigners and their treatment in Jordan' (May 2003) HRW Index No. E1504; AI, 'Iraq: US/UK forces must protect refugees' (2 May 2003) AI Index MDE 14/107/2003.

[82] HRW, 'Nowhere to flee: the perilous situation of Palestinians in Iraq' (September 2006) HRW Index No. E1804, p. 12.

[83] *Ibid.*, p. 16. [84] *Ibid.*, p. 18.

Between April 2003 and 28 June 2004, the situation in Iraq was that of a foreign military occupation, with the United States and its coalition partners acting as occupying powers under the command of the Coalition Provisional Authority (CPA).[85] In the early days of an occupation, one of the most pressing tasks for an occupying force is the restoration and the maintenance of law and order. Article 43 of the 1907 Hague Regulations clearly states that:

> The authority of the legitimate power having in fact passed into the hands of the occupant, the latter *shall take all the measures in his power to restore, and ensure, as far as possible, public order and safety*, while respecting, unless absolutely prevented, the laws in force in the country. [my italic]

While it is clear that the coalition forces were not responsible for acts of violence committed against Palestinian refugees and other non-Iraqi nationals, they nonetheless had a duty to exercise due diligence in order to ensure the protection of all civilians under their power, including refugees. In addition, by virtue of Article 27 of the Fourth Geneva Convention, refugees and other foreigners 'shall be protected especially against all acts of violence or threats thereof and against insults and public curiosity'. The occupying power must take all measures to protect the inhabitants of occupied territory from acts of violence by members of its own armed forces, as well as by private groups or individuals.[86] The coalition forces therefore had a clear duty to prevent Iraqis from attacking, threatening or forcibly displacing civilians, especially the 60–90,000 Palestinian refugees believed to be living in Iraq.[87]

The refugee in the hands of its country of origin or one of its allies

The precarious situation in which many refugees find themselves in when their state of asylum is occupied may become particularly dangerous and life-threatening when the occupying power turns out to be their own state of origin or, to a lesser extent, when the occupying power is an ally of their country of origin. In the latter case, the refugees' state of origin may apply pressure on the occupant to prosecute them or deport them back into its territory.[88] As an ally, the occupying power may readily concede

85 UNSC Res. 1483 of 22 May 2003; UN Doc. S/RES/1483 (2003); UNSC Res. 1546 of 8 June 2004; UN Doc. S/RES/1546 (2004).

86 Gasser, 'Protection of the civilian population', p. 248.

87 UNHCR (press release), 'UNHCR sends aid to evicted Palestinian refugees in Baghdad' (9 May 2003).

88 Obradovic cites the case of some five million Russians who found themselves in German and Austrian territories, occupied by the Western powers at the end of the Second

these demands. As explained earlier, refugee nationals of a co-belligerent of the occupying power do not come within the ambit of Article 4 of the Civilians Convention and thus do not benefit from the protection of the Conventions, unless they fulfil the conditions laid down in Article 73 of the First Protocol.

Even more worrying for refugees is the situation in which the state from which they fled persecution occupies their state of asylum, where they thought they had found safety. The most obvious example is that of German Jews and other German nationals who fled Germany to France and other neighbouring countries, only to find themselves in the hands of the state they so desperately tried to escape, once it invaded and subsequently occupied most of Europe.

It is the *raison d'être* of the Geneva Conventions to protect individuals against arbitrary treatment by the enemy. Therefore, the whole population in occupied territory benefits from the status of 'protected person' under Article 4 and is protected against abuse from the occupant. Since refugees are nationals of the occupying power, they do not fall within the definition of 'protected persons'. However, conscious of the necessity to protect individuals who, like refugees, had relinquished all links with their country of origin, the drafters of the Geneva Conventions adopted a provision to remedy the inconsistency. Article 70(2) of the Fourth Convention states that:

> Nationals of the Occupying Power who, before the outbreak of the hostilities, have sought refuge in the territory of the occupied State, shall not be arrested, prosecuted, convicted or deported from the occupied territory, except for offences committed after the outbreak of hostilities, or for offences under common law committed before the outbreak of hostilities which, according to the law of the occupied State, would have justified extradition in time of peace.

This article is the only provision in the whole of the Geneva Conventions which directly departs from the fundamental principle of non-interference in a state's internal affairs and aims to protect an individual against his own state. Article 70(2) is based on the idea that the right to asylum enjoyed by refugees before the occupation began 'must continue to be respected by their home country, when it takes over control as Occupying Power in the territory of the country of asylum'.[89] Indeed, the duty

World War. When the Soviet government insisted on the repatriation of all Russian nationals, many were forcibly returned to a country which they had fled and with which they had relinquished all links ('La protection des réfugiés dans les conflits armés internationaux', p. 155).

[89] Pictet, *Commentary* (1958), p. 351.

to respect the laws in force in the occupied country is a fundamental rule of the law of belligerent occupation.[90] Accordingly, decisions taken before the beginning of hostilities granting refugee status to nationals of the occupying power must be respected.

The occupying power may not arrest, prosecute, convict or deport refugees from the occupied territory. The purpose of this article is to prevent trials for political or military offences and instances of racial or religious discrimination.[91] However, this rule contains a number of limitations. First, the occupying authorities are permitted to arrest, prosecute, convict or deport refugees when they commit offences against their country of origin after the outbreak of hostilities. According to commentary on the ICRC, such offences include any action prejudicial to the refugee's home country, such as propaganda broadcasts and attacks in articles of the press, which amounts to treason when committed in wartime.[92] In other words, 'political agitation' in peacetime is permitted, but should be put an end to as soon as the hostilities break out, or run the risk of being prosecuted for treason against one's country of origin.[93]

The second exception concerns the arrest, prosecution, conviction or deportation of refugees for ordinary common offences, committed before the war, provided they are extraditable under the law of the occupied state in time of peace. The purpose of this exception is to draw a clear distinction between genuine refugees and common criminals who sought refuge in the occupied territory in order to avoid the consequences of their action.[94] If a refugee committed, before the war, an ordinary, non-political crime, as determined by the law of the occupied state, the occupying authorities may arrest the refugee, take him back to his country and bring him before its courts. However, the reference to 'the law of the occupied State' is an important guarantee for the refugee. The occupying power cannot arbitrarily arrest and deport refugees from the occupied territory based on an alleged offence committed before the war. They must produce sufficient proof that the offence would have justified extradition in peacetime under the law of the occupied state.[95]

In addition to these two exceptions, Article 70(2) is only applicable to nationals of the occupying power who sought refuge 'before the outbreak of the hostilities'. Consequently, those who entered the occupied territory

[90] Hague Regulations, Art. 43.
[91] Dinstein, 'Belligerent occupation and human rights', 108.
[92] Pictet, *Commentary* (1958), p. 351.
[93] Dinstein, 'Belligerent occupation and human rights', 105.
[94] Pictet, *Commentary* (1958), p. 351. [95] *Ibid.*, p. 352.

after the beginning of the hostilities, but before the occupation began, are excluded from the ambit of Article 70(2) and thus are in great danger of acts of revenge and persecution by the occupying authorities. This arbitrary distinction between refugees, based on the precise time when refuge was sought is thus to be deplored.

Articles 70(2) and 44 of the Civilians Convention are complementary: Article 44 deals with the refugees' relations with the authorities of the country of asylum, Article 70(2) governs their position vis-à-vis their country of origin when it becomes the occupying power.[96] Like Article 44, which is restricted to measures of control towards refugees, Article 70(2) does not cover all situations affecting refugees in occupied territory. In fact, it offers an even more limited protection, as it deals with arrest, prosecution, conviction and deportation. No reference is made to other measures which may be taken against refugees, such as the confiscation of property or denial of religious freedoms.[97] Nevertheless, in accordance with Article 73 of the First Protocol, refugees in occupied territory now benefit from the protection of the whole of the Fourth Geneva Convention. Among other improvements, refugees will therefore enjoy the immunity provided by the first paragraph of Article 70 against arrest, prosecution or conviction for acts committed before the occupation, except for breaches of the laws and customs of war. As observed by Bothe *et al.*, 'the reach of a Party's treason laws against its dissident nationals who became refugees before the outbreak of hostilities is substantially reduced'.[98]

Additionally, by virtue of Article 73, refugees may not be subjected to acts of violence,[99] torture,[100] collective penalties or reprisals against their person or their property.[101] They may be entitled to receive individual relief consignments[102] and they may not be forcibly displaced or deported from the occupied territory.[103] This provision is an important safeguard for refugees against deportation in the case of the occupying power being an ally of their country of origin. If the occupying power complied with its ally's demands to deport all refugees back into its territory, it would commit a war crime under Article 8(b)(viii) of the 1998 ICC Statute. Finally, and although they still owe allegiance to the occupant, refugees may not be compelled to serve in armed or auxiliary forces of the occupying power.[104]

[96] *Ibid.*, p. 350. [97] Dinstein, 'Belligerent occupation and human rights', 104.
[98] Bothe *et al.*, *New Rules for Victims of Armed Conflicts*, p. 449.
[99] Geneva Convention IV, Art. 27. [100] *Ibid.*, Art. 32. [101] *Ibid.*, Art. 33.
[102] *Ibid.*, Art. 62. [103] *Ibid.*, Art. 49. [104] *Ibid.*, Art. 51.

Article 73 of the First Protocol significantly improves the protection of refugees in occupied territory. Provided that they sought refugee status before the beginning of the hostilities, refugees should be considered as 'protected persons' and treated as such, irrespective their nationality. Whether the occupying power is their country of origin, or one of its allies, it is bound by conventional and customary international humanitarian law to ensure protection and fair treatment to all inhabitants of the occupied territory, including refugees.

The fundamental principle of non-refoulement

Article 45(4) of the Fourth Geneva Convention provides that:

> In no circumstance shall a protected person be transferred to a country where he or she have reason to fear persecution for his or her political opinion or religious beliefs.

This provision establishes, in international humanitarian law, the fundamental principle of *non-refoulement*, according to which 'no refugee shall be returned to any country where he or she is likely to face persecution, other ill-treatment or torture'.[105] This cornerstone principle of international refugee law is enshrined in Article 33(1) of the 1951 Refugee Convention, which declares that:

> No Contracting State shall expel or return ('refouler') a refugee in any manner whatsoever to the frontiers of territories where his life or freedom would be threatened on account of his race, religion, nationality, membership of a particular social group or political opinion.[106]

While the language of the provision corresponds to the definition of 'refugee' contained in Article 1A(2) of the Convention, it has been argued that the nature of the threat in the context of *refoulement* should be interpreted more broadly, in order to include an unqualified threat of persecution and a threat to life, physical integrity or liberty, as well as an application in situations of generalized violence and armed conflict.[107]

The principle of *non-refoulement* is also recognized by human rights law as a component of the prohibition on torture or cruel, inhuman or degrading treatment or punishment.[108] Article 3(1) of the Convention against Torture provides that:

[105] Goodwin-Gill and McAdam, *Refugee in International Law*, p. 201.
[106] See also OAU Refugee Convention, Art. II(3); ACHR, Art. 22(8).
[107] Lauterpacht and Bethlehem, 'Scope and content', 2003, pp. 126, 150.
[108] *Ibid.*, p. 92.

No State Party shall expel, return ('refouler') or extradite a person to another State where there are substantial grounds for believing that he would be in danger of being subjected to torture.[109]

The HRC has interpreted the prohibition on torture and cruel, inhuman or degrading treatment or punishment enshrined in Article 7 of the ICCPR as including a prohibition on *refoulement*:

States parties must not expose individuals to the danger of torture or cruel, inhuman or degrading treatment or punishment upon return to another country by way of their extradition, expulsion or *refoulement*.[110]

Similarly, the European Court of Human Rights has recognized that the principle of *non-refoulement* is implicitly contained in Article 3 of the European Convention, which prohibits torture and cruel treatment or punishment.[111] Thus, states are barred from expelling or returning an individual to his or her country of origin where there is a real risk that he or she may be subjected to torture or cruel treatment or punishment. Additionally, there is a case for arguing that states parties to international instruments abolishing the death penalty, such as the Second Optional Protocol to the ICCPR,[112] or Protocol No. 13 to the ECHR,[113] should refrain from transferring persons to situations where they may face the death penalty.[114]

The principle of *non-refoulement* is widely recognized as a customary principle of international law.[115] The question thus arises as to

[109] Convention against Torture or Other Cruel, Inhuman or Degrading Treatment or Punishment, 10 December 1984, 1465 UNTS 85.

[110] HRC, General Comment No. 20, Compilation of General Comments and General Recommendations Adopted by Human Rights Treaty Bodies, 28 July 1994, UN Doc. HRI/GEN/1/Rev.1, para. 9.

[111] *Soering* v. *United Kingdom*, Series A, No.161, 11 EHRR 439: 'It would hardly be compatible with the underlying values of the Convention, that "common heritage of political traditions, ideals, freedom and the rule of law" to which the Preamble refers, were a Contracting State knowingly to surrender a fugitive to another State where there were substantial grounds for believing that he would be in danger of being subjected to torture, however heinous the crime allegedly committed' (para. 88).

[112] Second Optional Protocol to the ICCPR aiming at the abolition of the death penalty, 15 December 1989, 1642 UNTS 414.

[113] Protocol No. 13 to the Convention for the Protection of Human Rights and Fundamental Freedoms, concerning the abolition of the death penalty in all circumstances, 3 May 2002, ETS No. 187.

[114] Gillard, 'No place like home', 2008, 721.

[115] Lauterpacht and Bethlehem, 'Scope and content', pp. 149–64. See also EXCOM Conclusion No. 6 (XXVIII) 'Non-refoulement' (1977): '*Recalling* that the fundamental humanitarian principle of *non-refoulement* has found expression in various

the particular relevance of relying on *non-refoulement* as a norm of international humanitarian law, rather than, or as well as, a fundamental norm of refugee protection.

Specificity and relevance of the principle of non-refoulement *in IHL*

Absoluteness of the principle

While the prohibition of *refoulement* in international humanitarian law and human rights law is absolute, Lauterpacht and Bethlehem observe that:

> there may be some circumstances of overriding importance that would, within the framework of [the 1951 Refugee Convention], legitimately allow the removal or rejection of individual refugees or asylum-seekers.[116]

Article 33(2) of the Refugee Convention indeed provides that a refugee can exceptionally be returned if there are reasonable grounds for regarding him or her as a danger to the national security of the host country, or if he or she has been convicted of a particularly serious crime and thus constitutes a danger to the community of that country. It should be noted, however, that the exceptions to *non-refoulement* should be interpreted restrictively and in strict compliance with due process of law.[117] Moreover, derogation from the principle of *non-refoulement* is not permitted, even under refugee law, if there are reasons to believe that the person concerned faces a danger of torture, or cruel, inhuman or degrading treatment or a risk coming within the scope of non-derogable principles of human rights upon return.[118]

In time of national emergency, such exceptions may be easily abused by a government, which finds itself overwhelmed by mass refugee flows pouring in from a neighbouring country. Provided that the situation amounts to an international armed conflict and the refugees concerned are regarded as 'protected persons' within the meaning of the Fourth Geneva Convention, the host state will not be able to avail itself of such grounds of exception, given the absolute character of the prohibition.[119] Consequently, in time of national emergency, and war in particular, the protection afforded by the Geneva Conventions, although not as comprehensive as that of the Refugee Convention, appears more effective.

international instruments adopted at the universal and regional levels and is generally accepted by States'.

116 Lauterpacht and Bethlehem, 'Scope and content', p. 133.

117 *Ibid.*, p. 134. 118 *Ibid.*, p. 133. 119 Pictet, *Commentary* (1958), p. 269.

Beneficiaries of the protection from *refoulement*

The scope of application of the refugee law principle of *non-refoulement* is subject to debate among refugee lawyers. Indeed, opinions differ as to whether the principle is limited to those formally recognized as refugees, in accordance with Article 1A(2) of the 1951 Refugee Convention, or whether it extends to asylum-seekers waiting to be formally recognized and other non-Convention refugees, such as refugees fleeing en masse from situations of civil wars.[120] According to the UNHCR, the principle of *non-refoulement* applies not only to recognized refugees, but also to those who have not had their status formally declared:

> Given that a person is a refugee within the meaning of the 1951 Convention as soon as he or she fulfills the criteria contained in the refugee definition, refugee status determination is declaratory in nature: a person does not become a refugee because of recognition, but is recognized because he or she is a refugee.[121]

Irrespective of the outcome of the debate, the principle of *non-refoulement* is clearly aimed at protecting 'refugees', namely persons who do not in fact enjoy the protection of the government of their country of origin.[122]

Article 45(4), on the other hand, is directed at 'protected persons', namely aliens in the territory of a party to the conflict. This category therefore not only includes refugees, but also all foreigners settled in a host country at war, or merely there on a temporary basis, provided that they meet the nationality requirement of Article 4 of the Fourth Geneva Convention. Thus, all foreigners in unoccupied territory are protected, in accordance with the *non-refoulement* principle, from forcible return to a place where they may be subjected to persecution, irrespective of their formal status. There is no equivalent provision applicable in situations of occupation. However, while transfers and expulsions of aliens are permitted in time of armed conflict,[123] subject to the prohibition on *refoulement*,

[120] Lauterpacht and Bethlehem, 'Scope and content', pp. 115–21. For two diverging opinions, see K. Hailbronner, '*Non-refoulement* and "humanitarian" refugees: customary international law or wishful thinking?', *Virginia J. Intl. L.*, 26 (1986), 857; G. Goodwin-Gill, '*Non-refoulement* and the new asylum-seekers', *Virginia J. Intl. L.*, 26 (1986), 897, 901.

[121] UNHCR, 'Advisory Opinion on the Extraterritorial Application of *Non-Refoulement* Obligations under the 1951 Convention relating to the Status of Refugees and its 1967 Protocol', 27 January 2007, para. 8, www.unhcr.org/refworld/pdfid/45f17a1a4.pdf (accessed 24 October 2011).

[122] Goodwin-Gill and McAdam, *Refugee in International Law*, p. 205.

[123] Deportation of enemy aliens in time of war, although permitted, should remain an exceptional measure. It should be carried out on an individual basis, for security

individual or mass forcible transfers and deportations within and from occupied territory are clearly and absolutely prohibited. Refugees in occupied territory could have nonetheless benefited from an additional safeguard against *refoulement* with a clear and express prohibition of transfers amounting to *refoulement* in Article 49 of Fourth Geneva Convention.

Nature of the threat

Article 45(4) prohibits *refoulement* only when the protected person has reason to fear political or religious persecution. In contrast, the principle of *non-refoulement* as expressed in the 1951 Refugee Convention offers a broader protection from *refoulement*, as it prohibits the expulsion or return of a refugee to a territory where 'his life or freedom would be threatened on account of his race, religion, nationality, membership of a particular social group or political opinion', while international human rights law prohibits the transfer of any person who faces a risk of torture, or cruel, inhuman or degrading treatment or punishment.

However, Article 45(4) is complemented by Article 45(3), which, although not expressly referring to *non-refoulement*, provides that:

> Protected persons may be transferred by the Detaining Power only to a Power which is a party to the present Convention and after the Detaining Power has satisfied itself of the willingness and ability of such transferee Power to apply the present Convention.[124]

Article 45(3) not only prohibits the transfer of a protected person to a state that is not party to the Fourth Geneva Convention, but also to one that is unwilling or unable to apply and respect all the protections in the Convention.[125] Accordingly, aliens in the territory of an international armed conflict benefit from a greater protection than that normally granted by the principle of *non-refoulement*, as their transfer to another power will be prohibited if they have reason to fear persecution, or if it appears that *any* of the rights and protections in the Fourth Geneva Convention cannot be assured in the country of transfer.[126]

reasons, and in accordance with the principles of fair trial and humanity. If collective deportation of aliens is nevertheless unavoidable, it may remain lawful only inasmuch as it constitutes a collection of individual deportations. Deportation en masse of aliens is prohibited under international humanitarian law, as constituting a discriminatory and arbitrary measure.

124 Geneva Convention III, Article 12 contains an identical provision for prisoners of war.

125 Gillard, 'No place like home', 724; Droege, 'Transfers of detainees: legal framework, *non-refoulement* and contemporary challenges', 2008.

126 Gillard, 'No place like home', 710.

By way of conclusion, it should therefore be noted that the principle of *non-refoulement*, although limited in scope and not as developed as in international refugee law and human rights law, is clearly established in international humanitarian law, at least in so far as the situation is one of international armed conflict. However, although widely accepted as a principle of customary international law, its application may be problematic in the context of an armed conflict, particularly as a belligerent's duties in this regard are rather vague and general. By failing to address the issue of *refoulement* in its study on customary international humanitarian law,[127] the ICRC clearly missed an opportunity to clarify and further develop the principle under international humanitarian law.[128]

The principle of non-refoulement *in non-international armed conflicts*

During the 1990s, tens of thousands of refugees escaped the civil war in Liberia to Côte d'Ivoire and settled near the border, in small Ivorian towns and villages. When an armed conflict broke out in September 2002, the situation of Liberian refugees in Côte d'Ivoire became seriously affected. Accused of supporting the rebels in the west of the country, forcibly recruited by various armed groups, including the government forces of former President Gbagbo, and generally viewed with suspicion by the Ivorian population,[129] many Liberian refugees had no choice but to flee once again. As observed by Human Rights Watch:

> In the absence of protection from the government in Côte d'Ivoire and offers for resettlement to another country, many refugees were forced to choose between two untenable solutions: return to Liberia or survival in an increasingly violent environment.[130]

Thus, tens of thousands of Liberian refugees and Ivorian nationals sought refuge in Liberia, despite the potential danger awaiting them there. When

[127] The ICRC erroneously mentioned Article 45(4) in support of its Rule 129A on the prohibition of forced displacement in situations of occupation. As mentioned above, Article 45(4) addresses the treatment of aliens in the territory of an international armed conflict and is therefore not relevant for the protection of the civilian population of an occupied territory. Nevertheless, the principle of *non-refoulement* under refugee and human rights law is generally regarded as a customary principle of international law, applicable at all times. Piotrowicz, 'Displacement and displaced persons', pp. 345–6.

[128] Greer, 'A critique of the ICRC's customary rules', 2007,124.

[129] AI, 'No escape: Liberian refugees in Côte d'Ivoire' (24 June 2003), AI Index AFR 31/012/2003.

[130] HRW, 'Trapped between two wars: violence against civilians in western Côte d'Ivoire' (5 August 2003), HRW Index No. A1514.

the situation deteriorated in eastern Liberia in February 2003, and neighbouring countries temporarily closed their borders, most of these refugees were forced to return to Côte d'Ivoire. These events in the West African region accurately illustrate the plight of many refugees in internal armed conflicts. Caught in the crossfire of two or more civil wars and confronted with security issues and lack of protection from their state of asylum, many refugees are trapped in a continuous cycle of displacement, in search of safety, wherever they can find it. Such a situation could effectively amount to *refoulement*, as these Liberian and Ivorian refugees were forced to go back to a region where they risked being the victims of serious human rights abuses.[131]

International humanitarian law does not specifically address the issue of refugees in non-international armed conflicts and there is no equivalent to Article 45(3) in Common Article 3 or Protocol II. Yet, as the above example shows, refugees are in urgent need of protection from multiple displacements and forced repatriation to their country of origin by government forces or rebel armed groups.

As civilians, all refugees on the territory of a country involved in an internal armed conflict should be entitled to protection under Common Article 3 to the four Geneva Conventions, Protocol II and customary international law. Both Common Article 3 and Article 4(2) of Protocol II prohibit violence to life and person, in particular cruel treatment and torture, as well as outrages upon personal dignity, including humiliating and degrading treatment. In *Furundžija*, the Yugoslav Tribunal held that torture in armed conflict was prohibited by a general rule of international law.[132] In addition, the prohibition of torture not only imposes upon states obligations *erga omnes*, that is, obligations towards the international community as whole, but it also constitutes a peremptory norm, or *jus cogens*, from which no derogation is possible.[133] As rightly noted by one commentator, if human rights law acknowledges that the importance of the prohibition is such that it also prohibits *refoulement* to torture or cruel, inhumane or degrading treatment or punishment, there is no reason why the prohibition in international humanitarian law should not be interpreted the same way.[134] Thus, an absolute prohibition of *refoulement* also exists in the context of a non-international armed conflict, where the individual concerned faces a danger of torture or other ill-treatment.

131 AI, 'No escape', 19.

132 *Prosecutor* v. *Furundžija*, Trial Judgment, IT-95-17/1, 10 December 1998, para. 139.

133 *Ibid.*, paras. 151, 153.

134 Droege, 'Transfers of detainees', 675.

In addition, Article 17 Protocol II clearly states that refugees shall not be forcibly displaced, except for security or imperative military reasons, or compelled to leave the country for reasons connected with the conflict.[135] This provision should act as a barrier against multiple displacements of populations, whether within or outside the borders of a country, and prevent the *refoulement* of refugees to situations of violence where they face a risk of persecution.

It should also be reminded that an asylum state's duties towards its refugees, as well as its general obligations under international human rights law, do not cease in time of armed conflict, whether international or non-international. Consequently, the principle of *non-refoulement* remains applicable in situations of armed conflict. However, for refugees caught up in an internal armed conflict, particularly if they find themselves in rebel-controlled territory, international humanitarian law clearly constitutes the first line of protection against abuse, not only due to its *lex specialis* character, but also because, unlike human rights and refugee law, it is widely regarded as binding upon states and non-state actors alike. It is therefore essential that the principle of *non-refoulement* be clearly established, not as a residual protection derived from other provisions of the Geneva Conventions, but as a self-standing, fully applicable principle of international humanitarian law to which recourse might be made in non-international armed conflicts and binding on all parties to the conflict.

135 See above Chapter 2.

6 Internally displaced persons as civilians in time of war

Internally displaced persons constitute a particularly vulnerable category of victims of war. They have been forced to leave their homes, belongings and relatives behind in search of safety. Instead, they often find themselves stranded in refugee or IDP camps, in appalling conditions of living, viewed with suspicion by the local population and regularly exposed to abuses by the parties to the conflict.

International humanitarian law does not specifically address the plight of internally displaced persons. Nevertheless, as long as they do not take direct part in the hostilities,[1] internally displaced persons benefit from the general rules of protection of international humanitarian law afforded to the civilian population as a whole. These rules will be complemented by the relevant rules of international human rights law, which applies, in principle, at all times, even in time of war. The purpose of this chapter is to derive, from the cumulative application of international human rights law and international humanitarian law, a basic regime of protection for IDPs caught up in armed conflict.

As noted throughout this study, international humanitarian law primarily seeks to protect non-nationals in the hands of a party to an armed conflict. Thus, as civilians displaced within their own territory, internally displaced persons are excluded from the scope of protection of humanitarian law, unless this territory is subsequently occupied by the enemy. IDPs in non-international armed conflicts are protected as civilians, but the extent of this protection is less detailed and developed than that offered by international humanitarian law in international armed conflicts. Thus, although international humanitarian law specifically provides for the provision of food and other basic subsistence needs in armed conflict, a

[1] For a definition of 'direct participation in hostilities', see below Chapter 7 below.

number of victims will fall short of this protection. In this case, international human rights law will play an essential role in compensating for this lack of protection. Conversely, international humanitarian law contains provisions of particular interest to internally displaced persons in armed conflict, such as family dispersion and reunification, as well as humanitarian assistance, which are covered in a more general manner by international human rights law.[2] In addition, the rules of international humanitarian law are non-derogable and unequivocally binding on all belligerents in an armed conflict.[3] These various issues will be considered below.[4]

Basic subsistence needs of displaced persons in armed conflict

Internally displaced persons in camps are often denied access to the most basic essentials necessary for an adequate standard of living, such as food, water, clothing or shelter, as well as proper medical care and sanitation.[5] Unlike human rights law, international humanitarian law does not explicitly recognize a right to an adequate standard of living.[6] It does, however, impose duties on belligerents to the effect that civilians are provided with food, water, clothing, shelter and adequate health care in situations of armed conflict. In fact, some of these provisions are more detailed and comprehensive than the human rights provisions applicable in peacetime.[7]

The specific needs of IDPs in relation to food, water, health clothing and shelter

According to the OCHA: 'A principal cause of mortality for internally displaced persons, as with refugees and other war-affected populations, is malnutrition. Lack of food kills on its own and malnourished individuals are more susceptible to disease.'[8]

[2] Phuong, *International Protection of Internally Displaced Persons*, p. 46.
[3] Pejić, 'The right to food in armed conflict', 2001, 1097–8.
[4] It should be noted that the issues addressed below have been isolated for specific consideration due to their particular relevance for the present study, as inherent in the plight of displaced persons in armed conflict. The present chapter, however, does not claim to exhaustively address all issues of concern for IDPs caught up in armed conflict.
[5] UNCHR, 'Report of the Representative of the Secretary-General on Internally Displaced Persons, Mr Francis Deng: Compilation and Analysis of Legal Norms' (5 December 1995), E/CN.4/1996/52/Add.2, 47.
[6] Kälin, *Guiding Principles on Internal Displacement: Annotations*, 2008, p. 99.
[7] Alston, 'The human right to food', 1984, p. 26.
[8] OCHA, *Handbook for Applying the Guiding Principles*, p. 37.

During his visit to Sudan in October 2005, the Representative of the Secretary-General on Internally Displaced Persons reported that food insecurity had reached an 'outrageous dimension' within the IDP community of southern Sudan (now the Republic of South Sudan), and that among the poor of Sudan, IDPs were the worst affected by malnutrition, with some 3.2 million dependent on food aid.[9] The Representative also reported on the extreme shortages of drinking water, with less than 40 per cent of the southern population having access, and every fourth child dying of preventable and water-borne diseases before the age of 5.[10] Overall, the Internal Displacement Monitoring Centre notes that in many countries, including Angola, Burma, Colombia, Ethiopia and Iraq, IDP access to clean water and sanitation is inferior to that of the general population.[11] As a result, contaminated water supplies combined with the absence of adequate sanitation facilities contribute to the spread of water-borne diseases, with devastating consequences on the health of the displaced.

In many cases, the poor food and water conditions in IDP camps are due to a variety of factors, including the geographical situation of the camps, which are often in conflict areas or in remote parts of the country, or a lack of adequate support from the concerned government and the international community.[12] In other cases however, food insecurity and malnutrition are part of a deliberate strategy of war. In a 2002 report on Sudan, the International Crisis Group noted:

> Instead of adopting a 'hearts and minds' strategy to peel away [rebel group] SPLA popular support, the government has consistently targeted the 'stomachs and feet' of civilians . . . Famine in the war-torn regions is not a by-product of indiscriminate fighting but a government objective that has largely been achieved through manipulation, diversion and denial of international humanitarian relief.[13]

Moreover, displaced persons are particularly vulnerable to displacement-related diseases caused by malnutrition, inadequate sanitation facilities and overall deplorable conditions of living. Nevertheless, internally displaced persons are often unable to access basic health services. According to the Internal Displacement Monitoring Centre, the existing IDP-specific health data suggest that in more than half the countries affected by

[9] UNCHR, 'Report of the Representative of the Secretary-General on Internally Displaced Persons: Mission to Sudan' (13 February 2006), E/CN.4/2006/71/Add.6, para. 36.

[10] *Ibid.*, para. 37. [11] IDMC, *Global Overview 2006*, p. 74. [12] *Ibid.*, p. 73.

[13] ICG, 'Ending starvation as a weapon of war in Sudan' (14 November 2002), www.crisisgroup.org/en/regions/africa/horn-of-africa/sudan/054-ending-starvation-as-a-weapon-of-war-in-sudan.aspx (accessed 28 October 2011).

internal displacement, including practically all African and Asian countries, IDPs have no access to adequate health care.[14] Most of the diseases to which displaced persons are exposed are preventable.[15] Yet, without proper health care and access to medication, many displaced persons affected by these diseases, mostly children, die.

The reasons for lack of access to adequate medical and health care are numerous. They include lack of financial resources, IDP camps' remote location and breakdown of health services in war-affected areas.[16] In Darfur for instance, the Office of the UN Resident and Humanitarian Coordinator explained that 'access restraints due to insecurity constituted the major challenge for the delivery of regular primary health care and services'.[17] In other countries, including Burma, Somalia and the OPT, IDPs face discrimination in gaining access to health care due to their ethnic origin or because of restricted freedom of movement.[18]

Provisions of IHL applicable to the civilian population as a whole

The prohibition of starvation as a method of warfare

One of the most fundamental principles of international humanitarian law is that civilians shall enjoy general protection against the dangers of war.[19] Consequently, belligerents should distinguish between civilians and combatants, and between civilian objects and military objectives at all times. In addition, 'the right of the Parties to the conflict to choose methods and means of warfare is not unlimited'[20] and certain methods of combat are expressly prohibited, precisely because they are clearly incompatible with the principle of civilian immunity.

Starvation of civilians as a method of warfare is prohibited during both international and non-international armed conflicts.[21] As explained by the Red Cross, to use starvation as a method of warfare would be 'to provoke it deliberately, causing the population to suffer hunger, particularly by depriving it of its sources of food or supplies'.[22] Consequently, it is prohibited to attack, destroy, remove or render useless, for that purpose, objects indispensable to the survival of the civilian population, such as foodstuffs, agricultural areas for the production of foodstuffs, crops,

[14] IDMC, *Global Overview 2006*, p. 72. [15] *Ibid.* [16] *Ibid.*
[17] OCHA, 'Darfur humanitarian profile no. 27' (1 April 2007), www.unsudanig.org/docs/Darfur%20Humanitarian%20Profile%20Narrative_1%20April%202007.pdf (accessed 28 October 2011).
[18] IDMC, *Global Overview 2006*, p. 72. [19] Protocol I, Art. 51(1) and Protocol II, Art. 13(1).
[20] Protocol I, Art. 35(1). [21] Protocol I, Art. 54(1) and Protocol II, Art. 14.
[22] Sandoz *et al.*, *Commentary on the Protocols*, p. 653.

livestock, drinking-water installations and supplies and irrigation works.[23] However, foodstuffs may nevertheless be attacked in international armed conflict if they are used as sustenance solely for combatants or in direct support of military action.[24]

Objects indispensable to survival evidently include foodstuffs and clean water. However, the commentary on the Protocols notes that the list of protected objects is merely illustrative and that, as a result of climate or other circumstances, objects such as shelter or clothing should be considered as indispensable to survival.[25] With reference to the displacement crisis in the Sudan, the OCHA reported in 2005 that:

> Lack of shelter threatens the health status of the population in a number of ways including extreme exposure to sun and dust and to colder temperature at night. Although night temperatures have now risen, from May onwards exposure to rains will increase with a corresponding risk of communicable diseases and sanitation concerns. Unconfirmed reports already indicate a rise in morbidity and mortality indicators.[26]

Protection of the wounded and sick

It is a fundamental principle of international humanitarian law that all the wounded, sick and shipwrecked shall be respected and protected. While Common Article 3 to the four Conventions merely provides that 'the wounded and sick shall be collected and cared for', Article 10(1) of Protocol I and Article 7(1) of Protocol II reaffirm and develop this customary norm of international law.

The protection of the sick and the wounded in based on the principle of non-discrimination. When caring for the wounded, sick and shipwrecked, 'no distinction shall be made between members of the armed forces and civilians or according to whether they belong to one party or another; the obligation to respect and protect is general and absolute'.[27] Paragraph 2 of Article 10 of Protocol I and Article 7 of Protocol II require that in all circumstances patients be 'treated humanely and . . . receive, to the fullest extent practicable and with the least possible delay, the medical care and attention required by their condition'. No distinction founded on any

[23] Protocol I, Art. 54(2) and Protocol II, Art. 14. [24] Protocol I, Art. 54(3).

[25] Sandoz *et al.*, *Commentary on the Protocols*, p. 655.

[26] OCHA, 'Darfur humanitarian profile no. 13 – shelter sector' (April 2005), cited in IDMC, 'Sudan: outlook for IDPs remains bleak' (12 October 2007), www.internal-displacement.org/8025708F004CE90B/(httpCountries)/F3D3CAA7CBEBE276802570A7004B87E4?OpenDocument (accessed 28 October 2011).

[27] Sandoz *et al.*, *Commentary on the Protocols*, p. 1410.

ground other than medical ones may be made between patients.[28] In other words, 'only urgent medical reasons will authorize priority in the order of treatment to be administered'.[29] In addition, all possible measures must be taken to search for and collect the wounded, sick and shipwrecked, and to protect them against pillage and ill-treatment.[30] Consequently, in situations of international and non-international armed conflict, all belligerents have a duty to collect and care for sick and wounded displaced persons who fall under their control.

Protection of women and children

Finally, it should be noted that displaced women and children, who constitute some 80 per cent of the world's refugees and displaced persons,[31] are among the most vulnerable categories of victims of war. Sexual and gender-based violence against women and young girls is often used as a strategy of war by armed actors, and can constitute a way to assert their power over the population or a means of ethnic cleansing. In the Democratic Republic of Congo, Chad and Sudan, there have been numerous reports of rape and sexual violence against displaced women and girls.[32] Gender-based violence may have serious implications for the health of displaced women, including an increased risk of infection from HIV/AIDS and other sexually transmitted infections (STIs), as well as unwanted pregnancies. Displaced women also lack access to adequate obstetric and reproductive health services.[33] Both conventional and customary international humanitarian law recognize that women and children shall be the object of special respect and protection.[34] However, as regards the specific medical needs of women, the protection offered by international humanitarian law is somewhat limited. By virtue of Article 16 of the Fourth Geneva Convention, expectant mothers are entitled to particular protection and respect. Pregnant women are included within the definition of 'the wounded and sick' because of their particular 'state of weakness which demands special consideration'.[35] However, the Geneva

[28] *Ibid.*, p. 1411. [29] Geneva Conventions I and II, Art. 12(3).

[30] Geneva Convention IV, Art. 16 and Protocol II, Art. 8.

[31] The United Nations Fourth World Conference on Women, 'Platform for Action: Women and Armed Conflict' (Beijing, September 1995), para. 136.

[32] IDMC, *Global Overview 2006*, p. 67.

[33] Inter-Agency Working Group, 'Reproductive health services for displaced persons: a decade in progress', November 2004, p. 67, http://iawg.net/resources/2004_global_eval (accessed 28 October 2011).

[34] Protocol I, Art. 76(1) and 77(1); Protocol II, Art. 4(2)(e).

[35] Pictet, *Commentary* (1958), p. 134.

Convention does not consider other women-specific health needs, such as access to reproductive health care.[36] Both morbidity and mortality could be reduced if displaced populations in conflict situations had access to proper medical treatment and high-quality reproductive health services, including emergency obstetric care, HIV/AIDS and other STIs prevention and treatment, as well as a gender-based violence medical response.[37]

Duty of the occupying power to provide for the basic subsistence needs of the occupied population

As well as general provisions for the protection of the civilian population as a whole, international humanitarian law contains a number of more specific and detailed provisions relating to the duties of the occupying power towards the occupied civilian population. These provisions are particularly relevant for internally displaced persons, because they address their specific needs in the most comprehensive way.[38]

Article 55 of the Fourth Convention charges the occupying power with the duty of ensuring the food and medical supplies of the population. The occupier should, in particular, bring in the necessary foodstuffs, medical stores and other articles if the resources of the occupied territory are inadequate. Article 69(1) of the First Protocol extends the scope of this obligation to cover 'the provision of clothing, bedding, means of shelter and other supplies essential to the survival of the civilian population of the occupied territory and objects necessary for religious worship'. It should be noted, however, that this duty is not absolute and only binds the occupying power 'to the fullest extent of the means available to it'.

The occupying power must also ensure and maintain, with the cooperation of national local authorities, the medical and hospital establishments and services, as well as a high level of public health and hygiene in the occupied territory.[39] By extension, this duty also applies to IDP camps situated in occupied territory. Article 56 refers in particular to the adoption and application of 'the prophylactic and preventive measures necessary to combat the spread of contagious diseases and epidemics'. According to the ICRC commentary, such measures include supervision of public health, the distribution of medicines, the organization of medical examinations and disinfection, the establishment of stock and medical supplies,

[36] UNCHR, 'Compilation and Analysis of Legal Norms', para. 212.

[37] Reproductive Health, Information and Services in Emergencies (RAISE), www.raiseinitiative.org (accessed 28 October 2011).

[38] Cohen and Deng, *Masses in Flight*, p. 84.

[39] Geneva Convention IV, Art. 56(1).

the dispatch of medical teams where epidemics are raging, the isolation and accommodation in hospital of people suffering from communicable diseases.[40]

Satisfactory conditions of living during displacement

International humanitarian law imposes an obligation upon the occupying power or, if evacuations are carried out within the context of a non-international armed conflict, any authorities in charge of the displaced civilian population, to take all possible measures to ensure that the civilians concerned are received under satisfactory conditions of shelter, hygiene, health, safety and nutrition.[41] The occupying power must also ensure that proper accommodation is provided to the evacuees.

The Guiding Principles on Internal Displacement further develop this duty of care towards the internally displaced population. Principle 18 requires that competent authorities must provide internally displaced persons with and ensure safe access to essential food and potable water, basic shelter and housing, appropriate clothing and essential medical services and sanitation.[42]

Complementary protection under IHRL and IHL

The cumulative application of international humanitarian law and human rights law considerably enhances the protection of individuals in armed conflict. With regard to living conditions in armed conflict, international humanitarian law explicitly prohibits starvation as a method of combat and imposes specific duties upon the belligerents. However, the value of such rules for all internally displaced persons in limited in several important respects. First, while the Fourth Convention and Protocol I contain a number of technical provisions detailing the obligations of the occupying power in terms of food, health, housing and clothing, they are only applicable 'to the fullest extent of the means available to it', and thus impose a duty of means rather than an absolute duty of result upon the occupying power, leaving it with a wide margin of appreciation as to the food and health needs of the occupied population. In addition, these provisions are only applicable in situations of occupation. Consequently, parties to an international armed conflict do not have similar duties of

[40] Pictet, *Commentary* (1958), p. 314.
[41] Geneva Convention IV, Art. 49(3) and Protocol II, Art. 17.
[42] Guiding Principles on Internal Displacement, Principle 18(1).

care towards their own population, including internally displaced persons. In an internal armed conflict, while the authorities in charge have a basic duty to ensure that displacement is carried out in satisfactory conditions of shelter, hygiene, health, safety and nutrition, this obligation is not complemented by the more detailed and comprehensive duties contained in Articles 55 and 56 of the Fourth Convention. Finally, as rightly noted by Sylvain Vité, although these rules set important basic requirements in terms of food, health, clothing and housing, 'they do not give precise indications about the objectives which have to be achieved'.[43]

Thus, international human rights law has an important role to play in the determination and formulation of states' obligations in terms of economic, social and cultural rights in time of armed conflict. More specifically, the duties of an occupying power in terms of health care or the provision of food should be interpreted in light of the right to health and the right to an adequate standard of living, as contained in the ICESCR.[44] Of particular relevance in this regard is the work of Committee on Economic, Social and Cultural Rights, especially the General Comments it issued in relation to each of the rights contained in the Covenant, which, although not legally binding, provide authoritative interpretations of these rights and a detailed and valuable understanding of states' obligations.[45]

It is worth noting that, as Special Rapporteur to the UN Commission on Human Rights on the Situation of Human Rights in Occupied Kuwait, Walter Kälin came to the conclusion that the destruction of the Kuwaiti health system by Iraqi occupying armed forces, which caused the death of elderly, handicapped and infant patients, was a violation not only of Articles 55 and 56 of the Fourth Geneva Convention, but also, and particularly, of the right to health, as guaranteed by Article 12 of the ICESCR. According to Kälin, the conclusion that the occupier had violated Articles 55 and 56 did not allow for a real assessment of the gravity and seriousness of these violations: 'The true significance of these events was only elucidated by recourse to the concept of the right to health as guaranteed by the Covenant on Economic, Social and Cultural Rights.'[46]

Moreover, the normative gap which exists in international humanitarian law with regard to the lack of explicit duties imposed on belligerents

[43] Vité, 'Interrelation of the law of occupation and economic, social and cultural rights', 2008, 637.
[44] Heintze, 'On the relationship between human rights law and international humanitarian law', 795.
[45] Lubell, 'Challenges in applying human rights', 2005, 751.
[46] Kälin, *Human Rights in Time of Occupation*, 1994, p. 28.

towards their own nationals is in part alleviated by the applicability of the core obligations of the right to an adequate standard of living, including adequate food, clothing and housing, and the right to the highest attainable standard of health, which are applicable in all circumstances.[47]

Relief and humanitarian assistance

As a general principle, the primary responsibility for the protection and assistance of internally displaced persons lies with each individual state.[48] In the context of an armed conflict, belligerents have a duty to ensure that the civilian population on their territory is adequately provided with food, medical supplies and other basic needs. However, if a party is unable or unwilling to fulfil this obligation, humanitarian access to the affected populations is essential. While a right to humanitarian assistance has not yet been explicitly recognized by human rights instruments,[49] international humanitarian law contains a number of provisions on humanitarian assistance and relief actions on behalf of civilians in armed conflict. These rules are particularly relevant for internally displaced persons caught up in war. Having fled from their homes, they are often gathered in camps, ignored by the state authorities, and continuously subjected to threats and attacks by both sides of the conflict. Living in deplorable conditions and with very little means of survival, they depend on international humanitarian assistance to survive. In 2005 in northern Uganda, for instance, 90 per cent of the population of the districts of Gulu, Pader and Kitgum was displaced, and over 1.45 million of the approximately 1.8 million internally displaced in northern Uganda relied almost entirely on external assistance for survival.[50]

The principle of humanitarian assistance to civilians in need

During an international armed conflict, Article 23 of the Fourth Convention, which deals with blockade situations, requires high contracting

47 The CESCR has stated in several General Comments that states parties to the ICESCR have a 'core obligation to ensure the satisfaction, or at the very least, minimum essential levels' of the right to an adequate standard of living, including adequate food, clothing and housing, and the right to the highest attainable standard of health, which are non-derogable. See, for instance, CESCR, 'General Comment No. 14, The right to the highest attainable standard of health', 11 August 2000, UN Doc. E/C.12/2000/4, para. 43.

48 Guiding Principles on Internal Displacement, Principle 3(1).

49 UNCHR, 'Compilation and Analysis of Legal Norms', para. 380.

50 UNSC, 'Report of the Secretary-General on the protection of civilians in armed conflict' (28 November 2005), S/2005/740, para. 18.

parties 'to allow the free passage of all consignments of medical and hospital stores' intended only for civilians of another state, even if this may be the adversary state. In addition, the belligerents must permit the free passage of all consignments of essential foodstuffs, clothing and tonics[51] intended for children under 15, expectant mothers and maternity cases, provided that a number of strict conditions are met.[52] This provision is generally considered as inadequate, as it only provides for transit of very limited categories of goods, under very restrictive conditions, and says nothing about a duty to provide or to accept relief.[53]

Article 70 of Protocol I, described as 'the new general regulation for *relief in non-occupied territories*',[54] considerably extends the rules of humanitarian assistance in international armed conflict. It states the basic principle that relief actions shall be undertaken if the civilian population of any territory under the control of a party to the conflict, other than occupied territory, is not adequately provided with basic supplies, including food, medical supplies and other items essential to their survival. In addition, when distributing relief, priority shall be given to children, expectant mothers, maternity cases and nursing mothers. As stated by a commentary on the Protocol, this priority provision has a twofold purpose:

> On the one hand, it is intended to ensure that the relief goes to the weakest parts of the population. This is the humanitarian aspect. On the other hand, it is intended to prevent civilian war labour forces and civilians who work closely with the Armed Forces getting priority in distribution, which would affect legitimate military interests of an adverse Party. This is the military aspect.[55]

The parties to the conflict and all states party to the Protocol must 'allow and facilitate rapid and unimpeded passage of all relief consignments, equipments and personnel'[56] and must 'encourage and facilitate effective international coordination of the relief actions'.[57] In addition, the party

[51] According to the ICRC commentary, 'essential foodstuffs' means 'basic foodstuffs, necessary to the health and normal physical and mental development of the persons for whom they are intended' while 'tonics' covers 'any pharmaceutical products which are intended to restore normal vitality in the human organism' (Pictet, *Commentary* (1958), pp. 180–1).

[52] According to Article 23(2), the obligation of a high contracting party to allow the free passage of consignments is subject to the condition that 'this Party shall be satisfied that there are no serious reasons for fearing: (a) that the consignments may be diverted from their destination; (b) that the control may not be effective; (c) that a definite advantage may accrue to the military efforts or economy of the enemy through the substitution of the . . . consignments for goods'.

[53] Bothe *et al.*, *New Rules for Victims of Armed Conflicts*, p. 426.

[54] *Ibid.*, p. 432.

[55] *Ibid.*, p. 435.

[56] Protocol I, Art. 70(2).

[57] Protocol I, Art. 70(5).

receiving the relief has a duty to protect relief consignments and facilitate their rapid distribution.[58]

International humanitarian law also provides for relief actions in favour of the civilian population in occupied territory.[59] If the whole or part of the population of an occupied territory is inadequately supplied, Article 59 of the Fourth Convention imposes a duty on the occupying power to agree relief schemes on behalf of the population, consisting, in particular, of the provision of consignments of foodstuffs, medical supplies and clothing. The obligation on the occupying power to accept collective relief is unconditional.[60] All states party to the Geneva Conventions must permit the free passage of these consignments and guarantee their protection. Furthermore, the occupying power has a duty to facilitate the relief schemes by all means at its disposal and must refrain from diverting relief consignments from their intended purposes, except in cases of urgent necessity, in the interests of the population of the occupied territory.[61] For instance, humanitarian aid specifically intended for displaced populations in IDP camps in occupied territory shall imperatively be directed at such populations. The occupying authorities have no discretionary power in this matter and may not divert the relief consignments, unless the diversion is due to urgent necessity, in the interests of a more vulnerable population in the occupied territory. In this case, the requirement of the consent of the protecting power is an essential safeguard against arbitrary and discriminatory judgments on the worth of the recipients of humanitarian aid.

Article 18(2) of Protocol II, which deals with the organization of humanitarian assistance in non-international armed conflict, similarly provides that:

> If the civilian population is suffering undue hardship owing to a lack of supplies essential for its survival, such as foodstuffs and medical supplies, relief actions for the civilian population which are of an exclusively humanitarian and impartial nature and which are conducted without any adverse distinction shall be undertaken subject to the consent of the High Contracting Party concerned.

Relief actions in international and non-international armed conflict must be humanitarian and impartial in character and conducted without any adverse distinction.[62] The humanitarian element of the relief action is

[58] Protocol I, Art. 70(4).
[59] Geneva Convention IV, Arts. 59–62 and Protocol II, Arts. 68, 69 and 71.
[60] Pictet, *Commentary* (1958), p. 320. [61] Geneva Convention IV, Art. 60.
[62] Protocol I, Art. 70(1) and Protocol II, Art. 8(2).

fulfilled once it is clear that the action is aimed at bringing relief to victims,[63] in this case internally displaced persons, in need of basic supplies. The relief action must also observe the principles of non-discrimination and impartiality. Both principles are intrinsically linked, and the impartial character of the relief action may be assumed on the basis of fulfilling the obligation to conduct the action 'without any adverse distinction'.[64] Thus, in this context, impartiality means that those providing the relief 'must resist any temptation to divert relief consignments or to favour certain groups or individuals rather than others because of personal preferences'.[65]

Denial of humanitarian assistance in armed conflict

In recent conflicts, humanitarian access to vulnerable populations has been consistently hindered by the parties to the conflict. As noted by the UN Secretary-General:

> In 1992 in Somalia, for instance, the parties to the conflict deliberately impeded the delivery of essential food and medical supplies, while during the siege of the enclaves in Bosnia and Herzegovina, civilians were systematically deprived of assistance necessary for their survival.[66]

Denial of humanitarian assistance can take several forms. The state concerned may prevent aid agencies from entering the country altogether, or refuse permission to access certain regions under the control of rebel forces.[67] An effective way of impeding humanitarian relief is to state that the security of aid workers cannot be guaranteed.[68] Humanitarian access may also simply be hindered by general conditions of insecurity.

In contemporary armed conflicts, in particular those of an internal character, civilians are increasingly targeted. Denial of humanitarian assistance thus forms part of a deliberate strategy of war, with the starvation of civilians as its ultimate aim. In addition, relief consignments may also be confiscated by belligerents for the benefit of their own forces, or looted by criminal gangs for the sole purpose of making profit.[69] In 2004, United Nations agencies were denied access to an estimated 10 million people in need of assistance and protection.[70] As a result, the plight of those

[63] Sandoz *et al.*, *Commentary on the Protocols*, p. 817. [64] *Ibid.* [65] *Ibid.*

[66] UNSC, 'Report of the Secretary-General on the protection of civilians in armed conflict' (8 September 1999) S/1999/957, para. 19.

[67] Rottensteiner, 'Denial of humanitarian assistance', 1999, 555. [68] *Ibid.* [69] *Ibid.*

[70] UNSC, 'Report of the Secretary-General on the protection of civilians in armed conflict' (2005), para. 6.

populations is further exacerbated and the consequences are often devastating. Internally displaced populations are particularly affected. They are under the responsibility of a state who is unable or unwilling to provide for their basic needs. In addition, as opposed to refugees, there is no established system of international protection and assistance for internally displaced persons. Consequently, the response to their needs has often been inconsistent and ineffective.[71] In 2005, an estimated one-third of the total 25 million internally displaced persons were effectively denied access to humanitarian assistance.[72] Considering the persistent denial of humanitarian aid to civilians in armed conflict, the relevant question is thus: do states and non-state actors have an obligation under international humanitarian law to accept humanitarian assistance to displaced persons and other victims of war?

The principle of consent of the parties concerned

According to Bothe *et al.*, '[t]he basic rule is that relief actions . . . "shall be undertaken"'.[73] Furthermore, Article 59 of the Fourth Convention states that the occupying power 'shall agree' to humanitarian relief. Consequently, states have an obligation to accept relief.[74] Nevertheless, international humanitarian law expressly requires the consent of the state concerned for the provision of humanitarian relief to civilians in need, both in international and non-international armed conflict. Article 70(1) of Protocol I stipulates that relief actions are 'subject to the agreement of the Parties concerned'. As stated in a commentary:

> the clause states the obvious. A person or an organization willing to undertake a relief action cannot just rush from one country through another country to a third country without asking the competent authorities for their permission.[75]

In accordance with Article 18 of Protocol II, humanitarian assistance must be 'subject to the consent of the high contracting party concerned', namely the government in power. However, in exceptional cases when it is not possible to determine who the authorities are, consent is to be presumed in view of the fact that assistance for the victims is of paramount

[71] UNSC, 'Report of the Secretary-General on the protection of civilians in armed conflict' (30 March 2001), S/2001/331, para. 22.
[72] UNSC, 'Report of the Secretary-General on the protection of civilians in armed conflict' (2005), para. 19.
[73] Bothe *et al.*, *New Rules for Victims of Armed Conflicts*, p. 433.
[74] Bothe, 'Relief actions', 1989, p. 92.
[75] Bothe *et al.*, *New Rules for Victims of Armed Conflicts*, p. 434.

importance and should not suffer any delay.[76] It is rather noteworthy that only the consent of the government in power is required, even if relief action is to be carried out in rebel-controlled territory. In practice however, there is no doubt that safe and unimpeded humanitarian access to civilian populations in rebel territory could not be guaranteed without the consent of the armed groups concerned. In addition, this also raises the question of whether the consent of the established government is necessary even in cases where the relief consignment does not pass through territory controlled by that government.[77] Bothe *et al.* emphasize the importance of the qualifier 'concerned' and argue that the established government, the 'high contracting party', is concerned only if it receives relief or grants transit for relief destined for the adverse party.[78] Thus, in theory, where the population in rebel-controlled territory is directly accessible, the consent of the state should not be required. However, the practice of donor states and international organizations show that humanitarian relief is very rarely provided in rebel-controlled areas without the prior consent of the state involved.[79]

Limitations on the right to refuse relief assistance

Nevertheless, the decision to accept or refuse relief actions is not left entirely to the discretion of the parties concerned. In this respect, the ICRC commentary on the Protocols explains that:

> If the survival of the population is threatened and a humanitarian organization fulfilling the conditions of impartiality and non-discrimination is able to remedy this situation, relief actions must take place.[80]

In 1995, the 26th International Conference of the Red Cross and the Red Crescent stressed the obligation of all parties to a conflict 'to accept, under the conditions prescribed by international humanitarian law, impartial humanitarian relief operations for the civilian population when it lacks

[76] Sandoz *et al.*, *Commentary on the Protocols*, p. 1479.
[77] Bothe *et al.*, *New Rules for Victims of Armed Conflicts*, p. 696.
[78] *Ibid.* This argument is based on a comparison between Article 18 Protocol II and Article 70(1) Protocol I. Indeed, with respect to Article 70, the 'Parties concerned' only consist of the state from whose territory the relief is being sent, the transit state and the receiving state. An adverse party to that receiving relief, but through whose territory relief consignments do not have to pass is not included (Sandoz *et al.*, *Commentary on the Protocols*, p. 819). See also Bothe, 'Relief actions', p. 94.
[79] Abril-Stoffels, 'Regulation of humanitarian assistance in armed conflict', 2004, 535.
[80] Sandoz *et al.*, *Commentary on the Protocols*, p. 1479.

supplies essential for its survival'.[81] Accordingly, the parties concerned may only refuse to give their consent to humanitarian assistance 'for valid reasons, not for arbitrary or capricious ones'.[82]

On the other hand, relief actions may legitimately be refused if they do not meet either of the conditions set out in Article 70 of Protocol I and Article 18 of Protocol II, namely that they should be 'humanitarian and impartial in character and conducted without any adverse distinction'. Valid reasons may also include imperative considerations of military necessity.[83] However, the provisions on humanitarian assistance should always be read in conjunction with Article 54 of Protocol I and Article 14 of Protocol II, which prohibit the use of starvation as a method of warfare.[84] In this regard, the ICRC commentary on the Second Protocol stresses that the prohibition on using starvation against civilians is a rule from which no derogation may be made, not even for imperative military reasons.[85] Consequently, the deliberate obstruction of humanitarian aid, in order to weaken the enemy by depriving the civilian population of food and other basic needs would be a violation of the prohibition of starvation as a method of warfare. In addition, 'wilfully impeding relief supplies' as part of the use of starvation of civilians as a method of warfare is a war crime in international armed conflict.[86]

Humanitarian assistance and the principle of non-intervention

The parties to a conflict often deny humanitarian access on the basis that it constitutes an unwanted interference in the conflict. Article 70(1) thus expressly stipulates that offers of relief shall not be regarded as 'interference in the armed conflict or as unfriendly acts'. This sentence is important, as it automatically excludes such arguments as reasons for refusing humanitarian aid. Although there is no such provision in Article 18 of the Second Protocol, Common Article 3 to the four Conventions suggests that 'an impartial body, such as the International Committee of the Red Cross, may offer its services to the Parties to the conflict'. Article 3 thus effectively acknowledges that an offer of humanitarian

81 ICRC, 26th International Conference of the Red Cross and the Red Crescent (Geneva, 3–7 December 1995), Resolution II – Protection of the civilian population in period of armed conflict, para. E(b).

82 Sandoz *et al.*, *Commentary on the Protocols*, p. 819.

83 Bothe mentions 'the case where the foreign relief personnel may hamper military operations or can be suspected of unneutral behaviour in favour of the other party to the conflict' ('Relief actions', p. 95).

84 Sandoz *et al.*, *Commentary on the Protocols*, pp. 819, 1479.

85 *Ibid.*, p. 1456.

86 ICC Statute, Art. 8(2)(b)(xxv).

assistance to victims of internal armed conflicts may no longer be seen by the parties to the conflict as an unfriendly act or an inadmissible attempt to interfere in the conflict.[87] Indeed, being essentially humanitarian and impartial in character, relief action cannot be seen as a hostile act and thus should not be qualified as such. This interpretation was confirmed by the International Court of Justice, regarding the 'humanitarian assistance' provided by the United States to the Contras in Nicaragua. In the *Case concerning military and paramilitary activities in and against Nicaragua*, the Court held that:

> There can be no doubt that the provision of strictly humanitarian aid to persons or forces in another country, whatever their political affiliations or objectives cannot be regarded as unlawful intervention, or as any other way contrary to international law.[88]

The Court also underlined the paramount importance of the principles of humanity, impartiality and neutrality in the provision of humanitarian aid. In this respect, the Court stated that:

> In the view of the Court, if the provision of humanitarian assistance is to escape condemnation as an intervention in the internal affairs of Nicaragua, not only must it be limited to the purposes hallowed in the practice of the Red Cross, namely 'to prevent and alleviate human suffering', and 'to protect life and health and to ensure respect for the human being'; it must also, and above all, be given without discrimination to all in need in Nicaragua, not merely to the *contras* and their dependents.[89]

Accordingly, the Court concluded that the activities of the United States in relation to the activities of the Contras constituted 'prima facie acts of intervention' in the internal affairs of Nicaragua.

The provisions of international humanitarian law on humanitarian assistance are of great significance for the protection of internally displaced persons in armed conflict. Indeed, as they do not benefit from an international system of protection and assistance, internally displaced persons are specifically concerned by these provisions and are entirely dependent on their full respect by the parties to the conflict for their survival. Internally displaced persons, like any other victim of war, have a right, under international humanitarian law, to receive humanitarian assistance. When they are unable or unwilling to provide for the

[87] Pictet, *Commentary on the Geneva Conventions*, 1952, p. 58.
[88] *Military and paramilitary activities in and against Nicaragua*, para. 242.
[89] *Ibid.*, para. 243.

basic needs of the populations under their control, parties to an international or non-international conflict have a duty to allow and facilitate rapid and unimpeded humanitarian relief, which is impartial in character and conducted without any adverse distinction, subject to their right of control.[90]

Family unity and displacement

During displacement, the preservation of family unity is essential for the well-being of displaced persons. The importance of family life is upheld in international human rights[91] and humanitarian law.[92] Similarly, the principle of the unity of the family has been affirmed by the UNHCR Executive Committee in a number of conclusions in the context of refugee protection.[93]

In application of the principle of respect for family life, international humanitarian law stipulates that members of the same family shall not be separated from one another during the evacuation of a given area in occupied territory.[94] Nevertheless, families often get dispersed as a result of armed conflict and displacement. Children are particularly vulnerable and at risk of neglect, violence, forced recruitment, sexual assault and other abuses when separated from their family.[95] In the Great Lakes region, following the conflict in Rwanda in 1994, more than 100,000 children were registered as unaccompanied, both inside and outside their countries of origin.[96]

Accordingly, international humanitarian law contains a number of provisions aimed at the reunification of families dispersed by war. First, family members should know the fate and whereabouts of their missing

90 Henckaerts and Doswald-Beck, *Customary International Humanitarian Law*, vol. 1, Rule 55, p. 193.

91 UDHR, Art. 16(3), ICCPR, Art. 23(1) and ACHR, Art. 11(1) declare that: 'The family is the natural and fundamental group unit of society and is entitled to protection by society and the State'. ECHR, Art. 8(1) states that: 'Everyone has the right to respect for his private and family life.'

92 Geneva Convention IV, Arts. 25, 26 27(1), 49(3), 82(2) and Protocol I, Arts. 74, 75(5), 77(4).

93 E.g. EXCOM Conclusion No. 9 (XXVIII) – 1977 on family reunion, and EXCOM Conclusion No. 24 (XXXII) – 1981 on family reunification, which states that: 'In application of the Principle of the unity of the family and for obvious humanitarian reasons, every effort should be made to ensure the reunification of separated refugee families.'

94 Geneva Convention IV, Art. 49(3).

95 UNGA, 'Report of the expert of the Secretary-General, Ms Graça Machel: impact of armed conflict on children' (26 August 1996), A/51/306, para. 69.

96 *Ibid.*

relatives. Second, dispersed family members should also be able to communicate with each other and exchange family news, and ultimately be reunited.

The right to know the fate and whereabouts of family members

During displacement, families are split up and loved ones go missing, due to the confusion and disorder reigning at the time. Separated from the rest of their families, displaced persons often do not know if their relatives have arrived in another location or camp, or if they have died during their flight.[97] Human rights law in this regard has mostly developed in the context of enforced disappearances and is not directly applicable to the incidental disappearance of a family member during displacement.[98] In contrast, international humanitarian law has developed an important body of rules relating to the missing and the right of families to know the fate of their relatives.[99]

In accordance with Article 32 of the First Protocol, families have a right to know the fate of their relatives. In order to guarantee this right, parties to a conflict must take all feasible measures to search and transmit information about missing persons.[100] In the context of international humanitarian law, 'missing persons' shall be understood to mean 'those whose whereabouts are unknown to their families and/or who, on the basis of reliable information, have been reported missing in connection with an international or non-international armed conflict'.[101]

In addition, Article 34 provides in particular that gravesites must be marked in such a way that they can be located and recognized by relatives of the deceased. However, as mentioned in the ICRC commentary on Article 32, these provisions do not impose obligations on a state with respect to its own nationals.[102] Moreover, Article 33 only imposes an obligation on the parties to a conflict to search for 'persons who have been reported missing by an adverse Party'. Persons to be searched for should be nationals of the adverse party, in particular 'combatants from whom there has been no news, or civilians in occupied territory or enemy territory'.[103] Thus, as nationals of a belligerent power, internally displaced

97 OCHA, *Handbook for Applying the Guiding Principles*, p. 33.

98 Gulick, 'Protection of family life', 2010, p. 308.

99 Kälin, *Human Rights in Time of Occupation*, p. 28.

100 Protocol I, Art. 33.

101 ICRC Advisory Service, 'Missing persons and their families' (October 2003), www.icrc.org/web/eng/siteeng0.nsf/htmlall/section_ihl_missing_persons?OpenDocument (accessed 17 September 2007).

102 Sandoz et al., *Commentary on the Protocols*, p. 346.

103 *Ibid.*, p. 351.

persons are excluded from the application of this article. Nevertheless, both Article 16 of the Fourth Convention and Article 8 of Protocol II oblige parties to an international or non-international armed conflict to search for and collect the wounded and sick, irrespective of their nationality. In addition, Article 26 of the Fourth Convention, which applies to the whole civilian population in international armed conflict, requires each party to the conflict to 'facilitate enquiries made by members of families dispersed owing to war'. Accordingly, these provisions lay down an implicit duty to transmit information about missing persons to their relatives, regardless of their nationality.[104]

Consequently, the duty of the parties to a conflict to facilitate enquiries about the whereabouts of family members seems to imply the existence of a correlated right of dispersed families to know the fate of their relatives during displacement, at least during international armed conflict. Moreover, according to the Red Cross commentary, the recognition of such a right in international armed conflicts 'should have further repercussions, particularly with regard to the families of missing persons in non-international armed conflicts and in the framework of human rights, even during internal disturbances or tensions'.[105] The 2005 ICRC study on customary international humanitarian law found that the duty of belligerents to 'take all feasible measures to account for persons reported missing as a result of armed conflict and [to] provide their family members with any information it has on their fate' was a customary rule of international humanitarian law, applicable in international and non-international armed conflicts.[106]

In a 1974 resolution, the UN General Assembly stated that 'the desire to know the fate of loved ones lost in armed conflicts is a basic human need which should be satisfied to the greatest extent possible'.[107] In addition, referring to both international humanitarian law and human rights law, the UN General Assembly and the Human Rights Council have both recognized 'the right of families to know the fate of their relatives reported missing in connection with armed conflicts'.[108] Furthermore, human

104 Kälin, *Guiding Principles on Internal Displacement: Annotations*, p. 39.

105 Sandoz *et al.*, *Commentary on the Protocols*, p. 346, fn. 19.

106 Henckaerts and Doswald-Beck, *Customary International Humanitarian Law*, vol. 1, Rule 117, p. 421.

107 UNGA Resolution 3220(XXIX), 6 November 1974, preambular para. 8, as quoted in Henckaerts and Doswald-Beck, *Customary International Humanitarian Law*, vol. 1, p. 424.

108 UNGA Resolution 63/183, 'Missing persons', 17 March 2009, UN Doc. A/RES/63/183, para. 3; HRC Resolution 7/28, 28 March 2008, UN Doc. A/HRC/RES/7/28, para. 3.

rights-monitoring bodies now recognize a general right to be informed about the fate of missing relatives, as well as a correlative duty of states to investigate cases of disappearances, not only in situations of enforced disappearance, but also in cases of persons missing in the context of an armed conflict. In a case involving the relatives of Greek Cypriots who went missing during the invasion of Cyprus by Turkish forces in 1974, the European Court of Human Rights held that failure by the Turkish authorities to investigate the circumstances surrounding the disappearance of the missing persons and the continuing suffering of their families amounted to inhuman treatment within the meaning of Article 3 ECHR.[109]

The situation of missing people in armed conflict is a clear illustration of mutual complementarity between human rights and humanitarian law. Indeed, the detailed rules of international humanitarian law relating to the missing and the right of families to know the fate of their relatives have clearly and effectively reinforced the very general protection under international human rights law in this regard.[110] However, once again the limitation of the application of the Geneva Conventions and Protocol I to 'protected persons' highlights the existence of a normative gap in the protection of IDPs under international humanitarian law and the important role played by human rights bodies and the Guiding Principles on Internal Displacement in filling this gap.

Family reunification

International humanitarian law imposes specific and detailed obligations upon the belligerents in international and non-international conflict in order to facilitate the reunification of dispersed families.

Family members separated by armed conflict and displacement should be able to communicate with each other. Article 25 of the Fourth Convention enables persons living in a country at war to give and receive family news of a strictly personal nature, wherever they may be. In his commentary, Pictet observes that 'The right to give his family news of a personal nature and to receive personal news from them is one of the inalienable rights of man. It must be respected fully without reservations.'[111]

For this reason, this right belongs to the whole population of the countries engaged in the armed conflict,[112] including internally displaced

[109] *Case of Cyprus* v. *Turkey* (Application No. 25781/94), Judgment, 10 May 2001, para. 157.
[110] Kälin, *Human Rights in Time of Occupation*, p. 28.
[111] Pictet, *Commentary* (1958), p. 192. [112] *Ibid.*

persons. The Convention obliges parties to the conflict to forward such correspondence 'speedily and without undue delay'. Furthermore, Article 26 of the Fourth Convention, which is directly concerned with the plight of dispersed families, states that:

> Each Party to the conflict shall facilitate enquiries made by members of families dispersed owing to the war, with the object of renewing contact with one another and of meeting if possible.

While this provision is particularly relevant for displaced persons, it should be noted that it is only concerned with the re-establishing of family ties and therefore applies solely to members of dispersed families, not to all displaced persons.[113] The belligerents have an obligation of means; they must 'facilitate enquiries' about family members. According to the commentary, such duty would entail, for example, the organization of official information bureaux and centres,[114] notification by postal authorities of changes of address and possible places of evacuation, the arranging of broadcasts and the granting of facilities for forwarding requests for information and the replies.[115] In addition, Article 26 requires the parties to the conflict to encourage the work of organizations engaged in the task of reuniting family members.

In 1976, it was considered appropriate to go slightly further by urging governments to facilitate not only enquiries made by family members, but also the reunion of dispersed families.[116] Thus, Article 74 of the First Protocol reads:

> The high contracting parties and the Parties to the conflict shall facilitate in every possible way the reunion of families dispersed as a result of armed conflicts and shall encourage in particular the work of humanitarian organizations engaged in this task in accordance with the provisions of the Conventions and of this Protocol and in conformity with their respective security regulations.

[113] *Ibid.*, p. 196

[114] The Convention expressly provides for the establishment of official Information Bureaux and of a Central Information Agency (Geneva Convention IV, Arts. 136–141).

> Each party to the conflict shall establish an official Information Bureau responsible for receiving information and transmitting information in respect of protected persons who are in its power. Furthermore, a Central Information Agency shall be created in a neutral country to receive and transmit to their country or origin or residence any information obtained on protected persons. However, the Bureaux and Agency are only competent to deal with matters regarding protected persons. They are not responsible for information concerning a belligerent power's own nationals, unless the parties to the conflict have decided otherwise. (Pictet, *Commentary* (1958), p. 197)

[115] *Ibid.*, pp. 196–7.

[116] Sandoz *et al.*, *Commentary on the Protocols*, p. 859.

This article develops Article 26 of the Fourth Convention. The main innovation of Article 74 is that it also imposes a duty to facilitate the reunion of families on high contracting parties not involved in the conflict. This is quite logical, since many nationals of a country at war will seek refuge in a neutral country.[117] As Article 74 reaffirms and develops Article 26, it also applies to the whole civilian population, including a state's own nationals affected by the armed conflict.[118] International humanitarian law also addresses the fate of unaccompanied children. Article 24 of the Fourth Convention requires parties to the conflict to take the necessary measures to identify and protect children under 15, who are orphaned or separated from their families as a result of the war, and ensure that they are not left to their own resources. The belligerents must also facilitate the reception of these children in a neutral country for the duration of the conflict, with the consent of the protecting power, if any. In situations of non-international armed conflict, Article 4(3) of Protocol II lays down a general principle of protection for children. In particular, subparagraph (b) requires belligerents to take 'all appropriate steps' in order to 'facilitate the reunion of families temporarily separated'. Accordingly, parties to an internal armed conflict should not only allow members of dispersed families to undertake searches, but they should also facilitate them.[119]

Although international human rights law recognizes the importance of family life and family unity, it does not envisage an express right to family reunification.[120] International humanitarian law, on the other hand, explicitly provides for the reunification of families dispersed by armed conflict. Dispersed family members have a right to know the fate of their missing relatives and belligerents have the duty to enable, as far as possible, separated family members to communicate with each other and to facilitate their reunion. The Central Tracing Agency and national information bureaux are essential tools for the centralization of information, transmission of family news and the reunification of dispersed families, and should be envisaged in all situations of displacement as a result of armed conflict. In practice, the ICRC sets up and coordinates a network for the restoration of family links, in regions directly affected by conflict and those receiving displaced persons and refugees.[121] In all cases of

[117] *Ibid.* [118] Bothe *et al.*, *New Rules for Victims of Armed Conflicts*, p. 452.

[119] Sandoz *et al.*, *Commentary on the Protocols*, p. 1379.

[120] Gulick, 'Protection of family life', p. 308.

[121] ICRC, 'War and family links: a general overview', www.icrc.org/web/eng/siteeng0.nsf/html/57JQRA (accessed 4 November 2011).

war-related displacement, displaced persons shall be entitled to know the fate of their relatives, to give and receive family news and to be reunited with their loved ones, regardless of their nationality, whether they fled within or across borders and whether the armed conflict was of an international or internal character.

7 International humanitarian law and the protection of refugee and IDP camps

Introduction: armed attacks on refugee and IDP camps

The issue

On 13 August 2004 a group of armed combatants of the Forces pour la Libération Nationale, a predominantly Hutu rebel movement, entered Gatumba refugee camp in Burundi, and massacred or wounded hundreds of refugees.[1] The large majority of victims were ethnic Tutsi Congolese, commonly referred to as Banyamulenge.

Military and armed attacks on refugee camps and settlements are a relatively new phenomenon, which first came to public attention in the 1970s, with the attack by South African armed forces on the refugee camp of Kassinga in Angola, on 4 May 1978.[2] This phenomenon is further exacerbated by the internal nature of contemporary armed conflicts, whose violence and cruelty typically generate massive movements of populations into neighbouring countries. Such large-scale refugee flows often comprise mixed populations of genuine refugees and armed elements, thereby constituting a potential target for attacks and an increased threat to national security and regional stability. The Great Lakes refugee crisis (1994–6), the militarization of Rwandan refugee camps in eastern Zaire and the subsequent massacres of Hutu refugees during the first Congo War bear witness to the gravity of the problem.

The issue of physical security in camps does not only affect refugees. Internally displaced persons are constantly subjected to threats, harassment and attacks, on the part of both rebel groups and the government

[1] HRW, 'Burundi: the Gatumba massacre, war crimes and political agendas' (September 2004), http://hrw.org/backgrounder/africa/burundi/2004/0904 (accessed 24 October 2011).

[2] Othman-Chande, 'Armed attacks in refugee camps', 1990, 153.

forces of their own country. In the Sudanese province of Darfur, IDP camps have been the object of violent attacks by the government-backed militias, known as the 'Janjaweed'.[3] Similarly in northern Uganda, which has been torn apart by conflict since 1986, Joseph Kony's Lord's Resistance Army (LRA) regularly targets IDPs living in camps. As noted by the OCHA:

> Although the camps were initially created to protect civilians from rebel attacks, they have now become just as much of a target for these attacks as the villages once were. As the Acholi people have been forced to crowd together in camp, so the LRA, in their search for food and slaves, have followed them.[4]

Attacks on refugee and IDP camps may take various forms. Displaced persons may get caught in the crossfire of enemy parties, due to the proximity of the camps to combat zones.[5] However, more often than not, displaced persons are directly targeted. Direct attacks may involve aerial bombardments[6] or cross-border raids for the purpose of forced repatriation or hot pursuits by the refugees' country of origin or its agents.[7] In 1998, Burmese refugees in Thailand suffered a series of punitive raids carried out by the Burmese Army and allied militia groups.[8] In April 2007, refugees on the Thai border faced renewed threats as the government-backed ethnic Karen militias appeared to be positioning artillery and heavy machine guns overlooking the Mae La refugee camp.[9] Attacks on camps may also take the form of military raids by the forces of the host

[3] HRW, 'Empty promises? Continuing abuses in Darfur, Sudan' (August 11, 2004), http://hrw.org/backgrounder/africa/sudan/2004 (accessed 24 October 2011); AI, 'Sudan, Darfur: "too many people killed for no reason"' (3 February 2004), AI Index: AFR 54/008/2004.

[4] OCHA IRIN News, 'Crisis in northern Uganda' (September 2003), www.irinnews.org/InDepthMain.aspx?InDepthId=23&ReportId=65778 (accessed 24 October 2011).

[5] In 1998, HRW expressed concern for the fate of some 32,000 Sierra Leonean refugees in one camp in Lofa County, Liberia, who faced serious security threats due to their proximity to the border where fighting was taking place ('Human Rights Watch expresses concern for the fate of Sierra Leonean refugees in Liberia' (June 18, 1998), http://hrw.org/english/docs/1998/06/18/liberi1164.htm (accessed 25 October 2011).

[6] E.g., repeated bombing by Rhodesian forces on Zimbabwean refugee camps in Manica province, Mozambique, August 1976 and December 1977 (Mtango, 'Attacks on refugee camps', 1990, p. 93).

[7] E.g., incursions by the armed forces of Burundi into refugee-populated areas of Tanzania, in order to apprehend combatants and 'subversives' (Crisp, 'Africa's refugees', 2000).

[8] HRW, 'Human Rights Watch condemns attack on Burmese refugee camps' (11 March 1998), http://hrw.org/english/docs/1998/03/11/burma1075.htm (accessed 24 October 2011).

[9] HRW, 'Burma: army and its proxies threaten refugee camps – Thailand should protect refugees and civilians fleeing conflict' (14 April 2007), http://hrw.org/english/docs/2007/04/14/burma15691.htm (accessed 24 October 2011).

country,[10] or armed raids by rebel groups for their resources, such as food and medical supplies, or for the purposes of forced recruitment[11] or reprisals.

The search for a legal basis for the prohibition of armed attacks on refugee and IDP camps

The physical security of displaced persons is first and foremost the responsibility of the state of asylum or, in the case of internally displaced persons, their own state. National laws of the host country are therefore the primary legal basis for the protection of the physical security of displaced persons. As it stands today, international law does not specifically address the issue of military and armed attacks on refugee camps. Certain rules and provisions with some relevance to the subject can be found in a number of international instruments, but there is no international instrument entirely dedicated to the protection of refugees and IDPs from military and armed attacks. Indeed, because of the relatively recent character of armed attacks on camps, the 1951 Refugee Convention does not include provisions on the physical security of refugees. The issue was later addressed in regional instruments, such as the 1969 OAU Convention.[12] In relation to internally displaced persons, the 1998 Guiding Principles on Internal Displacement expressly provide, in Principle 10(2), that:

> Attacks or other acts of violence against internally displaced persons who do not or no longer participate in hostilities are prohibited in all circumstances. Internally displaced persons shall be protected, in particular, against:
>
> (d) Attacks against their camps or settlements;

The UNHCR has been working on the development of a legal framework for the protection of refugee camps and settlements for over thirty years, ever since it first condemned armed attacks on refugee camps in Southern Africa in 1979.[13] In 1983, former UN Commissioner for Refugees, Felix

[10] In August 1985, the military forces of Honduras carried out a violent attack on the Salvadoran refugee camp of Colomoncagua, Honduras, in search of refugees engaged in subversive activities (Mtango, 'Attacks on refugee camps', p. 96).

[11] In Côte d'Ivoire, Liberian refugees, including children, are forcibly recruited by armed opposition groups and even by government forces (AI, 'No escape, Liberian refugees in Côte d'Ivoire' (24 June 2003)).

[12] Recognizing that the physical safety of refugees depends on the demilitarization of refugee camps, Article 3 of the 1969 OAU Refugee Convention is entirely dedicated to the prohibition of subversive activities.

[13] UNHCR EXCOM Conclusion No. 14 (XXX) (1979).

Schnyder, submitted a proposal for a draft declaration on the prohibition of military or armed attacks against refugee camps and settlements to be submitted for adoption to the UN General Assembly.[14] The declaration, which proclaimed that 'camps and settlements accommodating refugees shall not be the object of military or armed attacks', drew upon existing principles of international human rights and refugee law, the law of armed conflicts and the general principles of international law. Despite the initial enthusiasm for the report, Members of the Executive Committee struggled to reach an agreement on the declaration, as it soon became obvious that political and strategic considerations prevailed over humanitarian concern.[15] Eventually in 1987, the Executive Committee adopted Conclusion No. 48 (XXXVIII), which merely condemned 'all violations of the rights and safety of refugees and asylum-seekers and in particular military or armed attacks on refugee camps and settlements', thus leaving unanswered the question of the legal basis of the prohibition.

The issue of the prohibition of armed attacks on camps has also been addressed in the literature,[16] particularly in relation to the protection of refugees and the fundamental principle of the civilian and humanitarian character of asylum. The militarization of refugee and IDP camps and the presence of armed elements among the civilian population seriously compromise the civilian character of the camps and endanger the life and security of their inhabitants. Indeed, militarized camps may more readily prompt attacks from the refugees' country of origin, armed bands or even regular forces of the host country. Consequently, most discussions on the prohibition of armed attacks on refugee camps and settlements have revolved around the duty of the state of asylum to separate armed elements from genuine refugees in order to preserve the civilian and humanitarian character of refugee camps.[17] The host state's duty to

[14] EXCOM, 'Report by Ambassador Felix Schnyder on military attacks on refugee camps and settlements in Southern Africa and elsewhere', Annex: Draft Declaration on the prohibition of military or armed attacks against refugee camps or settlements (15 March 1983), Doc. No. EC/SCP/26.

[15] Mtango, 'Attacks on refugee camps', p. 98.

[16] The most thorough study on the subject is the work of Mtango, which provides a detailed account on the relevant principles of international law for the protection of refugees from military and armed attacks. Further studies include Othman-Chande, 'Armed attacks in refugee camps'; G. Coles, 'Informal note on the problem of military attacks on refugee camps', UNHCR Doc. (on my file).

[17] Mtango, 'Armed attacks on refugee camps'; Othman-Chande, 'International law and armed attacks in refugee camps'; Beyani, 'International legal criteria', 2000, 251; Da Costa, 'Maintaining the civilian and humanitarian character of asylum', 2004.

separate may be derived from principles of international refugee law,[18] the law of neutrality[19] and the UN Charter prohibition of the use of force.[20]

However, the issue has rarely been explored in relation with international humanitarian law.[21] Yet, many attacks against refugee and IDP camps have been carried out during international or internal armed conflicts. Alternatively, military activities fomented inside the camps may provoke an armed conflict with the state of origin or the host state.[22] In both contexts, international humanitarian law applies. The principles and rules regulating the conduct of hostilities, and the principle of civilian immunity in particular, should thus provide significant protection against attacks.[23] Moreover, these rules are of particular significance for internally displaced persons in situations of armed conflict, whose lives and physical security depend solely on IHL for their protection.

[18] The duty of the state of asylum to separate armed elements from genuine refugees is articulated explicitly in Article 3(2) of the OAU Refugee Convention, which places a duty on state parties to prohibit refugees living on their territory from attacking any other member state, 'by any activity likely to cause tension between Member States, and in particular by use of arms, through the press, or by radio'. Article 9 of the 1951 refugee convention may also provide a legal basis for a right (as opposed to an obligation) of asylum states to separate and intern combatants and armed elements (Beyani, 'International legal criteria', 259–65).

[19] Article 11 of the Fifth Hague Convention of 1907 respecting the rights and duties of neutral powers and persons in case of war on land places a duty on the neutral power which receives troops on its territory troops to 'intern them, as far as possible, at a distance from the theatre of war. It may keep them in camps and even confine them in fortresses or in places set apart for this purposes.'

[20] Indeed, as noted during the UNHCR Global Consultations on international protection: 'When persons engaged in armed conflict cross an international border without genuinely having laid down their arms, they are deemed to be carrying out a military agenda. Allowing the pursuit of such an agenda is inconsistent with the obligations of member states to maintain international peace and security, and friendly relations between States, as defined in the Charter and the United Nations General Assembly resolutions' ('The civilian character of asylum: separating armed elements form refugees' (1st meeting, 19 February 2001), EC/GC/01/5).

[21] Korsinik, 'Protection des camps de réfugiés', 1984, pp. 387–93.

[22] The International Institute of Humanitarian Law (IIHL) in cooperation with the ICRC, XXVIIth Round Table on Current Problems of International Humanitarian Law, 'International humanitarian law and other legal regimes: interplay in situations of violence' (summary report, 23 November 2003), 9, www.icrc.org/eng/assets/files/other/irrc_851_kellenberger.pdf (accessed 1 November 2011).

[23] For the purpose of the study, the term 'attacks' should be understood as 'acts of violence against the adversary, whether in offence or in defence', within the meaning of Article 49 Protocol I.

The fundamental principle of civilian immunity and the prohibition of attacks on refugee and IDP camps

While international humanitarian law deals with certain issues facing refugees in armed conflicts,[24] it does not address the specific problem of armed attacks on refugee and IDP camps. However, as civilians, refugees and IDPs benefit from the general protection granted to the civilian population against the effect of hostilities. The regulation of the conduct of hostilities in armed conflict will thus form the legal basis from which to derive a general prohibition on attacks on refugee and IDP camps.

The conduct of hostilities is governed by the cardinal principle that the parties to a conflict do not have an unlimited choice of means and methods of warfare.[25] Article 48 of Protocol I lays down the basic rule of the law of armed conflict, according to which:

> In order to ensure respect for and protection of the civilian population and civilian objects, the Parties to the conflict shall at all times distinguish between the civilian population and combatants and between civilian objects and military objectives and accordingly shall direct their operations only against military objectives.

Also known as the principle of distinction, this customary rule of international humanitarian law is applicable in international and non-international armed conflicts.[26] It is supplemented by two fundamental principles of international humanitarian law: the prohibition on direct attacks on civilians and civilian objects and the prohibition of indiscriminate attacks. In addition, in accordance with the principle of proportionality, even military objectives may not be attacked if the attack is expected to cause civilian casualties or damage which would be excessive in relation to the concrete and direct military advantage anticipated.[27] In its 1996 Advisory Opinion on the *Legality of the Threat or Use of Nuclear Weapons*, the ICJ qualified the above-mentioned principles as 'the cardinal principles . . . constituting the fabric of humanitarian law'.[28] It further added that 'these fundamental rules are to be observed by all States whether or not they have ratified the conventions that contain them, because they constitute intransgressible principles of international customary law'.[29]

[24] See above Chapter 5. [25] Protocol I, Art. 35.

[26] Henckaerts and Doswald-Beck, *Customary International Humanitarian Law*, vol. 1, Rules 1 and 7, pp. 3, 15.

[27] Protocol I, Arts. 51(5) and 57(2)(a)(iii).

[28] *Legality of the Threat or Use of Nuclear Weapons*, para. 78. [29] *Ibid.*, para. 79.

Furthermore, belligerents must always act in accordance with the fundamental principle of humanity, as stated in Common Article 3 to the Four Geneva Conventions, which constitutes a 'minimum yardstick' in the event of non-international, as well as international conflicts.[30]

Refugee and IDP camps are regularly targeted for attacks by rebels and government forces. Justifications commonly advanced by belligerents include the militarization of the camps and the presence of combatants within the civilian refugee population, thus depriving them of their immunity. Belligerents also often invoke the proximity of the camps near dangerous zones of combats or the killing of civilians as lawful collateral damage. In addition, armed raids on camps for the purpose of forced recruitment are common practice, particularly in countries torn by civil wars. It will be argued that the fundamental principles of international humanitarian law governing the conduct of hostilities should provide refugees and internally displaced persons with adequate protection against attacks, as long as they do not take any active part in the hostilities.

Direct and deliberate attacks on refugee and IDP camps

Camps for displaced persons are often the object of direct and deliberate attacks, particularly in civil wars, where armed groups target the camps in order to access their resources, abduct or forcibly recruit civilians and terrorize the population. In northern Uganda for instance, the LRA regularly attack 'protected villages' of internally displaced persons, suspected of being against the LRA and pro-government.[31] Similarly, there have been many reports of Janjaweed attacks on camps for internally displaced persons in western Darfur[32] and recently across the border, in eastern Chad.[33]

Both additional protocols expressly prohibit the deliberate targeting of civilians.[34] In addition, Article 52(1) Protocol I provides that '[c]ivilian

30 *Military and paramilitary activities in and against Nicaragua*, para. 218.

31 HRW, 'Abducted and abused: renewed conflict in northern Uganda' (July 2003), HRW Index No. A1512.

32 In 2005 for instance, UNHCR reported 'an unprecedented attack' by a group of 250–300 armed Arab men on a camp for thousands of internally displaced persons, that reportedly left 29 people dead and another 10 seriously wounded ('UNHCR gravely concerned over attack on Darfur' (29 September 2005), www.unhcr.org/cgi-bin/texis/vtx/news/opendoc.htm?tbl=NEWS&id=433bf1004 (accessed 25 October 2011).

33 UNSC, 'Report of the Secretary-General on Chad and the Central African Republic' (23 February 2007), S/2007/97, para. 28.

34 Protocol I, Art. 51(2); Protocol II, Art. 13(2): 'The civilian population as such, as well as individual civilians, shall not be the object of attack. Acts or threats of violence the

objects shall not be the object of attack'. The prohibition of direct attacks on civilians and civilian objects is a fundamental principle of customary international law, binding on all parties to a conflict, both states and non-state actors alike. Article 85 of the First Protocol qualifies as a grave breach of the Protocol the act of wilfully making the civilian population or individual civilians the object of attack if it causes death or serious injury to body or health. Similarly, the intentional direct attack against the civilian population as such or against individual civilians not taking direct part in hostilities is a war crime in both international and non-international armed conflict.[35]

Additional Protocol I prohibits attacks against the civilian population, civilians or civilian objects by way of reprisals in international armed conflicts.[36] However, as Solf explains, this prohibition breaks new grounds and thus cannot be considered as a reaffirmation of customary law.[37] Indeed, Article 33(3) of the Fourth Geneva Convention prohibits reprisals against 'protected civilians', namely civilians who are in the hands of a party of which they are not nationals. Civilians under the control of their own state, including internally displaced persons, are not protected against reprisals under the Geneva Conventions.[38] Consequently, the prohibition of reprisals against the civilian population as a whole will only be binding on states party to the First Protocol. Protocol II does not contain a similar provision applicable in internal armed conflicts, but collective punishments against civilians in internal armed conflicts are expressly prohibited under Article 4(2)(b). In the ICRC's view, 'to include the prohibition of collective punishments amongst the acts unconditionally prohibited by Article 4 is virtually equivalent to prohibiting "reprisals" against protected persons'.[39]

In northern Uganda, the attacks perpetrated by the LRA against IDP camps were deliberately targeted. Rebel leader, Joseph Koni, was said to feel that the Acholi population needed to be 'punished' for having turned their back on the LRA.[40] These attacks constitute a blatant violation of

primary purpose of which is to spread terror among the civilian population is prohibited.'

35 ICC Statute, Arts. 8(2)(b)(i) and (e)(i).

36 Protocol I, Arts. 51(6), 52(1).

37 Solf, 'Protection of civilians against the effects of hostilities', 1986, 131.

38 *Ibid.*

39 Sandoz *et al.*, *Commentary on the Protocols*, p. 1374.

40 Willet Weeks, 'Pushing the envelope: moving beyond "protected villages" in northern Uganda', report submitted to the UN Office for the Coordination of Humanitarian Affairs (March 2002), www.internal-displacement.org/8025708F004CE90B/(httpDocuments)/328D3C51889A4384802570B7005A55F3/$file/Weeks+march+2002.pdf (accessed 26 October 2011).

the laws of war. No attempt was made to deny or justify them. They were carried out in complete disregard for human life and for the sole purpose of punishment. However, in most cases of attacks on refugee or IDP camps, the perpetrators are anxious to explain their actions. In the case of cross-border raids in particular, states will often try to justify the attacks as the exercise of their right of 'anticipatory self-defence'[41] or their right of 'hot pursuit'.[42] As these arguments pertain to the realm of *jus ad bellum*, they will not be considered in the present study. Nevertheless, the militarization of camps and the presence of armed elements among the civilian displaced population are common *jus in bello* justifications, the value of which will be addressed below.

Militarization of refugee and IDP camps and the fundamental principle of distinction

The perpetrators of attacks against refugee or IDP camps often argue that the presence of armed elements within the camp compromises its civilian and humanitarian nature and, consequently, its immunity under international humanitarian law. Moreover, belligerents may also contend that civilian casualties in refugee or IDP camps are the incidental result of legitimate attacks against military objectives. For the sake of clarity, it is useful the recount the events of one of the most notorious cases of attacks against refugees in the context of an armed conflict.

Case study: attacks on Rwandan refugee camps in Zaire

Following the 1994 Rwandan genocide, an estimated 1.2 million Rwandans sought refuge in Zaire (now the Democratic Republic of Congo, or DRC), where they settled in large camps in the Kivu provinces, along the eastern border.[43] In the camps, refugees intermingled with *génocidaires* of the former regime. Despite appeals from the UNHCR and the Rwandan

[41] On 2 December 1975, 30 Israeli aircraft attacked three major Palestinian refugee camps in northern and southern Lebanon, killing more than 80 Palestinian refugees and injuring a further 117. Israel justified its actions as the exercise of its inherent right of self-defence, qualifying the raid as a 'preventive action'. Israel's arguments have been systematically rejected by the members of the Security Council. The raid against Palestinian camps in 1975 was widely condemned by the international community. All members of the Security Council condemned the attack. See 29 *UNYB* (1975), 226.

[42] In 1985, South Africa attempted to claim a right of hot pursuit in Botswana, but the argument was rejected by the Security Council, which denounced and rejected 'racist South Africa's practice of "hot pursuit" to terrorise and destabilise Botswana and other countries in Southern Africa' (Res. 568 (1985) of 21 June 1985).

[43] UNHCR, *The State of the World's Refugees*, 2000, p. 246.

government, the international community failed to support efforts to separate combatants from genuine refugees.[44] Political leaders, soldiers of the former Armed Forces of Rwanda (ex-FAR), and Interahamwe militias maintained strict control over the population in the camps. They had control over the distribution of food and relief supplies and resorted to threats and intimidation to prevent people from returning to Rwanda.[45] They quickly rearmed and reorganized, with the clear intention of continuing their genocidal agenda against ethnic Tutsi in Zaire and Rwanda. From 1995 and throughout 1996, Rwandan military groups in refugee camps mounted a series of cross-border raids into Rwanda.[46] Meanwhile in Zaire, the Banyamulenge, a Zairean Tutsi group, faced a number of discriminatory measures and abuses on the part of the Mobutu government.[47] In October 1996, they organized in a rebel coalition, the Alliance des Forces Démocratiques pour la Libération du Congo-Zaïre (AFDL), led by Laurent-Désiré Kabila, and marched on Kinshasa. The AFDL forces captured the capital in May 1997 and Kabila declared himself President of a newly named Democratic Republic of Congo. Shortly after that, human rights organizations, foreign news agencies and the UN accused Kabila's troops of the massacres of more than 200,000 refugees during his march to power.[48]

Between mid-October and mid-November 1996, AFDL troops, with the support of the Rwandan Patriotic Army, systematically attacked Hutu refugee camps. The first camps to be attacked were those in south Kivu, which hosted around 220,000 Burundian refugees, including Hutu rebel group Forces de Défense de le Démocratie (FDD), as well as ex-FAR and Interahamwe.[49] They then went on to attack the Rwandan refugee camps near Goma, in north Kivu. One of the objectives of these attacks was to force the refugee population in the camps to return to Rwanda, thus eliminating the Hutu threat.[50] However, large-scale killings of civilian refugees, including women and children, were committed during these attacks. While some 600,000 Hutu refugees returned to Rwanda, hundreds

[44] UNSC, 'Report of the Secretary-General on the causes of conflict and the promotion of durable peace and development in Africa' (13 April 1998), S/1998/318, para. 53.

[45] UNHCR, *State of the World's Refugees* (2000), p. 250; UNSC, 'Report of the Secretary-General on security in the Rwandese refugee camps' (18 November 1994), S/1994/1308, paras. 6–11.

[46] UNHCR, *State of the World's Refugees* (2000), p. 254. [47] *Ibid.*, p. 262.

[48] Emizet, 'The massacre of refugees in Congo', 2000, 169.

[49] UNHCR, *State of the World's Refugees* (2000), p. 263.

[50] UNSC, 'Report of the Secretary-General's Investigative Team charged with investigating serious violations of human rights and international humanitarian law in the Democratic Republic of Congo' (29 June 1998), S/1998/581, para. 96.

of thousands fled westward, into the interior of the country, where they were relentlessly hunted down and killed by ADFL troops and Mai-Mai militias.[51] Between February and May 1997, a number of camps set up in the interior of the country to receive those who had fled the attacks in the Kivus were attacked.[52]

In July 1997, the UN Secretary-General appointed an investigative team in order to investigate 'gross violations of Human Rights and International Humanitarian Law committed in the Democratic Republic of Congo (formerly Zaire) from 1 March 1993'.[53] The DRC government systematically prevented the investigative team from carrying out its mandate, employing the tactics of non-cooperation to deliberately obstruct the investigation.[54] Nevertheless, the team was able to reach important conclusions and to confirm that certain violations of international humanitarian law had been committed. In particular, while it was unable to reach conclusions about the possible violations of humanitarian law resulting from the attacks on the camps as such, the team found that the deliberate execution of unarmed civilians during and after the attacks on camps of displaced Rwandans by AFDL troops violated international humanitarian law and, because of their systematic nature, could well constitute crimes against humanity.[55]

Both the DRC government and the government of Rwanda rejected the conclusions of the investigative team and denied that massacres of civilians were ever committed under their command. According the DRC government, the sole purpose behind the attacks on refugee camps was 'to liberate the refugees held hostages by armed gangs who were using them as a human shield'.[56] In relation to the civilian casualties, it noted:

> The Government wishes to state that when camps were being cleared, bullets were aimed at the armed forces, not at civilians. If some civilians died or were hit by bullets, that was not intentional. They would, unfortunately, be war victims, within the meaning of the 1949 Geneva Conventions.[57]

[51] *Ibid.*, para. 81. [52] *Ibid.*, para. 86.

[53] UNSC, 'Letter dated 1 August 1997 from the Secretary-General addressed to the President of the Security Council' (S/1997/617).

[54] Emizet, 'Massacre of refugees in Congo', 170.

[55] UNSC, 'Report of the Investigative Team', pp. 6, 24.

[56] UNSC, 'Letter dated 25 June 1998 from the Permanent Representative of the Democratic Republic of the Congo to the United Nations addressed to the Secretary-General' (S/1998/582), para. 119. See also UNSC, 'Letter dated 25 June 1998 from the Permanent Representative of Rwanda to the United Nations addressed to the Secretary-General' (S/1998/583).

[57] 'Letter from Permanent Representative of the DRC', para. 92.

In other words, the attacks on refugee camps were aimed at legitimate military objectives within the civilian population and civilian deaths caused by the AFDL were unavoidable collateral damage. The presence of combatants or armed elements within a civilian displaced population is often invoked by belligerents as a legitimate ground for attack on a refugee or IDP camp. However, international humanitarian law strictly regulates the conduct of hostilities and the 'collateral damage' argument is clearly limited.

The prima facie civilian status of refugee and IDP camps

Refugee and IDP camps and settlements qualify as both civilian objects, in so far as they constitute dwellings used by civilians, and civilian populations, in so far as the displaced persons that comprise them are recognized as civilians.[58] As such, they are entitled to civilian immunity and are protected by the basic rules of international humanitarian law governing the conduct of hostilities, and the principle of distinction in particular. However, this civilian status is not absolute or irreversible, and refugee and IDP camps may lose their immunity, at least partially, if it becomes clear that such camps are in fact used for military purposes.

Refugee and IDP camps as civilian objects

In application of the fundamental principle of distinction, 'Civilian objects are protected against attack, unless and for such time as they are military objectives.'[59] 'Military objectives' are defined in Article 52(2) of Protocol I as 'objects which by their nature, location, purpose or use make an effective contribution to military action and whose total or partial destruction, capture or neutralization, in the circumstances ruling at the time, offers a definite military advantage'.

In addition, Article 52(3) states that:

> In case of doubt whether an object which is normally dedicated to civilian purposes, such as a place of worship, a house or other dwelling or a school, is being used to make an effective contribution to military action, it shall be presumed not to be so used.

As dwellings hosting persons considered as civilians, refugee and IDP camps clearly enter the category of objects 'normally dedicated to civilian

[58] Jacquemet, 'Under what circumstances?', 2004, p. 32.

[59] Henckaerts and Doswald-Beck, *Customary International Humanitarian Law*, vol. 1, Rule 10, p. 34.

purposes'.[60] Thus, at least in international armed conflicts, there exists a presumption that camps of displaced persons located in or near conflict zones are not used by the armed forces. It is consequently prohibited to attack them, unless it is certain that they accommodate enemy combatants or military objects.[61] According to the ICRC commentary, this constitutes 'an essential step forward . . . in that belligerents can no longer arbitrarily and unilaterally declare as a military objective any civilian object'.[62]

While the customary status of this rule is not entirely clear in non-international armed conflict, the ICRC nevertheless contends that, in case of doubt, a careful assessment has to be made as to whether there are sufficient indications to warrant an attack. 'It cannot automatically be assumed that any object that appears dubious may be subject to lawful attack.'[63]

Refugee and IDP camps as 'civilian populations'

As noted, refugee and IDP camps also constitute 'civilian populations', within the meaning of Article 50(2) of Protocol I[64] and are protected against attack. In addition, refugees and internally displaced persons are considered as civilians[65] and, as such, are entitled to the general protection of IHL against the effects of hostilities. However, both the displaced persons and the camps that shelter them may lose this immunity in two specific and clearly limited situations.

Direct participation of civilians in hostilities and consequent loss of protection

All civilians in situations of armed conflict shall enjoy general protection against dangers arising from military operations.[66] In return, civilians are strictly prohibited from participating in hostilities. If they do, they may be

60 Jacquemet, 'Under what circumstances?', 2004, p. 33.

61 Sandoz *et al.*, *Commentary on the Protocols*, p. 638. It should be noted, however, that this conclusion cannot be extended to non-international armed conflicts, as civilian objects do not enjoy the same protection under the Second Protocol. Only objects indispensable to the survival of the civilian population are protected.

62 Sandoz *et al.*, *Commentary on the Protocols*, p. 638.

63 Henckaerts and Doswald-Beck, *Customary International Humanitarian Law*, vol. 1, Rule 10, p. 36.

64 Protocol I, Art. 52(2): 'The civilian population comprises all persons who are civilians.'

65 Article 50(1) defines civilians negatively, by providing that a civilian is any person who is not a combatant within the meaning of Article 4 Geneva Convention III and Article 43 Protocol I. In addition, 'in case of doubt whether a person is a civilian, that person shall be considered to be a civilian'.

66 Protocol I, Art. 51(1); Protocol II, Art. 13(1).

lawfully targeted by the enemy for as long as they take a direct part in hostilities.[67] The rationale behind this rule is that unlawful participation in hostilities unduly threatens the principle of distinction between civilians and combatants, resulting in an increased risk to the civilian population. It is therefore vitally important to be able to clearly identify what constitutes 'direct participation in hostilities', and when and for how long an individual engaging in such activity may be lawfully targeted. However, although generally accepted as a customary rule of international law,[68] the principle of loss of immunity as a result of unlawful participation in hostilities is subject to 'much ambiguity'.[69] Indeed, Protocol I does not define 'direct participation in hostilities' and no clear and uniform definition of the concept has emerged from state practice.[70] In 2009, the ICRC attempted to clarify the concept of 'direct participation' and to shed light on the issue, with the publication of its 'Interpretive Guidance on the Notion of Direct Participation in Hostilities under International Humanitarian Law'.[71]

The ICRC's Interpretive Guidance has adopted a broader definition of 'direct participation in hostilities' than that in the commentary to the Protocols, which defined direct participation as 'acts of war which by their nature or purpose are likely to cause actual harm to the personnel and equipment of the enemy armed forces'.[72] In contrast, the 2009 Interpretive Guidance not only includes in the definition acts intended to cause harm of a 'specifically military nature',[73] but also acts directed at civilians or civilian objects, if they are likely to inflict death, injury or destruction.[74] In addition, there must be a direct causal link between the

[67] Protocol I, Art. 51(3); Protocol II, Art. 13(3).

[68] Henckaerts and Doswald-Beck, *Customary International Humanitarian Law*, vol. 1, Rule 6, p. 19.

[69] Akande, 'Clearing the fog of war?', 2010, 180.

[70] Henckaerts and Doswald-Beck, *Customary International Humanitarian Law*, vol. 2, pp. 107–13.

[71] ICRC, Interpretive Guidance on the Notion of Direct Participation in Hostilities under International Humanitarian Law (Geneva 2009), www.icrc.org/eng/resources/documents/publication/p0990.htm (accessed 15 October 2011).

[72] Sandoz *et al.*, *Commentary to the Protocols*, p. 618.

[73] ICRC, Interpretive Guidance on Direct Participation in Hostilities, p. 47. In the commentary to the Interpretive Guidance, the ICRC explains that 'military harm should be interpreted as encompassing not only the infliction of death, injury, or destruction on military personnel and objects but essentially any consequence adversely affecting the military operations or military capacity of a party to the conflict'.

[74] As noted in the commentary, '[t]he most uncontroversial examples of acts that can qualify as direct participation in hostilities even in the absence of military harm are

act of an individual and the harm caused, as well as an intention to cause harm.[75] According to the ICRC, this means that the harm that results, or is intended to result, from the act of an individual must be brought about 'in one causal step'.[76]

The consequence of direct civilian participation in hostilities is a loss of protection against direct attack for 'the duration of each specific act amounting to direct participation in hostilities'.[77] The ICRC thus clearly rejects the continuous direct participation approach,[78] adopted by a number of legal scholars, including Yoram Dinstein and Michael Schmitt, who consider that a civilian remains a valid target 'until unambiguously opting out through extended non-participation or an affirmative act of withdrawal'.[79] Instead, the ICRC adopts the narrow 'revolving-door' approach, according to which 'civilians lose and regain protection against direct attack in parallel with the intervals of their engagement in direct participation in hostilities'.[80] However, it should be noted that if the individual concerned is regarded, through its continuous action, as belonging to an organized armed group, he or she will lose protection against direct attack, 'for as long as they assume their continuous combat function'.[81]

Thus, in the present context, refugees or internally displaced persons who directly and deliberately engage in hostile activities against government armed forces and military installations or a group of civilians belonging to a different ethnic group will be considered as directly participating in hostilities and may, as a result, be legitimately targeted, for as long as they actively participate in hostilities. It should be noted, however, that 'direct participation' should be narrowly construed, and that displaced persons should always benefit from a presumption of civilian status.

attacks directed against civilians and civilian objects' (ICRC, Interpretive Guidance on the Notion of Direct Participation in Hostilities, 47).

75 *Ibid.*, p. 46. 76 *Ibid.*, p. 52. 77 *Ibid.*, p. 70.

78 Akande, 'Clearing the fog of war?', 189.

79 Schmitt, 'Direct participation in hostilities', 2005, 512; Dinstein, 'Distinction and loss of civilian protection', 2008, 10.

80 ICRC, Interpretive Guidance on Direct Participation in Hostilities, p. 70. The ICRC has justified its position by the fact that the behaviour of civilians is difficult to anticipate. 'Even the fact that a civilian has repeatedly taken a direct part in hostilities, either voluntarily or under pressure, does not allow a reliable prediction as to future conduct. As the concept of direct participation in hostilities refers to specific hostile acts, IHL restores the civilian's protection against direct attack each time his or her engagement in a hostile act ends.'

81 *Ibid.*

Presence of combatants within the civilian displaced population

Nevertheless, in accordance with Article 50(3), the presence of armed elements within a displaced civilian community does not deprive the population of its civilian character. Accordingly, a refugee or IDP containing a small number of armed elements within its population must still be considered as a whole, and retain its civilian character. As explained by the ICRC:

> Unless the definition of the civilian population were to lose all substance and the protection to which it was entitled were to be invalidated, it must be recognised that the presence of *single individuals* not answering the definition of civilians should not in any way modify the character of the civilian population.[82]

There is no equivalent of this provision in Protocol II, presumably because of the difficulty in distinguishing between rebels and civilians in internal armed conflicts. Nevertheless, as pointed out in the Red Cross commentary, if the mere presence of some armed elements were to permit an attack against a whole group of civilians, the protection enjoyed by the civilian population would become totally illusory.[83] The silence of the Protocol on this point 'should not be considered to be a licence to attack'.[84]

The application of Article 50(3) is limited to situations where small numbers of combatants mingle with the civilian population. Indeed, the ICRC notes that 'if whole contingents of troops moved among a peaceful population, the Parties to conflict involved would avoid total war only by applying the precautionary principle measures in attack laid down in Article 57'.[85] Regarding the Rwandan refugee camps in eastern Zaire, although estimates vary, there were reports of some 230 Rwandese political leaders, 50,000 ex-FAR and more than 10,000 Interahamwe militias.[86] There is no doubt that the military presence in the refugee camps could not be considered as 'single individuals'. However, it should also be borne in mind that the total refugee population in Zaire was estimated to be between 1 and 1.25 million. As noted by one commentator, the proportion of armed elements in the total refugee population therefore represented less than 6 per cent.[87] In any case, genuine individual civilians within a mixed population never lose their protected status. Consequently, any

[82] ICRC, 1973 Commentary on the Draft Protocols, p. 56, cited in Bothe *et al.*, *New Rules for Victims of Armed Conflicts*, p. 296.

[83] Sandoz et al., *Commentary on the Protocols*, p. 1452. [84] *Ibid.*

[85] ICRC, 1973 Commentary on the Draft Protocols, p. 56.

[86] UNSC, 'Report of the Secretary-General on security in the Rwandese camps', paras. 8–10.

[87] Emizet, 'Massacre of refugees in Congo', 166.

targeted attack against Hutu armed elements in the camps will only be regarded as lawful, if in strict compliance with the fundamental principles of distinction and proportionality, as codified in Articles 51(4) and 57(2) of the First Protocol.[88]

The prohibition of indiscriminate attacks and the rule of proportionality

International humanitarian law expressly prohibits indiscriminate attacks, i.e. attacks which strike military objectives and civilians or civilian objects without distinction.[89] The principle of discrimination as laid down in Article 51 of the first protocol is a fundamental principle of customary international law, applicable in international and non-international armed conflicts.[90] Furthermore, in application of the customary principle of proportionality, an attack on a refugee or IDP camp composed of a mixed population of armed elements and civilians will be considered indiscriminate and therefore unlawful if the incidental killings and injuries to the displaced civilians outweigh the military advantage anticipated.[91] The act of wilfully 'launching an indiscriminate attack affecting a civilian population or civilian objects in the knowledge that such attack will cause excessive loss to civilian life, injury to civilians or damage to civilian objects' is a grave breach of Protocol I[92] and a war crime under the ICC Statute.[93]

There have been many reports of heavy shelling of refugee camps and indiscriminate killings by the AFDL.[94] The attack on the Bukavu refugee camp in south Kivu, reportedly included the indiscriminate bombing of residential areas.[95] According to Amnesty International:

[88] During its investigation, the Secretary-General's Investigative Team failed to reach conclusions about the possible violations of humanitarian law resulting from the attacks on the camps as such. In its report, the team explained that it was unable to obtain reliable information about the degree of military presence in the camps and that there was credible testimony that forces located in the camps returned fire during the attacks on some of the camps. It added: 'This makes it impossible to determine whether the attacks on the camps had any legitimate military objective, or were simply attacks on the civilian population as such' (UNSC, 'Report of the Investigative Team', para. 88).

[89] Protocol I, Art. 51(4).

[90] Henckaerts and Doswald-Beck, *Customary International Humanitarian Law*, vol. 1, Rule 1, p. 3.

[91] Protocol I, Arts. 51(5) and 57(2)(a)(iii).

[92] Protocol I, Art. 85(3)(b).

[93] ICC Statute, Art. 8(2)(b)(iv).

[94] HRW, 'What Kabila is hiding: civilian killings and impunity in Congo' (October 1997), 15, HRW Index No. A905.

[95] UNSC, 'Report of the Investigative Team', para. 29.

The numerous testimonies of eye-witnesses indicate a reckless disregard for civilian lives on the part of AFDL: in some cases, soldiers had already evacuated the areas before the attack took place, in others, they fled early in the course of the attack. Further, there does not appear to have been any attempt to distinguish civilian and specific military targets.[96]

Upon entry in the camps, the AFDL reportedly separated the men from the women, children and the elderly, who were encouraged to return to Rwanda. The remaining male refugees were then executed.[97] During early 1997, as the refugees fled into the interior of the country and settled in temporary camps, they were hunted down and indiscriminately massacred by AFDL troops and Mai-Mai militias. The UN Investigative Team received many testimonies of Rwandan refugees, including women and children, systematically killed as they were trying to flee and offered no armed resistance.[98] Such massacres demonstrate that the killings of Rwandan refugees were not only indiscriminate, but also deliberate and intentional.

If belligerents in international and internal armed conflicts respected the fundamental principle of distinction, many refugee, internally displaced person and civilian deaths would be avoided. In addition, the location of refugee and IDP camps within dangerous zones of combat is often an important factor contributing to, or encouraging, the militarization and consequent vulnerability of these camps to armed attacks.

Location of camps within dangerous zones of combat

In time of war, many refugees and internally displaced persons are likely to be killed because of the proximity of their camps to international borders, dangerous combat zones or important military objectives. The Gatumba refugee transit centre, for instance, was located on the border of Burundi and the DRC, a high-risk zone, which had been under phase four of the five-stage system of security alert in the UN.[99] From the outset of the influx, UNHCR had expressed concern at the security situation and had been urging the Burundian government to relocate the refugees away from the volatile borders. The camp was finally closed in the aftermath of the massacres, and the refugees moved to more secure locations inside the

96 AI, 'Hidden from scrutiny: human rights abuses in eastern Zaire' (19 December 1996), AI Index AFR 62/029/1996.

97 UNSC, 'Report of the Investigative Team', paras. 91–3.

98 *Ibid*., paras. 102–9.

99 UNHCR, 'Burundi: agreement reached with government on second site for transit camp Congolese' (20 August 2004), www.unhcr.org/news/NEWS/4125d6260.html (accessed 27 October 2011)

country. The lives and safety of refugees and IDPs are also put at risk when their camps are established in conflict zones within a country. Sudanese refugees in northern Uganda live in constant fear for their lives, not only because of the location of their settlements close to the border with the country from which they have fled, but also because they have been settled in a particularly dangerous conflict zone,[100] where the rebel LRA has been spreading terror among the civilian population for over twenty years. Sudanese refugees in northern Uganda are regularly targeted by the LRA, which has been associated with the Khartoum government since 1994.

States are often unable or unwilling to locate refugee or IDP camps away from insecure borders or conflict zones. Governments, fearing instability, may prefer to contain the problem at the border for security reasons.[101] Refugees themselves may be reluctant to move away from the borders, wishing to be able to return to their country of origin if needed.[102] Internally displaced persons may find themselves caught in the crossfire, with no other possibility than to remain where they are. Host states in unstable regions, overwhelmed by their own internal difficulties, may have trouble setting up refugee camps in safe locations. Neighbour countries Liberia and Côte d'Ivoire, for instance, have been torn by regional conflicts and civil wars for years, with Liberian and Ivorian refugees shifting between borders depending of the state of the conflict within these countries. This constant flow of refugees crossing and recrossing the border threatens to further destabilize the region and the camps situated close to the border are frequently subjected to attacks by rebel fighters.

The location of refugee camps away from volatile international borders or conflict zones is not only prescribed by refugee law,[103] it is also a duty of the parties to a conflict under international humanitarian law. In the conduct of military operations, it is a rule of customary international law that constant care shall be taken to spare the civilian population,

[100] Bagenda and Hovil, 'Sudanese refugees in northern Uganda', 2003, 15.

[101] UNSC, 'Report of the Secretary-General to the Security Council on the protection of civilians in armed conflict' (26 November 2002), S/2002/1300, para. 36.

[102] *Ibid.*

[103] The Cartagena Declaration endorses the principle of safe location of refugee camps and stipulates that: 'Refugee camps and settlements located in frontier areas should be set up inland at a reasonable distance from the frontier with a view to improving the protection afforded to refugees, safeguarding their human rights and implementing projects aimed at their self-sufficiency and integration into the host society' (Point 6). Article 2(6) of the OAU Convention provides that countries shall, as far as possible, settle refugees at a reasonable distance from the frontier of their country of origin.

civilians and civilian objects.[104] Consequently, belligerents are required to take precautionary measures not only in attack,[105] but also against the effects of attacks, in order to avoid, or at least minimize, collateral loss or damage to civilians and civilian objects.[106] In accordance with Article 58 Protocol I the parties to a conflict have a duty to take precautionary measures to ensure that all civilians under their control, including refugees and IDPs, are protected against the effects of attacks from their adversary. Such measures include removing the civilian displaced population from the vicinity of military objectives and avoiding locating military objectives within or near densely populated areas. Other necessary precautions could also involve the building of camps or shelters for the protection of civilian refugees and displaced persons. With regard to a claim by Eritrea that Ethiopia's aerial attacks on IDP camps had resulted in excessive civilian deaths and destruction of civilian property, the Eritrea–Ethiopia Claims Commission observed that a number of civilian casualties and losses could have been avoided 'if Eritrea had done more to keep civilians and military objectives further apart'.[107] In its 2000 *Kupreskić* judgment, the ICTY held that Article 57 and 58 of Protocol I 'are now part of customary international law, not only because they specify and flesh out general pre-existing norms, but also they do not appear to be contested by any State, including those which have not ratified the Protocol'.[108]

This rule is not replicated in Protocol II. However, the ICRC study on customary international humanitarian law found that belligerents had a general customary obligation to take all possible precautions to protect the civilian population against the effects of attacks.[109]

In parallel, international humanitarian law also prohibits the forced movement of civilians in order to shield military objectives from attacks.[110] In accordance with Article 51(7) of Protocol I:

> The presence or movements of the civilian population or individual civilians shall not be used to render certain points or areas immune from military operations, in particular in attempts to shield military objectives from attacks or to shield, favour or impede military operations. The Parties to the conflict shall not direct the movement of the civilian population or individual civilians in order to attempt to shield military objectives from attacks or to shield military operations.

104 Protocol I, Art. 57(1). 105 Protocol I, Art. 57. 106 Protocol I, Art. 58.

107 Eritrea–Ethiopia Claims Commission, *Western Front, aerial bombardment and related claims*, Eritrea's Claim 26, para. 96.

108 ICTY, *Prosecutor* v. *Kupreskic et al.*, Trial Judgment, IT-95-16-T, 14 January 2000, para. 524.

109 Henckaerts and Doswald-Beck, *Customary International Humanitarian Law*, vol. 1, Rule 22, pp. 68–76.

110 Korsinik, 'Protection des camps de réfugiés', 392.

The use of human shields by belligerents is an abuse of the fundamental principle of civilian immunity. In terms of protection of refugees and displaced persons, the prohibition has several implications. First of all, parties to the conflict must not forcibly displace civilians or direct their movement in order to shield military objectives from attacks. There are nonetheless many instances of civilians forcibly displaced by a belligerent and placed near a military objective, in order to render it immune from attacks. For example, in 1999 Amnesty International reported that groups of Hutu displaced persons in Burundi were kept around military posts, thus surrounding and protecting the soldiers.[111] Furthermore, belligerents must refrain from deliberately placing a military objective in the middle of, or close to, a civilian area.[112] As was the case in eastern Zaire in 1994–6, militarized refugee and IDP camps are often used by armed elements as bases from which to launch their attacks. In addition, during the confrontations with AFDL troops, members of the former Rwandan armed forces and Interahamwe militias reportedly used Rwandan refugees as human shields, causing many deaths in the crossfire.[113]

The prohibition on the use of human shields is a corollary of the customary principle of civilian immunity in hostilities, and is thus binding on the parties to an international armed conflict, as well as both the government and the rebels in control of a territory in a non-international armed conflict. Moreover, 'utilizing the presence of a civilian or other protected person to render certain points, areas, or military forces immune from military operations' is a war crime in international armed conflict, under Article 8(2)(b)(xxiii) of the ICC Statute.

Forced recruitment of refugees and IDPs

A further threat to the personal safety of refugees and internally displaced persons is the growing practice of forced recruitment in refugee and IDP camps, particularly in internal armed conflicts. In 2003, Amnesty International denounced the forcible recruitment of Liberian refugees by the government forces of President Gbagbo in Côte d'Ivoire.[114] Armed opposition groups also forcibly recruit from within refugee and IDP

111 AI, 'Burundi – no respite without justice' (17 August 1999), AI Index AFR 16/012/1999.

112 Quéguiner, 'Precautions', 2006, 812.

113 HRW, 'Uncertain course: transition and human rights violations in the Congo' (December 1997), HRW Index No. A909.

114 AI, 'No escape, Liberian refugees in Côte d'Ivoire' (2003).

camps, sometimes with the support or at least tacit approval of the host government.[115]

Forced recruitment of displaced persons threatens the civilian character of the camps and seriously compromises the security of their inhabitants. Children are the most vulnerable to forced recruitment, particularly if they have been separated from their parents during their flight.[116] In 2010, forced recruitment of children by national armed forces and/or militias took place in Colombia, North Kivu (in DRC), Afghanistan and Chad among others.[117] The UN Secretary-General, in a 2007 report on children and armed conflict in Chad, claimed that the majority of the twelve Sudanese refugee camps in eastern Chad have experienced forced recruitment of Sudanese children, mainly by the Sudanese Liberation Army and the Justice and Equality Movement.[118] The recruitment of children, forcible or voluntary, is prohibited by international humanitarian law. Both Protocols expressly state that children under 15 should not take part in hostilities and should not be recruited.[119] Furthermore, the act of conscripting or enlisting children into the national armed forces or armed groups or using them to participate actively in hostilities constitutes a war crime in international and non-international armed conflict.[120]

International humanitarian law does not afford a similar protection to adults. Yet, adult refugees and IDPs are just as vulnerable to forced conscription. There have been many reports of forced recruitment of civilians in camps for internally displaced persons in Darfur and Chad, and in Sudanese refugee camps in eastern Chad.[121] A large number of those forcibly or voluntarily recruited in refugee camps are young men and adolescents and thus do not benefit from the protection of the 1977 Protocols. The 2000 Optional Protocol to the Convention of the Rights of the Child on the involvement of children in armed conflict[122] partially remedies this legal gap, by requiring that state parties ensure that persons under the

[115] HRW, 'Youth, blood and poverty: the legacy of West Africa's regional warriors' (April 2005), HRW Index No. A1705.

[116] UNGA, 'Report of the expert of the Secretary-General, Ms Graça Machel' (26 August 1996), para. 69.

[117] IDMC, *Global overview 2010*, p. 24.

[118] UNSC, 'Report of the Secretary-General on children and armed conflict in Chad' (3 July 2007), S/2007/400, para. 30.

[119] Protocol I, Art. 77(2); Protocol, Art. 4(3)(c) Protocol II.

[120] ICC Statute, Art. 8(2)(b)(xxvi) and (e)(vii).

[121] AFP, 'UNHCR probes forced recruitment of Chad refugees: source' (29 March 2006), http://reliefweb.int/node/203826 (accessed 24 October 2011).

[122] Optional Protocol to the Convention of the Rights of the Child on the involvement of children in armed conflict, New York, 25 May 2000, 2173 UNTS 222.

age of 18 are not compulsorily recruited into their armed forces. However, 15-year-olds may still join government armed forces *voluntarily*.[123]

The UN General Assembly has repeatedly denounced the forced recruitment of refugees. In Resolution 46/106 of 16 December 1991, the General Assembly condemned 'all violations of the rights and safety of refugees and asylum-seekers, in particular those perpetrated by military and armed attacks against refugee camps and settlements and forced recruitment into armed forces'.[124] Furthermore, the Guiding Principles on Internal Displacement state that:

> Internally displaced persons shall be protected against discriminatory practices of recruitment into any armed forces or groups as a result of their displacement. In particular any cruel, inhuman or degrading practices that compel compliance or punish non-compliance with recruitment are prohibited in all circumstances.[125]

Although displaced adults are not protected against forced recruitment into armed forces or armed groups, they are nevertheless protected against discriminatory recruitment practices specifically directed at them because they are displaced, as well as enslavement practices,[126] including forced labour.

Conclusion on the principle of civilian immunity

International humanitarian law plays an important role in the comprehensive legal framework for the protection of refugee and IDP camps against armed attacks, along with principles of international human rights and refugee law and general principles of international law. In the context of an armed conflict, the rules regulating the conduct of combatants are designed to protect refugees, internally displaced persons and other victims of war from attacks, as long as they do not take a direct part in the hostilities. It is thus the responsibility of states hosting refugees or accommodating internally displaced persons to ensure that the civilian and humanitarian character of the camps is respected. Indeed, separating out armed elements from civilian displaced populations will not only guarantee their immunity under the rules of international humanitarian

[123] ICRC, 'The ICRC says "no" to the recruitment of child soldiers' (6 February 2007), www.icrc.org/web/eng/siteeng0.nsf/html/children-statement-060207 (accessed 24 October 2011).

[124] UNGA Res. 46/106 (16 December 1991).

[125] Guiding Principles on Internal Displacement, Principle 13.

[126] Protocol II, Art. 4(2).

law, but also encourage the belligerents to agree on the creation of protected zones, free from attacks.

Protected zones for refugees and displaced persons

As well as establishing rules and principles for the protection of civilians against the effects of hostilities, international humanitarian law provides for the creation of special zones aimed at protecting the civilian population and individual civilians from the effects of war. These protected zones are specifically designated areas which may not be the object of attacks, provided that they have been established in accordance with the relevant provisions of the Geneva Conventions and Protocol I.[127] International humanitarian law provides for three main types of protected zones: hospital zones, neutralized zones and demilitarized zones.[128]

The idea of a zone benefiting from a protected status under international humanitarian law and where civilians could regroup and be protected from the hostilities is worth investigating in connection with the present issue under discussion. In fact, as early as 1983, the Schnyder report on military attacks on refugee camps and settlements considered the creation of protected zones for refugee camps. The Draft Declaration annexed to the report indeed requested that:

> States in cooperation with UNHCR and ICRC should examine whether and to what extent protection similar to that provided in the IVth Geneva Convention of 12 August 1949 (article 14: Sanitary and Safety Zones and Localities; article 15: Neutralized Zones) and Protocol I of 8 June 1977 (article 59: Non-protected Localities; article 60: De-militarized Zones) can be applied to refugee camps and settlements.[129]

Furthermore, the post-Cold War era saw the emergence of a new type of internationally sanctioned 'Safety Zones' for the protection of internally displaced persons in armed conflict.[130] This emerging concept, although based loosely on international humanitarian law, differs greatly from the traditional protected zones, as envisaged by the Geneva Conventions and the First Protocol.[131]

127 Sandoz, 'Localités et zones sous protection spéciales', 1985, p. 35.
128 Geneva Convention I, Art. 23; Geneva Convention IV, Arts. 14, 15; Protocol I, Arts. 59, 60.
129 Draft Declaration on the prohibition of military or armed attacks against refugee camps and settlements, para. 5.
130 Hyndman, 'Preventive, palliative, or punitive?', 2003, 168.
131 Landgren, 'Safety zones', 1995, 441.

This discussion on 'Safety Zones' for the protection of refugees and IDP camps against armed attacks should commence with an analysis of the relevant provisions of international humanitarian law, immediately followed by an exploration of the emerging concept of a UN-imposed safety zone, or 'safe area', for the protection of internally displaced persons, including its benefits and flaws. It will then be argued that refugee and IDP camps in situations of armed conflict could both benefit from the protection of 'protected zones' under strict conditions.

Protected zones in international humanitarian law

The essence of the notion of protected zones in international humanitarian law is that of 'a location within the disputed country or territory, neutral and free of belligerent activity, to which humanitarian access is ensured'.[132]

The Geneva Conventions provide for the creation of two types of zones for the protection of civilians in international armed conflict. First of all, Article 14 Geneva Convention IV foresees the creation of hospital and safety zones and localities for the protection of civilian sick and wounded, as well as especially vulnerable categories of civilians, such as the aged, children under 15, expectant mothers and mothers of young children under 7.[133] These zones are generally of a permanent character and established outside the combat zone in order to shelter certain categories of civilians from long-range weapons, especially aerial bombardment.[134] However, they cannot have any legal existence, or enjoy protection under the Convention, until they have been mutually recognized in an agreement by the parties concerned.[135] In addition, Article 15 of the Fourth Convention opens the possibility for belligerents to conclude agreements on the creation of temporary neutralized zones in the regions where fighting is taking place to protect the wounded and sick, combatants and non-combatants, and 'civilian persons who take no part in the hostilities and who perform no work of a military character'. The zones are therefore open to all civilians provided they engage in no military activity, which is, according to Yves Sandoz, 'a self-evident precondition for securing the agreement of the adverse party'.[136]

[132] *Ibid.*, 438.

[133] Similarly, Art. 23 Geneva Convention I provides for the creation of similar hospital zones and localities to protect *military* wounded and sick.

[134] Pictet, *Commentary* (1958), p. 120. [135] *Ibid.*, p. 127.

[136] Sandoz, 'Safety zones', p. 124.

Despite the formalization of the system of protected zones, Sandoz observes that there has not been any proliferation of such zones during conflicts that have arisen since 1949.[137] Moreover, the few instances of protected zones in armed conflict, such as the neutralized zones of Nicosia in 1974, and Saigon and Phnom Penh in 1975, 'have been established in dire emergency and fall only very roughly into the categories envisaged in the Geneva Conventions, if at all'.[138]

Protocol I extends the concept of neutralized zones and provides for two further places of refuge for the civilian population: non-defended localities and demilitarized zones. As noted by Yves Sandoz:

> Unlike Article 15 of the Fourth Geneva Convention, however, such places of refuge are not created to enable the population to seek shelter there; instead the idea is to ensure that a place in which a large number of persons are already assembled is recognized and protected.[139]

In virtue of Article 59 of the Protocol, 'it is prohibited for the Parties to the conflict to attack, by any means whatsoever, non-defended localities'. This paragraph codifies and confirms a customary rule of international law.[140] A party to a conflict may unilaterally declare as a non-defended locality 'any inhabited place near or in a zone where armed forces are in contact which is open for occupation by an adverse Party', provided that it fulfils four conditions:

(a) all combatants, as well as mobile weapons and mobile military equipments must have been evacuated;
(b) no hostile use shall be made of fixed military installations or establishments;
(c) no acts of hostility shall be committed by the authorities or by the population; and
(d) no activities in support of military operations shall be undertaken.

Finally, Article 60 of the Protocol provides for the creation of demilitarized zones in which populations can be sheltered from hostilities in an organized manner, and not on the improvised basis which characterizes the establishment of neutralized zones under Article 15 of the Fourth Convention.[141] Demilitarized zones must fulfil the same preconditions as those laid down for non-defended localities. Moreover, the establishment

137 *Ibid.* 138 *Ibid.* 139 *Ibid.*, p. 126.

140 Sandoz *et al.*, *Commentary on the Protocols*, p. 700. Article 25 of the Hague Regulations of 1907 provides that: 'The attack or bombardment, by whatever means, of towns, villages, dwellings, or buildings which are undefended, is prohibited.'

141 Sandoz, 'Safety zones', p. 127.

of such zones must be the subject of an express agreement, which may be concluded verbally or in writing, either in peacetime or after the outbreak of hostilities and should define the limits of the demilitarized zone and the methods of supervision.[142]

Accordingly, traditional protected zones within the meaning of international humanitarian law must be based on the consent of the parties concerned and the complete demilitarization of the zone. The combination of these elements is the only guarantee to ensure that the immunity of the protected zone will be respected by the belligerents. These provisions have rarely been applied in practice.[143] It wasn't until 1991 that a new type of ad hoc safety zone emerged, which differed fundamentally from the establishment of protected zones as provided for under international humanitarian law.[144]

Safety zones for the protection of internally displaced persons

During the 1990s, the concept of protected zones evolved into that of the safety zone, which Chimni defines as 'a clearly demarcated space in which individuals fleeing danger can seek safety within their own country'.[145] Primarily designed to provide physical protection to displaced persons within their own country, the safety zone may have another less explicit objective, which is to divert potential cross-border movements into other countries towards the safe areas.[146] As explained by Leonardo Franco:

> The idea, put simply, is that persons facing armed conflict, internal disturbances or fearing persecution, rather than departing their own country in large numbers, should remain in that country, in defined and policed zones where their security and material well-being would be assured, whether by the authorities of that country or through international supervision. But the zones should also be available to refugees as initial safe havens upon voluntary repatriation.[147]

The first instance of such a safety zone was the 'safe havens' in northern Iraq for the protection of Kurdish Iraqis. Following the 1991 Gulf War and Saddam Hussein's repression of the Kurdish uprising, over 450,000

142 Protocol I, Art. 60(2).

143 Sandoz mentions the creation of protected zones in Nicaragua in 1979, opened to the civilian population as well as members of the government armed forces wishing to lay down their arms. During the Falklands conflict of 1982, a neutralized zone was planned, but never used, because active hostilities ceased almost immediately ('Safety zones', p. 128).

144 *Ibid.* 145 Chimni, 'Deconstructing safety zones', 1995, p. 825.

146 Phuong, *International Protection of Internally Displaced Persons*, p. 137.

147 Franco, 'An examination of safety zones for internally displaced persons', 1995, p. 877.

Kurdish people fled towards the Turkish border.[148] Faced with a mass influx of refugees, the Turkish government closed its borders, leaving several hundred thousand Kurds stranded in inhospitable conditions along the Iraqi–Turkish border.[149] On 5 April 1991, the Security Council adopted Resolution 688 which condemned the 'the repression of the Iraqi civilian population in many parts of Iraq, including most recently in Kurdish-populated areas, the consequences of which threaten international peace and security in the region' and demanded that Iraq immediately end this repression. Shortly afterwards, a US-led coalition launched Operation Provide Comfort, aimed at creating a 'safe haven' zone for displaced Kurds, about 150 kilometres long and 25 kilometres deep, north of the 36th Parallel, over which military flights were forbidden.[150] Operation Provide Comfort has attracted some criticism, primarily for lacking a plausible legal basis.[151] Indeed, although Resolution 688 mentioned Article 2(7) of the UN Charter, it made no reference to Chapter VII or the creation of safety zones, and thus, could not have justified the use of force in northern Iraq.[152]

These new types of safety zones differ greatly from the traditional notion of protected zones under international humanitarian law. As Landgren explains:

> The two elements which have tended to distinguish current safety zones so sharply from their conception in international humanitarian law are that *they need not be based on the consent of the parties to the conflict*, and that *they are not required to have an exclusively civilian character*.[153]

As opposed to protected zones under international humanitarian law, most of the safety zones established in the 1990s were indeed not based on the express agreement of the parties to the conflict, but imposed on them through multilateral action.[154] Perhaps one of the most notorious – and infamous – instances of safety zones created by the Security Council is that

148 UNHCR, *State of the World's Refugees* (2000), p. 212. 149 *Ibid.*

150 Sandoz, 'Safety zones', p. 129; Chimni, 'Deconstructing safety zones', p. 837.

151 Chimni, 'Deconstructing safety zones', pp. 830–1; Landgren, 'Safety zones', 442–3; Subedi, '"Safe havens" in "zones of turmoil"', 1999, 28. Subedi however argues that while Resolution 688 did not justify an action by the US, Great Britain and France, independently of the UN, it did provide 'somewhat plausible grounds for the Security Council's intervention in the Kurdish affair and the form of such intervention could have been the creation of a safe haven or an enclave or something consistent with the express and implied powers of the UN'.

152 Hutchinson, 'Restoring hope', 1993, 633. 153 Landgren, 'Safety zones', 441.

154 Chimni, 'Deconstructing safety zones', p. 827.

of the six 'safe areas' established in 1993 in Bosnia and Herzegovina. On 16 April 1993, in response to the intolerable situation prevailing around Srebrenica and constant armed attacks against civilians by Bosnian Serb forces, the Security Council, acting under Chapter VII of the UN Charter, adopted Resolution 819 which demanded that:

> all parties and others concerned treat Srebrenica and its surroundings as a safe area which should be free from any armed attack or any other hostile act.

This decision was rapidly followed by Resolution 824 of 6 May 1993, in which the Security Council declared Sarajevo, Bihac, Tuzla, Zepa and Gorazde as 'safe areas'. In this context, the safe areas were envisaged to be 'areas free from armed attacks and from any other hostile acts that would endanger the well-being and the safety of their inhabitants and where the unimpeded delivery of humanitarian assistance to the civilian population would be ensured'.[155]

However, although the Security Council acted under Chapter VII, it had provided no resources or mandate for the UN Protection Force (UNPROFOR) to impose its demands on the parties.[156] As a result, the 'safe area' concept in Bosnia and Herzegovina lacked a vital enforcement component.[157] Moreover, while the Secretary-General had indicated that approximately 34,000 troops would be required 'to obtain deterrence through strength', the Security Council opted for a 'light option' of about 7,600 troops.[158] As recognized by the UN Secretary-General in 1999:

> The safe areas were established by the Security Council without the consent of the parties to the conflict and without the provision of any credible military deterrent. They were neither protected areas nor safe havens in the sense of international humanitarian law, nor safe areas in any militarily meaningful sense.[159]

155 UNSC, 'Report of the Secretary-General pursuant to Resolution 844 (1993)' (9 May 1994), S/1994/555, para. 2.

156 UNGA, 'Report of the Secretary-General pursuant to General Assembly Resolution 53/35 – the fall of Srebrenica' (15 November 1999), A/54/549, para. 56.

157 UNSC, 'Report of the Secretary-General pursuant to Security Council Resolutions 982(1995) and 987(1995)' (30 May 1995) S/1995/444, para. 33.

158 UNSC, 'Report of the Secretary-General pursuant to Security Council Resolutions 982(1995) and 987(1995)', para. 33; in his report of 9 May 1994, the Secretary-General explained that while this option could not, in itself, completely guarantee the defence of the safe areas, it would provide a basic level of deterrence, assuming the consent and cooperation of the parties ('Report of the Secretary-General pursuant to Resolution 844(1993)', para. 6).

159 'Report of the Secretary-General on the fall of Srebrenica', para. 499.

Furthermore, the safe areas had not been demilitarized[160] and were used by Bosnian government forces as military bases from which to launch their attacks. Inevitably, the Bosnian Serb forces responded with disproportionate force, bombarding and shelling the safe areas.[161] The Bosnian Serb authorities also denied the people living in the areas freedom of movement through Serb-controlled territory, and frequently prevented humanitarian organizations from reaching them.[162] Finally, on 11 July 1995, the Bosnian Serb troops overran Srebrenica, forcing some 40,000 people to flee and summarily executing some 7,000 people, mostly Muslim men and boys.[163]

There have been other attempts to create safety zones for the protection of civilians in armed conflict, including a UN-sanctioned 'preventive zone' in Somalia in 1992,[164] as well as a 'safe humanitarian zone' established by French-led Operation Turquoise, towards the end of the civil conflict in Rwanda.[165] Despite some humanitarian benefits,[166] safety zones have been widely criticized for their failure to prevent armed attacks on the zone as a result of a lack of both the consent of the parties involved and a 'credible threat', as well as continued militarization of the zone.[167]

In contrast, open relief centres (ORCs) in Sri Lanka represent a somewhat different, and more successful, type of safety zone. An ORC has been broadly defined as 'a temporary place where displaced persons on the move can freely enter or leave and obtain essential relief assistance in a relatively safe environment'.[168] Between 1988 and 1990, following the end of hostilities in north and east Sri Lanka, the UNHCR had been assisting the Sri Lankan government in the repatriation and reintegration of returnees from south India. The returnee reintegration programme was

160 Indeed, part of UNPROFOR's mandate under Res. 836 (1993) was 'to promote the withdrawal of military or paramilitary units *other than those of the Bosnian Government* from the safe areas'.

161 UNSC, 'Report of the Secretary-General pursuant to Security Council Resolutions 982(1995) and 987(1995)', para. 38.

162 UNHCR, *State of the World's Refugees* (2000), p. 224.

163 *Ibid.*

164 Hyndman, 'Preventive, palliative, or punitive?', 176–8.

165 Landgren, 'Safety zones', 447–51; Chimni, 'Deconstructing safety zones', pp. 848–50.

166 Operation Provide Comfort in northern Iraq enabled over 1.5 million Kurdish refugees to return from Turkey, Iran and the border areas inside Iraq (Franco, 'An examination of safety zones', p. 879); the humanitarian zone in Rwanda protected the remaining Tutsi in the zone, as well as Hutu troops from revenge killings. It also stemmed refugee outflows into Zaire (Landgren, 'Safety zones', 450).

167 Landgren, 'Safety zones', 454; Sandoz, 'Safety zones', pp. 134–5.

168 Clarance, 'Open relief centres', 1991, 325.

undertaken within the framework of the UNCHR Statute, which calls upon the High Commissioner to seek 'permanent solutions to the problem of refugees by assisting Governments and ... private organizations to facilitate the voluntary repatriation of ... refugees'.[169] When hostilities resumed between the Sri Lankan government forces and the Liberation Tamil Tigers of Eelam (LTTE) in June 1990, many returnees and internally displaced persons found themselves on the road once again. As observed by Clarance, the UNHCR had a 'moral obligation towards those returnees whom it had been assisting with reintegration'.[170] Moreover, while it had no statutory competence for internally displaced persons, internal displacement was fuelling refugee exodus to south India. In this context, it would also have been 'morally unacceptable' for the UNHCR to draw a distinction between the two categories of displaced persons.[171]

Consequently, the ORCs were established in 1990, 'as a pragmatic response to the humanitarian needs emerging from the ground situation in Mannar District'.[172] According to Clarance:

> They differed significantly, both from closed camps and from government welfare centres, and did not and could not claim to constitute, at least *de jure*, 'safe havens'.[173]

What distinguishes ORCs in Sri Lanka from, for instance, the safe areas in Bosnia-Herzegovina is the fact the ORCs have become 'havens of safety, accepted and respected by both warring Parties'.[174] Initially, UNHCR explains, 'the establishment of the ORCs was based on an informal acceptance by the parties that humanitarian assistance to and physical safety of the population in the Centres would be respected'.[175] They were later formally recognized in a 1993 memorandum of understanding between

169 UNGA, 'Statute of the Office of the United Nations High Commissioner for Refugees', Res. 428(V) (14 December 1950), UN Doc. A/RES/428, para. 1; Clarance, 'Open relief centres', 321.

170 Clarance, 'Open relief centres', 324. 171 *Ibid.* 172 *Ibid.*

173 *Ibid.* Clarance notes that the possibility of establishing a 'safe haven' on Mannar Island was studied in July and August 1990 by the local delegation of the ICRC and the UNHCR Office in Sri Lanka on the one hand, and the Sri Lankan government on the other. The idea was rejected, as 'technical problems, particularly relating to entry/exit and internal security, precluded satisfactory implementation of such a concept in the then prevailing conditions'.

174 UNHCR, *The State of the World's Refugees*, 1993.

175 UNHCR, 'UNHCR's operational experience with internally displaced persons' (September 1994), www.unhcr.org/3d4f95964.html (accessed 20 September 2011), para. 152.

UNHCR and the Sri Lankan government. While the neutrality of the ORCs has often been challenged, especially by LTTE cadres, the ORCs have not been targeted for attack, or caught in the crossfire.[176] Despite incidents involving weapons in the ORCs and attempts to intimidate the residents, Landgren notes that the centres have not taken on a military character.[177] Finally, the open nature of these centres means that no restrictions have been imposed on freedom of movement to and from the centres.[178]

ORCs are closer to the traditional concept of protected zone than other recent instances of safety zones.[179] Thus, the question remains as to the desirability of such safety zones for the physical protection of internally displaced persons against armed attacks. Could the concept of ORCs in Sri Lanka serve as a model on which to base subsequent safety zones for IDPs? Or should efforts be concentrated on the establishment of protected zones within the meaning of international humanitarian law? Could the concept of protected zones be revisited in order to specifically protect refugee camps from armed attacks?

Protected zones for displaced persons in armed conflict

In a 1999 report, the UN Secretary-General declared that:

> Protected zones and safe areas can have a role in protecting civilians in armed conflict, but it is clear that either they must be demilitarized and established by the agreements of the belligerents, as in the case of the 'protected zones' and 'safe havens' recognised by international humanitarian law, or they must be truly safe areas, fully defended by a credible military deterrent.[180]

For safety zones to truly protect civilians fleeing the dangers of war and to be respected by the belligerents, they should be created, as much as possible, within the framework of international humanitarian law. Thus, it is essential that a protected zone be established with the consent of all parties concerned, in order to ensure effective protection from attacks. Indeed, a coerced party will be more likely to violate the immunity of the protected zone than if such a party agreed to it in the first place. Moreover, a safe area should imperatively be demilitarized, in accordance with

176 *Ibid.*; Landgren, 'Safety zones', 452. 177 Landgren, 'Safety zones', 453.

178 Islam, 'The least protection for the most vulnerable', 2006, 354; Landgren, 'Safety zones', 453.

179 Landgren, 'Safety zones', 441.

180 1999 Report of the Secretary-General on the fall of Srebrenica, para. 499.

the conditions laid down in Articles 59 and 60 of the First Protocol, as a way to preserve the civilian character of the area and the non-combatant status of its inhabitants, and thus ensure its immunity from attacks. Furthermore, protected zones should be established on the basis of precise criteria, such as the clear delimitation of the area, as provided by Article 60 of the First Protocol. In a 1994 report on safe areas in Bosnia-Herzegovina, the UN Secretary-General indeed noted that the effective implementation of the safe area concept had been facilitated, in the areas where an agreement was achieved, 'by a clear demarcation of the area concerned and a concise statement of the obligations that each party would respect'.[181]

Nevertheless, it should not be forgotten that contemporary armed conflicts tend to be mostly internal in nature. International humanitarian law does not make provision for protected zones in non-international armed conflict.[182] Thus, the creation of safety zones for the protection of civilians displaced by civil war must be envisaged on an ad hoc, case-by-case basis. However, many internal conflicts are characterized by mutual hatred, extreme violence, complete disregard for human life and lack of respect for international humanitarian law. In such situations, consent may be difficult to achieve[183] and a safety zone may have to be imposed on the belligerents by unilateral action sanctioned by the United Nations. In a 2000 resolution, the UN Security Council indeed indicated:

> its willingness to consider the appropriateness and feasibility of temporary security zones and safe corridors for the protection of civilians and the delivery of assistance in situations characterized by the threat of genocide, crimes against humanity and war crimes against the civilian population.[184]

However, such enforced safety zones should only be envisaged as a 'measure of last resort'.[185] As noted above, the success of a safe area depends first and foremost on the belligerents' acceptance of it and the belligerents' willingness to respect its protected status. Therefore, it is important that impartial humanitarian organizations, such as the ICRC or UNHCR, negotiate the creation of safe areas and enter into agreements with all

181 UNSC, 'Report of the Secretary-General pursuant to Resolution 844 (1993)', para. 12.
182 ICRC, 'The ICRC and internally displaced persons', IRRC 35 (1995), 181.
183 Landgren, 'Safety zones', 454; UNHCR, *State of the World's Refugees* (1997).
184 UNSC Res. 1296 (19 April 2000).
185 UNSC, 'Report of the Secretary-General on the protection of civilians in armed conflict' (8 September 1999), S/1999/957, Recommendation 39.

parties involved, including armed opposition groups, particularly if the safe areas are to be established in rebel-controlled territory. The 2004 Darfur Plan of Action between the Government of Sudan and the United Nations attracted criticism for its failure to incorporate rebel groups in the negotiations. As a result, the proposed plan to create 'safe areas' for displaced and resident civilians in Darfur[186] was accused by Human Rights Watch of consolidating the government's ethnic-cleansing policy, without offering real security for civilians.[187]

If consent is nevertheless impossible to obtain, imposed safety zones will only be effective if supported by a 'credible military deterrent'.[188] Indeed, without the adequate military force to back them up, safety zones will be more likely to be attacked, and the protection which these zones are intended to provide would then only be 'illusory'.[189] In order to avoid repeating the terrible debacle of the Srebrenica 'safe area', UN-sanctioned safety zones should thus require the availability, prior to their establishment, 'of sufficient and credible force to guarantee the safety of civilian populations making use of them'.[190] Moreover, extreme caution should be exercised, particularly in inter-ethnic conflict, so that UN-sponsored

186 The Darfur Plan of Action provides that:

> The GoS [Government of Sudan] would identify parts of Darfur that can be made secure and safe within 30 days.
>
> This could include existing IDP camps, and areas around certain towns and villages with a high concentration of local population. The GoS would then provide secure routes to and between these areas. These tasks should be carried out by Sudan police forces to maintain confidence already created by the redeployment of GoS armed forces. This will allow people to reach the areas initially and also conduct business essential to life support. (Text of the Darfur Plan of Action, at: http://news.bbc.co.uk/1/hi/world/africa/3543740.stm (accessed 7 October 2011))

187 HRW, 'Darfur: UN "safe areas"' offer no real security' (1 September 2004), http://hrw.org/english/docs/2004/09/01/darfur9286.htm (accessed 7 October 2011):

> The proposed 'safe areas' in the Darfur Plan of Action ignore key considerations for the genuine security of civilians. It is a bilateral agreement between the Sudanese government and the United Nations that lacks the consent of the rebel forces. The proposed locations of the areas, the lack of specificity regarding modalities of protection – beyond the use of Sudanese police that have already proven to be more likely to commit abuses than prevent them – and their open-ended duration risk that these proposed safe areas become permanent resettlement sites aimed at controlling the civilian population, rather than providing genuine security.

188 'Report of the Secretary-General on the fall of Srebrenica', para. 499.

189 Sandoz, 'Safety zones', 134.

190 'Report of the Secretary-General on the protection of civilians in armed conflict', Recommendation 39.

'safe areas' cannot be used by the belligerents to justify the forced relocation of IDPs in continuation of a policy of ethnic cleansing. Most importantly, the creation of safety zones should not deprive internally displaced persons of their right to leave the country and seek refuge in another country.[191]

In addition, the creation of protected zones could be considered for the protection of refugee camps in conflict zones. In his 1983 report, Ambassador Felix Schnyder indeed envisaged the possibility of refugee camps and settlements enjoying a status similar to that of protected zones in international humanitarian law.[192] Similarly, in 1996 international emergency relief agency Médecins Sans Frontières (MSF) called for an immediate UN military intervention to set up safe areas in eastern Zaire in order to ensure protection of Rwandan and Burundian refugees and Zaireans, and access for relief agencies.[193]

Two situations could be identified. First, a refugee camp may have been established in the territory of a host state before it became engulfed in an armed conflict, but then finds itself in the conflict zone once the hostilities have begun. As long as the refugee camp has been completely demilitarized, remains exclusively civilian in character and is not used as a base from which to launch hostile actions, parties to the conflict may agree to declare the camp and surrounding area a demilitarized zone within the meaning of Article 60 of the First Protocol. Alternatively, refugees fleeing the dangers of war may seek asylum in a country itself involved in an armed conflict. Belligerents may agree on the creation of a temporary neutralized zone in virtue of Article 15 of the Fourth Geneva Convention, in order to accommodate refugees and protect them from the effects of hostilities. However, such zones may only protect civilians who do not engage in military activity. It is therefore essential that effective separation of armed elements be undertaken, in order to ensure maximum protection to genuine civilian refugees in armed conflict.

Like safe areas for the protection of civilians displaced by a conflict, protected zones for refugees should be based on the consent of the parties to the conflict and be clearly established for the protection of genuine civilian refugees. In addition, they should be strictly monitored by a neutral

191 Chimni, 'Deconstructing safety zones', p. 853.

192 Draft Declaration on the prohibition of military or armed attacks against refugee camps and settlements, para. 5.

193 ReliefWeb, 'Doctors without Borders calls for international military intervention to create safe zones in Zaire' (4 November 1996), http://reliefweb.int/node/27827 (accessed 7 October 2011).

organization such as the ICRC or UNHCR, which would control the civilian character of the camps and prevent weapons from getting in. If imposed on the belligerents, it is imperative that these zones are protected by an international force, with a clear mandate and adequate enforcement powers.

Concluding remarks

A number of important conclusions may be derived from this study on the protection of refugees and internally displaced persons under international humanitarian law.

The imperative need to ensure respect and compliance with existing rules of IHL for the protection of displaced persons in armed conflict

First, in many respects, international humanitarian law constitutes a comprehensive corpus of protection for refugees and other displaced persons in armed conflict. It indeed adequately protects civilians from forced displacement in situations of occupation and non-international armed conflict, which arguably constitute the most common instances in which displacement takes place. Furthermore, the rules of humanitarian law governing the conduct of hostilities, including the fundamental principle of civilian immunity, provide adequate safeguards against armed attacks by belligerents and should, if respected, guarantee the physical safety of displaced persons. Similarly, the standards of general application for the protection of all civilians in armed conflict provide for certain displacement-related needs, including the provision of food, health care and other basic necessities, humanitarian assistance and family reunification.

Nevertheless, most of these essential rules are often blatantly ignored. Civilians are deliberately displaced, humanitarian assistance is intentionally diverted and refugee and IDP camps are regularly targeted by armed forces and armed groups. In addition, states will often contest the applicability of the Geneva Conventions, by denying either that a situation of internal unrest amounts to an internal armed conflict, or that a belligerent occupation is actually taking place. In turn, armed opposition groups will also be reluctant to comply with their obligations, if the government disregards its obligations.[1] Thus, the problem is not so much a lack of rules, but rather a lack of will on the part of the belligerents to abide by their obligations.[2] Current efforts must therefore be directed towards ensuring better compliance with existing rules of international humanitarian law and encouraging states and armed groups to abide by their obligations.

Assessment of IHL implementation mechanisms as effective means of protection

Current implementation mechanisms of international humanitarian law have been often qualified as 'underdeveloped' and 'fairly ineffective'.[3] The system of protecting powers depends upon the consent of the parties concerned and has very rarely been used by belligerents,[4] and the International Fact-Finding Commission relies on both state acceptance and state initiative for its operation.[5] In addition, apart from the ICRC's right of initiative,[6] none of the existing IHL supervision mechanisms are expressly mandated to address situations of internal armed conflicts. The most effective means of enforcing IHL is the prosecution and punishment of war criminals within national or international criminal jurisdictions.[7] However, this enforcement mechanism is designed to address and repress violations of international humanitarian law post-conflict. Thus, prosecution of war crimes, although an extremely useful deterrent mechanism for future conflicts, does not constitute, in itself, a protection mechanism against abuses at, or near to, the time that they are being committed.[8]

In parallel, universal and regional human rights bodies have increasingly considered issues of international humanitarian law. Two reasons

1 Moir, *Law of Internal Armed Conflict*, p. 232.
2 *Ibid.*; Hulme, 'Armed conflict and the displaced', 91.
3 Heintze, 'On the relationship between human rights law and international humanitarian law', 798.
4 Cassese, 'Current trends', 1998, 4.
5 ICRC Expert Seminars, 'Improving compliance with international humanitarian law', Report prepared by the ICRC (October 2003), www.icrc.org/eng/resources/documents/report/ihl-respect-report-011003.htm (accessed 20 November 2011), p. 20.
6 Under Common Art. 3 of the Geneva Conventions and Art. 18 Protocol II, the ICRC may offer its services to the parties to the conflict 'for the performance of their traditional functions in relation to the victims of the armed conflict'.
7 Cassese, 'Current trends', 17.
8 Moir, *Law of Internal Armed Conflict*, p. 272.

may be advanced to justify this development. First, human rights bodies are often required to report or render decisions on situations of human rights abuses taking place within the context of an armed conflict. Second, there is an undisputable overlap between the substantive norms of the two bodies of law, particularly in relation with issues such as the right to life, the prohibition of torture, or the principle of non-discrimination.[9] Regional human rights bodies, especially the European Court of Human Rights and the Inter-American Commission for Human Rights, have participated greatly in the promotion and enforcement of international humanitarian law, by applying the rules of international humanitarian law either as a tool for interpretation of human rights provisions or directly to the case before them.[10] Although the practice of human rights bodies in this regard is a 'welcome addition' to the limited and arguably rather ineffective means of enforcement of international humanitarian law,[11] a number of non-negligible limitations should be highlighted. First, it has been argued that human rights bodies may lack adequate knowledge of international humanitarian law.[12] In addition, the lengthy investigations and deliberations involved in most human rights supervision processes means that violations are usually addressed long after they were committed, which, in terms of protection of victims of

[9] Kalshoven and Zegveld, *Constraints on the Waging of War*, 2001, p. 200.

[10] For instance, in the *La Tablada* case, the Commission considered that a concerted attack by an armed group on a barracks of the Argentine Armed Forces constituted a non-international armed conflict, which triggered the application of Common Article 3 and other rules of IHL relevant to internal armed conflicts. The Commission explained its decision to apply rules of international humanitarian law directly by saying that the American Convention on Human Rights, although applicable in situations of armed conflict, did not specifically regulate the conduct of hostilities:

> For example, both Common Article 3 and Article 4 of the American Convention protect the right to life and, thus, prohibit, *inter alia*, summary executions in all circumstances. Claims alleging arbitrary deprivations of the right to life attributable to State agents are clearly within the Commission's jurisdiction. But the Commission's ability to resolve claimed violations of this non-derogable right arising out of an armed conflict may not be possible in many cases by reference to Article 4 of the American Convention alone. This is because the American Convention contain no rules that either define or distinguish civilians from combatants and other military targets, much less, specificity when a civilian can be lawfully attacked or when civilian casualties are a lawful consequence of military operations. (*Abella* v. *Argentina*, Report No. 55/97, Annual Report of the Inter-American Commission on Human Rights 1997, OEA/Ser.L/V/II.98, paras. 157, 161)

[11] Kalshoven and Zegveld, *Constraints on the Waging of War*, p. 201.

[12] *Ibid.*; ICRC Report on the expert seminars, p. 16.

armed conflict, is clearly insufficient.[13] Finally, human rights bodies lack competence to effectively address alleged violations by non-state actors. Accordingly, 'while interest in international humanitarian law should be supported and encouraged, their activities in this area do not remove the need to develop supervisory mechanisms specifically mandated to enforce compliance with humanitarian norms'.[14]

There is indeed a clear and urgent need for contemporaneous IHL implementation mechanisms which are not dependent upon state sovereignty and consent and effectively protect civilians and other war victims, including refugees and internally displaced persons, irrespective of their nationality, the qualification of the armed conflict or the will of the authorities on whose territory they find themselves. Alternatives to existing implementation mechanisms have been considered by the ICRC and legal scholars. Krzysztof Drzewicki, for instance, has suggested the introduction of reporting systems for legislative implementation of humanitarian law, with a mild supervisory role for the ICRC.[15] Another option would be the creation of an ad hoc reporting system, where states engaged in active armed conflict would report on alleged violations of international humanitarian law.[16] However, as demonstrated by the reporting procedure of the Human Rights Committee and other human rights treaty bodies, reliance on state reporting for the protection of human rights is 'deeply flawed', particularly in situations of internal armed conflicts.[17] First, many governments embroiled in an armed conflict are unable to submit their reports on time, and many reports are long overdue.[18] Second, when they do submit a report, there is a strong likelihood of it being economical with the truth, given that its authors are usually the very perpetrators of abuse.[19]

The participants in a series of expert seminars organized by the ICRC on improving compliance with international humanitarian law also pondered proposals for the creation of an IHL Commission or Office of the High Commissioner for International Humanitarian Law.[20] Such Commission would have functions similar to those found in existing human

[13] Moir, *Law of Internal Armed Conflict*, p. 272.
[14] Kalshoven and Zegveld, *Constraints on the Waging of War*, p. 201.
[15] Drzewicki, 'National legislation and international humanitarian law', 1989, pp. 109–31.
[16] ICRC Report on the expert seminars, p. 18.
[17] Moir, *Law of Internal Armed Conflict*, p. 259.
[18] *Ibid.*; Heintze, 'On the relationship between human rights law and international humanitarian law', 798–9.
[19] Moir, *Law of Internal Armed Conflict*, p. 259.
[20] ICRC Report on the expert seminars, p. 17.

rights bodies, including a reporting system and an individual complaints mechanism.[21] The creation of an independent international humanitarian law supervision mechanism would indeed be highly desirable. As noted, denial of the existence of an armed conflict is one of the main tools used by belligerents to avoid their obligations under international humanitarian law.[22] The creation of an impartial body, which would authoritatively characterize the conflict and determine the legal regime applicable, would be a good means of forcing all belligerents to abide by their obligations and ensuring that international humanitarian law is respected in international and non-international armed conflicts.

In the meantime, it is the responsibility of the international community as a whole 'to respect and ensure respect' for the Conventions in all circumstances.[23] High contracting parties have a duty to ensure that the rules of international humanitarian law, as well as other essential rules for the protection of human beings, are duly respected by all parties to the conflict and must act accordingly. As far as non-international armed conflicts are concerned, the priority is to try to engage non-state actors to encourage them to comply with norms of international humanitarian law.

Engaging non-state actors towards compliance with international humanitarian law

Rebels and other members of armed opposition groups do not have a specific status under international law and are generally considered criminals under domestic law. Unlike combatants in international armed conflicts, who benefit from the so-called 'combatant privilege', captured rebels may be prosecuted for mere participation in the conflict, murder or treason and be punished accordingly. Consequently, without the benefit of the combatant privilege and prisoner of war status, rebels have very little incentive to comply with the laws of war.[24] In fact, they will probably use the most brutal tactics in order to ensure military victory and avoid prosecution. '[W]ithout the Geneva Conventions to either protect them or restrain them, there is no reason for victory-starved insurgents to defer to any of the Conventions' humanitarian provisions.'[25]

During the ICRC expert seminar, the participants discussed at length the potential incentives that could be given to armed groups in order to encourage compliance with the rules of international humanitarian

[21] *Ibid.* [22] See above, Chapters 2 and 3. [23] Geneva Conventions, Common Article 1.
[24] Solf, 'Problems with the application of norms', 1983, 292.
[25] Lopez, 'Uncivil wars', 935.

law. In particular, they saw great potential in the grant of immunity from prosecution for participation in the armed conflict.[26] Indeed, under Article 6(5) of Protocol II, states are encouraged to grant the 'broadest possible' amnesty to persons who have taken part in hostilities, at the end of an armed conflict. Although the purpose of this provision was initially 'to encourage gestures of reconciliation',[27] it is clear that it could also be used as an effective way of encouraging armed groups to comply with the laws of war. However, amnesties should only be granted for participation in hostilities and other war-like acts not constituting serious violations of international humanitarian law. War crimes and other international crimes, subject to universal jurisdiction, cannot be annulled by the grant of an amnesty. This was confirmed by the Appeals Chamber of the Special Court for Sierra Leone, which held that: 'A State cannot bring into oblivion and forgetfulness a crime, such as a crime against international law, which other States are entitled to keep alive and remember.'[28] Thus, it found that the blanket amnesties granted to all participants in the Sierra Leone civil war by the Lomé Peace Agreement did not prevent the prosecution of international crimes before the Special Court.

Furthermore, if armed groups were given the opportunity to express their consent to be bound by the treaty provisions, they would be more willing to comply with international obligations agreed to during negotiations in which they took no part. The conclusion of special agreements between armed groups and state parties, as envisaged in Common Article 3, would be one solution. By these agreements, the parties to a non-international armed conflict declare their intention to comply with all or part of the provisions of Geneva Conventions. Such agreements were concluded between the belligerents in the conflicts in former Yugoslavia. Similarly, the conclusion of special agreements between the ICRC and armed groups, for the delivery of humanitarian relief or for access and visits to detainees and prisoners of war in areas under their control, is common practice.[29]

Alternatively, rebel armed groups may issue a unilateral declaration of their commitment to abide by the rules of international humanitarian

[26] ICRC Report on the expert seminars, p. 22.

[27] Sandoz *et al.*, *Commentary on the Protocols*, p. 1400.

[28] *Prosecutor* v. *Morris Kallon and Brima Buzzy Kamara*, SCSL-2004-15-AR72(E) and SCSL-2004-16-AR72(E), para. 67, as cited by S. Meisenberg, 'Legality of amnesties in international humanitarian law: the Lomé Amnesty Decision of the Special Court for Sierra Leone', IRRC, 856 (2004), 837, 842.

[29] Ewumbue-Monono, 'Armed non-state actors in Africa', 2006, 911.

law. The aim of this declaration would be to provide 'a self-disciplining effect' on the armed groups.[30] One such example is the Declaration of 23 May 1968 by the rebel Biafran authorities, pledging to respect civilian populations, give the ICRC facilities for the delivery of humanitarian assistance and organize the exchange of prisoners of war through the ICRC.[31] Furthermore, in 2000, the non-governmental organization Geneva Call launched an innovative initiative, encouraging non-state actors to express adherence to the norms of the Ottawa anti-personnel mine ban treaty through the signature of a 'Deed of Commitment for Adherence to a Total Ban on Anti-Personnel Mines and for Cooperation in Mine Action'. The 'Deed of Commitment' also contains an accountability provision which binds signatory groups to both allow and cooperate in the monitoring of their commitment to a total ban on anti-personnel mines.[32] As of 2011, forty-one armed non-state actors had signed Geneva Call's 'Deed of Commitment' banning anti-personnel landmines.[33] Such mechanism appears to be a very effective way of encouraging armed groups to take an active role in the protection of civilians in areas under their control and should be replicated in other areas of the laws of war.[34]

Issues inherent in the very nature of IHL and the need for reform

Although the substantive norms of international humanitarian law form an adequate body of rules for the protection of refugees and internally displaced persons, international humanitarian law, as a legal regime, contains two very clear deficiencies, which inevitably affect the situation of displaced persons in armed conflict. As mentioned throughout this study, international humanitarian law is essentially rooted in a traditional conception of interstate armed conflicts. Its development has been intrinsically tied in with concern for state sovereignty, while the applicability of its rules depends on the characterization of the conflict, on the

30 ICRC Report on the expert seminar, p. 21.

31 Ewumbue-Monono, 'Armed non-state actors in Africa', 907.

32 Geneva Call, 'Engaging non-state actors toward compliance with humanitarian norms', workshop summary report (15 July 2001), 4 www.genevacall.org/resources/conference-reports/f-conference-reports/2001–2010/gc-2001–15jul01-geneva.pdf (accessed 10 November 2011).

33 Geneva Call, *Annual Report 2010*, 8, www.genevacall.org/resources/annual-reports/f-annual-reports/2001-2010/gc_annual_report_2010.pdf (accessed 10 November 2011).

34 A second 'Deed of commitment for the protection of children from the effects of armed conflict' opened for signature at the end of 2010, and a deed on gender-based violence is currently under preparation (Geneva Call, *Annual Report 2010*, 7).

one hand, and on the determination of the victim of war as 'protected person', on the other.

Inadequacy of the dichotomy

International humanitarian law is based upon a distinction between international and non-international armed conflicts and conventional international humanitarian law of international armed conflicts is much more developed than the law applicable to internal armed conflicts. The implication of this is a significant discrepancy between the two regimes, particularly in terms of protection of refugees in armed conflict. The dichotomy between the two regimes, described as 'problematic'[35] and an 'outdated phenomenon',[36] has been widely criticized.[37] In addition, situations of internal disturbances and tensions are excluded from the scope of application of international humanitarian law and thus remain within the realm of a state's domestic jurisdiction. As states may also derogate from their human rights obligations during times of public emergency, it is clear that the protection of civilians from and during displacement in such situations will be inexorably affected.

Nevertheless, the past decades have seen the gradual attenuation of the distinction between international and non-international armed conflicts. First, the characterization of an armed conflict as international or non-international may be difficult to establish, as contemporary armed conflicts often find themselves outside this so-called 'two-box' system.[38] Wars of national liberation, once considered as strictly internal matters, have been elevated to the status of international armed conflicts, governed by Protocol I.[39] In addition, non-international armed conflicts have increasingly become internationalized, as a result of the direct or indirect intervention of a third state or a multinational force in the conflict. There is a multitude of a relationships involved in an internationalized internal armed conflict – e.g. between the rebels and the intervening state, between the intervening state and the host state, and between the rebels and the host state – and the question of whether such conflict should

35 Schindler, 'The different types of armed conflict', 1979, 126.

36 Kwakwa, *Personal and Material Fields of Application*, 1992, p. 23.

37 For an in-depth criticism of the current distinction, see J. G. Stewart, 'Towards a single definition of armed conflict in international humanitarian law: a critique of internationalized armed conflict', IRRC, 85 (2003), 313–50.

38 Boelaert-Suominen, 'The Yugoslav Tribunal and the common core of humanitarian law', 2000, 619.

39 Protocol I, Art. 1(4).

be governed by the rules applicable to international or non-international armed conflicts, or both, is widely debated.[40]

Second, on a substantive level, the jurisprudence of the ICTY has greatly contributed to the blurring of the distinction between the rules applicable in international and non-international armed conflicts. In the first case before the Yugoslav Tribunal, the Appeals Chamber indeed asked:

> Why protect civilians from belligerent violence, or ban rape, torture or the wanton destruction of hospitals, churches, museums or private property, as well as proscribe weapons causing unnecessary suffering when two sovereign States are engaged in war, and yet refrain from enacting the same bans or providing the same protection when armed violence has erupted 'only' within the territory of a sovereign State? If international law, while of course duly safeguarding the legitimate interests of States, must gradually turn to the protection of human beings, it is only natural that the aforementioned dichotomy should gradually lose its weight.[41]

Since then, the ICTY has recognized the existence of 'a corpus of customary international law applicable to all armed conflicts irrespective of their characterization as international or non-international armed conflicts'.[42] Furthermore, the ICRC study on customary international humanitarian law identified a large number of substantive rules applicable both in international and non-international armed conflicts, irrespective of their characterization. Thus, as stated by Lindsay Moir:

> we would appear to be moving tentatively towards the position whereby the legal distinction between international and non-international armed conflict is becoming outmoded. If this trend continues, then there may shortly be a body of international humanitarian law which applies to *all* armed conflicts. What will matter as regards legal regulation will not be whether an armed conflict is international or internal, but simply whether an armed conflict exists *per se*.[43]

Such a development is highly anticipated. Civilians, whether they are caught in the fighting between two states, between their government armed forces and an armed opposition group, or between two armed groups, deserve equal and effective protection. In parallel, states should also agree on a set of binding, non-derogable, minimum humanitarian standards applicable at all times, so that no state can escape their

[40] Pejić, 'Status of armed conflicts', 2007, p. 84.

[41] *Tadić*, Appeals on Jurisdiction, para. 97.

[42] *Prosecutor* v. *Martić*, Rule 61 Decision, IT-95-11, 8 March 1996, para. 11.

[43] Moir, *Law of Internal Armed Conflict*, pp. 51–2.

obligations towards individuals under their control, irrespective of the characterization of the situation.

Irrelevance of the concept of 'protected persons' for the protection of war victims in contemporary armed conflicts

Armed conflicts are continuously evolving. In particular, conflicts are increasingly fought along ethnic lines and civilians are becoming the main victims of atrocities committed in the name of an ideology. The Yugoslav wars for instance were characterized by the extensive displacement of populations as part of a wider policy of 'ethnic cleansing'. Yet, international humanitarian law remains based on a traditional, state-oriented concept of the victim of armed conflict. There is a major gap in the law as regards the protection of a state's own nationals in inter-ethnic conflicts. Similarly, internally displaced persons are not explicitly protected against arbitrary treatment and other unlawful practices committed by their own country. International humanitarian law is clearly no longer adapted to the demands of contemporary armed conflicts. The ICTY has indeed recognized that the concept of 'protected persons' needs to be redefined in order to guarantee a more effective protection to all victims of armed conflicts.

Would this redefinition of 'protected persons', based on allegiance as opposed to nationality, be applicable to all international armed conflicts? At first sight, the answer seems to be negative. However, owing to the disintegration of states into several smaller states, it has become clear that even interstate armed conflicts are not as straightforward as they seem. In certain cases, it may be difficult to clearly ascertain the nationality, and hence the protection regime, of the civilians concerned. The notion of allegiance, although difficult to determine, may be a valid ground for protection. As a matter of fact, the drafters of the Geneva Conventions considered it as early as 1949, in relation to refugees of enemy nationality. It seemed absurd to consider those persons as enemy nationals if they had themselves sought to renounce all nationality link with their state of origin and declared allegiance to their state of residence. The situation of nationals of enemy descent differs in a number of ways and allegiance to their own state may be more difficult to ascertain, especially in the case of newly separated countries. They should nevertheless benefit from some protection, akin to that of refugees, based on a presumption of allegiance.

A persuasive argument can be made for the introduction of an international instrument which would take into consideration the evolution of international armed conflicts. So far, non-international armed conflicts and wars of national liberation have been placed on the international scene. It is now time for international humanitarian law to acknowledge the fact that international armed conflicts have also evolved. In particular, the practice of deportations and forcible transfers by a state of its own nationals should be recognized as such and regulated.

Relevance of a complementarity of legal regimes for the protection of refugees and IDPs in armed conflict

The issue of the protection of displaced persons in time of war clearly demonstrates the importance of the complementarity of three branches of international law, as a way to ensure that the best protection possible is afforded to displaced persons in the midst of an armed conflict.

First of all, with regard to the protection from displacement, the explicit rules of international humanitarian law prohibiting the forced displacement of civilians both in situations of occupation and in non-international armed conflict complement and strengthen the implicit human rights law protection derived from the freedom of movement and residence. Second, international humanitarian law, human rights law and refugee law all contain certain rules of particular relevance for the protection and assistance of displaced persons. These bodies of law will complement and reinforce each other, and the relevant rules should be applied cumulatively in order to provide the greatest protection to internally displaced civilians and refugees. For instance, the duties of the occupying power in relation to food and health care in occupied territory should be analysed in light of the more explicit provisions of the International Covenant on Economic, Social and Cultural Rights. Alternatively, the detailed body of rules pertaining to the 'Missing' and reunification of families in international humanitarian law will undoubtedly serve to complement and bring into effect the more limited provisions of international human rights and refugee law in this regard. Finally, international humanitarian law, international human rights law and international refugee law provide complementary protection against *refoulement* within their respective scope of application.[44]

A new instrument for the protection of 'displaced persons' in armed conflict?

Should refugees and internally displaced persons be recognized as a specific category of victims of war in need of protection and become the

[44] Droege, 'Transfers of detainees', 676.

subject of a new instrument, entirely dedicated to the protection of 'displaced persons' in times of war? As noted throughout this study, refugees and internally displaced persons, although not specifically protected by international humanitarian law, nevertheless benefit from it, as long as they are affected by an armed conflict and do not actively participate in the hostilities. In addition, international human rights and refugee law continue to apply in time of war. It has therefore been argued that the adoption of a further instrument would add to the confusion and undermine the existing law.[45] Moreover, issues of internal displacement, refugees and armed conflict, each taken separately, are already contentious issues, especially as they touch upon aspects of the law within the realm of states' domestic jurisdiction. It is therefore highly unlikely that states would agree to the adoption of a binding instrument which would combine such sensitive subjects and potentially mean relinquishing part of their sovereignty.

However, the option of a non-binding instrument, on the model of the Guiding Principles on Internal Displacement, is worth considering. Not only would it restate, in a comprehensive and methodical manner, existing principles of humanitarian law applicable to refugees and IDPs, but it would also fill certain legal gaps in the protection offered to displaced persons in armed conflict. Additionally, such an instrument would be particularly useful as a guiding tool, when engaging non-state actors towards the protection and respect for the rights of refugees and other displaced persons.

45 Lavoyer, 'Refugees and internally displaced persons', 162; Bugnion, 'Réfugiés, personnes déplacées et droit international humanitaire', 286.

Bibliography

Abebe, A. M., 'Displacement of civilians during armed conflict in light of the case law of the Eritrea–Ethiopia Claims Commission', *LJIL*, 22 (2009), 823.

Abril-Stoffels, R., 'Legal regulation of humanitarian assistance in armed conflict: achievements and gaps', *IRRC*, 86 (2004), 515.

Akande, D., 'Clearing the fog of war? The ICRC's interpretative guidance on direct participation in hostilities', *ICLQ*, 59 (2010), 180.

Akhavan, P., 'Reconciling crimes against humanity with the laws of war: human rights, armed conflict and the limits of progressive jurisprudence', *JICJ*, 6 (2008), 21.

Alston, P., 'International law and the human right to food', in P. Alston and K. Tomaševski (eds.), *The Right to Food* (Utrecht: Martinus Nijhoff, 1984).

Arai-Takahashi, Y., *The Law of Occupation: Continuity and Change of International Humanitarian Law, and Its Interaction with International Human Rights Law* (Leiden: Martinus Nijhoff, 2009).

Bagenda, E. and Hovil, L., 'Sudanese refugees in northern Uganda: from one conflict to the next', *FMR*, 16 (2003), 15.

Bassiouni, M. C., *Crimes against Humanity in International Criminal Law* (2nd edn, The Hague: Kluwer Law International, 1999).

The Law of the International Criminal Tribunal for the Former Yugoslavia (New York: Transnational Publishers, Inc., 1996).

Bayefski, A. F. and Fitzpatrick, J. (eds), *Human Rights and Forced Displacement* (The Hague: Kluwer Law International, 2000).

Benvenisti, E., *The International Law of Occupation* (Princeton: Princeton University Press, 1993).

Beyani, C., 'International legal criteria for the separation of members of armed forces, armed bands and militia from refugees in the territories of host states', *IJRL*, 12 (2000), 251.

Bill, B. J., 'The Rendulic "rule": military necessity, commander's knowledge and methods of warfare', *YBIHL*, 12 (2009), 119.

Blum, Y., 'The missing reversioner: reflections on the status of Judea and Samaria', *Israel L. Rev.*, 3 (1968), 279.

Boelaert-Suominen, S., 'The Yugoslav Tribunal and the common core of humanitarian law applicable at all armed conflicts', *LJIL*, 13 (2000), 619.

Bothe, M., 'Relief actions: the position of the recipient state', in F. Kalshoven (ed.), *Assisting the Victims of Armed Conflict and Other Disasters* (Dordrecht: Martinus Nijhoff, 1989), pp. 91–8.

Bothe, M., Partsch, K. J. and Solf, W. A., *New Rules for Victims of Armed Conflicts, Commentary on the Two 1977 Protocols Additional to the Geneva Conventions of 1949* (The Hague: Martinus Nijhoff, 1982).

Brett, R. and Lester, E., 'Refugee law and international humanitarian law: parallels, lessons and looking ahead', *IRRC*, 83 (2001), 713.

Brownlie, I. and Goodwin-Gill, G. S. (Opinion), 'The protection afforded by international humanitarian law to the indigenous population of the West Bank and the Gaza Strip and to foreign citizens therein, with particular reference to the application of the 1949 Fourth Geneva Convention relative to the Protection of Civilian Persons in Time of War' (18 September 2003) (on file with author).

Bugnion, F., 'Droit de Genève et droit de La Haye', *IRRC*, 83 (2001), 901–22.

'Refugees, displaced persons and international humanitarian law', *Fordham Int'l L. J.*, 28 (2004), 139.

'Réfugiés, personnes déplacées et droit international humanitaire', *Revue Suisse de Droit International et de Droit Européen*, 3 (2001), 277.

Carey, C. M., 'Internal displacement: is prevention through accountability possible? A Kosovo case study', *Am. U. L. Rev.*, 49 (1999), 243.

Casanovas, O., 'La protection internationale des réfugiés et des personnes déplacées dans les conflits armés', *Recueil des Cours de l'Académie de La Haye*, 306 (2003), 13.

Cassese, A., 'Civil war and international law', in P. Gaeta and S. Zappalà (eds.), *The Human Dimension of International Law: Selected Papers of Antonio Cassese* (Oxford: Oxford University Press, 2008), pp. 110–27.

'The Geneva Protocols of 1977 on the humanitarian law of armed conflict and customary international law', *UCLA Pac. Basin L. J.*, 3 (1984), 55.

'On the current trends towards criminal prosecution and punishment of breaches of IHL', *EJIL*, 9 (1998), 2.

'Powers and duties of an occupant in relation to land and natural resources', in E. Playfair (ed.), *International Law and the Administration of Occupied Territories – Three Decades of Israeli Occupation of the West Bank and Gaza Strip* (Oxford: Clarendon, 1992), pp. 419–42.

'The status of rebels under the 1977 Geneva Protocol on non-international armed conflicts', *ICLQ*, 30 (1981), 416.

Chimni, B. S., 'The incarceration of victims: deconstructing safety zones', in N. Al-Nauimi and R. Meese (eds.), *International Legal Issues Arising under the United Nations Decade of International Law*, proceedings of the Qatar International Law Conference 1994 (Boston: Martinus Nijhoff, 1995), pp. 823–54.

Clapham, A., 'Human rights obligations of non-state actors in conflict situations', *IRRC*, 88 (2006), 491.

Clarance, W. D., 'Open relief centres: a pragmatic approach to emergency relief and monitoring during conflict in a country of origin', *IJRL*, 3 (1991), 320.

Cohen, R., 'The development of international standards to protect internally displaced persons', in A.F. Bayefski and J. Fitzpatrick (eds.), *Human Rights and Forced Displacement* (The Hague: Kluwer Law International, 2000), pp. 76–85.

'The Guiding Principles on Internal Displacement: an innovation in international standard setting', *Global Governance*, 10 (2004), 459.

Cohen, R. and Deng F. (eds.), *Masses in Flight: The Global Crisis of Internal Displacement* (Washington, DC: Brookings Institution Press, 1998).

Cohn, E. J., 'Legal aspects of internment', *MLR*, 4 (1941), 206.

Crisp, J., 'Africa's refugees: patterns, problems and policy challenges' (August 2000), UNHCR New issues in refugee research, Working Paper No. 28 (Geneva: UNHCR).

Da Costa, R., 'Maintaining the civilian and humanitarian character of asylum', UNHCR Legal and Protection Policy Research Series (Geneva: UNHCR, 2004).

Dayanim, B., 'The Israeli Supreme Court and the deportations of Palestinians: the interaction of law and legitimacy', *Stan. J. Int'l L.*, 30 (1994), 115.

Deng, F. M., 'The global challenge of internal displacement', *Wash. U. J. L. & Pol'y*, 5 (2001), 141.

Dingwall, J., 'Unlawful confinement as a war crime: the jurisprudence of the Yugoslav Tribunal and the common core of international humanitarian law applicable to contemporary armed conflicts', *JCSL*, 9 (2004), 133.

Dinstein, Y., *The Conduct of Hostilities under the Law of International Armed Conflict* (Cambridge: Cambridge University Press, 2004).

'Distinction and loss of civilian protection in international armed conflicts', *Isr. Y. B. Hum. Rts.*, 38 (2008), 1.

'The international law of belligerent occupation and human rights', *Isr. Y. B. Hum. Rts.*, 8 (1978), 104.

'The Israeli Supreme Court and the law of belligerent occupation: deportations', *Isr. Y. B. Hum. Rts.*, 23 (1993), 1.

'Refugees and the law of armed conflict', *Isr. Y. B. Hum. Rts.*, 12 (1982), 94.

Dörmann, K., *Elements of War Crimes under the Rome Statute of the International Criminal Court – Sources and Commentary* (Cambridge: Cambridge University Press, 2002).

Doswald-Beck, L. and Vité, S., 'International humanitarian law and human rights law', *IRRC*, 33 (1993), 94.

Dowty, A. and Loescher, G., 'Refugee flows as grounds for international action', *International Security*, 21 (1996), 43.

Draper, G. I. A. D., 'The Geneva Conventions of 1949', *Recueil des Cours de l'Académie de Droit International*, 96 (1965).

Droege, C., 'Elective affinities? Human rights and humanitarian law', *IRRC*, 90 (2008), 501.

'Transfers of detainees: legal framework, *non-refoulement* and contemporary challenges', *IRRC*, 90 (871) (2008), 669.

Drzewicki, K., 'National legislation and international humanitarian law', in F. Kalshoven and Y. Sandoz (eds.), *Implementation of International Humanitarian Law* (Dordrecht: Martinus Nijhoff, 1989), pp. 109–31.

Dupuis, M. D., Heywood, J. Q. and Sarko, M. Y. F., 'The Sixth Annual American Red Cross Conference on international humanitarian law: a workshop on customary international law and the 1977 Protocols additional to the 1949 Geneva Conventions', *Am. Uni. J. Int'l L. & Pol'y*, 2 (1987), 415.

Eide, A., Rosas, A. and Meron, T., 'Combating lawlessness in grey zone conflicts through humanitarian standards', *AJIL*, 89 (1995), 215.

El Kouhene, M., *Les garanties fondamentales de la personne en droit humanitaire et droits de l'homme* (Dordrecht: Martinus Nijhoff, 1986).

Emizet, K., 'The massacre of refugees in Congo: a case of UN peacekeeping failure and international law', *Journal of Modern African Studies*, 38 (2000), 163.

Ewumbue-Monono, C., 'Respect for international humanitarian law by armed non-state actors in Africa', *IRRC*, 88 (2006), 905.

Fenrick, W. J., 'Crimes in combat: the relationship between crimes against humanity and war crimes', *Guest Lecture Series of the Office of the Prosecutor of the ICC* (2004), 11, available at: www.icc-cpi.int/NR/rdonlyres/E7C759C8-C5A4-4AD3-8AB5-EF6ED68AC1D4/0/Fenrick.pdf (accessed 6 July 2011).

Franco, L., 'An examination of safety zones for internally displaced persons as a contribution toward prevention and solution of refugee problems', in N. Al-Nauimi and R. Meese (eds.), *International Legal Issues Arising under the United Nations Decade of International Law*, proceedings of the Qatar International Law Conference 1994 (Boston: Martinus Nijhoff, 1995), pp. 871–97.

Frulli, M., 'Are crimes against humanity more serious than war crimes?', *EJIL*, 12 (2001), 32.

Gasser, H.-P., 'Protection of the civilian population', in D. Fleck (ed.), *The Handbook of Humanitarian Law in Armed Conflicts* (Oxford: Oxford University Press 1995).

Gillard, E.-C., 'The role of international humanitarian law in the protection of internally displaced persons', *Refugee Survey Quarterly*, 24 (2005), 37.

'There's no place like home: states' obligations in relation to transfers of persons', *IRRC*, 90 (2008), 703.

Goodwin-Gill, G. S., '*Non-refoulement* and the new asylum-seekers', *Virginia J. Intl. L.*, 26 (1986), 897.

Goodwin-Gill, G. S. and McAdam, J., *The Refugee in International Law* (3rd edn, Oxford: Oxford University Press, 2007).

Grahl-Madsen, A., *Commentary on the 1951 Refugee Convention* (Geneva: UNHCR, 1997).

Grant, S., 'A just treatment for enemy aliens', *NLJ*, 141 (1991), 305.

Greenwood, C., 'Customary law status of the 1977 Geneva Protocols', in A. Delissen and G. Tanja (eds.), *Humanitarian Law of Armed Conflict – Challenges Ahead: Essays in Honour of Frits Kalshoven* (Dordrecht: Martinus Nijhoff, 1991), pp. 93–114.

'New world order or old? The invasion of Kuwait and the rule of law', *MLR*, 55 (1992), 153.
'Rights at the frontier – protecting the individual in time of war', in B. A. K. Ryder (ed.), *Law at the Centre – The Institute of Advanced Legal Studies at Fifty* (London: Kluwer Law International, 1999), pp. 277–92.
Greer, J. L., 'A critique of the ICRC's customary rules concerning displaced persons: general accuracy, conflation, and a missed opportunity', *Military Law Review*, 192 (2007), 116.
Gulick, K., 'Protection of family life', in W. Kälin, R. C. Williams, K. Koser and A. Solomon (eds.), *Incorporating the Guiding Principles on Internal Displacement into Domestic Law: Issues and Challenges* (Washington, DC: American Society of International Law, 2010), pp. 291–335.
Hadden, T. and Harvey, C., 'The law of internal crisis and conflict – an outline prospectus for the merger of international human rights law, the law of armed conflict, refugee law and the law on humanitarian intervention', *IRRC*, 81 (1999), 119.
Hailbronner, K., '*Non-refoulement* and "humanitarian" refugees: customary international law or wishful thinking?', *Virginia J. Intl. L.*, 26 (1986), 857.
Hathaway, J. C., *The Law of Refugee Status* (Toronto: Butterworths, 1991).
The Rights of Refugees under International Law (Cambridge: Cambridge University Press, 2005).
Heintze, H.-J., 'On the relationship between human rights law protection and international humanitarian law', *IRRC*, 86 (2004), 789.
Henckaerts, J. M., 'Deportation and the transfer of civilians in time of war', *Vanderbilt J. Transnatl. L.*, 26 (1993–4), 469.
Mass Expulsion in Modern International Law and Practice (Dordrecht: Kluwer Law International, 1995).
Henckaerts, J. M. and Doswald-Beck, L., *Customary International Humanitarian Law*, 2 vols. (Cambridge: Cambridge University Press, 2005).
Hulme, K., 'Armed conflict and the displaced', *JRL*, 17 (2005), 91.
Human Security Centre, *Human Security Report 2005 – War and Peace in the 21st Century* (New York: Oxford University Press, 2005).
Hutchinson, M. R., 'Restoring hope: UN Security Council resolutions for Somalia and an expanded doctrine of humanitarian intervention', *Harv. Int'l L. J.*, 34 (1993), 624.
Hyndman, J., 'Preventive, palliative, or punitive? Safe spaces in Bosnia-Herzegovina, Somalia and Sri Lanka', *JRS*, 16 (2003), 167.
ICRC, 'The ICRC and internally displaced persons', *IRRC*, 35 (1995), 181.
'ICRC protection and assistance activities in situations not covered by international humanitarian law', *IRRC*, 28 (1988), 9.
IDMC, *Internal Displacement – Global Overview of Trends and Developments in 2005* (Geneva: IDMC–Norwegian Refugee Council, 2006).
Internal Displacement – Global Overview of Trends and Developments in 2006 (Geneva: IDMC–Norwegian Refugee Council, 2007).

Internal Displacement – Global Overview of Trends and Developments in 2010 (Geneva: IDMC–Norwegian Refugee Council, 2010).

Imseis, A., 'Critical reflections on the international humanitarian law aspects of the ICJ *Wall* Advisory Opinion', *AJIL*, 99 (2005), 102.

Islam, R., 'The Sudanese refugee crisis and internally displaced persons in international law: the least protection for the most vulnerable', *IJRL*, 18 (2006), 354.

Jacquemet, S., 'The cross-fertilization of international humanitarian law and international refugee law', *IRRC*, 83 (2001), 651.

'Under what circumstances can a person who has taken an active part in the hostilities of an international or a non-international armed conflict become an asylum seeker?', UNHCR Legal and Protection Policy Research Series (Geneva: UNHCR, 2004).

Kälin, W., 'Flight in times of war', *IRRC*, 83 (2001), 628.

Guiding Principles on Internal Displacement: Annotations, Studies in Transnational Legal Policy, No.38 (Washington, DC: American Society of International Law, 2008).

'The Guiding Principles on internal displacement as international minimum standard and protection tool', *Refugee Survey Quarterly*, 24 (2005), 27.

'How hard is soft law? The Guiding Principles on Internal Displacement and the need for a normative framework', presentation at roundtable meeting, Ralph Bunche Institute for International Studies, CUNY Graduate Center, 19 December 2001, available at: www.brookings.edu/fp/projects/idp/articles/Kaelin12-19-01.pdf (accessed 7 October 2011).

Human Rights in Time of Occupation: The Case of Kuwait (Berne: Law Books Europe, 1994).

Kalshoven, F. and Zegveld, L., *Constraints on the Waging of War: An Introduction to International Humanitarian Law* (Geneva: ICRC, 2001).

Kempner, R., 'The enemy alien problem in the present war', *AJIL*, 34 (1940), 443.

Korsinik, R., 'Droit international humanitaire et protection des camps de réfugiés', in C. Swinarski (ed.), *Etudes et essais sur le droit international humanitaire et sur les principes de la Croix-Rouge* (Geneva: ICRC, 1984), pp. 387–93.

Kretzmer, D., 'The Advisory Opinion: the light treatment of international humanitarian law', *AJIL*, 99 (2005), 88.

The Occupation of Justice: The Supreme Court of Israel and the Occupied Territories (Albany: State University of New York Press, 2002).

Krieger, H., 'A conflict of norms: the relationship between humanitarian law and human rights law in the ICRC customary law study', *JCSL*, 11 (2006), 265.

Krill, F., 'ICRC action in aid of refugees', *IRRC*, 265 (1988), 328.

'The ICRC's policy on refugees and internally displaced civilians' *IRRC*, 83 (2001), 607.

Kwakwa, E., *The International Law of Armed Conflict: Personal and Material Fields of Application* (Dordrecht: Martinus Nijhoff, 1992).

La Haye, E., *War Crimes in Internal Armed Conflicts* (Cambridge: Cambridge University Press, 2008).
Landgren, L., 'Safety zones and international protection: a dark grey area', *IJRL*, 7 (1995), 436.
Lapidoth, R., 'The Advisory Opinion and the Jewish settlements', *Israel L. Rev.*, 38 (2005), 292.
'The expulsion of civilians from areas which came under Israeli control in 1967: some legal issues', *EJIL*, 2 (1990), 97.
Lauterpacht, E. and Bethlehem, D., 'The scope and content of the principle of non-refoulement', in E. Feller, V. Turk and F. Nicholson (eds.), *Refugee Protection in International Law – UNHCR's Global Consultations on International Protection* (Cambridge: Cambridge University Press, 2003).
Lavoyer, J.-P., 'Refugees and internally displaced persons: International humanitarian law and the role of the ICRC', *IRRC*, 35 (1995), 162.
Lesch, A., 'Israeli deportation of Palestinians from the West Bank and the Gaza Strip, 1967–1978', *Journal of Palestine Studies*, 8 (1979), 101.
Lischer, S. K., *Dangerous Sanctuaries: Refugee Camps, Civil War and the Dilemmas of Humanitarian Aid* (Ithaca, NY: Cornell University Press, 2005).
Lopez, L., 'Uncivil wars: the challenge of applying international humanitarian law to internal armed conflicts', *NYU L. Rev.*, 69 (1994), 916.
Lubell, N., 'Challenges in applying human rights law to armed conflict', *IRRC*, 87 (2005), 737.
Mallison, W. T. and Mallison, S. V., 'A juridical analysis of the Israeli settlements in the occupied territories', *Palestine Yearbook of International Law*, 10 (1998–9), 19.
Meindersma C., 'Legal issues surrounding population transfers in conflict situations', *NILR*, 41 (1994), 31.
'Population exchanges: international law and state practice – part 2', *IJRL*, 9 (1997), 613.
Meisenberg, S., 'Legality of amnesties in international humanitarian law: the *Lomé Amnesty* decision of the Special Court for Sierra Leone', *IRRC*, 856 (2004), 837.
Meron, T., 'Deportation of civilians as a war crime under customary law', in D. Gomien (ed.), *Broadening the Frontiers of Human Rights – Essays in Honour of Asbjørn Eide* (Oslo: Scandinavian University Press, 1993), pp. 201–18.
'Draft model declaration on internal strife', *IRRC*, 28 (1988), 59.
The Humanization of International Law (Leiden: Martinus Nijhoff, 2006).
Human Rights and Humanitarian Norms as Customary Law (Oxford: Clarendon, 1989).
Human Rights in Internal Strife: Their International Protection (Cambridge: Grotius, 1987).
'International criminalization of internal atrocities', *AJIL*, 89 (1995), 554.
'On the inadequate reach of humanitarian and human rights law and the need for a new instrument', *AJIL*, 77 (1983), 589.

'West Bank and Gaza: human rights and humanitarian law in the period of transition', *Isr. Y. B. Hum. Rts.*, 9 (1978), 106.

Mettraux, G., *International Crimes and the Ad Hoc Tribunals* (Oxford: Oxford University Press, 2005).

Moir, L., 'Grave breaches and internal armed conflict', *JICJ*, 7 (2009), 763.

The Law of Internal Armed Conflict (Cambridge: Cambridge University Press, 2002).

Mtango, E.-E., 'Military and armed attacks on refugee camps', in G. Loescher and L. Monahan (eds.), *Refugees and International Relations* (New York: Oxford University Press, 1990), pp. 87–121.

Neff, D., 'Settlements in US policy', *Journal of Palestine Studies*, 23 (1994), 53.

Obradovic, K., 'La protection des réfugiés dans les conflits armés internationaux', in *The Refugee Problem on Universal, Regional and National Level, Thesaurus Acroasium*, vol. 13 (Thessaloniki: Institute of International Public Law and International Relations of Thessaloniki, 1987), pp. 147–61.

Olson, L. M., 'Practical challenges of implementing the complementarity between international humanitarian and human rights law – demonstrated by the procedural regulation of internment in non-international armed conflict', *Case W. Res. J. Int. L.*, 40 (2009), 437.

Oppenheim, L., *International Law – A Treatise*, vol. II: *Disputes, War and Neutrality* (London: Longmans, Green and Co., 1952).

Othman-Chande, M., 'International law and armed attacks in refugee camps', *Nord. J. Intl. L.*, 59 (1990), 153.

Partsch, K. K., 'The protection of refugees in armed conflict and internal disturbances by Red Cross organs', *Revue du Droit Pénal Militaire et du Droit de la Guerre*, 22 (1983), 419.

Patrnogic, J., 'International protection of refugees in armed conflict', *Annales de Droit International Medical*, 29 (1981), 1.

Pejić, J., 'The right to food in situations of armed conflict: the legal framework', *IRRC*, 83 (2001), 1097.

'Status of armed conflicts', in E. Wilmshurst and S. Breau (eds.), *Perspectives on the ICRC Study on Customary International Humanitarian Law* (Cambridge: Cambridge University Press, 2007), pp. 77–100.

Pellet, A., 'The destruction of Troy will not take place', in E. Playfair (ed.), *International Law and the Administration of Occupied Territories – Three Decades of Israeli Occupation of the West Bank and Gaza Strip* (Oxford: Clarendon, 1992), pp. 169–204.

Phuong, C., *The International Protection of Internally Displaced Persons* (Cambridge: Cambridge University Press, 2004).

Pictet, J., *Commentary on the Geneva Conventions of 12 August 1949 Convention for the Amelioration of the Condition of Wounded, Sick and Shipwrecked Members of the Armed Forces in the Field* (Geneva: ICRC, 1952).

Commentary on the Geneva Conventions of 12 August 1949 Convention for the Amelioration of the Condition of Wounded, Sick and Shipwrecked Members of the Armed Forces at Sea (Geneva: ICRC, 1960).

Commentary on the Geneva Conventions of 12 August 1949 Convention relative to the Protection of Civilian Persons in Time of War (Geneva: ICRC, 1958).
Development and Principles of International Humanitarian Law (Dordrecht: Martinus Nijhoff, 1982).
Le droit humanitaire et la protection des victimes de la guerre (Leiden: Sijthoff, 1973).
Piotrowicz, R., 'Displacement and displaced persons', in E. Wilmshurst and S. Breau (eds.), *Perspectives on the ICRC Study on Customary International Humanitarian Law* (Cambridge: Cambridge University Press, 2007), pp. 327–53.
Plattner, D., 'The penal repression of violations of international humanitarian law applicable in non-international armed conflicts', *IRRC*, 278 (1990), 409.
Provost, R., *International Human Rights and Humanitarian Law* (Cambridge: Cambridge University Press, 2002).
Quéguiner, J.-F., 'Dix ans après la création du Tribunal pénal international pour l'ex-Yougoslavie: évaluation de l'apport de sa jurisprudence en droit international humanitaire', *IRRC*, 85 (2003), 271.
'Precautions under the law governing the conduct of hostilities', *IRRC*, 88 (2006), 793.
Randelzhoffer, A., 'Nationality', in R. Bernhardt (ed.), *Encyclopedia of Public International Law*, vol. 3 (Oxford: Oxford University Press, 1997).
Roberts, A., 'Prolonged military occupation: the Israeli-occupied territories 1967–1988', in E. Playfair (ed.), *International Law and the Administration of Occupied Territories – Three Decades of Israeli Occupation of the West Bank and Gaza Strip* (Oxford: Clarendon, 1992), pp. 25–85.
Robinson, D. and von Hebel, H., 'War crimes in internal conflicts: Article 8 of the ICC Statute', *YIHL*, 2 (1999), 193.
Roch, M. P. 'Forced displacement in the former Yugoslavia: a crime under international law?', *Dick. J. Int'l L.*, 14 (1995), 2.
Rottensteiner, C., 'The denial of humanitarian assistance as a crime under international law', *IRRC*, 39 (1999), 555.
Salehyan, I. and Gleditsch, K. S., 'Refugees and the spread of civil war', *International Organization*, 60 (2006), 335.
Sandoz, Y., 'The establishment of safety zones for persons displaced within their country of origin', Conference on the international legal issues arising under the United Nations decade of international law (Doha, Qatar, 22–5 March 1994) (on file with author).
'Localités et zones sous protection spéciales', in *Quatre Études de Droit International Humanitaire* (Geneva: Institut Henry Dunant, 1985), pp. 35–47.
Sandoz, Y., Swinarski, C. and Zimmermann, B. (eds.), *Commentary on the Additional Protocols of 8 June 1977 to the Geneva Conventions of 12 August 1949* (Geneva: ICRC–Martinus Nijhoff, 1987).
Sassòli, M., 'The implementation of international humanitarian law: current and inherent challenges', *YIHL*, 10 (2007), 45.
Sassòli, M. and Olson, L. M., 'The relationship between international humanitarian law and human rights law where it matters: admissible

killing and internment of fighters in non-international armed conflicts', *IRRC*, 90 (2008), 599.
Schabas, W. A., '*Lex specialis*? Belt and suspenders? The parallel operation of human rights law and the law of armed conflict, and the conundrum of *jus ad bellum*', *Isr. L. Rev.*, 40 (2007), 592.
Schachter, O., *International Law in Theory and Practice* (Dordrecht: Martinus Nijhoff, 1991).
Schindler, D., 'The different types of armed conflict according to the Geneva Conventions and Protocols', *Recueil des Cours de l'Académie de Droit International*, 163 (1979), 151.
Schindler, D. and Toman, J. (eds.), *The Laws of Armed Conflict* (Leiden: Martinus Nijhoff, 2004).
Schmitt, M., 'Humanitarian law and direct participation in hostilities by private contractors or civilian employees', *CJIL*, 5 (2005), 511.
Schwarzenberger, G., *International Law as Applied by International Courts and Tribunals*, Vol. 2, *The Law of Armed Conflict* (London: Stevens, 1989).
Shany, Y., 'Capacities and inadequacies: a look at the two Separation Barrier cases', *Israel L. Rev.*, 38 (2005), 220.
'Head against the Wall? Israel's rejection of the Advisory Opinion on the legal consequence of the construction of a wall in the occupied Palestinian territories', *YIHL*, 7 (2004), 352.
Sohn, L. B. and Buergenthal, T. (eds.), *The Movement of Persons Across Borders* (Washington, DC: American Society of International Law, 1992).
Solf, W. A., 'Problems with the application of norms governing inter-state armed conflict to non-international armed conflict', *Ga. J. Intl. & Comp. L.*, 13 (1983), 291.
'Protection of civilians against the effects of hostilities under customary international law and under Protocol I', *Am. U. J. Int'l. L. & Pol'y*, 1 (1986), 117.
Stewart J., 'Towards a single definition of armed conflict in international humanitarian law: A critique of internationalized armed conflict', *IRRC*, 85 (2003), 313–50.
Stone, J., *Israel and Palestine: Assault on the Law of Nations* (Baltimore: Johns Hopkins University Press, 1981).
Storey, H. and Wallace, R., 'War and peace in refugee law jurisprudence', *AJIL*, 95 (2001), 349.
Subedi, S., 'The legal competence of the international community to create "safe havens" in "zones of turmoil"', *JRS*, 12 (1999), 23.
UK Ministry of Defence, *The Manual of the Law of Armed Conflict* (Oxford: Oxford University Press, 2004).
UNHCR, *Global Trends 2010* (Geneva: UNHCR, 2011).
The State of the World's Refugees: The Challenge of Protection (Geneva: UNHCR, 1993).
The State of the World's Refugees – Fifty Years of Humanitarian Action (Oxford: Oxford University Press, 2000).
The State of the World's Refugees – A Humanitarian Agenda (Oxford: Oxford University Press, 1997).

US Committee for Refugees and Immigrants, *World Refugee Survey 2006* (Washington, DC: USCRI, 2007).
Vinuesa, R. E., 'Interface, correspondence and convergence of human rights and international humanitarian law', *YIHL*, 1 (1998), 69.
Vité, S., 'The interrelation of the law of occupation and economic, social and cultural rights', *IRRC*, 90 (2008), 629.
Watkin, K., 'Controlling the use of force: a role for human rights norms in contemporary armed conflict', *AJIL*, 98 (2004), 1.
Watson, G. R., *The Oslo Accords: International Law and the Israeli–Palestinian Peace Agreements* (Oxford: Oxford University Press 2000).
'The "Wall" decisions in legal and political context', *AJIL*, 99 (2005), 6.
Weiner, M., 'Bad neighbors, bad neighborhoods: An inquiry into the cause of refugee flows', *International Security*, 21(1) (1996), 5.
Weis, P., *Nationality and Statelessness in International Law* (2nd edn, Alphen aan den Rijn: Sitjhoff & Nordhoff, 1979).
The Refugee Convention, 1951 (Cambridge: Cambridge University Press, 1995).
Werle, G., *Principles of International Criminal Law* (The Hague: TMC Asser Press, 2005).
Willms, J., 'Without order, anything goes? The prohibition of forced displacement in non-international armed conflict', *IRRC*, 91 (2009), 547.
Wills, S., 'The obligations due to former "protected persons" in conflicts that have ceased to be international: the People's Mujahedin Organization of Iran', *JCSL*, 15 (2010), 117.
Yingling, R. T. and Ginnane, R. W., 'The Geneva Conventions of 1949', *AJIL*, 46 (1952), 393.
de Zayas, A., 'The Annan Plan and the implantation of Turkish settlers in the occupied territory of Cyprus' (24 July 2005), available at: www.alfreddezayas.com/Articles/cyprussettlers.shtml (accessed 26 October 2011).
'Ethnic cleansing: applicable norms, emerging jurisprudence, implementable remedies', available at: www.alfreddezayas.com/Chapbooks/Ethn_clean.shtml (accessed 26 October 2011).
'International law and mass population transfers', *Harv. Int'l. L. J.*, 16 (1975), 207.
'Population, expulsion and transfer', in R. Bernhardt (ed.), *Encyclopedia of Public International Law*, vol. 3 (Oxford: Oxford University Press, 1997), p. 1062.
Zegveld, L., *Accountability of Armed Opposition Groups in International Law* (Cambridge: Cambridge University Press, 2002).
Zimmermann, A., 'War crimes', para. 2(c)–(f), in O. Triffterer (ed.), *Commentary on the Rome Statute of the International Criminal Court* (2nd edn, Oxford: Hart, 2008).

Index

CAMBRIDGE STUDIES IN INTERNATIONAL AND COMPARATIVE LAW

Books in the series

Armed Conflict and Displacement: The Protection of Refugees and Displaced Persons under International Humanitarian Law Mélanie Jacques
Foreign Investment and the Environment in International Law Jorge Viñuales
The Human Rights Treaty Obligations of Peacekeepers Kjetil Larsen
Cyberwarfare and the Laws of War Heather Harrison Dinniss
The Right to Reparation in International Law for Victims of Armed Conflict: The Role of the UN in Advocating for State Responsibility Christine Evans
Global Public Interest in International Investment Law Andreas Kulick
State Immunity in International Law Xiaodong Yang
Reparations and Victim Support in the International Criminal Court Conor McCarthy
Reducing Genocide to Law: Definition, Meaning, and the Ultimate Crime Payam Akhavan
Decolonizing International Law: Development, Economic Growth and the Politics of Universality Sundhya Pahuja
Complicity and the Law of State Responsibility Helmut Philipp Aust
State Control over Private Military and Security Companies in Armed Conflict Hannah Tonkin
'Fair and Equitable Treatment' in International Investment Law Roland Kläger
The UN and Human Rights: Who Guards the Guardians? Guglielmo Verdirame
Sovereign Defaults before International Courts and Tribunals Michael Waibel
Making the Law of the Sea: A Study in the Development of International Law James Harrison
Science and the Precautionary Principle in International Courts and Tribunals: Expert Evidence, Burden of Proof and Finality Caroline E. Foster
Transition from Illegal Regimes in International Law Yaël Ronen
Access to Asylum: International Refugee Law and the Globalisation of Migration Control Thomas Gammeltoft-Hansen
Trading Fish, Saving Fish: The Interaction between Regimes in International Law Margaret Young
The Individual in the International Legal System: Continuity and Change in International Law Kate Parlett
The Participation of States in International Organisations: The Role of Human Rights and Democracy Alison Duxbury
'Armed Attack' and Article 51 of the UN Charter: Evolutions in Customary Law and Practice Tom Ruys
Science and Risk Regulation in International Law: The Role of Science, Uncertainty and Values Jacqueline Peel
Theatre of the Rule of Law: The Theory, History and Practice of Transnational Legal Intervention Stephen Humphreys
The Public International Law Theory of Hans Kelsen: Believing in Universal Law Jochen von Bernstorff

Vicarious Liability in Tort: A Comparative Perspective Paula Giliker
Legal Personality in International Law Roland Portmann
Legitimacy and Legality in International Law: An Interactional Account Jutta Brunnée and Stephen J. Toope
The Concept of Non-International Armed Conflict in International Humanitarian Law Anthony Cullen
The Challenge of Child Labour in International Law Franziska Humbert
Shipping Interdiction and the Law of the Sea Douglas Guilfoyle
International Courts and Environmental Protection Tim Stephens
Legal Principles in WTO Disputes Andrew D. Mitchell
War Crimes in Internal Armed Conflicts Eve La Haye
Humanitarian Occupation Gregory H. Fox
The International Law of Environmental Impact Assessment: Process, Substance and Integration Neil Craik
The Law and Practice of International Territorial Administration: Versailles to Iraq and Beyond Carsten Stahn
Cultural Products and the World Trade Organization Tania Voon
United Nations Sanctions and the Rule of Law Jeremy Farrall
National Law in WTO Law: Effectiveness and Good Governance in the World Trading System Sharif Bhuiyan
The Threat of Force in International Law Nikolas Stürchler
Indigenous Rights and United Nations Standards Alexandra Xanthaki
International Refugee Law and Socio-Economic Rights Michelle Foster
The Protection of Cultural Property in Armed Conflict Roger O'Keefe
Interpretation and Revision of International Boundary Decisions Kaiyan Homi Kaikobad
Multinationals and Corporate Social Responsibility: Limitations and Opportunities in International Law Jennifer A. Zerk
Judiciaries within Europe: A Comparative Review John Bell
Law in Times of Crisis: Emergency Powers in Theory and Practice Oren Gross and Fionnuala Ní Aoláin
Vessel-Source Marine Pollution: The Law and Politics of International Regulation Alan Tan
Enforcing Obligations Erga Omnes in International Law Christian J. Tams
Non-Governmental Organisations in International Law Anna-Karin Lindblom
Democracy, Minorities and International Law Steven Wheatley
Prosecuting International Crimes: Selectivity and the International Law Regime Robert Cryer
Compensation for Personal Injury in English, German and Italian Law: A Comparative Outline Basil Markesinis, Michael Coester, Guido Alpa, Augustus Ullstein
Dispute Settlement in the UN Convention on the Law of the Sea Natalie Klein
The International Protection of Internally Displaced Persons Catherine Phuong
Imperialism, Sovereignty and the Making of International Law Antony Anghie
Necessity, Proportionality and the Use of Force by States Judith Gardam
International Legal Argument in the Permanent Court of International Justice: The Rise of the International Judiciary Ole Spiermann

Great Powers and Outlaw States: Unequal Sovereigns in the International Legal Order Gerry Simpson
Local Remedies in International Law C. F. Amerasinghe
Reading Humanitarian Intervention: Human Rights and the Use of Force in International Law Anne Orford
Conflict of Norms in Public International Law: How WTO Law Relates to Other Rules of International Law Joost Pauwelyn
Transboundary Damage in International Law Hanqin Xue
European Criminal Procedures Edited by Mireille Delmas-Marty and John Spencer
The Accountability of Armed Opposition Groups in International Law Liesbeth Zegveld
Sharing Transboundary Resources: International Law and Optimal Resource Use Eyal Benvenisti
International Human Rights and Humanitarian Law René Provost
Remedies Against International Organisations Karel Wellens
Diversity and Self-Determination in International Law Karen Knop
The Law of Internal Armed Conflict Lindsay Moir
International Commercial Arbitration and African States: Practice, Participation and Institutional Development Amazu A. Asouzu
The Enforceability of Promises in European Contract Law James Gordley
International Law in Antiquity David J. Bederman
Money Laundering: A New International Law Enforcement Model Guy Stessens
Good Faith in European Contract Law Reinhard Zimmermann and Simon Whittaker
On Civil Procedure J. A. Jolowicz
Trusts: A Comparative Study Maurizio Lupoi
The Right to Property in Commonwealth Constitutions Tom Allen
International Organizations Before National Courts August Reinisch
The Changing International Law of High Seas Fisheries Francisco Orrego Vicuña
Trade and the Environment: A Comparative Study of EC and US Law Damien Geradin
Unjust Enrichment: A Study of Private Law and Public Values Hanoch Dagan
Religious Liberty and International Law in Europe Malcolm D. Evans
Ethics and Authority in International Law Alfred P. Rubin
Sovereignty over Natural Resources: Balancing Rights and Duties Nico Schrijver
The Polar Regions and the Development of International Law Donald R. Rothwell
Fragmentation and the International Relations of Micro-States: Self-Determination and Statehood Jorri Duursma
Principles of the Institutional Law of International Organizations C. F. Amerasinghe

Lightning Source UK Ltd.
Milton Keynes UK
UKHW022158280720
367335UK00006B/105

9 781107 538399